FORD EDGE & ... X
2007-14 ...

CHILTON'S

Covers U.S. and Canadian models of
Ford Edge & Lincoln MKX
2007 through 2014

by Jeff Killingsworth

CHILTON *Automotive Books*

PUBLISHED BY **HAYNES NORTH AMERICA, Inc.**

Printed in Malaysia
©2013, 2016 Haynes North America, Inc.
ISBN-13: 978-1-62092-275-0
ISBN-10: 1-62092-275-4
Library of Congress Control Number 2016957190

Haynes Publishing Group
Sparkford Nr Yeovil
Somerset BA22 7JJ England

Haynes North America, Inc
859 Lawrence Drive
Newbury Park
California 91320 USA

ABCDE
FGHIJ
KLMNO
PQR

10U1

Contents

Mechanic and photographer with a 2012 Ford Edge

ACKNOWLEDGEMENTS

Technical writers who contributed to this project include Trip Aiken and John Wegmann.

We are grateful to Valley Forge Technical Information Services for providing Wiring Diagrams.

About this manual

ITS PURPOSE

The purpose of this manual is to help you get the best value from your vehicle. It can do so in several ways. It can help you decide what work must be done, even if you choose to have it done by a dealer service department or a repair shop; it provides information and procedures for routine maintenance and servicing; and it offers diagnostic and repair procedures to follow when trouble occurs.

We hope you use the manual to tackle the work yourself. For many simpler jobs, doing it yourself may be quicker than arranging an appointment to get the vehicle into a shop and making the trips to leave it and pick it up. More importantly, a lot of money can be saved by avoiding the expense the shop must pass on to you to cover its labor and overhead costs. An added benefit is the sense of satisfaction and accomplishment that you feel after doing the job yourself.

USING THE MANUAL

The manual is divided into Chapters. Each Chapter is divided into numbered Sections. Each Section consists of consecutively numbered paragraphs.

At the beginning of each numbered Section you will be referred to any illustrations which apply to the procedures in that Section. The reference numbers used in illustration captions pinpoint the pertinent Section and the Step within that Section. That is, illustration 3.2 means the illustration refers to Section 3 and Step (or paragraph) 2 within that Section.

Procedures, once described in the text, are not normally repeated. When it's necessary to refer to another Chapter, the reference will be given as Chapter and Section number. Cross references given without use of the word "Chapter" apply to Sections and/or paragraphs in the same Chapter. For example, "see Section 8" means in the same Chapter.

References to the left or right side of the vehicle assume you are sitting in the driver's seat, facing forward.

Even though we have prepared this manual with extreme care, neither the publisher nor the author can accept responsibility for any errors in, or omissions from, the information given.

➡ NOTE

A *Note* provides information necessary to properly complete a procedure or information which will make the procedure easier to understand.

❈ CAUTION

A *Caution* provides a special procedure or special steps which must be taken while completing the procedure where the Caution is found. Not heeding a Caution can result in damage to the assembly being worked on.

❈ WARNING

A *Warning* provides a special procedure or special steps which must be taken while completing the procedure where the Warning is found. Not heeding a Warning can result in personal injury.

Introduction

This manual covers the Ford Edge and Lincoln MKX. The available engines are: The 2.0L turbocharged in-line four-cylinder engine, 3.5L V6 engine or 3.7L V6 engine.

The engine drives the front wheels through a six-speed automatic transaxle via independent driveaxles. On All-Wheel Drive (AWD) models, the rear wheels are also propelled via a driveshaft, rear differential, and two rear driveaxles.

Suspension is independent at all four wheels. The front suspension uses strut/coil spring assemblies with lower control arms. The rear uses a multi-link design with shock absorbers and coil springs. The rack-and-pinion steering unit is mounted on the suspension crossmember.

The brakes are disc at the front and rear, with power assist standard. An Anti-lock Brake System (ABS) is standard equipment.

Vehicle identification numbers

Modifications are a continuing and unpublicized process in vehicle manufacturing. Since spare parts manuals and lists are compiled on a numerical basis, the individual vehicle numbers are essential to correctly identify the component required.

VEHICLE IDENTIFICATION NUMBER (VIN)

This very important identification number is stamped on a plate attached to the dashboard inside the windshield on the driver's side of the vehicle (see illustration). The VIN also appears on the Vehicle Certificate of Title and Registration. It contains information such as where and when the vehicle was manufactured, the model year and the body style.

MANUFACTURER'S CERTIFICATION REGULATION LABEL

The Manufacturer's Certification Regulation label is attached to the driver's side door opening (see illustration). The label contains the name of the manufacturer, the month and year of production, the Gross Vehicle Weight Rating (GVWR), the Gross Axle Weight Rating (GAWR) and the certification statement.

VIN ENGINE CODE

Counting from the left, the engine code letter designation is the 8th character. On all models covered by this manual the engine codes are:

9 2.0L four-cylinder engine
C 3.5L V6 engine
K 3.7L V6 engine

VIN MODEL YEAR CODE

Counting from the left, the model year code letter designation is the 10th character. On all models covered by this manual the model year

codes are:

7 2007
8 2008
9 2009
A 2010
B 2011
C 2012
D 2013
E 2014

ENGINE NUMBER

The engine identification numbers are on a sticker attached to the front side of the valve cover (see illustration).

TRANSAXLE IDENTIFICATION

The transaxle identification code is listed at the bottom of the Manufacturer's Certification Regulation label, under the heading "TR." The codes are as follows:

6 6-speed automatic transaxle
J 6-speed automatic transaxle

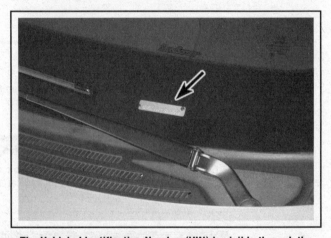

The Vehicle Identification Number (VIN) is visible through the driver's side of the windshield

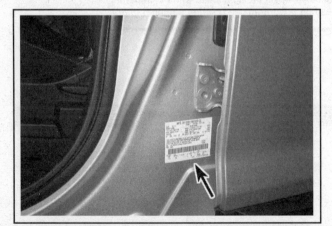

The Manufacturer's Certification Regulation label is located on the driver's door opening

Location of the engine identification number - four-cylinder engine shown, other engines similar

Recall information

Vehicle recalls are carried out by the manufacturer in the rare event of a possible safety-related defect. The vehicle's registered owner is contacted at the address on file at the Department of Motor Vehicles and given the details of the recall. Remedial work is carried out free of charge at a dealer service department.

If you are the new owner of a used vehicle which was subject to a recall and you want to be sure that the work has been carried out, it's best to contact a dealer service department and ask about your individual vehicle - you'll need to furnish them your Vehicle Identification Number (VIN).

The table below is based on information provided by the National Highway Traffic Safety Administration (NHTSA), the body which oversees vehicle recalls in the United States. The recall database is updated constantly.

For the latest information on vehicle recalls, check the NHTSA website at www.nhtsa.gov, www.safercar.gov, or call the NHTSA hotline at 1-888-327-4236.

Recall date	Recall campaign number	Model(s) affected	Concern
JULY 03, 2008	08V301000	2008 Edge	On some models, the fuel tank weld fixture may have been exposed to a contaminant during production which could cause a dimple in the bottom of the fuel tank at a spot weld. This dimple could result in a fuel leak or a fuel drip from the tank. Fuel leakage, in the presence of an ignition source, could result in a fire.
OCT 27, 2010	10V516000	2011 Edge and Lincoln MKX	Some models were shipped with incorrectly configured electronic module settings that disable the locking function of the liftgate. Accordingly, the vehicles fail to conform to the requirements of Federal Motor Vehicle Safety Standard No. 206, "door locks and door retention components." The liftgate lock may be disabled and the driver may not be able to lock the liftgate using interior lock switches or remote key fob buttons.
DEC 29, 2010	10V659000	2011 Edge and Lincoln MKX	On some models, the Body Control Module may have the potential for an internal short. If an electrical short develops, an overheating condition may occur which can result in a vehicle fire.
FEB 24, 2011	11V128000	2011 Edge	On some models, the Body Control Module may have the potential for an internal short. If an electrical short develops, an overheating condition may occur which can result in a vehicle fire.
SEP 07, 2012	12V428000	2012 Edge	On some models, the fuel line pulse damper metal housing may crack as a result of an improper manufacturing process. A cracked fuel line pulse damper housing may result in a combination of fuel odor, weepage, or a continuous leak while the fuel system is pressurized. A fuel leak in the presence of an ignition source may result in a fire.

Recall date	Recall campaign number	Model(s) affected	Concern
JAN 06, 2014	14V002000	2012, 2013 Ford Edge	On some models equipped with a four-cylinder engine, the fuel line pulse damper metal housing may crack. This may result in a combination of fuel odor, weepage, or a continuous leak while the fuel system is pressurized, which could result in a fire.
JUL 02, 2014	14V393000	2012 – 2014 Ford Edge, Lincoln MKX	On some models, the driveaxle retention circlip may not have been properly installed, and as a result, the driveaxle may move outward and disengage from the intermediate shaft while driving. If the driveaxle and intermediate shaft separate while driving, power will no longer be transmitted to the wheels, increasing the risk of a crash. Additionally, if the parking brake is not applied before exiting the vehicle, the vehicle may roll away despite the transmission being placed in 'Park', increasing the risk of injury to exiting occupants and bystanders.
OCT 29, 2014	14V682000	2007, 2008 Ford Edge, Lincoln MKX	On some models the fuel tank can corrode to the point of leakage, which could result in a fire.
JAN 09, 2015	15V005000	2014 Ford Edge	Improper nickel plating of components within the fuel pump on some models may result in the fuel pump failing. If the fuel pump fails, the vehicle may stall, increasing the risk of a crash.
OCT 27, 2015	15V712000	2009, 2010 Ford Edge, Lincoln MKX	On some models, due to corrosion from salt water exposure such as from road salt use, the affected vehicles may leak fuel from the fuel tank seam weld under the tank mounting reinforcement brackets, which could result in a fire.

Buying parts

Replacement parts are available from many sources, which generally fall into one of two categories - authorized dealer parts departments and independent retail auto parts stores. Our advice concerning these parts is as follows:

Retail auto parts stores: Good auto parts stores will stock frequently needed components which wear out relatively fast, such as clutch components, exhaust systems, brake parts, tune-up parts, etc. These stores often supply new or reconditioned parts on an exchange basis, which can save a considerable amount of money. Discount auto parts stores are often very good places to buy materials and parts needed for general vehicle maintenance such as oil, grease, filters, spark plugs, belts, touch-up paint, bulbs, etc. They also usually sell tools and general accessories, have convenient hours, charge lower prices and can often be found not far from home.

Authorized dealer parts department: This is the best source for parts which are unique to the vehicle and not generally available elsewhere (such as major engine parts, transmission parts, trim pieces, etc.).

Warranty information: If the vehicle is still covered under warranty, be sure that any replacement parts purchased - regardless of the source - do not invalidate the warranty!

To be sure of obtaining the correct parts, have engine and chassis numbers available and, if possible, take the old parts along for positive identification.

MAINTENANCE TECHNIQUES

There are a number of techniques involved in maintenance and repair that will be referred to throughout this manual. Application of these techniques will enable the home mechanic to be more efficient, better organized and capable of performing the various tasks properly, which will ensure that the repair job is thorough and complete.

Fasteners

Fasteners are nuts, bolts, studs and screws used to hold two or more parts together. There are a few things to keep in mind when working with fasteners. Almost all of them use a locking device of some type, either a lockwasher, locknut, locking tab or thread adhesive. All threaded fasteners should be clean and straight, with undamaged threads and undamaged corners on the hex head where the wrench fits. Develop the habit of replacing all damaged nuts and bolts with new ones. Special locknuts with nylon or fiber inserts can only be used once. If they are removed, they lose their locking ability and must be replaced with new ones.

Rusted nuts and bolts should be treated with a penetrating fluid to ease removal and prevent breakage. Some mechanics use turpentine in a spout-type oil can, which works quite well. After applying the rust penetrant, let it work for a few minutes before trying to loosen the nut or bolt. Badly rusted fasteners may have to be chiseled or sawed off or removed with a special nut breaker, available at tool stores.

If a bolt or stud breaks off in an assembly, it can be drilled and removed with a special tool commonly available for this purpose. Most automotive machine shops can perform this task, as well as other repair procedures, such as the repair of threaded holes that have been stripped out.

Flat washers and lockwashers, when removed from an assembly, should always be replaced exactly as removed. Replace any damaged washers with new ones. Never use a lockwasher on any soft metal surface (such as aluminum), thin sheet metal or plastic.

Fastener sizes

For a number of reasons, automobile manufacturers are making wider and wider use of metric fasteners. Therefore, it is important to be able to tell the difference between standard (sometimes called U.S. or SAE) and metric hardware, since they cannot be interchanged.

All bolts, whether standard or metric, are sized according to diameter, thread pitch and length. For example, a standard 1/2 - 13 x 1 bolt is 1/2 inch in diameter, has 13 threads per inch and is 1 inch long. An M12 - 1.75 x 25 metric bolt is 12 mm in diameter, has a thread pitch of 1.75 mm (the distance between threads) and is 25 mm long. The two bolts are nearly identical, and easily confused, but they are not interchangeable.

In addition to the differences in diameter, thread pitch and length, metric and standard bolts can also be distinguished by examining the bolt heads. To begin with, the distance across the flats on a standard bolt head is measured in inches, while the same dimension on a metric bolt is sized in millimeters (the same is true for nuts). As a result, a standard wrench should not be used on a metric bolt and a metric wrench should not be used on a standard bolt. Also, most standard bolts have slashes radiating out from the center of the head to denote the grade or strength

of the bolt, which is an indication of the amount of torque that can be applied to it. The greater the number of slashes, the greater the strength of the bolt. Grades 0 through 5 are commonly used on automobiles. Metric bolts have a property class (grade) number, rather than a slash, molded into their heads to indicate bolt strength. In this case, the higher the number, the stronger the bolt. Property class numbers 8.8, 9.8 and 10.9 are commonly used on automobiles.

Strength markings can also be used to distinguish standard hex nuts from metric hex nuts. Many standard nuts have dots stamped into one side, while metric nuts are marked with a number. The greater the number of dots, or the higher the number, the greater the strength of the nut.

Metric studs are also marked on their ends according to property class (grade). Larger studs are numbered (the same as metric bolts), while smaller studs carry a geometric code to denote grade.

It should be noted that many fasteners, especially Grades 0 through 2, have no distinguishing marks on them. When such is the case, the only way to determine whether it is standard or metric is to measure the thread pitch or compare it to a known fastener of the same size.

Standard fasteners are often referred to as SAE, as opposed to metric. However, it should be noted that SAE technically refers to a non-metric fine thread fastener only. Coarse thread non-metric fasteners are referred to as USS sizes.

Since fasteners of the same size (both standard and metric) may have different strength ratings, be sure to reinstall any bolts, studs or nuts removed from your vehicle in their original locations. Also, when replacing a fastener with a new one, make sure that the new one has a strength rating equal to or greater than the original.

Tightening sequences and procedures

Most threaded fasteners should be tightened to a specific torque value (torque is the twisting force applied to a threaded component such as a nut or bolt). Overtightening the fastener can weaken it and cause it to break, while undertightening can cause it to eventually come loose. Bolts, screws and studs, depending on the material they are made of and their thread diameters, have specific torque values, many of which are noted in the Specifications at the end of each Chapter. Be sure to follow the torque recommendations closely. For fasteners not assigned a specific torque, a general torque value chart is presented here as a guide. These torque values are for dry (unlubricated) fasteners threaded into steel or cast iron (not aluminum). As was previously mentioned, the size and grade of a fastener determine the amount of torque that can safely be applied to it. The figures listed here are approximate for Grade 2 and Grade 3 fasteners. Higher grades can tolerate higher torque values.

Fasteners laid out in a pattern, such as cylinder head bolts, oil pan bolts, differential cover bolts, etc., must be loosened or tightened in sequence to avoid warping the component. This sequence will normally be shown in the appropriate Chapter. If a specific pattern is not given, the following procedures can be used to prevent warping.

Initially, the bolts or nuts should be assembled finger-tight only. Next, they should be tightened one full turn each, in a criss-cross or diagonal pattern. After each one has been tightened one full turn, return to the first one and tighten them all one-half turn, following the same

Grade 1 or 2 Grade 5 Grade 8

Bolt strength marking (standard/SAE/USS; bottom - metric)

Standard hex nut strength markings

Metric hex nut strength markings

Metric stud strength markings

00-1 HAYNES

pattern. Finally, tighten each of them one-quarter turn at a time until each fastener has been tightened to the proper torque. To loosen and remove the fasteners, the procedure would be reversed.

Component disassembly

Component disassembly should be done with care and purpose to help ensure that the parts go back together properly. Always keep track of the sequence in which parts are removed. Make note of special characteristics or marks on parts that can be installed more than one way, such as a grooved thrust washer on a shaft. It is a good idea to lay the disassembled parts out on a clean surface in the order that they were removed. It may also be helpful to make sketches or take instant photos of components before removal.

When removing fasteners from a component, keep track of their locations. Sometimes threading a bolt back in a part, or putting the washers and nut back on a stud, can prevent mix-ups later. If nuts and bolts cannot be returned to their original locations, they should be kept in a compartmented box or a series of small boxes. A cupcake or muffin tin is ideal for this purpose, since each cavity can hold the bolts and nuts from a particular area (i.e. oil pan bolts, valve cover bolts, engine

Metric thread sizes

	Ft-lbs	Nm
M-6	6 to 9	9 to 12
M-8	14 to 21	19 to 28
M-10	28 to 40	38 to 54
M-12	50 to 71	68 to 96
M-14	80 to 140	109 to 154

Pipe thread sizes

1/8	5 to 8	7 to 10
1/4	12 to 18	17 to 24
3/8	22 to 33	30 to 44
1/2	25 to 35	34 to 47

U.S. thread sizes

1/4 - 20	6 to 9	9 to 12
5/16 - 18	12 to 18	17 to 24
5/16 - 24	14 to 20	19 to 27
3/8 - 16	22 to 32	30 to 43
3/8 - 24	27 to 38	37 to 51
7/16 - 14	40 to 55	55 to 74
7/16 - 20	40 to 60	55 to 81
1/2 - 13	55 to 80	75 to 108

00-2 HAYNES

Standard (SAE and USS) bolt dimensions/grade marks

G   Grade marks (bolt strength)
L   Length (in inches)
T   Thread pitch (number of threads per inch)
D   Nominal diameter (in inches)

Metric bolt dimensions/grade marks

P   Property class (bolt strength)
L   Length (in millimeters)
T   Thread pitch (distance between threads in millimeters)
D   Diameter

mount bolts, etc.). A pan of this type is especially helpful when working on assemblies with very small parts, such as the carburetor, alternator, valve train or interior dash and trim pieces. The cavities can be marked with paint or tape to identify the contents.

Whenever wiring looms, harnesses or connectors are separated, it is a good idea to identify the two halves with numbered pieces of masking tape so they can be easily reconnected.

Gasket sealing surfaces

Throughout any vehicle, gaskets are used to seal the mating surfaces between two parts and keep lubricants, fluids, vacuum or pressure contained in an assembly.

Many times these gaskets are coated with a liquid or paste-type gasket sealing compound before assembly. Age, heat and pressure can sometimes cause the two parts to stick together so tightly that they are very difficult to separate. Often, the assembly can be loosened by striking it with a soft-face hammer near the mating surfaces. A regular hammer can be used if a block of wood is placed between the hammer and the part. Do not hammer on cast parts or parts that could be easily damaged. With any particularly stubborn part, always recheck to make sure that every fastener has been removed.

Avoid using a screwdriver or bar to pry apart an assembly, as

Micrometer set

Dial indicator set

they can easily mar the gasket sealing surfaces of the parts, which must remain smooth. If prying is absolutely necessary, use an old broom handle, but keep in mind that extra clean up will be necessary if the wood splinters.

After the parts are separated, the old gasket must be carefully scraped off and the gasket surfaces cleaned. Stubborn gasket material can be soaked with rust penetrant or treated with a special chemical to soften it so it can be easily scraped off.

✳✳ CAUTION:

Never use gasket removal solutions or caustic chemicals on plastic or other composite components.

A scraper can be fashioned from a piece of copper tubing by flattening and sharpening one end. Copper is recommended because it is usually softer than the surfaces to be scraped, which reduces the chance of gouging the part. Some gaskets can be removed with a wire brush, but regardless of the method used, the mating surfaces must be left clean and smooth. If for some reason the gasket surface is gouged, then a gasket sealer thick enough to fill scratches will have to be used during reassembly of the components. For most applications, a non-drying (or semi-drying) gasket sealer should be used.

Hose removal tips

✳✳ WARNING:

If the vehicle is equipped with air conditioning, do not disconnect any of the A/C hoses without first having the system depressurized by a dealer service department or a service station.

Hose removal precautions closely parallel gasket removal precautions. Avoid scratching or gouging the surface that the hose mates against or the connection may leak. This is especially true for radiator hoses. Because of various chemical reactions, the rubber in hoses can bond itself to the metal spigot that the hose fits over. To remove a hose, first loosen the hose clamps that secure it to the spigot. Then, with slip-joint pliers, grab the hose at the clamp and rotate it around the spigot. Work it back and forth until it is completely free, then pull it off. Silicone or other lubricants will ease removal if they can be applied

between the hose and the outside of the spigot. Apply the same lubricant to the inside of the hose and the outside of the spigot to simplify installation.

As a last resort (and if the hose is to be replaced with a new one anyway), the rubber can be slit with a knife and the hose peeled from the spigot. If this must be done, be careful that the metal connection is not damaged.

If a hose clamp is broken or damaged, do not reuse it. Wire-type clamps usually weaken with age, so it is a good idea to replace them with screw-type clamps whenever a hose is removed.

TOOLS

A selection of good tools is a basic requirement for anyone who plans to maintain and repair his or her own vehicle. For the owner who has few tools, the initial investment might seem high, but when compared to the spiraling costs of professional auto maintenance and repair, it is a wise one.

To help the owner decide which tools are needed to perform the tasks detailed in this manual, the following tool lists are offered: *Maintenance and minor repair, Repair/overhaul* and *Special.*

The newcomer to practical mechanics should start off with the *maintenance and minor repair* tool kit, which is adequate for the simpler jobs performed on a vehicle. Then, as confidence and experience grow, the owner can tackle more difficult tasks, buying additional tools as they are needed. Eventually the basic kit will be expanded into the *repair and overhaul* tool set. Over a period of time, the experienced do-it-yourselfer will assemble a tool set complete enough for most repair and overhaul procedures and will add tools from the special category when it is felt that the expense is justified by the frequency of use.

Maintenance and minor repair tool kit

The tools in this list should be considered the minimum required for performance of routine maintenance, servicing and minor repair work. We recommend the purchase of combination wrenches (box-end and open-end combined in one wrench). While more expensive than open end wrenches, they offer the advantages of both types of wrench.

Combination wrench set (1/4-inch to 1 inch or 6 mm to 19 mm)
Adjustable wrench, 8 inch
Spark plug wrench with rubber insert

Dial caliper

Hand-operated vacuum pump

Timing light

Compression gauge with spark plug hole adapter

Damper/steering wheel puller

General purpose puller

Hydraulic lifter removal tool

Spark plug gap adjusting tool
Feeler gauge set
Brake bleeder wrench
Standard screwdriver (5/16-inch x 6 inch)
Phillips screwdriver (No. 2 x 6 inch)
Combination pliers - 6 inch
Hacksaw and assortment of blades
Tire pressure gauge
Grease gun

Oil can
Fine emery cloth
Wire brush
Battery post and cable cleaning tool
Oil filter wrench
Funnel (medium size)
Safety goggles
Jackstands (2)
Drain pan

Valve spring compressor

Valve spring compressor

Ridge reamer

Piston ring groove cleaning tool

Ring removal/installation tool

Ring compressor

Cylinder hone

Brake hold-down spring tool

➡ Note: If basic tune-ups are going to be part of routine maintenance, it will be necessary to purchase a good quality stroboscopic timing light and combination tachometer/dwell meter. Although they are included in the list of special tools, it is mentioned here because they are absolutely necessary for tuning most vehicles properly.

Repair and overhaul tool set

These tools are essential for anyone who plans to perform major repairs and are in addition to those in the maintenance and minor repair tool kit. Included is a comprehensive set of sockets which, though expensive, are invaluable because of their versatility, especially when various extensions and drives are available. We recommend the 1/2-inch drive over the 3/8-inch drive. Although the larger drive is bulky and more expensive, it has the capacity of accepting a very wide range of large sockets. Ideally, however, the mechanic should have a 3/8-inch drive set and a 1/2-inch drive set.

Torque angle gauge

Clutch plate alignment tool

Socket set(s)
Reversible ratchet
Extension - 10 inch
Universal joint
Torque wrench (same size drive as sockets)
Ball peen hammer - 8 ounce
Soft-face hammer (plastic/rubber)
Standard screwdriver (1/4-inch x 6 inch)
Standard screwdriver (stubby - 5/16-inch)
Phillips screwdriver (No. 3 x 8 inch)
Phillips screwdriver (stubby - No. 2)
Pliers - vise grip
Pliers - lineman's
Pliers - needle nose
Pliers - snap-ring (internal and external)
Cold chisel - 1/2-inch
Scribe
Scraper (made from flattened copper tubing)
Centerpunch
Pin punches (1/16, 1/8, 3/16-inch)
Steel rule/straightedge - 12 inch
Allen wrench set (1/8 to 3/8-inch or 4 mm to 10 mm)
A selection of files
Wire brush (large)
Jackstands (second set)
Jack (scissor or hydraulic type)

➡ **Note: Another tool which is often useful is an electric drill with a chuck capacity of 3/8-inch and a set of good quality drill bits.**

Special tools

The tools in this list include those which are not used regularly, are expensive to buy, or which need to be used in accordance with their manufacturer's instructions. Unless these tools will be used frequently, it is not very economical to purchase many of them. A consideration would be to split the cost and use between yourself and a friend or friends. In addition, most of these tools can be obtained from a tool rental shop on a temporary basis.

This list primarily contains only those tools and instruments widely available to the public, and not those special tools produced by the vehicle manufacturer for distribution to dealer service departments. Occasionally, references to the manufacturer's special tools are included in the text of this manual. Generally, an alternative method of doing the job without the special tool is offered. However, sometimes there is no alternative to their use. Where this is the case, and the tool cannot be purchased or borrowed, the work should be turned over to the dealer service department or an automotive repair shop.

Valve spring compressor
Piston ring groove cleaning tool
Piston ring compressor
Piston ring installation tool
Cylinder compression gauge
Cylinder ridge reamer
Cylinder surfacing hone
Cylinder bore gauge
Micrometers and/or dial calipers
Hydraulic lifter removal tool
Balljoint separator
Universal-type puller
Impact screwdriver
Dial indicator set
Stroboscopic timing light (inductive pick-up)
Hand operated vacuum/pressure pump
Tachometer/dwell meter
Universal electrical multimeter
Cable hoist
Brake spring removal and installation tools
Floor jack

Tap and die set

Buying tools

For the do-it-yourselfer who is just starting to get involved in vehicle maintenance and repair, there are a number of options available when purchasing tools. If maintenance and minor repair is the extent of the work to be done, the purchase of individual tools is satisfactory. If, on the other hand, extensive work is planned, it would be a good idea to purchase a modest tool set from one of the large retail chain stores. A set can usually be bought at a substantial savings over the individual tool prices, and they often come with a tool box. As additional tools are needed, add-on sets, individual tools and a larger tool box can be purchased to expand the tool selection. Building a tool set gradually allows the cost of the tools to be spread over a longer period of time and gives the mechanic the freedom to choose only those tools that will actually be used.

Tool stores will often be the only source of some of the special tools that are needed, but regardless of where tools are bought, try to avoid cheap ones, especially when buying screwdrivers and sockets, because they won't last very long. The expense involved in replacing cheap tools will eventually be greater than the initial cost of quality tools.

Care and maintenance of tools

Good tools are expensive, so it makes sense to treat them with respect. Keep them clean and in usable condition and store them properly when not in use. Always wipe off any dirt, grease or metal chips before putting them away. Never leave tools lying around in the work area. Upon completion of a job, always check closely under the hood for tools that may have been left there so they won't get lost during a test drive.

Some tools, such as screwdrivers, pliers, wrenches and sockets, can be hung on a panel mounted on the garage or workshop wall, while others should be kept in a tool box or tray. Measuring instruments, gauges, meters, etc. must be carefully stored where they cannot be damaged by weather or impact from other tools.

When tools are used with care and stored properly, they will last a very long time. Even with the best of care, though, tools will wear out if used frequently. When a tool is damaged or worn out, replace it. Subsequent jobs will be safer and more enjoyable if you do.

HOW TO REPAIR DAMAGED THREADS

Sometimes, the internal threads of a nut or bolt hole can become stripped, usually from overtightening. Stripping threads is an all-too-common occurrence, especially when working with aluminum parts, because aluminum is so soft that it easily strips out.

Usually, external or internal threads are only partially stripped. After they've been cleaned up with a tap or die, they'll still work. Sometimes, however, threads are badly damaged. When this happens, you've got three choices:

1) *Drill and tap the hole to the next suitable oversize and install a*

larger diameter bolt, screw or stud.
2) *Drill and tap the hole to accept a threaded plug, then drill and tap the plug to the original screw size. You can also buy a plug already threaded to the original size. Then you simply drill a hole to the specified size, then run the threaded plug into the hole with a bolt and jam nut. Once the plug is fully seated, remove the jam nut and bolt.*
3) *The third method uses a patented thread repair kit like Heli-Coil or Slimsert. These easy-to-use kits are designed to repair damaged threads in straight-through holes and blind holes. Both are available as kits which can handle a variety of sizes and thread patterns. Drill the hole, then tap it with the special included tap. Install the Heli-Coil and the hole is back to its original diameter and thread pitch.*

Regardless of which method you use, be sure to proceed calmly and carefully. A little impatience or carelessness during one of these relatively simple procedures can ruin your whole day's work and cost you a bundle if you wreck an expensive part.

WORKING FACILITIES

Not to be overlooked when discussing tools is the workshop. If anything more than routine maintenance is to be carried out, some sort of suitable work area is essential.

It is understood, and appreciated, that many home mechanics do not have a good workshop or garage available, and end up removing an engine or doing major repairs outside. It is recommended, however, that the overhaul or repair be completed under the cover of a roof.

A clean, flat workbench or table of comfortable working height is an absolute necessity. The workbench should be equipped with a vise that has a jaw opening of at least four inches.

As mentioned previously, some clean, dry storage space is also required for tools, as well as the lubricants, fluids, cleaning solvents, etc. which soon become necessary.

Sometimes waste oil and fluids, drained from the engine or cooling system during normal maintenance or repairs, present a disposal problem. To avoid pouring them on the ground or into a sewage system, pour the used fluids into large containers, seal them with caps and take them to an authorized disposal site or recycling center. Plastic jugs, such as old antifreeze containers, are ideal for this purpose.

Always keep a supply of old newspapers and clean rags available. Old towels are excellent for mopping up spills. Many mechanics use rolls of paper towels for most work because they are readily available and disposable. To help keep the area under the vehicle clean, a large cardboard box can be cut open and flattened to protect the garage or shop floor.

Whenever working over a painted surface, such as when leaning over a fender to service something under the hood, always cover it with an old blanket or bedspread to protect the finish. Vinyl covered pads, made especially for this purpose, are available at auto parts stores.

Jacking and towing

JACKING

> ※ **WARNING:**
>
> **The jack supplied with the vehicle should only be used for changing a tire or placing jackstands under the frame. Never work under the vehicle or start the engine while this jack is being used as the only means of support.**

The vehicle should be on level ground. Place the shift lever in Park. Block the wheel diagonally opposite the wheel being changed. Set the parking brake.

Remove the spare tire and jack from stowage. Remove the wheel cover and trim ring (if so equipped) with the tapered end of the lug nut wrench by inserting and twisting the handle and then prying against the back of the wheel cover. Loosen, but do not remove, the lug nuts (one-half turn is sufficient).

Place the scissors-type jack under the vehicle and adjust the jack height until it engages with the proper jacking point. There is a front and rear jacking point on each side of the vehicle (see illustration).

Turn the jack handle clockwise until the tire clears the ground. Remove the lug nuts and pull the wheel off, then install the spare.

Install the lug nuts with the beveled edges facing in. Tighten them snugly. Don't attempt to tighten them completely until the vehicle is lowered or it could slip off the jack. Turn the jack handle counterclockwise to lower the vehicle. Remove the jack and tighten the lug nuts in a diagonal pattern.

Stow the tire, jack and wrench. Unblock the wheels.

TOWING

Two-wheel drive models can be towed from the front with the front wheels off the ground, using a wheel lift type tow truck. If towed from the rear, the front wheels must be placed on a dolly. All-wheel drive models must be towed with all four wheels off the ground. A sling-type tow truck cannot be used, as body damage will result. The best way to tow the vehicle is with a flat-bed car carrier.

In an emergency the vehicle can be towed a short distance with a cable or chain attached to one of the towing eyelets located under the front or rear bumpers. The driver must remain in the vehicle to operate the steering and brakes (remember that power steering and power brakes will not work with the engine off).

Place the jack between the raised welts on the rocker pane flange

Booster battery (jump) starting

Observe these precautions when using a booster battery to start a vehicle:

a) *Before connecting the booster battery, make sure the ignition switch is in the Off position.*

b) *Turn off the lights, heater and other electrical loads.*

c) *Your eyes should be shielded. Safety goggles are a good idea.*

d) *Make sure the booster battery is the same voltage as the dead one in the vehicle.*

e) *The two vehicles MUST NOT TOUCH each other!*

f) *Make sure the transaxle is in Neutral (manual) or Park (automatic).*

g) *If the booster battery is not a maintenance-free type, remove the vent caps and lay a cloth over the vent holes.*

Connect the red jumper cable to the positive (+) terminals of each battery (see illustration).

Connect one end of the black jumper cable to the negative (-) terminal of the booster battery. The other end of this cable should be connected to a good ground on the vehicle to be started, such as a bolt or bracket on the body.

Start the engine using the booster battery, then, with the engine running at idle speed, disconnect the jumper cables in the reverse order of connection.

Make the booster battery cable connections in the numerical order shown (note that the negative cable of the booster battery is NOT attached to the negative terminal of the dead battery)

Automotive chemicals and lubricants

A number of automotive chemicals and lubricants are available for use during vehicle maintenance and repair. They include a wide variety of products ranging from cleaning solvents and degreasers to lubricants and protective sprays for rubber, plastic and vinyl.

CLEANERS

Carburetor cleaner and choke cleaner is a strong solvent for gum, varnish and carbon. Most carburetor cleaners leave a dry-type lubricant film which will not harden or gum up. Because of this film it is not recommended for use on electrical components.

Brake system cleaner is used to remove brake dust, grease and brake fluid from the brake system, where clean surfaces are absolutely necessary. It leaves no residue and often eliminates brake squeal caused by contaminants.

Electrical cleaner removes oxidation, corrosion and carbon deposits from electrical contacts, restoring full current flow. It can also be used to clean spark plugs, carburetor jets, voltage regulators and other parts where an oil-free surface is desired.

Demoisturants remove water and moisture from electrical components such as alternators, voltage regulators, electrical connectors and fuse blocks. They are non-conductive and non-corrosive.

Degreasers are heavy-duty solvents used to remove grease from the outside of the engine and from chassis components. They can be sprayed or brushed on and, depending on the type, are rinsed off either with water or solvent.

LUBRICANTS

Motor oil is the lubricant formulated for use in engines. It normally contains a wide variety of additives to prevent corrosion and reduce foaming and wear. Motor oil comes in various weights (viscosity ratings) from 0 to 50. The recommended weight of the oil depends on the season, temperature and the demands on the engine. Light oil is used in cold climates and under light load conditions. Heavy oil is used in hot climates and where high loads are encountered. Multi-viscosity oils are designed to have characteristics of both light and heavy oils and are available in a number of weights from 0W-20 to 20W-50.

Gear oil is designed to be used in differentials, manual transmissions and other areas where high-temperature lubrication is required.

Chassis and wheel bearing grease is a heavy grease used where increased loads and friction are encountered, such as for wheel bearings, ball-joints, tie-rod ends and universal joints.

High-temperature wheel bearing grease is designed to withstand the extreme temperatures encountered by wheel bearings in disc brake equipped vehicles. It usually contains molybdenum disulfide (moly), which is a dry-type lubricant.

White grease is a heavy grease for metal-to-metal applications where water is a problem. White grease stays soft under both low and high temperatures (usually from -100 to +190-degrees F), and will not wash off or dilute in the presence of water.

Assembly lube is a special extreme pressure lubricant, usually containing moly, used to lubricate high-load parts (such as main and rod bearings and cam lobes) for initial start-up of a new engine. The assembly lube lubricates the parts without being squeezed out or washed away until the engine oiling system begins to function.

Silicone lubricants are used to protect rubber, plastic, vinyl and nylon parts.

Graphite lubricants are used where oils cannot be used due to contamination problems, such as in locks. The dry graphite will lubricate metal parts while remaining uncontaminated by dirt, water, oil or acids. It is electrically conductive and will not foul electrical contacts in locks such as the ignition switch.

Moly penetrants loosen and lubricate frozen, rusted and corroded fasteners and prevent future rusting or freezing.

Heat-sink grease is a special electrically non-conductive grease that is used for mounting electronic ignition modules where it is essential that heat is transferred away from the module.

SEALANTS

RTV sealant is one of the most widely used gasket compounds. Made from silicone, RTV is air curing, it seals, bonds, waterproofs, fills surface irregularities, remains flexible, doesn't shrink, is relatively easy to remove, and is used as a supplementary sealer with almost all low and medium temperature gaskets.

Anaerobic sealant is much like RTV in that it can be used either to seal gaskets or to form gaskets by itself. It remains flexible, is solvent resistant and fills surface imperfections. The difference between an anaerobic sealant and an RTV-type sealant is in the curing. RTV cures when exposed to air, while an anaerobic sealant cures only in the absence of air. This means that an anaerobic sealant cures only after the assembly of parts, sealing them together.

Thread and pipe sealant is used for sealing hydraulic and pneumatic fittings and vacuum lines. It is usually made from a Teflon compound, and comes in a spray, a paint-on liquid and as a wrap-around tape.

CHEMICALS

Anti-seize compound prevents seizing, galling, cold welding, rust and corrosion in fasteners. High-temperature anti-seize, usually made with copper and graphite lubricants, is used for exhaust system and exhaust manifold bolts.

Anaerobic locking compounds are used to keep fasteners from vibrating or working loose and cure only after installation, in the absence of air. Medium strength locking compound is used for small nuts, bolts and screws that may be removed later. High-strength locking compound is for large nuts, bolts and studs which aren't removed on a regular basis.

Oil additives range from viscosity index improvers to chemical treatments that claim to reduce internal engine friction. It should be noted that most oil manufacturers caution against using additives with their oils.

Gas additives perform several functions, depending on their chemical makeup. They usually contain solvents that help dissolve gum and varnish that build up on carburetor, fuel injection and intake parts. They also serve to break down carbon deposits that form on the inside surfaces of the combustion chambers. Some additives contain upper cylinder lubricants for valves and piston rings, and others contain chemicals to remove condensation from the gas tank.

MISCELLANEOUS

Brake fluid is specially formulated hydraulic fluid that can withstand the heat and pressure encountered in brake systems. Care must be taken so this fluid does not come in contact with painted surfaces or plastics. An opened container should always be resealed to prevent contamination by water or dirt.

Weatherstrip adhesive is used to bond weatherstripping around doors, windows and trunk lids. It is sometimes used to attach trim pieces.

Undercoating is a petroleum-based, tar-like substance that is designed to protect metal surfaces on the underside of the vehicle from corrosion. It also acts as a sound-deadening agent by insulating the bottom of the vehicle.

Waxes and polishes are used to help protect painted and plated surfaces from the weather. Different types of paint may require the use of different types of wax and polish. Some polishes utilize a chemical or abrasive cleaner to help remove the top layer of oxidized (dull) paint on older vehicles. In recent years many non-wax polishes that contain a wide variety of chemicals such as polymers and silicones have been introduced. These non-wax polishes are usually easier to apply and last longer than conventional waxes and polishes.

CONVERSION FACTORS

LENGTH (distance)

Inches (in)	X	25.4	= Millimeters (mm)	X 0.0394	= Inches (in)
Feet (ft)	X	0.305	= Meters (m)	X 3.281	= Feet (ft)
Miles	X	1.609	= Kilometers (km)	X 0.621	= Miles

VOLUME (capacity)

Cubic inches (cu in; in^3)	X	16.387	= Cubic centimeters (cc; cm^3)	X 0.061	= Cubic inches (cu in; in^3)
Imperial pints (Imp pt)	X	0.568	= Liters (l)	X 1.76	= Imperial pints (Imp pt)
Imperial quarts (Imp qt)	X	1.137	= Liters (l)	X 0.88	= Imperial quarts (Imp qt)
Imperial quarts (Imp qt)	X	1.201	= US quarts (US qt)	X 0.833	= Imperial quarts (Imp qt)
US quarts (US qt)	X	0.946	= Liters (l)	X 1.057	= US quarts (US qt)
Imperial gallons (Imp gal)	X	4.546	= Liters (l)	X 0.22	= Imperial gallons (Imp gal)
Imperial gallons (Imp gal)	X	1.201	= US gallons (US gal)	X 0.833	= Imperial gallons (Imp gal)
US gallons (US gal)	X	3.785	= Liters (l)	X 0.264	= US gallons (US gal)

MASS (weight)

Ounces (oz)	X	28.35	= Grams (g)	X 0.035	= Ounces (oz)
Pounds (lb)	X	0.454	= Kilograms (kg)	X 2.205	= Pounds (lb)

FORCE

Ounces-force (ozf; oz)	X	0.278	= Newtons (N)	X 3.6	= Ounces-force (ozf; oz)
Pounds-force (lbf; lb)	X	4.448	= Newtons (N)	X 0.225	= Pounds-force (lbf; lb)
Newtons (N)	X	0.1	= Kilograms-force (kgf; kg)	X 9.81	= Newtons (N)

PRESSURE

Pounds-force per square inch (psi; lbf/in^2; lb/in^2)	X	0.070	= Kilograms-force per square centimeter (kgf/cm^2; kg/cm^2)	X 14.223	= Pounds-force per square inch (psi; lbf/in^2; lb/in^2)
Pounds-force per square inch (psi; lbf/in^2; lb/in^2)	X	0.068	= Atmospheres (atm)	X 14.696	= Pounds-force per square inch (psi; lbf/in^2; lb/in^2)
Pounds-force per square inch (psi; lbf/in^2; lb/in^2)	X	0.069	= Bars	X 14.5	= Pounds-force per square inch (psi; lbf/in^2; lb/in^2)
Pounds-force per square inch (psi; lbf/in^2; lb/in^2)	X	6.895	= Kilopascals (kPa)	X 0.145	= Pounds-force per square inch (psi; lbf/in^2; lb/in^2)
Kilopascals (kPa)	X	0.01	= Kilograms-force per square centimeter (kgf/cm^2; kg/cm^2)	X 98.1	= Kilopascals (kPa)

TORQUE (moment of force)

Pounds-force inches (lbf in; lb in)	X	1.152	= Kilograms-force centimeter (kgf cm; kg cm)	X 0.868	= Pounds-force inches (lbf in; lb in)
Pounds-force inches (lbf in; lb in)	X	0.113	= Newton meters (Nm)	X 8.85	= Pounds-force inches (lbf in; lb in)
Pounds-force inches (lbf in; lb in)	X	0.083	= Pounds-force feet (lbf ft; lb ft)	X 12	= Pounds-force inches (lbf in; lb in)
Pounds-force feet (lbf ft; lb ft)	X	0.138	= Kilograms-force meters (kgf m; kg m)	X 7.233	= Pounds-force feet (lbf ft; lb ft)
Pounds-force feet (lbf ft; lb ft)	X	1.356	= Newton meters (Nm)	X 0.738	= Pounds-force feet (lbf ft; lb ft)
Newton meters (Nm)	X	0.102	= Kilograms-force meters (kgf m; kg m)	X 9.804	= Newton meters (Nm)

VACUUM

Inches mercury (in. Hg)	X	3.377	= Kilopascals (kPa)	X 0.2961	= Inches mercury
Inches mercury (in. Hg)	X	25.4	= Millimeters mercury (mm Hg)	X 0.0394	= Inches mercury

POWER

Horsepower (hp)	X	745.7	= Watts (W)	X 0.0013	= Horsepower (hp)

VELOCITY (speed)

Miles per hour (miles/hr; mph)	X	1.609	= Kilometers per hour (km/hr; kph)	X 0.621	= Miles per hour (miles/hr; mph)

FUEL CONSUMPTION *

Miles per gallon, Imperial (mpg)	X	0.354	= Kilometers per liter (km/l)	X 2.825	= Miles per gallon, Imperial (mpg)
Miles per gallon, US (mpg)	X	0.425	= Kilometers per liter (km/l)	X 2.352	= Miles per gallon, US (mpg)

TEMPERATURE

Degrees Fahrenheit = (°C x 1.8) + 32   Degrees Celsius (Degrees Centigrade; °C) = (°F - 32) x 0.56

*It is common practice to convert from miles per gallon (mpg) to liters/100 kilometers (l/100km), where mpg (Imperial) x l/100 km = 282 and mpg (US) x l/100 km = 235

FRACTION/DECIMAL/MILLIMETER EQUIVALENTS

DECIMALS TO MILLIMETERS

Decimal	mm	Decimal	mm
0.001	0.0254	0.500	12.7000
0.002	0.0508	0.510	12.9540
0.003	0.0762	0.520	13.2080
0.004	0.1016	0.530	13.4620
0.005	0.1270	0.540	13.7160
0.006	0.1524	0.550	13.9700
0.007	0.1778	0.560	14.2240
0.008	0.2032	0.570	14.4780
0.009	0.2286	0.580	14.7320
		0.590	14.9860
0.010	0.2540		
0.020	0.5080		
0.030	0.7620		
0.040	1.0160	0.600	15.2400
0.050	1.2700	0.610	15.4940
0.060	1.5240	0.620	15.7480
0.070	1.7780	0.630	16.0020
0.080	2.0320	0.640	16.2560
0.090	2.2860	0.650	16.5100
		0.660	16.7640
0.100	2.5400	0.670	17.0180
0.110	2.7940	0.680	17.2720
0.120	3.0480	0.690	17.5260
0.130	3.3020		
0.140	3.5560		
0.150	3.8100		
0.160	4.0640	0.700	17.7800
0.170	4.3180	0.710	18.0340
0.180	4.5720	0.720	18.2880
0.190	4.8260	0.730	18.5420
		0.740	18.7960
0.200	5.0800	0.750	19.0500
0.210	5.3340	0.760	19.3040
0.220	5.5880	0.770	19.5580
0.230	5.8420	0.780	19.8120
0.240	6.0960	0.790	20.0660
0.250	6.3500		
0.260	6.6040		
0.270	6.8580	0.800	20.3200
0.280	7.1120	0.810	20.5740
0.290	7.3660	0.820	21.8280
		0.830	21.0820
0.300	7.6200	0.840	21.3360
0.310	7.8740	0.850	21.5900
0.320	8.1280	0.860	21.8440
0.330	8.3820	0.870	22.0980
0.340	8.6360	0.880	22.3520
0.350	8.8900	0.890	22.6060
0.360	9.1440		
0.370	9.3980		
0.380	9.6520		
0.390	9.9060		
		0.900	22.8600
0.400	10.1600	0.910	23.1140
0.410	10.4140	0.920	23.3680
0.420	10.6680	0.930	23.6220
0.430	10.9220	0.940	23.8760
0.440	11.1760	0.950	24.1300
0.450	11.4300	0.960	24.3840
0.460	11.6840	0.970	24.6380
0.470	11.9380	0.980	24.8920
0.480	12.1920	0.990	25.1460
0.490	12.4460	1.000	25.4000

FRACTIONS TO DECIMALS TO MILLIMETERS

Fraction	Decimal	mm	Fraction	Decimal	mm
1/64	0.0156	0.3969	33/64	0.5156	13.0969
1/32	0.0312	0.7938	17/32	0.5312	13.4938
3/64	0.0469	1.1906	35/64	0.5469	13.8906
1/16	0.0625	1.5875	9/16	0.5625	14.2875
5/64	0.0781	1.9844	37/64	0.5781	14.6844
3/32	0.0938	2.3812	19/32	0.5938	15.0812
7/64	0.1094	2.7781	39/64	0.6094	15.4781
1/8	0.1250	3.1750	5/8	0.6250	15.8750
9/64	0.1406	3.5719	41/64	0.6406	16.2719
5/32	0.1562	3.9688	21/32	0.6562	16.6688
11/64	0.1719	4.3656	43/64	0.6719	17.0656
3/16	0.1875	4.7625	11/16	0.6875	17.4625
13/64	0.2031	5.1594	45/64	0.7031	17.8594
7/32	0.2188	5.5562	23/32	0.7188	18.2562
15/64	0.2344	5.9531	47/64	0.7344	18.6531
1/4	0.2500	6.3500	3/4	0.7500	19.0500
17/64	0.2656	6.7469	49/64	0.7656	19.4469
9/32	0.2812	7.1438	25/32	0.7812	19.8438
19/64	0.2969	7.5406	51/64	0.7969	20.2406
5/16	0.3125	7.9375	13/16	0.8125	20.6375
21/64	0.3281	8.3344	53/64	0.8281	21.0344
11/32	0.3438	8.7312	27/32	0.8438	21.4312
23/64	0.3594	9.1281	55/64	0.8594	21.8281
3/8	0.3750	9.5250	7/8	0.8750	22.2250
25/64	0.3906	9.9219	57/64	0.8906	22.6219
13/32	0.4062	10.3188	29/32	0.9062	23.0188
27/64	0.4219	10.7156	59/64	0.9219	23.4156
7/16	0.4375	11.1125	15/16	0.9375	23.8125
29/64	0.4531	11.5094	61/64	0.9531	24.2094
15/32	0.4688	11.9062	31/32	0.9688	24.6062
31/64	0.4844	12.3031	63/64	0.9844	25.0031
1/2	0.5000	12.7000	1	1.0000	25.4000

Safety first!

Regardless of how enthusiastic you may be about getting on with the job at hand, take the time to ensure that your safety is not jeopardized. A moment's lack of attention can result in an accident, as can failure to observe certain simple safety precautions. The possibility of an accident will always exist, and the following points should not be considered a comprehensive list of all dangers. Rather, they are intended to make you aware of the risks and to encourage a safety conscious approach to all work you carry out on your vehicle.

ESSENTIAL DOS AND DON'TS

DON'T rely on a jack when working under the vehicle. Always use approved jackstands to support the weight of the vehicle and place them under the recommended lift or support points.

DON'T attempt to loosen extremely tight fasteners (i.e. wheel lug nuts) while the vehicle is on a jack - it may fall.

DON'T start the engine without first making sure that the transmission is in Neutral (or Park where applicable) and the parking brake is set.

DON'T remove the radiator cap from a hot cooling system - let it cool or cover it with a cloth and release the pressure gradually.

DON'T attempt to drain the engine oil until you are sure it has cooled to the point that it will not burn you.

DON'T touch any part of the engine or exhaust system until it has cooled sufficiently to avoid burns.

DON'T siphon toxic liquids such as gasoline, antifreeze and brake fluid by mouth, or allow them to remain on your skin.

DON'T inhale brake lining dust - it is potentially hazardous (see Asbestos below).

DON'T allow spilled oil or grease to remain on the floor - wipe it up before someone slips on it.

DON'T use loose fitting wrenches or other tools which may slip and cause injury.

DON'T push on wrenches when loosening or tightening nuts or bolts. Always try to pull the wrench toward you. If the situation calls for pushing the wrench away, push with an open hand to avoid scraped knuckles if the wrench should slip.

DON'T attempt to lift a heavy component alone - get someone to help you.

DON'T rush or take unsafe shortcuts to finish a job.

DON'T allow children or animals in or around the vehicle while you are working on it.

DO wear eye protection when using power tools such as a drill, sander, bench grinder, etc. and when working under a vehicle.

DO keep loose clothing and long hair well out of the way of moving parts.

DO make sure that any hoist used has a safe working load rating adequate for the job.

DO get someone to check on you periodically when working alone on a vehicle.

DO carry out work in a logical sequence and make sure that everything is correctly assembled and tightened.

DO keep chemicals and fluids tightly capped and out of the reach of children and pets.

DO remember that your vehicle's safety affects that of yourself and others. If in doubt on any point, get professional advice.

STEERING, SUSPENSION AND BRAKES

These systems are essential to driving safety, so make sure you have a qualified shop or individual check your work. Also, compressed suspension springs can cause injury if released suddenly - be sure to use a spring compressor.

AIRBAGS

Airbags are explosive devices that can CAUSE injury if they deploy while you're working on the vehicle. Follow the manufacturer's instructions to disable the airbag whenever you're working in the vicinity of airbag components.

ASBESTOS

Certain friction, insulating, sealing, and other products - such as brake linings, brake bands, clutch linings, torque converters, gaskets, etc. - may contain asbestos or other hazardous friction material. Extreme care must be taken to avoid inhalation of dust from such products, since it is hazardous to health. If in doubt, assume that they do contain asbestos.

FIRE

Remember at all times that gasoline is highly flammable. Never smoke or have any kind of open flame around when working on a vehicle. But the risk does not end there. A spark caused by an electrical short circuit, by two metal surfaces contacting each other, or even by static electricity built up in your body under certain conditions, can ignite gasoline vapors, which in a confined space are highly explosive. Do not, under any circumstances, use gasoline for cleaning parts. Use an approved safety solvent.

Always disconnect the battery ground (-) cable at the battery before working on any part of the fuel system or electrical system. Never risk spilling fuel on a hot engine or exhaust component. It is strongly recommended that a fire extinguisher suitable for use on fuel and electrical fires be kept handy in the garage or workshop at all times. Never try to extinguish a fuel or electrical fire with water.

FUMES

Certain fumes are highly toxic and can quickly cause unconsciousness and even death if inhaled to any extent. Gasoline vapor falls into this category, as do the vapors from some cleaning solvents. Any draining or pouring of such volatile fluids should be done in a well ventilated area.

When using cleaning fluids and solvents, read the instructions on the container carefully. Never use materials from unmarked containers.

Never run the engine in an enclosed space, such as a garage. Exhaust fumes contain carbon monoxide, which is extremely poisonous. If you need to run the engine, always do so in the open air, or at least have the rear of the vehicle outside the work area.

THE BATTERY

Never create a spark or allow a bare light bulb near a battery. They normally give off a certain amount of hydrogen gas, which is highly explosive.

Always disconnect the battery ground (-) cable at the battery before working on the fuel or electrical systems.

If possible, loosen the filler caps or cover when charging the battery from an external source (this does not apply to sealed or maintenance-free batteries). Do not charge at an excessive rate or the battery may burst.

Take care when adding water to a non maintenance-free battery and when carrying a battery. The electrolyte, even when diluted, is very corrosive and should not be allowed to contact clothing or skin.

Always wear eye protection when cleaning the battery to prevent the caustic deposits from entering your eyes.

HOUSEHOLD CURRENT

When using an electric power tool, inspection light, etc., which operates on household current, always make sure that the tool is correctly connected to its plug and that, where necessary, it is properly grounded. Do not use such items in damp conditions and, again, do not create a spark or apply excessive heat in the vicinity of fuel or fuel vapor.

SECONDARY IGNITION SYSTEM VOLTAGE

A severe electric shock can result from touching certain parts of the ignition system (such as the spark plug wires) when the engine is running or being cranked, particularly if components are damp or the insulation is defective. In the case of an electronic ignition system, the secondary system voltage is much higher and could prove fatal.

HYDROFLUORIC ACID

This extremely corrosive acid is formed when certain types of synthetic rubber, found in some O-rings, oil seals, fuel hoses, etc. are exposed to temperatures above 750-degrees F (400-degrees C). The rubber changes into a charred or sticky substance containing the acid. *Once formed, the acid remains dangerous for years. If it gets onto the skin, it may be necessary to amputate the limb concerned.*

When dealing with a vehicle which has suffered a fire, or with components salvaged from such a vehicle, wear protective gloves and discard them after use.

Troubleshooting

CONTENTS

Section   Symptom

Engine

1   Engine will not rotate when attempting to start
2   Engine rotates but will not start
3   Engine hard to start when cold
4   Engine hard to start when hot
5   Starter motor noisy or excessively rough in engagement
6   Engine starts but stops immediately
7   Oil puddle under engine
8   Engine lopes while idling or idles erratically
9   Engine misses at idle speed
10   Engine misses throughout driving speed range
11   Engine stumbles on acceleration
12   Engine surges while holding accelerator steady
13   Engine stalls
14   Engine lacks power
15   Engine backfires
16   Pinging or knocking engine sounds during acceleration or uphill
17   Engine runs with oil pressure light on
18   Engine continues to run after switching off

Engine electrical systems

19   Battery will not hold a charge
20   Alternator light fails to go out
21   Alternator light fails to come on when key is turned on

Fuel system

22   Excessive fuel consumption
23   Fuel leakage and/or fuel odor

Cooling system

24   Overheating
25   Overcooling
26   External coolant leakage
27   Internal coolant leakage
28   Coolant loss
29   Poor coolant circulation

Automatic transaxle

30   Fluid leakage

Section   Symptom

31   Transaxle fluid brown or has burned smell
32   General shift mechanism problems
33   Transaxle slips, shifts roughly, is noisy or has no drive in forward or reverse gears

Driveaxles

34   Clicking noise in turns
35   Shudder or vibration during acceleration
36   Vibration at highway speeds

Brakes

37   Vehicle pulls to one side during braking
38   Noise (high-pitched squeal when the brakes are applied)
39   Brake roughness or chatter (pedal pulsates)
40   Excessive pedal effort required to stop vehicle
41   Excessive brake pedal travel
42   Dragging brakes
43   Grabbing or uneven braking action
44   Brake pedal feels spongy when depressed
45   Brake pedal travels to the floor with little resistance
46   Parking brake does not hold

Suspension and steering systems

47   Vehicle pulls to one side
48   Abnormal or excessive tire wear
49   Wheel makes a thumping noise
50   Shimmy, shake or vibration
51   Hard steering
52   Poor returnability of steering to center
53   Abnormal noise at the front end
54   Wander or poor steering stability
55   Erratic steering when braking
56   Excessive pitching and/or rolling around corners or during braking
57   Suspension bottoms
58   Cupped tires
59   Excessive tire wear on outside edge
60   Excessive tire wear on inside edge
61   Tire tread worn in one place
62   Excessive play or looseness in steering system
63   Rattling or clicking noise in rack and pinion

This section provides an easy reference guide to the more common problems which may occur during the operation of your vehicle. These problems and their possible causes are grouped under headings denoting various components or systems, such as Engine, Cooling system, etc. They also refer you to the chapter and/or section which deals with the problem.

Remember that successful troubleshooting is not a mysterious black art practiced only by professional mechanics. It is simply the result of the right knowledge combined with an intelligent, systematic approach to the problem. Always work by a process of elimination, starting with the simplest solution and working through to the most complex - and never overlook the obvious. Anyone can run the gas tank dry or leave the lights on overnight, so don't assume that you are exempt from such oversights.

Finally, always establish a clear idea of why a problem has occurred and take steps to ensure that it doesn't happen again. If the electrical system fails because of a poor connection, check the other connections in the system to make sure that they don't fail as well. If a particular fuse continues to blow, find out why - don't just replace one fuse after another. Remember, failure of a small component can often be indicative of potential failure or incorrect functioning of a more important component or system.

ENGINE

1 Engine will not rotate when attempting to start

1 Battery terminal connections loose or corroded (Chapter 1).
2 Battery discharged or faulty (Chapters 1 and 5).
3 Automatic transaxle not completely engaged in Park (Chapter 7).
4 Broken, loose or disconnected wiring in the starting circuit (Chapters 5 and 12).
5 Starter motor pinion jammed in flywheel ring gear (Chapter 5).
6 Starter solenoid faulty (Chapter 5).
7 Starter motor faulty (Chapter 5).
8 Ignition switch faulty (Chapter 12).
9 Starter pinion or flywheel teeth worn or broken (Chapter 5).

2 Engine rotates but will not start

1 Fuel tank empty.
2 Battery discharged (engine rotates slowly) (Chapter 5).
3 Battery terminal connections loose or corroded (Chapter 1).
4 Leaking fuel injector(s), faulty fuel pump, pressure regulator, etc. (Chapter 4).
5 Broken timing chain (Chapter 2A or 2B).
6 Ignition components damp or damaged (Chapter 5).
7 Worn, faulty or incorrectly-gapped spark plugs (Chapter 1).
8 Broken, loose or disconnected wiring in the starting circuit (Chapter 5).
9 Broken, loose or disconnected wires at the ignition coil or faulty coil (Chapter 5).
10 Defective crankshaft or camshaft sensor (Chapter 6).

3 Engine hard to start when cold

1 Battery discharged or low (Chapter 1).
2 Malfunctioning fuel system (Chapter 4).
3 Faulty coolant temperature sensor or intake air temperature sensor (Chapter 6).
4 Faulty ignition system (Chapter 5).

4 Engine hard to start when hot

1 Air filter clogged (Chapter 1).
2 Fuel not reaching the fuel injection system (Chapter 4).
3 Corroded battery connections (Chapter 1).
4 Faulty coolant temperature sensor or intake air temperature sensor (Chapter 6).

5 Starter motor noisy or excessively rough in engagement

1 Pinion or flywheel gear teeth worn or broken (Chapter 5).
2 Starter motor mounting bolts loose or missing (Chapter 5).

6 Engine starts but stops immediately

1 Insufficient fuel reaching the fuel injector(s) (Chapters 1 and 4).
2 Vacuum leak at the gasket between the intake manifold/plenum and throttle body (Chapter 4).

7 Oil puddle under engine

1 Oil pan gasket and/or oil pan drain bolt washer leaking (Chapter 2).
2 Oil pressure sending unit leaking (Chapter 2).
3 Valve cover leaking (Chapter 2).
4 Engine oil seals leaking (Chapter 2).
5 Oil pump housing leaking (Chapter 2).

8 Engine lopes while idling or idles erratically

1 Vacuum leakage (Chapters 2 and 4).
2 Leaking EGR valve (Chapter 6).
3 Air filter clogged (Chapter 1).
4 Malfunction in the fuel injection or engine control system (Chapters 4 and 6).
5 Leaking head gasket (Chapter 2).
6 Timing chain and/or sprockets worn (Chapter 2).
7 Camshaft lobes worn (Chapter 2).

9 Engine misses at idle speed

1 Spark plugs worn or not gapped properly (Chapter 1).
2 Faulty coil(s) (Chapter 1).
3 Vacuum leaks (Chapter 1).
4 Uneven or low compression (Chapter 2).
5 Problem with the fuel injection system (Chapter 4).

10 Engine misses throughout driving speed range

1 Fuel filter clogged and/or impurities in the fuel system (Chapters 1 and 4).
2 Low fuel pressure (Chapter 4).
3 Faulty or incorrectly gapped spark plugs (Chapter 1).
4 Faulty emission system components (Chapter 6).

5   Low or uneven cylinder compression pressures (Chapter 2).
6   Weak or faulty ignition system (Chapter 5).
7   Vacuum leak in fuel injection system, intake manifold, air control valve or vacuum hoses (Chapters 4 and 6).

11   Engine stumbles on acceleration

1   Spark plugs fouled (Chapter 1).
2   Problem with fuel injection or engine control system (Chapters 4 and 6).
3   Fuel filter clogged (Chapters 1 and 4).
4   Intake manifold air leak (Chapters 2 and 4).
5   Problem with the emissions control system (Chapter 6).

12   Engine surges while holding accelerator steady

1   Intake air leak (Chapter 4).
2   Fuel pump or fuel pressure regulator faulty (Chapter 4).
3   Problem with the fuel injection system (Chapter 4).
4   Problem with the emissions control system (Chapter 6).

13   Engine stalls

1   Idle speed incorrect (Chapter 1).
2   Fuel filter clogged and/or water and impurities in the fuel system (Chapters 1 and 4).
3   Faulty emissions system components (Chapter 6).
4   Faulty or incorrectly-gapped spark plugs (Chapter 1).
5   Vacuum leak in the fuel injection system, intake manifold or vacuum hoses (Chapters 2 and 4).

14   Engine lacks power

1   Obstructed exhaust system (Chapter 4).
2   Faulty or incorrectly-gapped spark plugs (Chapter 1).
3   Problem with the fuel injection system (Chapter 4).
4   Dirty air filter (Chapter 1).
5   Brakes binding (Chapter 9).
6   Automatic transaxle fluid level incorrect (Chapter 1).
7   Clutch slipping (Chapter 8).
8   Fuel filter clogged and/or impurities in the fuel system (Chapters 1 and 4).
9   Emission control system not functioning properly (Chapter 6).
10 Low or uneven cylinder compression pressures (Chapter 2).

15   Engine backfires

1   Emission control system not functioning properly (Chapter 6).
2   Problem with the fuel injection system (Chapter 4).
3   Vacuum leak at fuel injector(s), intake manifold or vacuum hoses (Chapters 2 and 4).
4   Valve clearances incorrectly set (four-cylinder engines) and/or valves sticking (Chapter 2).

16   Pinging or knocking engine sounds during acceleration or uphill

1   Incorrect grade of fuel.
2   Fuel injection system faulty (Chapter 4).

3   Improper or damaged spark plugs or wires (Chapter 1).
4   Knock sensor defective (Chapter 6).
5   EGR valve not functioning (Chapter 6).
6   Vacuum leak (Chapters 2 and 4).

17   Engine runs with oil pressure light on

1   Low oil level (Chapter 1).
2   Idle rpm below specification (Chapter 1).
3   Short in wiring circuit (Chapter 12).
4   Faulty oil pressure sender (Chapter 2).
5   Worn engine bearings and/or oil pump (Chapter 2).

18   Engine continues to run after switching off

Defective ignition switch (Chapter 12).

ENGINE ELECTRICAL SYSTEMS

19   Battery will not hold a charge

1   Drivebelt or tensioner defective (Chapter 1).
2   Battery electrolyte level low (Chapter 1).
3   Battery terminals loose or corroded (Chapter 1).
4   Alternator not charging properly (Chapter 5).
5   Loose, broken or faulty wiring in the charging circuit (Chapter 5).
6   Short in vehicle wiring (Chapter 12).
7   Internally defective battery (Chapters 1 and 5).

20   Alternator light fails to go out

1   Faulty alternator or charging circuit (Chapter 5).
2   Drivebelt or tensioner defective (Chapter 1).

21   Alternator light fails to come on when key is turned on

1   Instrument cluster defective (Chapter 12).
2   Fault in the Smart Junction Box or wiring harness (Chapter 12).

FUEL SYSTEM

22   Excessive fuel consumption

1   Dirty air filter element (Chapter 1).
2   Emissions system not functioning properly (Chapter 6).
3   Fuel injection system not functioning properly (Chapter 4).
4   Low tire pressure or incorrect tire size (Chapter 1).

23   Fuel leakage and/or fuel odor

1   Leaking fuel line (Chapters 1 and 4).
2   Tank overfilled.
3   Evaporative emissions control system problem (Chapters 1 and 6).
4   Problem with the fuel injection system (Chapter 4).

COOLING SYSTEM

24 Overheating

1 Insufficient coolant in system (Chapter 1).
2 Water pump drivebelt defective or out of adjustment (Chapter 1).
3 Radiator core blocked or grille restricted (Chapter 3).
4 Thermostat faulty (Chapter 3).
5 Electric coolant fan inoperative or blades broken (Chapter 3).
6 Expansion tank cap not maintaining proper pressure (Chapter 3).

25 Overcooling

1 Faulty thermostat (Chapter 3).
2 Inaccurate temperature gauge sending unit (Chapter 3).

26 External coolant leakage

1 Deteriorated/damaged hoses; loose clamps (Chapters 1 and 3).
2 Water pump defective (Chapter 3).
3 Leakage from radiator core or coolant reservoir (Chapter 3).
4 Engine drain or water jacket core plugs leaking (Chapter 2).

27 Internal coolant leakage

1 Leaking cylinder head gasket (Chapter 2).
2 Cracked cylinder bore or cylinder head (Chapter 2).

28 Coolant loss

1 Too much coolant in reservoir (Chapter 1).
2 Coolant boiling away because of overheating (Chapter 3).
3 Internal or external leakage (Chapter 3).
4 Faulty radiator cap (Chapter 3).

29 Poor coolant circulation

1 Inoperative water pump (Chapter 3).
2 Restriction in cooling system (Chapters 1 and 3).
3 Drivebelt or tensioner defective (Chapter 1).
4 Thermostat sticking (Chapter 3).

AUTOMATIC TRANSAXLE

➡ Note: Due to the complexity of the automatic transaxle, it is difficult for the home mechanic to properly diagnose and service this component. For problems other than the following, the vehicle should be taken to a dealer or transmission shop.

30 Fluid leakage

1 Automatic transaxle fluid is a deep red color. Fluid leaks should not be confused with engine oil, which can easily be blown onto the transaxle by air flow.

2 To pinpoint a leak, first remove all built-up dirt and grime from the transaxle housing with degreasing agents and/or steam cleaning. Then drive the vehicle at low speeds so air flow will not blow the leak far from its source. Raise the vehicle and determine where the leak is coming from. Common areas of leakage are:

a) Dipstick tube (Chapters 1 and 7).
b) Transaxle oil lines (Chapter 7).
c) Speed sensor (Chapter 6).
d) Driveaxle oil seals (Chapter 7).

31 Transaxle fluid brown or has a burned smell

Transaxle fluid overheated (Chapter 1).

32 General shift mechanism problems

1 Chapter 7A deals with checking and adjusting the shift cable on automatic transaxles. Common problems which may be attributed to poorly adjusted linkage are:

a) Engine starting in gears other than Park or Neutral.
b) Indicator on shifter pointing to a gear other than the one actually being used.
c) Vehicle moves when in Park.

2 Refer to Chapter 7A for the shift cable adjustment procedure.

33 Transaxle slips, shifts roughly, is noisy or has no drive in forward or reverse gears

There are many probable causes for the above problems, but the home mechanic should be concerned with only one possibility - fluid level. Before taking the vehicle to a repair shop, check the level and condition of the fluid as described in Chapter 1. Correct the fluid level as necessary or change the fluid and filter if needed. If the problem persists, have a professional diagnose the cause.

DRIVEAXLES

34 Clicking noise in turns

Worn or damaged outboard CV joint (Chapter 8).

35 Shudder or vibration during acceleration

1 Excessive toe-in (Chapter 10).
2 Worn or damaged inboard or outboard CV joints (Chapter 8).
3 Sticking inboard CV joint assembly (Chapter 8).

36 Vibration at highway speeds

1 Out-of-balance front wheels and/or tires (Chapters 1 and 10).
2 Out-of-round front tires (Chapters 1 and 10).
3 Worn CV joint(s) (Chapter 8).

BRAKES

➡ Note: Before assuming that a brake problem exists, make sure that:

a) The tires are in good condition and properly inflated (Chapter 1).
b) The front end alignment is correct.
c) The vehicle is not loaded with weight in an unequal manner.

37   Vehicle pulls to one side during braking

1   Incorrect tire pressures (Chapter 1).
2   Front end out of alignment (have the front end aligned).
3   Front, or rear, tire sizes not matched to one another.
4   Restricted brake lines or hoses (Chapter 9).
5   Malfunctioning caliper assembly (Chapter 9).
6   Loose suspension parts (Chapter 10).
7   Excessive wear of pad material or disc on one side (Chapter 9).
8   Contamination (grease or brake fluid) of brake pad material or disc on one side (Chapter 9).

38   Noise (high-pitched squeal when the brakes are applied)

Brake pads worn out. Replace pads with new ones immediately (Chapter 9).

39   Brake roughness or chatter (pedal pulsates)

1   Excessive lateral runout (Chapter 9).
2   Uneven pad wear (Chapter 9).
3   Defective disc (Chapter 9).

40   Excessive brake pedal effort required to stop vehicle

1   Malfunctioning power brake booster (Chapter 9).
2   Partial system failure (Chapter 9).
3   Excessively worn pads (Chapter 9).
4   Piston in caliper stuck or sluggish (Chapter 9).
5   Brake pads contaminated with oil or grease (Chapter 9).
6   Brake disc grooved and/or glazed (Chapter 9).

41   Excessive brake pedal travel

1   Partial brake system failure (Chapter 9).
2   Insufficient fluid in master cylinder (Chapters 1 and 9).
3   Air trapped in system (Chapter 9).

42   Dragging brakes

1   Incorrect adjustment of brake light switch (Chapter 9).
2   Master cylinder pistons not returning correctly (Chapter 9).
3   Caliper piston stuck (Chapter 9).
3   Restricted brakes lines or hoses (Chapter 9).
4   Incorrect parking brake adjustment (Chapter 9).

43   Grabbing or uneven braking action

1   Malfunction of proportioning valve (Chapter 9).
2   Binding brake pedal mechanism (Chapter 9).
3   Contaminated brake linings (Chapter 9).

44   Brake pedal feels spongy when depressed

1   Air in hydraulic lines (Chapter 9).

2   Master cylinder mounting bolts loose (Chapter 9).
3   Master cylinder defective (Chapter 9).

45   Brake pedal travels to the floor with little resistance

1   Little or no fluid in the master cylinder reservoir caused by leaking caliper piston(s) (Chapter 9).
2   Loose, damaged or disconnected brake lines (Chapter 9).

46   Parking brake does not hold

Parking brake improperly adjusted (Chapter 9).

SUSPENSION AND STEERING SYSTEMS

➡ **Note: Before attempting to diagnose the suspension and steering systems, perform the following preliminary checks:**

 a) *Tires for wrong pressure and uneven wear.*
 b) *Steering universal joints from the column to the rack and pinion for loose connectors or wear.*
 c) *Front and rear suspension and the rack-and-pinion assembly for loose or damaged parts.*
 d) *Out-of-round or out-of-balance tires, bent rims and loose and/or rough wheel bearings.*

47   Vehicle pulls to one side

1   Mismatched or uneven tires (Chapter 10).
2   Broken or sagging springs (Chapter 10).
3   Wheel alignment incorrect. Have the wheels professionally aligned.
4   Front brake dragging (Chapter 9).

48   Abnormal or excessive tire wear

1   Wheel alignment out-of-specification. Have the wheels professionally aligned.
2   Sagging or broken springs (Chapter 10).
3   Tire out-of-balance (Chapter 10).
4   Worn strut damper (Chapter 10).
5   Overloaded vehicle.
6   Tires not rotated regularly.

49   Wheel makes a thumping noise

1   Blister or bump on tire (Chapter 10).
2   Improper strut damper action (Chapter 10).

50   Shimmy, shake or vibration

1   Tire or wheel out-of-balance or out-of-round (Chapter 10).
2   Loose or worn wheel bearings (Chapter 10).
3   Worn tie-rod ends (Chapter 10).
4   Worn balljoints (Chapters 1 and 10).
5   Excessive wheel runout (Chapter 10).
6   Blister or bump on tire (Chapter 10).

51 Hard steering

1 Lack of lubrication at balljoints and/or tie-rod ends (Chapter 10).
2 Wheel alignment out-of-specifications. Have the wheels professionally aligned.
3 Low tire pressure(s) (Chapter 1).
4 Worn steering gear (Chapter 10).

52 Poor returnability of steering to center

1 Worn balljoints or tie-rod ends (Chapter 10).
2 Worn steering gear assembly (Chapter 10).
3 Wheel alignment out-of-specifications. Have the wheels professionally aligned.

53 Abnormal noise at the front end

1 Worn balljoints or tie-rod ends (Chapter 10).
2 Damaged shock absorber mounting (Chapter 10).
3 Worn control arm bushings or tie-rod ends (Chapter 10).
4 Loose stabilizer bar (Chapter 10).
5 Loose wheel nuts (Chapter 1).
6 Loose suspension bolts (Chapter 10).

54 Wander or poor steering stability

1 Mismatched or uneven tires (Chapter 10).
2 Lack of lubrication at balljoints and tie-rod ends (Chapters 1 and 10).
3 Worn shock absorber assemblies (Chapter 10).
4 Loose stabilizer bar (Chapter 10).
5 Broken or sagging springs (Chapter 10).
6 Wheels out of alignment. Have the wheels professionally aligned.

55 Erratic steering when braking

1 Wheel bearings worn (Chapter 10).
2 Broken or sagging springs (Chapter 10).
3 Leaking wheel cylinder or caliper (Chapter 10).
4 Excessive brake disc runout (Chapter 9).

56 Excessive pitching and/or rolling around corners or during braking

1 Loose stabilizer bar (Chapter 10).
2 Worn strut dampers or mountings (Chapter 10).
3 Broken or sagging springs (Chapter 10).
4 Overloaded vehicle.

57 Suspension bottoms

1 Overloaded vehicle.
2 Sagging springs (Chapter 10).

58 Cupped tires

1 Front wheel or rear wheel alignment out-of-specifications. Have the wheels professionally aligned.
2 Worn shock absorbers (Chapter 10).
3 Wheel bearings worn (Chapter 10).
4 Excessive tire or wheel runout (Chapter 10).
5 Worn balljoints (Chapter 10).

59 Excessive tire wear on outside edge

1 Inflation pressures incorrect (Chapter 1).
2 Excessive speed in turns.
3 Wheel alignment incorrect (excessive toe-in). Have professionally aligned.
4 Suspension arm bent or twisted (Chapter 10).

60 Excessive tire wear on inside edge

1 Inflation pressures incorrect (Chapter 1).
2 Wheel alignment incorrect (toe-out). Have professionally aligned.
3 Loose or damaged steering components (Chapter 10).

61 Tire tread worn in one place

1 Tires out-of-balance.
2 Damaged or buckled wheel. Inspect and replace if necessary.
3 Defective tire (Chapter 1).

62 Excessive play or looseness in steering system

1 Wheel bearing(s) worn (Chapter 10).
2 Tie-rod end loose (Chapter 10).
3 Steering gear loose (Chapter 10).
4 Worn or loose steering intermediate shaft U-joint (Chapter 10).

63 Rattling or clicking noise in steering gear

1 Steering gear loose (Chapter 10).
2 Steering gear defective.

Section

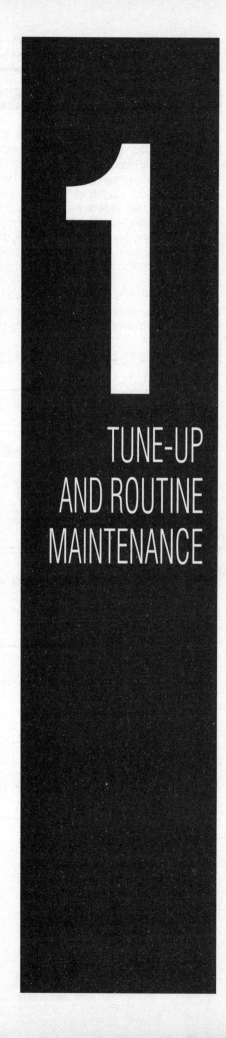

1

TUNE-UP
AND ROUTINE
MAINTENANCE

1 Maintenance schedule

The maintenance intervals in this manual are provided with the assumption that you, not the dealer, will be doing the work. These are the minimum maintenance intervals recommended by the factory for vehicles that are driven daily. If you wish to keep your vehicle in peak condition at all times, you may wish to perform some of these procedures even more often. Because frequent maintenance enhances the efficiency, performance and resale value of your car, we encourage you to do so. If you drive in dusty areas, tow a trailer, idle or drive at low speeds for extended periods or drive for short distances (less than four miles) in below freezing temperatures, shorter intervals are also recommended.

When your vehicle is new, it should be serviced by a factory authorized dealer service department to protect the factory warranty. In many cases, the initial maintenance check is done at no cost to the owner.

EVERY 250 MILES (400 KM) OR WEEKLY, WHICHEVER COMES FIRST

Check the engine oil level (Section 4)
Check the engine coolant level (Section 4)
Check the brake fluid level (Section 4)
Check the windshield washer fluid level (Section 4)
Check the power steering fluid level (Section 4)
Check the tires and tire pressures (Section 5)

EVERY 3000 MILES (4800 KM) OR 3 MONTHS, WHICHEVER COMES FIRST

All items listed above plus:
Change the engine oil and oil filter (Section 6)

EVERY 7500 MILES (12,000 KM) OR 6 MONTHS, WHICHEVER COMES FIRST

All items listed above plus:
Inspect (and replace, if necessary) the windshield wiper blades (Section 7)
Check and service the battery (Section 8)
Check the cooling system (Section 9)
Rotate the tires (Section 10)
Check the seat belts (Section 11)

EVERY 15,000 MILES (24,000 KM) OR 12 MONTHS, WHICHEVER COMES FIRST

All items listed above plus:
Check the automatic transaxle fluid level (Section 4)
Check all underhood hoses (Section 12)

Inspect the brake system (Section 13)*
Inspect the suspension, steering and driveaxle boots (Section 14)*
Check the fuel system (Section 15)
Check the transfer case lubricant level (AWD models) (Section 16)
Check (and replace, if necessary) the air filter (Section 17)*
Replace the cabin air filter (Section 18)

EVERY 30,000 MILES (48,000 KM) OR 24 MONTHS, WHICHEVER COMES FIRST

All items listed above plus:
Check the exhaust system (Section 19)
Service the cooling system (drain, flush and refill) (Section 20)
Change the brake fluid (Section 21)
Check/adjust the engine drivebelts (Section 22)

EVERY 60,000 MILES (72,420 KM) OR 48 MONTHS, WHICHEVER COMES FIRST

Replace the automatic transaxle fluid (Section 23)**
Replace the rear differential lubricant (AWD) (Section 24)**
Check (and replace, if necessary) the spark plugs (conventional, non-platinum or iridium type) (Section 26)

EVERY 100,000 MILES (160,000 KM)

Replace the spark plugs (iridium or platinum-tipped type) (Section 26)
*This item is affected by "severe" operating conditions as described below. If your vehicle is operated under "severe" conditions, perform all maintenance indicated with an asterisk (*) at 3000 mile/3 month intervals. Severe conditions are indicated if you mainly operate your vehicle under one or more of the following conditions:
Operating in dusty areas
Towing a trailer
Idling for extended periods and/or low speed operation
Operating when outside temperatures remain below freezing and when most trips are less than 4 miles
** If operated under one or more of the following conditions, change the automatic transaxle fluid and differential lubricant every 30,000 miles:
Operating in dusty areas
In heavy city traffic where the outside temperature regularly reaches 90-degrees F (32-degrees C) or higher
In hilly or mountainous terrain
On flex-fuel models, using E85 fuel more than 50% of the time

Typical engine compartment components (four-cylinder engine)

1	Automatic transaxle fluid filler tube	5	Air filter housing	9	Engine oil filler cap
2	Brake fluid reservoir	6	Radiator hose	10	Coolant expansion tank
3	Battery	7	Engine oil dipstick	11	Power steering fluid reservoir
4	Fuse/relay block	8	Windshield washer fluid reservoir		

Typical engine compartment underside components (four-cylinder engine)

1	Engine oil filter	3	Front disc brake caliper	5	Automatic transaxle drain plug
2	Driveaxle boot	4	Engine oil drain plug	6	Exhaust system

Typical rear underside components (2WD)

1   Rear disc brake caliper
2   Muffler
3   Coil springs

4   Stabilizer bar
5   Exhaust system hanger
6   Shock absorbers

7   Parking brake cables
8   Fuel tank

2 Introduction

This Chapter is designed to help the home mechanic maintain the Ford Edge or Lincoln MKX with the goals of maximum performance, economy, safety and reliability in mind.

Included is a master maintenance schedule, followed by procedures dealing specifically with each item on the schedule. Visual checks, adjustments, component replacement and other helpful items are included. Refer to the accompanying illustrations of the engine compartment and the underside of the vehicle for the locations of various components.

Servicing the vehicle, in accordance with the mileage/time maintenance schedule and the step-by-step procedures will result in a planned maintenance program that should produce a long and reliable service life. Keep in mind that it is a comprehensive plan, so maintaining some items but not others at the specified intervals will not produce the same results.

As you service the vehicle, you will discover that many of the procedures can - and should - be grouped together because of the nature of the particular procedure you're performing or because of the close proximity of two otherwise unrelated components to one another.

For example, if the vehicle is raised for chassis lubrication, you should inspect the exhaust, suspension, steering and fuel systems while you're under the vehicle. When you're rotating the tires, it makes good sense to check the brakes since the wheels are already removed. Finally, let's suppose you have to borrow or rent a torque wrench. Even if you only need it to tighten the spark plugs, you might as well check the torque of as many critical fasteners as time allows.

The first step in this maintenance program is to prepare yourself before the actual work begins. Read through all the procedures you're planning to do, then gather up all the parts and tools needed. If it looks like you might run into problems during a particular job, seek advice from a mechanic or an experienced do-it-yourselfer.

OWNER'S MANUAL AND VECI LABEL INFORMATION

Your vehicle owner's manual was written for your year and model and contains very specific information on component locations, specifications, fuse ratings, part numbers, etc. The Owner's Manual is an important resource for the do-it-yourselfer to have; if one was not supplied with your vehicle, it can generally be ordered from a dealer parts department.

Among other important information, the Vehicle Emissions Control Information (VECI) label contains specifications and procedures for applicable tune-up adjustments and, in some instances, spark plugs (see Chapter 6 for more information on the VECI label). The information on this label is the exact maintenance data recommended by the manufacturer. This data often varies by intended operating altitude, local emissions regulations, month of manufacture, etc.

This Chapter contains procedural details, safety information and more ambitious maintenance intervals than you might find in manufacturer's literature. However, you may also find procedures or specifications in your Owner's Manual or VECI label that differ with what's printed here. In these cases, the Owner's Manual or VECI label can be considered correct, since it is specific to your particular vehicle.

3 Tune-up general information

The term tune-up is used in this manual to represent a combination of individual operations rather than one specific procedure.

If, from the time the vehicle is new, the routine maintenance schedule is followed closely and frequent checks are made of fluid levels and high wear items, as suggested throughout this manual, the engine will be kept in relatively good running condition and the need for additional work will be minimized.

More likely than not, however, there will be times when the engine is running poorly due to lack of regular maintenance. This is even more likely if a used vehicle, which has not received regular and frequent maintenance checks, is purchased. In such cases, an engine tune-up will be needed outside of the regular routine maintenance intervals.

The first step in any tune-up or diagnostic procedure to help correct a poor running engine is a cylinder compression check. A compression check (see Chapter 2C) will help determine the condition of internal engine components and should be used as a guide for tune-up and repair procedures. If, for instance, a compression check indicates serious internal engine wear, a conventional tune-up will not improve the performance of the engine and would be a waste of time and money. Because of its importance, the compression check should be done by someone with the proper equipment and the knowledge to use it properly.

The following procedures are those most often needed to bring a generally poor running engine back into a proper state of tune.

MINOR TUNE-UP

Check all engine related fluids (Section 4)
Clean, inspect and test the battery (Section 8)
Check the cooling system (Section 9)
Check all underhood hoses (Section 12)
Check the fuel system (Section 15)
Check the air filter (Section 17)
Check the drivebelt (Section 22)

MAJOR TUNE-UP

All items listed under Minor tune-up, plus . . .
Replace the air filter (Section 17)
Replace the PCV valve (See Chapter 6)
Replace the spark plugs (Section 26)

4 Fluid level checks (every 250 miles or weekly)

1 Fluids are an essential part of the lubrication, cooling, brake and windshield washer systems. Because the fluids gradually become depleted and/or contaminated during normal operation of the vehicle, they must be periodically replenished. See "Recommended lubricants and fluids" in this Chapter's Specifications before adding fluid to any of the following components.

→ **Note: The vehicle must be on level ground when fluid levels are checked.**

ENGINE OIL

▶ **Refer to illustrations 4.2 and 4.4**

2 The oil level is checked with a dipstick, which is attached to the engine block (see illustration). The dipstick extends through a metal tube down into the oil pan.

3 The oil level should be checked before the vehicle has been driven, or about 5 minutes after the engine has been shut off. If the oil is checked immediately after driving the vehicle, some of the oil will remain in the upper part of the engine, resulting in an inaccurate reading on the dipstick.

4 Pull the dipstick out of the tube and wipe all the oil from the end with a clean rag or paper towel. Insert the clean dipstick all the way back into the tube and pull it out again. Note the oil at the end of the dipstick. At its highest point, the level should be between the MIN and MAX marks on the dipstick (see illustration).

5 It takes one quart of oil to raise the level from the MIN mark to the MAX mark on the dipstick. Do not allow the level to drop below the MIN mark or oil starvation may cause engine damage. Conversely, overfilling the engine (adding oil above the MAX mark) may cause oil fouled spark plugs, oil leaks or oil seal failures. Maintaining the oil level above the MAX mark can cause excessive oil consumption.

6 To add oil, remove the filler cap from the valve cover (see illustration 4.2). After adding oil, wait a few minutes to allow the level to stabilize, then pull out the dipstick and check the level again. Add more oil if required. Install the filler cap and tighten it by hand only.

7 Checking the oil level is an important preventive maintenance step. A consistently low oil level indicates oil leakage through damaged seals, defective gaskets or past worn rings or valve guides. If the oil looks milky in color or has water droplets in it, the cylinder head gasket(s) may be blown or the head(s) or block may be cracked. The engine should be checked immediately. The condition of the oil should

also be checked. Whenever you check the oil level, slide your thumb and index finger up the dipstick before wiping off the oil. If you see small dirt or metal particles clinging to the dipstick, the oil should be changed (see Section 6).

ENGINE COOLANT

▶ **Refer to illustrations 4.8 and 4.9**

✱ WARNING:

Do not allow antifreeze to come in contact with your skin or painted surfaces of the vehicle. Flush contaminated areas immediately with plenty of water. Don't store new coolant or leave old coolant lying around where it's accessible to children or pets - they're attracted by its sweet smell. Ingestion of even a small amount of coolant can be fatal! Wipe up garage floor and drip pan spills immediately. Keep antifreeze containers covered and repair cooling system leaks as soon as they're noticed.

8 All vehicles covered by this manual are equipped with a pressurized coolant recovery system. A plastic expansion tank located at the right front corner of the engine compartment is connected by hoses to the cooling system (see illustration). As the engine heats up during operation, the expanding coolant fills the tank.

4.2 Engine oil dipstick (A) and oil filler cap (B) locations - 2.0L four-cylinder engine

4.4 The oil level should be in the safe range - if it's below the MIN or ADD mark, add enough oil to bring it up to or near the MAX or FULL mark

4.8 The cooling system expansion tank is located at the right side of the engine compartment

4.9 When the engine is cold, the coolant level should be in the COLD FILL range

4.15 The brake fluid level should be kept between the MIN (A) and MAX (B) marks on the translucent plastic reservoir

9   The coolant level in the tank should be checked regularly.

⁕⁕ WARNING:

Do not remove the expansion tank cap to check the coolant level when the engine is warm!

The level in the tank varies with the temperature of the engine. When the engine is cold, the coolant level should be at the COLD FULL mark on the reservoir. If it isn't, remove the cap from the tank and add a 50/50 mixture of ethylene glycol-based antifreeze and water (see illustration).

10   Drive the vehicle, let the engine cool completely then recheck the coolant level. Don't use rust inhibitors or additives. If only a small amount of coolant is required to bring the system up to the proper level, water can be used. However, repeated additions of water will dilute the antifreeze and water solution. In order to maintain the proper ratio of antifreeze and water, always top up the coolant level with the correct mixture. An empty plastic milk jug or bleach bottle makes an excellent container for mixing coolant.

11   If the coolant level drops consistently, there may be a leak in the system. Inspect the radiator, hoses, filler cap, drain plugs and water pump (see Section 9). If no leaks are noted, have the expansion tank cap pressure tested by a service station.

12   If you have to remove the expansion tank cap wait until the engine has cooled completely, then wrap a thick cloth around the cap and unscrew it slowly, stopping if you hear a hissing noise. If coolant or steam escapes, let the engine cool down longer, then remove the cap.

13   Check the condition of the coolant as well. If it's brown or rust colored, the system should be drained, flushed and refilled. Even if the coolant appears to be normal, the corrosion inhibitors wear out, so it must be replaced at the specified intervals.

BRAKE FLUID

▶ **Refer to illustration 4.15**

14   The brake master cylinder is mounted on the front of the power booster unit in the engine compartment.

15   To check the fluid level, simply look at the MAX and MIN marks on the brake fluid reservoir (see illustration).

16   If the level is low, wipe the top of the reservoir cover with a clean rag to prevent contamination of the brake system before lifting the cover.

17   Add only the specified brake fluid to the reservoir (refer to "Recommended lubricants and fluids" in this Chapter's Specifications, or to your owner's manual). Mixing different types of brake fluid can damage the system. Fill the brake master cylinder reservoir only to the MAX line.

⁕⁕ WARNING:

Use caution when filling the reservoir - brake fluid can harm your eyes and damage painted surfaces. Do not use brake fluid that is more than one year old or has been left open. Brake fluid absorbs moisture from the air. Excess moisture can cause a dangerous loss of braking.

18   While the reservoir cap is removed, inspect the master cylinder reservoir for contamination. If deposits, dirt particles or water droplets are present, the system should be drained and refilled.

19   After filling the reservoir to the proper level, make sure the lid is properly seated to prevent fluid leakage.

20   The fluid in the brake master cylinder will drop slightly as the brake pads at each wheel wear down during normal operation. If the master cylinder requires repeated replenishing to keep it at the proper level, this is an indication of leakage in the brake system, which should be corrected immediately. If the brake system shows an indication of leakage check all brake lines and connections, along with the calipers and booster (see Section 13 for more information).

21   If, upon checking the brake master cylinder fluid level, you discover the reservoir empty or nearly empty, the systems should be bled (see Chapter 9).

WINDSHIELD WASHER FLUID

▶ **Refer to illustration 4.22**

22   Fluid for the windshield washer system is stored in a plastic reservoir located at the right front of the engine compartment (see illustration).

4.22 The windshield/rear window washer fluid reservoir is located in the right front corner of the engine compartment

4.25 The power steering fluid reservoir is located at the right rear corner of the engine compartment

4.28 At normal operating temperature, the power steering fluid level should be between the MAX (A) and MIN (B) marks

23 In milder climates, plain water can be used in the reservoir, but it should be kept no more than 2/3 full to allow for expansion if the water freezes. In colder climates, use windshield washer system antifreeze, available at any auto parts store, to lower the freezing point of the fluid. Mix the antifreeze with water in accordance with the manufacturer's directions on the container.

✳ CAUTION:

Do not use cooling system antifreeze - it will damage the vehicle's paint.

POWER STEERING FLUID

◗ **Refer to illustrations 4.25 and 4.28**

24 Check the power steering fluid level periodically to avoid steering system problems, such as damage to the pump.

✳ CAUTION:

DO NOT hold the steering wheel against either stop (extreme left or right turn) for more than five seconds. If you do, the power steering pump could be damaged.

25 The power steering reservoir, located at the right side of the engine compartment (see illustration), has MIN and MAX fluid level marks on the side. The fluid level can be seen without removing the reservoir cap.

26 Park the vehicle on level ground and apply the parking brake.

27 Run the engine until it has reached normal operating temperature. With the engine at idle, turn the steering wheel back and forth about 10 times to get any air out of the steering system. Shut the engine off with the wheels in the straight-ahead position.

28 Note the fluid level on the side of the reservoir. It should be between the two marks (see illustration).

29 Add small amounts of fluid until the level is correct.

✳ CAUTION:

Do not overfill the reservoir. If too much fluid is added, remove the excess with a clean syringe or suction pump.

30 Check the power steering hoses and connections for leaks and wear.

AUTOMATIC TRANSAXLE FLUID

➡ **Note: It isn't necessary to check the transaxle fluid weekly; every 15,000 miles or 12 months is adequate (unless fluid leakage is suspected).**

31 The level of the automatic transaxle fluid should be carefully maintained. Low fluid level can lead to slipping or loss of drive, while overfilling can cause foaming, loss of fluid and transaxle damage.

32 The transaxle fluid level should only be checked when the transaxle is hot (at its normal operating temperature). If the vehicle has just been driven over 10 miles (15 miles in a frigid climate), and the fluid temperature is 160 to 175-degrees Г, the transaxle is hot.

✳ CAUTION:

If the vehicle has just been driven for a long time at high speed or in city traffic in hot weather, or if it has been pulling a trailer, an accurate fluid level reading cannot be obtained. Allow the fluid to cool down for about 30 minutes.

33 If the vehicle has not just been driven, park the vehicle on level ground, set the parking brake and start the engine. While the engine is idling, depress the brake pedal and move the selector lever through all the gear ranges, beginning and ending in Park.

V6 models (6F50/6F55 transaxles)

34 With the engine still idling, remove the dipstick from its tube. Check the level of the fluid on the dipstick and note its condition.

35 Wipe the fluid from the dipstick with a clean rag and reinsert it back into the filler tube until the cap seats.

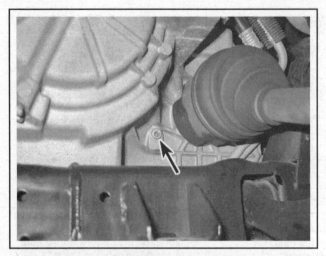

4.41 Location of the transaxle fluid leveling plug

4.42 Remove the cap from the transaxle fill tube to add transaxle fluid

36 Pull the dipstick out again and note the fluid level. The fluid level should be in the operating temperature range. If the level is at the low side of either range, remove the filler tube cap and add the specified automatic transmission fluid through the filler tube with a funnel.

➡ **Note: To access the filler tube, the air filter housing must be removed (see Chapter 4).**

37 Add just enough of the recommended fluid to fill the transaxle to the proper level. It takes about one pint to raise the level from the low mark to the high mark when the fluid is hot, so add the fluid a little at a time and keep checking the level until it is correct.

38 The condition of the fluid should also be checked along with the level. If the fluid at the end of the dipstick is black or a dark reddish brown color, or if it emits a burned smell, the fluid should be changed (see Section 23). If you are in doubt about the condition of the fluid, purchase some new fluid and compare the two for color and smell.

Four-cylinder models (6F35 transaxle)

▶ **Refer to illustrations 4.41 and 4.42**

39 Remove the engine splash shield fasteners and shield.

40 Raise the vehicle on a hoist or support it on four jackstands, keeping the vehicle in a level position, and place a drain pan under the transaxle.

41 Start the engine, depress the brake pedal and move the selector lever through all of the gear ranges, ending in the Park position. With the engine idling and in the park position, remove the oil leveling plug on the side of the transaxle (see illustration). Check the level of the fluid, it should be even with the bottom of the plug hole.

42 If the level is low, remove the filler tube cap (see illustration) and add the specified automatic transmission fluid through the filler tube with a funnel until the fluid starts to drip out of the oil leveling plug.

➡ **Note: Allow all excess fluid to drip out of the plug hole.**

43 Once the fluid is even with the oil leveling plug hole install the plug and tighten the plug to torque listed in this Chapter's Specifications.

44 The condition of the fluid should also be checked along with the level. If the fluid is black or a dark reddish brown color, or if it emits a burned smell, the fluid should be changed (see Section 23). If you are in doubt about the condition of the fluid, purchase some new fluid and compare the two for color and smell.

5 Tire and tire pressure checks (every 250 miles or weekly)

▶ **Refer to illustrations 5.2, 5.3, 5.4a, 5.4b and 5.8**

1 Periodic inspection of the tires may spare you the inconvenience of being stranded with a flat tire. It can also provide you with vital information regarding possible problems in the steering and suspension systems before major damage occurs.

2 The original tires on this vehicle are equipped with 1/2-inch wide bands that will appear when tread depth reaches 1/16-inch, at which point they can be considered worn out. Tread wear can be monitored with a simple, inexpensive device known as a tread depth indicator (see illustration).

3 Note any abnormal tread wear (see illustration). Tread pattern irregularities such as cupping, flat spots and more wear on one side than the other are indications of front end alignment and/or balance problems. If any of these conditions are noted, take the vehicle to a tire shop or service station to correct the problem.

4 Look closely for cuts, punctures and embedded nails or tacks. Sometimes a tire will hold air pressure for a short time or leak down

5.2 A tire tread depth indicator should be used to monitor tire wear - they are available at auto parts stores and service stations and cost very little

UNDERINFLATION

CUPPING

Cupping may be caused by:

• Underinflation and/or mechanical irregularities such as out-of-balance condition of wheel and/or tire, and bent or damaged wheel.
• Loose or worn steering tie-rod or steering idler arm.
• Loose, damaged or worn front suspension parts.

OVERINFLATION

INCORRECT TOE-IN OR EXTREME CAMBER

FEATHERING DUE TO MISALIGNMENT

5.3 This chart will help you determine the condition of your tires, the probable cause(s) of abnormal wear and the corrective action necessary

very slowly after a nail has embedded itself in the tread. If a slow leak persists, check the valve stem core to make sure it is tight (see illustration). Examine the tread for an object that may have embedded itself in the tire or for a plug that may have begun to leak (radial tire punctures are repaired with a plug that is installed in a puncture). If a puncture is suspected, it can be easily verified by spraying a solution of soapy water onto the puncture area (see illustration). The soapy solution will bubble if there is a leak. Unless the puncture is unusually large, a tire shop or service station can usually repair the tire.

5 Carefully inspect the inner sidewall of each tire for evidence of brake fluid leakage. If you see any, inspect the brakes immediately.

6 Correct air pressure adds miles to the life span of the tires, improves mileage and enhances overall ride quality. Tire pressure cannot be accurately estimated by looking at a tire, especially if it's a radial. A tire pressure gauge is essential. Keep an accurate gauge in the glove compartment. The pressure gauges attached to the nozzles of air hoses at gas stations are often inaccurate.

7 Always check tire pressure when the tires are cold. Cold, in this

5.4a If a tire loses air on a steady basis, check the valve core first to make sure it's snug (special inexpensive wrenches are commonly available at auto parts stores)

5.4b If the valve core is tight, raise the corner of the vehicle with the low tire and spray a soapy water solution onto the tread as the tire is turned slowly - slow leaks will cause small bubbles to appear

5.8 To extend the life of your tires, check the air pressure at least once a week with an accurate gauge (don't forget the spare!)

case, means the vehicle has not been driven over a mile in the three hours preceding a tire pressure check. A pressure rise of four to eight pounds is not uncommon once the tires are warm.

8 Unscrew the valve cap protruding from the wheel or hubcap and push the gauge firmly onto the valve stem (see illustration). Note the reading on the gauge and compare the figure to the recommended tire pressure shown on the tire placard on the driver's side door. Be sure to reinstall the valve cap to keep dirt and moisture out of the valve stem mechanism. Check all four tires and, if necessary, add enough air to bring them up to the recommended pressure.

9 Don't forget to keep the spare tire inflated to the specified pressure (refer to the pressure molded into the tire sidewall).

6 Engine oil and filter change (every 3000 miles or 3 months)

▶ Refer to illustrations 6.2, 6.7, 6.12 and 6.15

➡ **Note: Some models are equipped with an oil life indicator system that illuminates a light or message on the instrument panel when the system deems it necessary to change the oil. A number of factors are taken into consideration to determine when the oil should be considered worn out. Generally, this system will allow the vehicle to accumulate more miles between oil changes than the traditional 3000-mile interval, but we believe that frequent oil changes are cheap insurance and will prolong engine life. If you do decide not to change your oil every 3000 miles and rely on the oil life indicator instead, make sure you don't exceed 7,500 miles before the oil is changed, regardless of what the oil life indicator shows.**

1 Frequent oil changes are the most important preventive maintenance procedures that can be done by the home mechanic. As engine oil ages, it becomes diluted and contaminated, which leads to premature engine wear.

2 Make sure that you have all the necessary tools before you begin this procedure (see illustration). You should also have plenty of rags or newspapers handy for mopping up oil spills.

3 Access to the oil drain plug and filter will be improved if the vehicle can be lifted on a hoist, driven onto ramps or supported by jackstands.

✳✳ WARNING:

Do not work under a vehicle supported only by a jack - always use jackstands!

4 If you haven't changed the oil on this vehicle before, get under it and locate the oil drain plug and the oil filter. The exhaust components will be warm as you work, so note how they are routed to avoid touching them when you are under the vehicle.

5 Start the engine and allow it to reach normal operating tempera-

6.2 These tools are required when changing the engine oil and filter

1 *Drain pan* - It should be fairly shallow in depth, but wide in order to prevent spills
2 *Rubber gloves* - When removing the drain plug and filter, it is inevitable that you will get oil on your hands (the gloves will prevent burns)
3 *Breaker bar* - Sometimes the oil drain plug is pretty tight and a long breaker bar is needed to loosen it
4 *Socket* - To be used with the breaker bar or a ratchet (must be the correct size to fit the drain plug)
5 *Filter wrench* - This is a metal band-type wrench, which requires clearance around the filter to be effective
6 *Filter wrench* - This type fits on the bottom of the filter and can be turned with a ratchet or beaker bar (different size wrenches are available for different types of filters)

6.7 Use a proper size box-end wrench or socket to remove the oil drain plug and avoid rounding it off

6.12 Use an oil filter wrench to remove the filter (four-cylinder engine shown)

6.15 Lubricate the oil filter gasket with clean engine oil before installing the filter on the engine

ture - oil and sludge will flow out more easily when warm. If new oil, a filter or tools are needed, use the vehicle to go get them and warm up the engine/oil at the same time. Park on a level surface and shut off the engine when it's warmed up. Remove the oil filler cap from the valve cover.

6 Raise the vehicle and support it on jackstands. Make sure it is safely supported!

7 Being careful not to touch the hot exhaust components, position a drain pan under the plug in the bottom of the engine, then remove the plug (see illustration). It's a good idea to wear a rubber glove while unscrewing the plug the final few turns to avoid being scalded by hot oil.

8 It may be necessary to move the drain pan slightly as oil flow slows to a trickle. Inspect the old oil for the presence of metal particles.

9 After all the oil has drained, wipe off the drain plug with a clean rag. Any small metal particles clinging to the plug would immediately contaminate the new oil.

10 Clean the area around the drain plug opening, reinstall the plug and tighten it to the torque listed in this Chapter's Specifications.

11 Move the drain pan into position under the oil filter.

12 Loosen the oil filter by turning it counterclockwise with a filter wrench (see illustration). Any standard filter wrench will work. Some engines are equipped with a cartridge type oil filter. On these types, remove the oil filter cover and element.

13 Once the filter is loose, use your hands to unscrew it from the block. Just as the filter is detached from the block, immediately tilt the open end up to prevent the oil inside the filter from spilling out.

14 Using a clean rag, wipe off the mounting surface on the block. Also, make sure that none of the old gasket remains stuck to the mounting surface. It can be removed with a scraper if necessary.

15 Compare the old filter with the new one to make sure they are the same type. Smear some engine oil on the rubber gasket or O-ring seal of the new filter and screw it into place (see illustration). On typical filters, overtightening the filter will damage the gasket, so don't use a filter wrench. Most filter manufacturers recommend tightening the filter by hand only. Normally they should be tightened 3/4-turn after the gasket contacts the block, but be sure to follow the directions on the filter or

container. On cartridge type filters, install the new oil filter element and use the oil filter wrench to tighten the filter cover securely. Do not over-tighten the oil filter cover.

16 Remove all tools and materials from under the vehicle, being careful not to spill the oil in the drain pan, then lower the vehicle.

17 Add new oil to the engine through the oil filler cap. Use a funnel to prevent oil from spilling onto the top of the engine. Pour four quarts of fresh oil into the engine. Wait a few minutes to allow the oil to drain into the pan, then check the level on the dipstick (see Section 4 if necessary). If the oil level is in the OK range, install the filler cap.

18 Start the engine and run it for about a minute. While the engine is running, look under the vehicle and check for leaks at the oil pan drain plug and around the oil filter. If either one is leaking, stop the engine and tighten the plug or filter slightly.

19 Wait a few minutes, then recheck the level on the dipstick. Add oil as necessary to bring the level into the OK range.

20 During the first few trips after an oil change, make it a point to check frequently for leaks and proper oil level.

21 The old oil drained from the engine cannot be reused in its present state and should be disposed of. Check with your local auto parts store, disposal facility or environmental agency to see if they will accept the oil for recycling. After the oil has cooled it can be drained into a container (capped plastic jugs, topped bottles, milk cartons, etc.) for transport to one of these disposal sites. Don't dispose of the oil by pouring it on the ground or down a drain!

OIL LIFE MONITOR RESETTING

➡ **Note: Not all models are equipped with an oil life monitor.**

22 Press the SETUP button to display "OIL LIFE XXX% HOLD RESET=NEW."

23 Press and hold the RESET button for two seconds, then release it. The indicator should now read "OIL LIFE SET TO 100%," which is approximately a 7,500-mile interval. This interval can be shortened by pressing and releasing the RESET button; each push of the button reduces the interval by 10-percent.

7   Windshield wiper blade inspection and replacement (every 7500 miles or 6 months)

▶ **Refer to illustrations 7.4a and 7.4b**

1   The windshield wiper and blade assembly should be inspected periodically for damage, loose components and cracked or worn blade elements.

2   Road film can build up on the wiper blades and affect their efficiency, so they should be washed regularly with a mild detergent solution.

3   If the wiper blade elements are cracked, worn or warped, or no longer clean adequately, they should be replaced with new ones.

4   Lift the arm assembly away from the glass for clearance, press on the release lever, then slide the wiper blade assembly out of the hook in the end of the arm (see illustrations).

5   Attach the new wiper to the arm. Connection can be confirmed by an audible click.

7.4a To release the blade holder, push the release pin . . .

7.4b . . . and pull the wiper blade in the direction of the arrow to separate it from the arm

8   Battery check, maintenance and charging (every 7500 miles or 6 months)

▶ **Refer to illustrations 8.1, 8.6a, 8.6b, 8.7a, 8.7b and 8.8**

✳✳ WARNING:

Certain precautions must be followed when checking and servicing the battery. Hydrogen gas, which is highly flammable, is always present in the battery cells, so keep lighted tobacco and all other open flames and sparks away from the battery. The electrolyte inside the battery is actually diluted sulfuric acid, which will cause injury if splashed on your skin or in your eyes. It will also ruin clothes and painted surfaces. When removing the battery cables, always detach the negative cable first and hook it up last!

1   A routine preventive maintenance program for the battery in your vehicle is the only way to ensure quick and reliable starts. But before performing any battery maintenance, make sure that you have the proper equipment necessary to work safely around the battery (see illustration).

8.1 Tools and materials required for battery maintenance

1   ***Face shield/safety goggles*** - *When removing corrosion with a brush, the acidic particles can easily fly up into your eyes*

2   ***Rubber gloves*** - *Another safety item to consider when servicing the battery; remember that's acid inside the battery*

3   ***Battery post/cable cleaner*** - *This wire brush cleaning tool will remove all traces of corrosion from the battery posts and cable clamps*

4   ***Treated felt washers*** - *Placing one of these on each post, directly under the cable clamps, will help prevent corrosion*

5   ***Baking soda*** - *A solution of baking soda and water can be used to neutralize corrosion*

6   ***Petroleum jelly*** - *A layer of this on the battery posts will help prevent corrosion*

8.6a Battery terminal corrosion usually appears as light, fluffy powder

8.6b Removing a cable from the battery post with a wrench - sometimes a pair of special battery pliers are required for this procedure if corrosion has caused deterioration of the nut hex. Always remove the ground (-) cable first and hook it up last!

8.7a When cleaning the cable clamps, all corrosion must be removed (the inside of the clamp is tapered to match the taper on the post, so don't remove too much material)

8.7b Regardless of the type of tool used to clean the battery posts, a clean, shiny surface should be the result

8.8 Make sure the battery hold-down fastener is tight

2   There are also several precautions that should be taken whenever battery maintenance is performed. Before servicing the battery, always turn the engine and all accessories off and disconnect the cables from the negative terminal of the battery (see Chapter 5).

3   The battery produces hydrogen gas, which is both flammable and explosive. Never create a spark, smoke or light a match around the battery. Always charge the battery in a ventilated area.

4   Electrolyte contains poisonous and corrosive sulfuric acid. Do not allow it to get in your eyes, on your skin on your clothes. Never ingest it. Wear protective safety glasses when working near the battery. Keep children away from the battery.

5   Note the external condition of the battery. If the positive terminal and cable clamp on your vehicle's battery is equipped with a rubber protector, make sure that it's not torn or damaged. It should completely cover the terminal. Look for any corroded or loose connections, cracks in the case or cover or loose hold-down clamps. Also check the entire length of each cable for cracks and frayed conductors.

6   If corrosion, which looks like white, fluffy deposits (see illustration) is evident, particularly around the terminals, the battery should be removed for cleaning. Loosen the cable clamp bolts with a wrench,

being careful to remove the ground cable first, and slide them off the terminals (see illustration). Then disconnect the hold-down clamp bolt and nut, remove the clamp and lift the battery from the engine compartment.

7   Clean the cable clamps thoroughly with a battery brush or a terminal cleaner and a solution of warm water and baking soda (see illustration). Wash the terminals and the top of the battery case with the same solution but make sure that the solution doesn't get into the battery. When cleaning the cables, terminals and battery top, wear safety goggles and rubber gloves to prevent any solution from coming in contact with your eyes or hands. Wear old clothes too - even diluted, sulfuric acid splashed onto clothes will burn holes in them. If the terminals have been extensively corroded, clean them up with a terminal cleaner (see illustration). Thoroughly wash all cleaned areas with plain water.

8   Make sure that the battery tray is in good condition and the hold-down clamp fasteners are tight (see illustration). If the battery is removed from the tray, make sure no parts remain in the bottom of the tray when the battery is reinstalled. When reinstalling the hold-down clamp bolts, do not overtighten them.

9   Information on removing and installing the battery can be found

in Chapter 5. If you disconnected the cable(s) from the negative and/or positive battery terminals, the powertrain control module (PCM) must relearn its idle and fuel trim strategy for optimum driveability and performance (see Chapter 5 for this procedure). Information on jump starting can be found at the front of this manual.

CLEANING

10 Corrosion on the hold-down components, battery case and surrounding areas can be removed with a solution of water and baking soda. Thoroughly rinse all cleaned areas with plain water.

11 Any metal parts of the vehicle damaged by corrosion should be covered with a zinc-based primer, then painted.

CHARGING

> ✳✳ **WARNING:**
>
> **When batteries are being charged, hydrogen gas, which is very explosive and flammable, is produced. Do not smoke or allow open flames near a charging or a recently charged battery. Wear eye protection when near the battery during charging. Also, make sure the charger is unplugged before connecting or disconnecting the battery from the charger.**

12 Slow-rate charging is the best way to restore a battery that's discharged to the point where it will not start the engine. It's also a good way to maintain the battery charge in a vehicle that's only driven a few miles between starts. Maintaining the battery charge is particularly important in the winter when the battery must work harder to start the engine and electrical accessories that drain the battery are in greater use.

13 It's best to use a one or two-amp battery charger (sometimes called a trickle charger). They are the safest and put the least strain on the battery. They are also the least expensive. For a faster charge, you can use a higher amperage charger, but don't use one rated more than 1/10th the amp/hour rating of the battery. Rapid boost charges that claim to restore the power of the battery in one to two hours are hardest on the battery and can damage batteries not in good condition. This type of charging should only be used in emergency situations.

14 The average time necessary to charge a battery should be listed in the instructions that come with the charger. As a general rule, a trickle charger will charge a battery in 12 to 16 hours.

9   Cooling system check (every 7,500 miles or 6 months)

▶ **Refer to illustration 9.4**

1   Many major engine failures can be caused by a faulty cooling system.

2   The engine must be cold for the cooling system check, so perform the following procedure before the vehicle is driven for the day or after it has been shut off for at least three hours.

3   Remove the pressure-relief cap from the expansion tank at the right side of the engine compartment. Clean the cap thoroughly, inside and out, with clean water. The presence of rust or corrosion in the expansion tank means the coolant should be changed (see Section 20). The coolant inside the expansion tank should be relatively clean and transparent. If it's rust colored, drain the system and refill it with new coolant.

4   Carefully check the radiator hoses and the smaller diameter heater hoses (see illustrations in Chapter 3). Inspect each coolant hose along its entire length, replacing any hose which is cracked, swollen or deteriorated (see illustration). Cracks will show up better if the hose is squeezed. Pay close attention to hose clamps that secure the hoses to cooling system components. Hose clamps can pinch and puncture hoses, resulting in coolant leaks.

5   Make sure that all hose connections are tight. A leak in the cooling system will usually show up as white or rust colored deposits on the area adjoining the leak. If wire-type clamps are used on the hoses, it may be a good idea to replace them with screw-type clamps.

6   Clean the front of the radiator and air conditioning condenser with compressed air, if available, or a soft brush. Remove all bugs, leaves, etc. embedded in the radiator fins. Be extremely careful not to damage the cooling fins or cut your fingers on them.

7   If the coolant level has been dropping consistently and no leaks are detectable, have the expansion tank cap and cooling system pressure checked at a service station.

Check for a chafed area that could fail prematurely.

Check for a soft area indicating the hose has deteriorated inside.

Overtightening the clamp on a hardened hose will damage the hose and cause a leak.

Check each hose for swelling and oil-soaked ends. Cracks and breaks can be located by squeezing the hose.

9.4 Hoses, like drivebelts, have a habit of failing at the worst possible time - to prevent the inconvenience of a blown radiator or heater hose, inspect them carefully as shown here

10 Tire rotation (every 7,500 miles or 6 months)

◆ **Refer to illustration 10.2**

1   The tires should be rotated at the specified intervals and whenever uneven wear is noticed. Since the vehicle will be raised and the tires removed anyway, check the brakes also (see Section 13).

2   Radial tires must be rotated in a specific pattern (see illustration). Don't include the spare tire in the rotation pattern.

3   Refer to the information in "Jacking and towing" at the front of this manual for the proper procedure to follow when raising the vehicle and changing a tire. If the brakes must be checked, don't apply the parking brake as stated.

4   The vehicle must be raised on a hoist or supported on jackstands to get all four wheels off the ground. Make sure the vehicle is safely supported!

5   After the rotation procedure is finished, check and adjust the tire pressures as necessary and be sure to check the lug nut tightness.

10.2 The recommended tire rotation pattern for these vehicles (FWD and AWD)

11 Seat belt check (every 7,500 miles or 6 months)

1   Check seat belts, buckles, latch plates and guide loops for obvious damage and signs of wear.

2   See if the seat belt reminder light comes on when the key is turned to the Run or Start position. A chime should also sound.

3   The seat belts are designed to lock up during a sudden stop or impact, yet allow free movement during normal driving. Make sure the retractors return the belt against your chest while driving and rewind the belt fully when the buckle is unlatched.

4   If any of the above checks reveal problems with the seat belt system, replace parts as necessary.

12 Underhood hose check and replacement (every 15,000 miles or 12 months)

※ **WARNING:**

Replacement of air conditioning hoses must be left to a dealer service department or air conditioning shop that has the equipment to depressurize the system safely. Never remove air conditioning components or hoses until the system has been depressurized.

GENERAL

1   High temperatures under the hood can cause deterioration of the rubber and plastic hoses used for engine, accessory and emission systems operation. Periodic inspection should be made for cracks, loose clamps, material hardening and leaks.

2   Information specific to the cooling system hoses can be found in Section 9.

3   Most (but not all) hoses are secured to the fittings with clamps. Where clamps are used, check to be sure they haven't lost their tension, allowing the hose to leak. If clamps aren't used, make sure the hose has not expanded and/or hardened where it slips over the fitting, allowing it to leak.

PCV SYSTEM HOSE

4   To reduce hydrocarbon emissions, crankcase blow-by gas is vented through the PCV valve in the valve cover to the intake manifold via a rubber hose on most models. The blow-by gases mix with incoming air in the intake manifold before being burned in the combustion chambers.

5   Check the PCV hose for cracks, leaks and other damage. Remove the intake manifold (see Chapter 2) and disconnect it from the valve cover then check the inside for obstructions. If it's clogged, clean it out with solvent.

VACUUM HOSES

6   It's quite common for vacuum hoses, especially those in the emissions system, to be color coded or identified by colored stripes molded into them. Various systems require hoses with different wall thickness, collapse resistance and temperature resistance. When replacing hoses, be sure the new ones are made of the same material.

7   Often the only effective way to check a hose is to remove it completely from the vehicle. If more than one hose is removed, be sure to label the hoses and fittings to ensure correct installation.

8   When checking vacuum hoses, be sure to include any plastic T-fittings in the check. Inspect the fittings for cracks and the hose where it fits over each fitting for distortion, which could cause leakage.

9   A small piece of vacuum hose (1/4-inch inside diameter) can be used as a stethoscope to detect vacuum leaks. Hold one end of the hose to your ear and probe around vacuum hoses and fittings, listening for the hissing sound characteristic of a vacuum leak.

> ✳✳ **WARNING:**
>
> **When probing with the vacuum hose stethoscope, be careful not to come into contact with moving engine components such as drivebelts, the cooling fan, etc.**

FUEL HOSE

> ✳✳ **WARNING:**
>
> **Gasoline is flammable, so take extra precautions when you work on any part of the fuel system. Don't smoke or allow open flames or bare light bulbs near the work area, and don't work in a garage where a gas-type appliance (such as a water heater or clothes dryer) is present. Since fuel is carcinogenic, wear fuel-resistant gloves when there's a possibility of being exposed to fuel, and, if you spill any fuel on your skin, rinse it off immediately with soap and water. Mop up any spills immediately and do not store fuel-soaked rags where they could ignite. The fuel system is under constant pressure, so, if any fuel lines are to be disconnected, the fuel pressure in the system must be relieved first (see Chapter 4 for more information). When you perform any kind of work on the fuel system, wear safety glasses and have a Class B type fire extinguisher on hand.**

10   The fuel lines are usually under pressure, so if any fuel lines are to be disconnected be prepared to catch spilled fuel.

> ✳✳ **WARNING:**
>
> **Your vehicle is equipped with fuel injection and you must relieve the fuel system pressure before servicing the fuel lines. Refer to Chapter 4 for the fuel system pressure relief procedure.**

11   Check all flexible fuel lines for deterioration and chafing. Check especially for cracks in areas where the hose bends and just before fittings, such as where the fuel line attaches to the fuel rail.

12   When replacing a hose, use only hose that is specifically designed for your fuel injection system.

13   Some fuel lines use quick-connect fittings, which require a special tool to disconnect. See Chapter 4 for more information on these types of fittings.

METAL LINES

14   Sections of metal line are often used for fuel line that runs underneath the vehicle. Check carefully to make sure the line isn't bent, crimped or cracked.

15   If a section of metal fuel line must be replaced, use seamless steel tubing only, since copper and aluminum tubing do not have the strength necessary to withstand vibration caused by the engine.

16   Check the metal brake lines where they enter the master cylinder and brake proportioning unit (if used) for cracks in the lines and loose fittings. Any sign of brake fluid leakage calls for an immediate thorough inspection of the brake system.

13 Brake check (every 15,000 miles or 12 months)

> ✳✳ **WARNING:**
>
> **Dust created by the brake system is harmful to your health. Never blow it out with compressed air and don't inhale any of it. An approved filtering mask should be worn when working on brakes. Do not, under any circumstances, use petroleum-based solvents to clean brake parts. Use brake system cleaner only!**

1   The brakes should be inspected every time the wheels are removed or whenever a defect is suspected. Indications of a potential brake system problem include the vehicle pulling to one side when the brake pedal is depressed, noises coming from the brakes when they are applied, excessive brake pedal travel, a pulsating pedal and leakage of fluid, usually seen on the inside of the tire or wheel.

➡ **Note: It is normal for a vehicle equipped with an Anti-lock Brake System (ABS) to exhibit brake pedal pulsations during severe braking conditions.**

DISC BRAKES

◗ **Refer to illustrations 13.5a and 13.5b**

2   Disc brakes can be visually checked without removing any parts except the wheels. Remove the hub caps (if applicable) and loosen the wheel lug nuts a quarter turn each.

3   Raise the vehicle and place it securely on jackstands.

> ✳✳ **WARNING:**
>
> **Never work under a vehicle that is supported only by a jack!**

4   Remove the wheels. Now visible is the disc brake caliper which contains the pads. There is an outer brake pad and an inner pad. Both must be checked for wear.

➡ **Note: Usually the inner pad wears faster than the outer pad.**

13.5a You will find an inspection hole like this in each caliper through which you can view the thickness of remaining friction material for the inner pad

13.5b Check the thickness of the outer pad material, too

5   Measure the thickness of the outer pad at each end of the caliper and the inner pad through the inspection hole in the caliper body (see illustrations). Compare the measurement with the limit given in this Chapter's Specifications; if any brake pad thickness is less than specified, then all brake pads must be replaced (see Chapter 9).

6   If you're in doubt as to the exact pad thickness or quality, remove them for measurement and further inspection (see Chapter 9).

7   Check the disc for score marks, wear and burned spots. If any of these conditions exist, the disc should be removed for servicing or replacement (see Chapter 9).

8   Before installing the wheels, check all the brake lines and hoses for damage, wear, deformation, cracks, corrosion, leakage, bends and twists, particularly in the vicinity of the rubber hoses and calipers.

9   Install the wheels, lower the vehicle and tighten the wheel lug nuts to the torque given in this Chapter's Specifications.

PARKING BRAKE

10 Park the vehicle on a steep hill with the engine running (so you can apply the brakes if necessary) with the parking brake set and the transaxle in Neutral. If the parking brake cannot prevent the vehicle from rolling, it needs adjustment (see Chapter 9).

14   Steering, suspension and driveaxle boot check (every 15,000 miles or 12 months)

➡ Note: For detailed illustrations of the steering and suspension components, refer to Chapter 10.

SHOCK ABSORBER CHECK

▶ Refer to illustration 14.6

1   Park the vehicle on level ground, turn the engine off and set the parking brake. Check the tire pressures.

2   Push down at one corner of the vehicle, then release it while noting the movement of the body. It should stop moving and come to rest in a level position within one or two bounces.

3   If the vehicle continues to move up-and-down or if it fails to return to its original position, a worn or weak shock absorber is probably the reason.

4   Repeat the above check at each of the three remaining corners of the vehicle.

5   Raise the vehicle and support it securely on jackstands.

6   Check the shock absorbers for evidence of fluid leakage (see illustration). A light film of fluid is no cause for concern. Make sure that any fluid noted is from the shocks and not from some other source. If leakage is noted, replace the shocks as a set.

7   Check the shocks to be sure that they are securely mounted and

14.6 Check the shocks for leakage at the indicated area

undamaged. Check the upper mounts for damage and wear. If damage or wear is noted, replace the shocks as a set (front or rear).

8   If the shocks must be replaced, refer to Chapter 10 for the procedure.

14.11 To check a balljoint for wear, try to pry the control arm up and down to make sure there is no play in the balljoint (if there is, replace it)

14.12 Check the balljoint boots for damage

14.15 Flex the driveaxle boots by hand to check for cracks and/or leaking grease

STEERING AND SUSPENSION CHECK

▶ **Refer to illustrations 14.11 and 14.12**

9   Check the tires for irregular wear patterns and proper inflation. See Section 5 in this Chapter for information regarding tire wear and Chapter 10 for information on wheel bearing replacement.

10 Inspect the universal joint between the steering shaft and the steering gear housing. Check the steering gear housing for lubricant leakage. Make sure that the dust boots are not damaged and that the boot clamps are not loose. Check the tie-rod ends for excessive play. Look for loose bolts, broken or disconnected parts and deteriorated rubber bushings on all suspension and steering components. While an assistant turns the steering wheel from side to side, check the steering components for free movement, chafing and binding. If the steering components do not seem to be reacting with the movement of the steering wheel, try to determine where the slack is located.

11 Check the balljoints for wear by trying to move each control arm up and down with a prybar (see illustration) to ensure that its balljoint has no play. If any balljoint does have play, it's worn out. See Chapter 10 for the control arm replacement procedure (the balljoints aren't replaceable separately).

12 Inspect the balljoint boots for damage and leaking grease (see illustration).

13 At the rear of the vehicle, inspect the suspension arm bushings for deterioration. Additional information on suspension components can be found in Chapter 10.

DRIVEAXLE BOOT CHECK

▶ **Refer to illustration 14.15**

14 The driveaxle boots are very important because they prevent dirt, water and foreign material from entering and damaging the constant velocity (CV) joints. Oil and grease can cause the boot material to deteriorate prematurely, so it's a good idea to wash the boots with soap and water. Because it constantly pivots back and forth following the steering action of the front hub, the outer CV boot wears out sooner and should be inspected regularly.

15 Inspect the boots for tears and cracks as well as loose clamps (see illustration). If there is any evidence of cracks or leaking lubricant, they must be replaced as described in Chapter 8.

15 Fuel system check (every 15,000 miles or 12 months)

✲✲ WARNING:

Gasoline is flammable, so take extra precautions when you work on any part of the fuel system. Don't smoke or allow open flames or bare light bulbs near the work area, and don't work in a garage where a gas-type appliance (such as a water heater or clothes dryer) is present. Since fuel is carcinogenic, wear fuel-resistant gloves when there's a possibility of being exposed to fuel, and, if you spill any fuel on your skin, rinse it off immediately with soap and water. Mop up any spills immediately and do not store fuel-soaked rags where they could ignite. When you perform any kind of work on the fuel system, wear safety glasses and have a Class B type fire extinguisher on hand. The fuel system is under constant pressure, so, before any lines are disconnected, the fuel system pressure must be relieved (see Chapter 4).

1   If you smell gasoline while driving or after the vehicle has been sitting in the sun, inspect the fuel system immediately.

2   Remove the fuel filler cap and inspect if for damage and corrosion. The gasket should have an unbroken sealing imprint. If the gasket is damaged or corroded, install a new cap.

3   Inspect the fuel feed line for cracks. Make sure that the connections between the fuel lines and the fuel injection system, and between the fuel lines and the fuel tank (inspect from below) are tight and dry.

✲✲ WARNING:

Your vehicle is fuel injected, so you must relieve the fuel system pressure before servicing fuel system components. The fuel system pressure relief procedure is outlined in Chapter 4.

4   Since some components of the fuel system - the fuel tank and part of the fuel feed line, for example - are underneath the vehicle, they can be inspected more easily with the vehicle raised on a hoist. If that's not possible, raise the vehicle and support it on jackstands.

5   With the vehicle raised and safely supported, inspect the gas tank and filler neck for punctures, cracks and other damage. The connection between the filler neck and the tank is particularly critical. Sometimes a rubber filler neck will leak because of loose clamps or deteriorated rubber. Inspect all fuel tank mounting brackets and straps to be sure that the tank is securely attached to the vehicle.

❋❋ WARNING:

Do not, under any circumstances, try to repair a fuel tank (except rubber components). A welding torch or any open flame can easily cause fuel vapors inside the tank to explode.

6   Carefully check all rubber hoses and metal lines leading away from the fuel tank. Check for loose connections, deteriorated hoses, crimped lines and other damage. Repair or replace damaged sections as necessary (see Chapter 4).

16 Transfer case lubricant level check (AWD models)

➡ **Note: Do not service the transfer case fluid unless the vehicle is used in extreme off-road conditions or in sand.**

1   Raise the vehicle and support it securely on jackstands.

2   Using a ratchet or breaker bar, unscrew the check/fill plug from the transfer case.

3   Using your little finger, reach inside the housing to feel the lubricant level. The level should be at or near the bottom of the plug hole. If it isn't, add the recommended lubricant through the plug hole with a syringe or squeeze bottle.

4   Install and tighten the plug. Check for leaks after the first few miles of driving.

➡ **Note: The manufacturer states that if the transfer case is ever submerged in water, the entire unit must be replaced (see Chapter 7B). However, it may be worth trying to gain more service life from the unit (see Section 25) by draining the lubricant and refilling the unit with fresh lubricant.**

17 Air filter check and replacement (every 15,000 miles or 12 months)

▶ **Refer to illustrations 17.1a and 17.1b**

1   The air filter is located inside a housing at the left (driver's) side of the engine compartment. To remove the air filter, release the clamps that secure the two halves of the air filter housing together, then separate the cover halves and remove the air filter element (see illustrations).

2   Inspect the outer surface of the filter element. If it is dirty, replace it. If it is only moderately dusty, it can be reused by blowing it clean from the back to the front surface with compressed air. Because it is a pleated paper type filter, it cannot be washed or oiled. If it cannot be cleaned satisfactorily with compressed air, discard and replace it. While the cover is off, be careful not to drop anything down into the housing.

❋❋ CAUTION:

Never drive the vehicle with the air filter removed. Excessive engine wear could result and backfiring could even cause a fire under the hood.

3   Wipe out the inside of the air filter housing.

4   Place the new filter into the filter housing, making sure it seats properly.

5   Make sure the top half of the housing is seated properly, then secure it with the clamps.

17.1a Unlatch these clips . . .

17.1b . . . pull the cover out of the way and lift the element out

18 Cabin air filter replacement (every 15,000 miles or 12 months)

◆ Refer to illustrations 18.2a and 18.2b

➡ Note: Not all models were equipped from the factory with a cabin air filter. If a filter was not installed, a screen was installed in its place. Check with your local auto parts store or dealer parts department for a retrofit filter available for these models.

1 Unlatch the glove box door stop from the top, and lower the door.
2 Depress the tab on the left side of the filter door and pull the filter from the housing (see illustrations).
3 Installation is the reverse of removal.

18.2a Depress the latch and swing the access panel open . . .

18.2b . . . then remove the filter from the housing. When installing, make sure the pleated side is facing up

19 Exhaust system check (every 30,000 miles or 24 months)

◆ Refer to illustration 19.2

1 With the engine cold (at least three hours after the vehicle has been driven), check the complete exhaust system from the engine to the end of the tailpipe. Ideally, the inspection should be done with the vehicle on a hoist to permit unrestricted access. If a hoist isn't available, raise the vehicle and support it securely on jackstands.

2 Check the exhaust pipes and connections for evidence of leaks, severe corrosion and damage. Make sure that all brackets and hangers are in good condition and tight (see illustration).

3 At the same time, inspect the underside of the body for holes, corrosion, open seams, etc. which may allow exhaust gases to enter the passenger compartment. Seal all body openings with silicone or body putty.

4 Rattles and other noises can often be traced to the exhaust system, especially the mounts and hangers. Try to move the pipes, muffler and catalytic converter. If the components can come in contact with the body or suspension parts, secure the exhaust system with new mounts.

5 Check the running condition of the engine by inspecting inside the end of the tailpipe. The exhaust deposits here are an indication of engine

19.2 Check each exhaust system rubber hanger for damage

state-of-tune. If the pipe is black and sooty or coated with white deposits, the engine may need a tune-up, including a thorough fuel system inspection and adjustment.

20 Cooling system servicing (draining, flushing and refilling) (every 30,000 miles or 24 months)

✳✳ WARNING:

Do not allow antifreeze to come in contact with your skin or painted surfaces of the vehicle. Rinse off spills immediately with plenty of water. Antifreeze is highly toxic if ingested. Never leave antifreeze lying around in an open container or in puddles on the floor; children and pets are attracted by its sweet smell and may drink it. Check with local authorities about disposing of used antifreeze. Many communities have collection centers which will see that antifreeze is disposed of safely. Never dump used antifreeze on the ground or pour it into drains.

✳✳ CAUTION:

Do not mix coolants of different colors. Doing so might damage the cooling system and/or the engine. The manufacturer specifies either a green colored coolant or an orange colored coolant to be used in these systems. Read the warning label in the engine compartment for additional information.

➡ **Note: Non-toxic antifreeze is now manufactured and available at local auto parts stores, but even this type must be disposed of properly.**

1 Periodically, the cooling system should be drained, flushed and refilled to replenish the antifreeze mixture and prevent formation of rust and corrosion, which can impair the performance of the cooling system and cause engine damage. When the cooling system is serviced, all hoses and the expansion tank cap should be checked and replaced if necessary.

DRAINING

▶ **Refer to illustrations 20.4 and 20.5**

2 Apply the parking brake and block the wheels. If the vehicle has just been driven, wait several hours to allow the engine to cool down before beginning this procedure.

3 Once the engine is completely cool, remove the expansion tank cap.

4 On four-cylinder engines, loosen the cooling system bleed screw, located in a small hose attached to the water outlet at the left end (driver's side) of the cylinder head (see illustration).

➡ **Note: On models with a plastic bleed screw, it's only necessary to turn the screw counterclockwise about 1/4-turn.**

5 Move a large container under the radiator drain to catch the coolant. Attach a length of hose to the drain fitting to direct the coolant into the container, then turn the drain fitting 1/4-turn counterclockwise and pull it out to open it (a pair of pliers may be required) (see illustration).

6 While the coolant is draining, check the condition of the radiator hoses, heater hoses and clamps (refer to Section 9 if necessary). Replace any damaged clamps or hoses.

FLUSHING

7 Fill the cooling system with clean water, following the "Refilling" procedure (see Step 13).

8 Start the engine and allow it to reach normal operating temperature, then rev up the engine a few times.

9 Turn the engine off and allow it to cool completely, then drain the system as described earlier.

10 Repeat Steps 7 through 9 until the water being drained is free of contaminants.

11 In severe cases of contamination or clogging of the radiator, remove the radiator (see Chapter 3) and have a radiator repair facility clean and repair it if necessary.

12 Many deposits can be removed by the chemical action of a cleaner available at auto parts stores. Follow the procedure outlined in the manufacturer's instructions.

➡ **Note: When the coolant is regularly drained and the system refilled with the correct antifreeze/water mixture, there should be no need to use chemical cleaners or descalers.**

20.4 Location of the cooling system bleed screw (four-cylinder models)

20.5 The radiator drain fitting is located at the lower left corner of the radiator - before opening the valve, push a short length of rubber hose onto the plastic fitting to prevent the coolant from splashing

REFILLING

13 Close and tighten the radiator drain.

14 Place the heater temperature control in the maximum heat position.

15 On a four-cylinder engines, slowly add new coolant (a 50/50 mixture of water and antifreeze) until coolant flows from the bleed screw, then tighten the bleed screw and continue to fill the expansion tank to the MAX fill mark. On V6 engines, add coolant to the expansion tank until the level is at the MAX fill mark on the expansion tank.

16 Install the expansion tank cap and run the engine at 2500 rpm for ten minutes.

❋❋ CAUTION:

If at any time the engine begins to overheat, or the coolant level falls below the MIN fill line on the expansion tank, turn off the engine, allow it to cool completely, then add coolant to the expansion tank to the MAX fill line.

17 Turn the engine off and let it cool. Add more coolant mixture to bring the level to the MAX fill mark on the expansion tank.

18 Repeat Steps 16 and 17 if necessary.

19 Start the engine, allow it to reach normal operating temperature and check for leaks. Also, set the heater and blower controls to the maximum setting and check to see that the heater output from the air ducts is warm. This is a good indication that all air has been purged from the cooling system.

21 Brake fluid change (every 30,000 miles or 24 months)

❋❋ WARNING:

Brake fluid can harm your eyes and damage painted surfaces, so use extreme caution when handling or pouring it. Do not use brake fluid that has been standing open or is more than one year old. Brake fluid absorbs moisture from the air. Excess moisture can cause a dangerous loss of braking effectiveness.

1 At the specified intervals, the brake fluid should be drained and replaced. Since the brake fluid may drip or splash when pouring it, place plenty of rags around the master cylinder to protect any surrounding painted surfaces.

2 Before beginning work, purchase the specified brake fluid (see "Recommended lubricants and fluids" in this Chapter's Specifications).

3 Remove the cap from the master cylinder reservoir.

4 Using a hand suction pump or similar device, withdraw the fluid from the master cylinder reservoir.

5 Add new fluid to the master cylinder until it rises to the base of the filler neck.

6 Bleed the brake system (see Chapter 9) at all four brakes until new and uncontaminated fluid is expelled from the bleeder screw. Be sure to maintain the fluid level in the master cylinder as you perform the bleeding process. If you allow the master cylinder to run dry, air will enter the system.

7 Refill the master cylinder with fluid and check the operation of the brakes. The pedal should feel solid when depressed, with no sponginess.

❋❋ WARNING:

Do not operate the vehicle if you are in doubt about the effectiveness of the brake system.

22 Drivebelt check and replacement (every 30,000 miles or 24 months)

ACCESSORY DRIVEBELT

1 A single serpentine drivebelt is located at the front of the engine and plays an important role in the overall operation of the engine and its components. Due to its function and material make up, the belt is prone to wear and should be periodically inspected. On four-cylinder models, the serpentine belt drives the alternator, power steering pump, water pump and air conditioning compressor. On V6 models, the serpentine belt drives the alternator and air conditioning compressor; a second belt is used to drive the power steering pump. Although the belt should be inspected at the recommended intervals, replacement may not be necessary for more than 100,000 miles.

Check

▶ **Refer to illustrations 22.2 and 22.4**

2 Since the drivebelt is located very close to the right-hand side of the engine compartment, it is possible to gain better access by raising the front of the vehicle and removing the right-hand wheel, then removing the splash shield in the right fenderwell (see illustration). Be sure to support the front of the vehicle securely on jackstands.

3 With the engine stopped, inspect the full length of the drivebelt for cracks and separation of the belt plies. It will be necessary to turn the engine (using a wrench or socket and bar on the crankshaft pulley bolt, working clockwise only) in order to move the belt from the pulleys

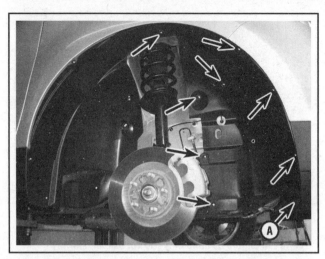

22.2 Remove the fasteners from the front area of the inner fender liner (A) then remove the remaining fasteners (arrows) and pull it back for access

22.4 Small cracks in the underside of a V-ribbed belt are acceptable - lengthwise cracks, or missing pieces that cause the belt to make noise, are cause for replacement

so that the belt can be inspected thoroughly. Twist the belt between the pulleys so that both sides can be viewed. Also check for fraying, and glazing which gives the belt a shiny appearance. Check the pulleys for nicks, cracks, distortion and corrosion.

4   Note that it is not unusual for a ribbed belt to exhibit small cracks in the edges of the belt ribs, and unless these are extensive or very deep, belt replacement is not essential (see illustration).

Replacement

Four-cylinder models

▶ **Refer to illustration 22.6**

5   Disconnect the cable from the negative terminal of the battery (see Chapter 5). Loosen the right front wheel lug nuts, then raise the front of the vehicle and support it securely on jackstands. Remove the right front wheel and the splash shield (see illustration 22.2).

6   Note how the drivebelt is routed, then remove the belt from the

22.6 Insert a 3/8-inch drive ratchet or breaker bar into the square hole (A) and rotate the tensioner arm to relieve belt tension. (B) indicates the tensioner mounting bolts (four-cylinder engines)

pulleys. Insert a 1/2-inch drive ratchet or breaker bar into the tensioner hole and pull the handle to release the drivebelt tension (see illustration). Once tension has been released, remove the belt from the pulleys.

7   Loosen the drivebelt tensioner mounting bolts and pull the tensioner away from the engine far enough to allow the belt to slide the belt past the tensioner pulley.

8   Slip the drivebelt past the tensioner pulley, then tighten the tensioner mounting bolts to the torque listed in this Chapter's Specifications.

9   Route the drivebelt around the crankshaft pulley, alternator pulley, air conditioning compressor pulley, power steering pump pulley, and the tensioner pulley. Rotate the tensioner to create slack in the belt and slip the belt over the water pump pulley. Make sure the drivebelt is correctly seated in all of the pulley grooves, then release the tensioner.

10 Install the splash shield and wheel, then lower the vehicle.

V6 models

11 Working under the hood, turn the drivebelt tensioner clockwise to release tension, then slip the belt off the alternator pulley.

12 Loosen the right front wheel lug nuts, then raise the front of the vehicle and support it securely on jackstands. Remove the wheel and the inner fender splash shield (see illustration 2.22).

13 Noting how it is routed, remove the belt from the remainder of the pulleys.

14 Route the new belt around the pulleys, making sure it seats properly in the pulley grooves. Have an assistant pull upwards on the belt (from above) so it doesn't fall off any of the pulleys.

15 Working from above, guide the belt around the tensioner pulley, then turn the tensioner clockwise and loop the belt over the alternator pulley. Release the tensioner.

16 Install the splash shield and wheel. Lower the vehicle and tighten the lug nuts to the torque listed in this Chapter's Specifications.

POWER STEERING PUMP DRIVEBELT (V6 ENGINES)

◆ **Refer to illustration 22.18**

17 The power steering drivebelt is located at the lower right rear of the engine. The belt is of a unique design, called a stretchy belt, which provides tension without the use of a mechanical tensioner.

18 Disconnect the cable from the negative terminal of the battery (see Chapter 5). Loosen the right front wheel lug nuts. Raise the vehicle and support it securely on jackstands, then remove the wheel and the right inner fender splash shield (see Chapter 11). Insert a length of flexible material such as a leather or plastic strap under the belt at the pulley at the end of the camshaft. Rotate the engine (clockwise) with a socket and breaker bar on the crankshaft pulley bolt, while you feed the remover strap between the belt and the pulley (see illustration). Pull the strap quickly to force the belt from the pulley on the camshaft.

※ **CAUTION:**

Do not use hard plastic or metal tools to pry the belt off; it can be easily damaged.

➡ **Note: If the belt is not going to be re-used, you can simply cut it off.**

19 Route the new belt under the drive pulley, then over the power steering pump pulley and rotate the engine again; the belt should pop over the pulley on the pump. Make sure the belt is positioned properly on both pulleys.

22.18 Typical stretchy belt removal (shown on a different model for illustrative purposes). Warning: *While doing this, rotate the engine by hand only (do not use the starter)*

ACCESSORY DRIVEBELT TENSIONER

20 On four-cylinder models, remove the two bolts securing the tensioner to the engine block (see illustration 22.6) and remove the tensioner.

21 On V6 models, remove the three bolts securing the tensioner to the timing chain cover, then detach the tensioner from the cover.

22 Installation is the reverse of removal. Tighten the tensioner bolt(s) to the torque listed in this Chapter's Specifications.

23 Automatic transaxle fluid change (every 60,000 miles or 48 months)

➡ **Note: For transaxle identification, refer to the "Vehicle Identification Numbers" information at the front of this manual.**

1 The automatic transaxle fluid should be changed at the recommended intervals.

2 Before beginning work, purchase the specified transmission fluid (see "Recommended lubricants and fluids" in this Chapter's Specifications).

3 Other tools necessary for this job include jackstands to support the vehicle in a raised position, wrenches, a drain pan, newspapers and clean rags.

4 The fluid should be drained immediately after the vehicle has been driven. Hot fluid is more effective than cold fluid at removing built-up sediment.

※ **WARNING:**

Fluid temperature can exceed 350-degrees F in a hot transaxle. Wear protective gloves.

5 After the vehicle has been driven to warm up the fluid, turn off engine and raise the front of the vehicle and support it securely on jackstands.

※ **WARNING:**

Never work under a vehicle that is supported only by a jack!

V6 MODELS (6F50/6F55 TRANSAXLE)

6 Place the drain pan under the drain plug in the transaxle and remove the drain plug. Once the fluid has drained, reinstall the drain plug and tighten it to the torque listed in this Chapter's Specifications.

7 Lower the vehicle and unscrew dipstick/cap from the fill tube on the top of the transaxle.

➡ **Note: On 2010 and later models, the dipstick/cap is mounted directly to the top of the transaxle fluid pan.**

8 Add five quarts of new fluid to the transaxle through the fill plug hole (see "Recommended lubricants and fluids" for the recommended fluid type), then install the fill plug and tighten it to the torque listed in this Chapter's Specifications.

9 Start the engine and, while depressing the brake pedal, cycle the shifter through each gear position and return it to Park. With the engine running, add fluid through the dipstick tube, 1/2-pint at a time as necessary (cycling the shifter through each gear position between additions) until the level is up to the COLD notch (the lowest notch) on the dipstick.

10 Drive the vehicle a few miles until the fluid is up to normal operating temperature, then recheck the fluid level (see Section 4); it should be in the range indicated on the dipstick. If not, add fluid a little at a time (cycling the shifter through each gear position between additions) until the level is correct. Tighten the dipstick/cap securely.

11 If you wish to flush the torque converter of old fluid, repeat Steps 6 through 10 one or two more times.

FOUR-CYLINDER MODELS (6F35 TRANSAXLE)

‣ **Refer to illustration 23.12**

➡ **Note: If you're working on a four-cylinder model, raise both ends of the vehicle and support it securely on jackstands (the vehicle must be level).**

12 Place the drain pan under the drain plug in the transaxle and remove the drain plug (see illustration). Once the fluid has drained, reinstall the drain plug and tighten it to the torque listed in this Chapter's Specifications.

13 Measure the amount of fluid drained and record this figure for reference when refilling.

14 Add new fluid (the amount measured in the previous Step) to the transaxle through the fill tube (see illustration 4.42).

15 Start the engine, depress the brake pedal, then move the selector lever through all of the gear ranges, ending in the Park position. Turn the engine off.

16 Repeat Steps 12 through 15 two more times to flush any contaminated fluid from the torque converter.

17 Place the drain pan under the transaxle. Start the engine.

18 With the engine idling and in the park position, remove the oil leveling plug on the side of the transaxle (see illustration 4.41). Check the level of the fluid, it should be even with the bottom of the plug hole.

19 If the level is low, remove the filler tube cap (see illustration 4.42) and add the specified automatic transmission fluid through the filler tube with a funnel until the fluid starts to drip out of the oil leveling plug.

➡ **Note: Allow all excess fluid to drip out of the plug hole.**

20 Once the fluid is even with the oil leveling plug hole install the plug and tighten the plug to torque listed in this Chapter's Specifications.

23.12 Location of the transaxle drain plug (6F35 transaxle)

21 Drive the vehicle a few miles until the fluid is up to normal operating temperature, then recheck the fluid level (see Section 4).

FLUID DISPOSAL

22 The old fluid drained from the transaxle cannot be reused in its present state and should be disposed of. Check with your local auto parts store, disposal facility or environmental agency to see if they will accept the fluid for recycling. After the fluid has cooled it can be drained into a container (capped plastic jugs, topped bottles, milk cartons, etc.) for transport to one of these disposal sites. Don't dispose of the fluid by pouring it on the ground or down a drain!

---

24 Differential lubricant change (AWD models) (every 60,000 miles or 48 months)

DRAIN

1 This procedure should be performed after the vehicle has been driven so the lubricant will be warm and therefore flow out of the differential more easily.

2 Raise the vehicle and support it securely on jackstands.

3 The easiest way to drain the differential is to remove the lubricant through the filler plug hole with a suction pump. If the differential cover gasket is leaking, it will be necessary to remove the cover to drain the lubricant (which will also allow you to inspect the differential).

Changing the lubricant with a suction pump

‣ **Refer to illustration 24.4**

4 Remove the filler plug from the differential (see illustration).

5 Insert the flexible hose.

6 Work the hose down to the bottom of the differential housing and pump the lubricant out.

24.4 Rear differential check/fill plug

Changing the lubricant by removing the cover

♦ **Refer to illustration 24.11**

7   Move a drain pan, rags, newspapers and wrenches under the vehicle.

8   Remove the bolts on the lower half of the cover. Loosen the bolts on the upper half and use them to loosely retain the cover. Allow the oil to drain into the pan, then completely remove the cover.

9   Using a lint-free rag, clean the inside of the cover and the accessible areas of the differential housing. As this is done, check for chipped gears and metal particles in the lubricant, indicating that the differential should be more thoroughly inspected and/or repaired.

10   Thoroughly clean the gasket mating surfaces of the differential housing and the cover plate. Use a gasket scraper or putty knife to remove all traces of the old gasket.

11   Apply a bead of RTV sealant to the cover flange (see illustration). Make sure the bolt holes align properly, then install the cover and tighten the fasteners to the torque listed in this Chapter's Specifications.

REFILL

12   Use a hand pump, syringe or funnel to fill the differential housing with the specified lubricant until it's within 1/8 to 3/16-inch (3 to 5 mm) from the bottom of the filler plug hole.

13   Install the fill plug and tighten it to the torque listed in this Chapter's Specifications.

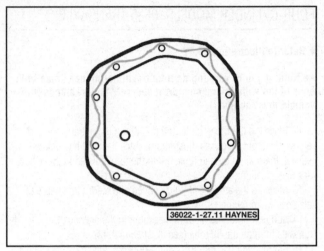

36022-1-27.11 HAYNES

24.11 Apply a continuous bead of RTV sealant to the cover

14   The old lubricant drained from the differential cannot be reused in its present state and should be disposed of. Check with your local auto parts store, disposal facility or environmental agency to see if they will accept the lubricant for recycling. After the lubricant has cooled, it can be drained into a container (capped plastic jugs, topped bottles, milk cartons, etc.) for transport to one of these disposal sites. Don't dispose of the lubricant by pouring it on the ground or down a drain!

25 Transfer case lubricant change (AWD models)

➡ **Note: Technically, the transfer case is filled for life; routine fluid changes aren't necessary unless the fluid somehow becomes contaminated.**

DRAIN

1   This procedure should be performed after the vehicle has been driven so the lubricant will be warm and therefore flow out of the transfer case more easily.

2   Raise the vehicle and support it securely on jackstands.

3   On models equipped with a drain plug, remove the drain plug and allow the fluid to drain.

4   On models without a drain plug, remove the filler plug and insert the flexible hose. Work the hose down to the bottom of the unit and pump the lubricant out.

REFILL

5   Use a hand pump, syringe or funnel to fill the housing with the specified lubricant until it's within 1/8 to 3/16-inch (3 to 5 mm) from the bottom of the filler plug hole.

6   Install the fill plug and tighten it to the torque listed in this Chapter's Specifications.

7   The old lubricant cannot be reused in its present state and should be disposed of. Check with your local auto parts store, disposal facility or environmental agency to see if they will accept the lubricant for recycling. After the lubricant has cooled, it can be drained into a container (capped plastic jugs, topped bottles, milk cartons, etc.) for transport to one of these disposal sites. Don't dispose of the lubricant by pouring it on the ground or down a drain!

26 Spark plug check and replacement (see Maintenance schedule for service intervals)

▶ **Refer to illustrations 26.2, 26.5, 26.6a, 26.6b, 26.8, 26.9, 26.10a and 26.10b**

1   The spark plugs are located in the center of the valve cover(s). Access to the rear cylinder bank spark plugs on V6 models requires removal of the upper intake manifold (see Chapter 2B).

2   In most cases, the tools necessary for spark plug replacement include a spark plug socket which fits onto a ratchet (spark plug sockets are padded inside to prevent damage to the porcelain insulators on the new plugs), various extensions and a gap gauge to check and adjust the gaps on the new plugs (see illustration). A torque wrench should be used to tighten the new plugs.

3   The best approach when replacing the spark plugs is to purchase the new ones in advance, adjust them to the proper gap and replace the plugs one at a time. When buying the new spark plugs, be sure to obtain the correct plug type for your particular engine. This information can be found in this Chapter's Specifications or in the factory owner's manual.

4   Allow the engine to cool completely before attempting to remove any of the plugs. These engines are equipped with aluminum cylinder heads, which can be damaged if the spark plugs are removed when the engine is hot. While you are waiting for the engine to cool, check the new plugs for defects and adjust the gaps.

5   The gap is checked by inserting the proper-thickness gauge between the electrodes at the tip of the plug (see illustration). The gap between the electrodes should be the same as the one specified in this Chapter's Specifications. The gauge should just slide between the electrodes with a slight amount of drag. If the gap is incorrect, use the adjuster on the gauge body to bend the curved side electrode slightly until the proper gap is obtained. If the side electrode is not exactly over the center electrode, bend it with the adjuster until it is. Check for cracks in the porcelain insulator (if any are found, the plug should not be used).

➡ **Note: We recommend using a wire-type thickness gauge when checking platinum- or iridium-type spark plugs. Other types of gauges may scrape the thin coating from the electrodes, thus dramatically shortening the life of the plugs.**

26.2 Tools required for changing spark plugs

1   **Spark plug socket** - *This will have special padding inside to protect the spark plug porcelain insulator*
2   **Torque wrench** - *Although not mandatory, use of this tool is the best way to ensure that the plugs are tightened properly*
3   **Ratchet** - *Standard hand tool to fit the plug socket*
4   **Extension** - *Depending on model and accessories, you may need special extensions and universal joints to reach one or more of the plugs*
5   **Spark plug gap gauge** - *This gauge for checking the gap comes in a variety of styles. Make sure the gap for your engine is included*

26.5 When checking the spark plug gap, the wire should slide between the electrodes with a slight drag

26.6a All models are equipped with individual coils which must be removed to access the spark plugs (four-cylinder shown, V6 similar)

26.6b Depress the tab (A) and disconnect the electrical connector, remove the coil retaining bolts (B), then pull the coil straight up to remove it

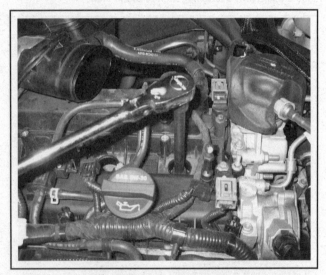

26.8 Use a ratchet and extension to remove the spark plugs

6 All models are equipped with individual ignition coils which must be removed first to access the spark plugs (see illustrations).

7 If compressed air is available, use it to blow any dirt or foreign material away from the spark plug hole. The idea here is to eliminate the possibility of debris falling into the cylinder as the spark plug is removed.

8 Place the spark plug socket over the plug and remove it from the engine by turning it in a counterclockwise direction (see illustration).

9 Compare the spark plug to those shown in this chart (see illustration) to get an indication of the general running condition of the engine.

10 Apply a small amount of anti-seize compound to the spark plug threads (see illustration). Install one of the new plugs into the hole until you can no longer turn it with your fingers, then tighten it with a torque wrench (if available) or the ratchet. It is a good idea to slip a short length of rubber hose over the end of the plug to use as a tool to thread it into place (see illustration). The hose will grip the plug well enough to turn it, but will start to slip if the plug begins to cross-thread in the hole - this will prevent damaged threads and the accompanying repair costs.

11 Repeat the procedure for the remaining spark plugs.

A normally worn spark plug should have light tan or gray deposits on the firing tip.

A carbon fouled plug, identified by soft, sooty, black deposits, may indicate an improperly tuned vehicle. Check the air cleaner, ignition components and engine control system.

An oil fouled spark plug indicates an engine with worn piston rings and/or bad valve seals allowing excessive oil to enter the chamber.

This spark plug has been **left in the engine too long,** as evidenced by the extreme gap- Plugs with such an extreme gap can cause misfiring and stumbling accompanied by a noticeable lack of power.

A physically damaged spark plug may be evidence of severe detonation in that cylinder. Watch that cylinder carefully between services, as a continued detonation will not only damage the plug, but could also damage the engine.

A bridged or almost bridged spark plug, identified by a build-up between the electrodes caused by excessive carbon or oil build-up on the plug.

26.9 Inspect the spark plug to determine engine running conditions

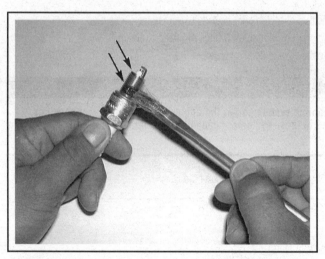

26.10a Apply a thin coat of anti-seize compound to the spark plug threads

26.10b A length of snug-fitting rubber hose will save time and prevent damaged threads when installing the spark plugs

Specifications

Recommended lubricants and fluids

➡ Note: Listed here are manufacturer recommendations at the time this manual was written. Manufacturers occasionally upgrade their fluid and lubricant specifications, so check with your local auto parts store for current recommendations.

Engine oil	
Type	API "certified for gasoline engines"
Viscosity	
Four-cylinder engine	SAE 5W-30
V6 engines	SAE 5W-20
Fuel	Unleaded gasoline, 87 octane
Automatic transaxle fluid	
2007 and 2008 models	MERCON V Automatic Transmission Fluid
2009 models	
Early build	MERCON V Automatic Transmission Fluid
Late build	MERCON LV Automatic Transmission Fluid
2010 and later models	MERCON LV Automatic Transmission Fluid

✳ CAUTION:

Do not mix MERCON V and MERCON LV fluids. Transaxle damage could occur.

Transfer case (AWD models)	MERCON LV Automatic Transmission Fluid
Rear differential lubricant (AWD models)	SAE 80W-90 Premium Rear Axle Lubricant
Brake fluid	DOT 3 brake fluid
Engine coolant	50/50 mixture of Motorcraft Specialty Green Engine Coolant (green colored) or Motorcraft Orange Antifreeze/Coolant (orange colored) and distilled water

✳ CAUTION:

Do not mix coolants of different colors. Doing so might damage the cooling system and/or the engine. The manufacturer specifies either a green colored coolant or an orange colored coolant to be used in these systems, depending on what was originally installed in the vehicle.

Power steering system	MERCON V automatic transmission fluid

Capacities*

Engine oil (including filter)	
Four-cylinder engine	5.7 quarts (5.4 liters)
V6 engines	6.0 quarts (5.7 liters)
Coolant	
Four-cylinder engine	
Without trailer tow option	Up to 11.3 quarts (10.7 liters)
With trailer tow option	Up to 11.5 quarts (10.9 liters)
V6 engines	
Without trailer tow option	Up to 11.7 quarts (11.1 liters)
With trailer tow option	Up to 11.9 quarts (11.3 liters)

*All capacities approximate. Add as necessary to bring up to appropriate level.

Capacities* (continued)

Automatic transaxle (dry fill)
    Four-cylinder models (6F35)   Up to 9 quarts (8.5 liters)
    V6 models (6F50/6F55)   Up to 11.1 quarts (10.5 liters)

➡ **Note: Since this is a dry-fill specification, the amount required during a routine fluid change will be substantially less. The best way to determine the amount of fluid to add during a routine fluid change is to measure the amount drained. Begin the refill procedure by initially adding 1/3 of the amount drained. Then, with the engine running, add 1/2-pint at a time (cycling the shifter through each gear position between additions) until the level is correct on the dipstick. It is important to not overfill the transaxle. You will, however, need to purchase a few extra quarts, since the fluid replacement procedure involves flushing the torque converter (see Section 23).**

Transfer case (AWD models)   Up to 18 ounces (0.53 liters)
Rear differential (AWD models)   Up to 2.43 pints (1.15 liters)

All capacities approximate. Add as necessary to bring up to appropriate level.

Ignition system

Spark plug type and gap
    Type
        Four-cylinder engine   Motorcraft CYFS-12Y-2 or equivalent
        V6 engines   Motorcraft 12405(SP-520) or equivalent
    Gap
        Four-cylinder engine   0.031 inch (0.8 mm)
        V6 engines   0.049 to 0.053 inch (1.25 to 1.35 mm)
Engine firing order
    Four-cylinder engine   1-3-4-2
    V6 engines   1-4-2-5-3-6

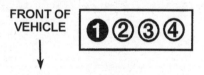

Cylinder location - four-cylinder engines

1-4-2-5-3-6

Cylinder location - V6 engines

Valve clearances (engine cold)

Four-cylinder engine
    Intake valve   0.0075 to 0.0122 inch (0.19 to 0.31 mm)
    Exhaust valve   0.0118 to 0.0165 inch (0.30 to 0.42 mm)
V6 engines
    Intake   0.006 to 0.010 inch (0.15 to 0.25 mm)
    Exhaust   0.014 to 0.018 inch (0.36 to 0.46 mm)

Brakes

Disc brake pad lining thickness (minimum)   1/8 inch (3 mm)

Torque specifications	Ft-lbs (unless otherwise indicated)	Nm

→ Note: One foot-pound (ft-lb) of torque is equivalent to 12 inch-pounds (in-lbs) of torque. Torque values below approximately 15 foot-pounds are expressed in inch-pounds, because most foot-pound torque wrenches are not accurate at these smaller values.

Engine oil drain plug	20	27
Automatic transaxle drain plug		
Four-cylinder models (6F35)	106 in-lbs	12
V6 models (6F50/6F55)	80 in-lbs	9
Automatic transaxle oil leveling plug		
(four-cylinder models - 6F35)	71 in-lbs	8
Rear differential cover bolts (AWD)	17	23
Rear differential check/fill plug (AWD)	21	29
Transfer case check/fill plug	177 in-lbs	20
Spark plugs		
Four-cylinder engine	106 in-lbs	12
V6 engines	133 in-lbs	15
Drivebelt tensioner bolts	18	25
Wheel lug nuts	100	135

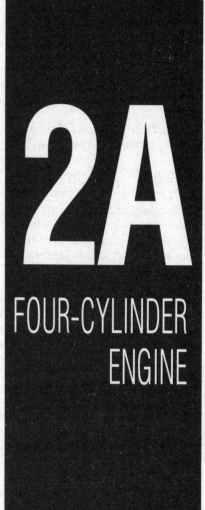

2A

FOUR-CYLINDER ENGINE

Section

Reference to other Chapters

1 General information

HOW TO USE THIS CHAPTER

This Part of Chapter 2 is devoted to repair procedures for the four-cylinder engine possible while the engine is still installed in the vehicle. Since these procedures are based on the assumption that the engine is installed in the vehicle, if the engine has been removed from the vehicle and mounted on a stand, some of the preliminary dismantling steps outlined will not apply.

Information concerning engine/transaxle removal and replacement and engine overhaul can be found in Part C of this Chapter.

ENGINE DESCRIPTION

These engines are sixteen-valve, double overhead camshaft (DOHC), four-cylinder, in-line type, mounted transversely at the front of the vehicle, with the transaxle on the left-hand end. They incorporate an aluminum cylinder head, an aluminum cylinder block, direct injection and a turbocharger.

The two camshafts are driven by a timing chain, each operating eight valves via conventional lifters. Each camshaft rotates in five bearings that are line-bored directly in the cylinder head and the (bolted-on) bearing caps. This means that the bearing caps are not available separately from the cylinder head, and must not be interchanged with caps from another engine. The exhaust manifold is integral with the cylinder head, and the turbocharger bolts directly to the cylinder head.

These engines incorporate an aluminum timing chain cover and oil pan, and the crankshaft main caps are part of a one-piece lower block support. When working on these engines, note that Torx-type (both male and female heads) and hexagon socket (Allen head) fasteners are widely used. A good selection of sockets, with the necessary adapters, will be required, so that these can be unscrewed without damage and, on reassembly, tightened to the specified torque settings.

LUBRICATION SYSTEM

The oil pump is driven via a chain from the front of the crankshaft. The pump forces oil through an externally mounted full-flow cartridge-type filter. From the filter, the oil is pumped into a main gallery in the cylinder block/crankcase, from where it is distributed to the crankshaft (main bearings) and cylinder head.

The connecting rod bearings are supplied with oil via internal drillings in the crankshaft. Each piston crown and connecting rod is cooled by a spray of oil.

The cylinder head is provided with two oil galleries, one on the intake side and one on the exhaust, to ensure constant oil supply to the camshaft bearings and lifters. A retaining valve (inserted into the cylinder head's top surface, in the middle, on the intake side) prevents these galleries from being drained when the engine is switched off. The valve incorporates a ventilation hole in its upper end, to allow air bubbles to escape from the system when the engine is restarted.

2 Repair operations possible with the engine in the vehicle

Many major repair operations can be accomplished without removing the engine from the vehicle.

Clean the engine compartment and the exterior of the engine with some type of degreaser before any work is done. It will make the job easier and help keep dirt out of the internal areas of the engine.

Depending on the components involved, it may be helpful to remove the hood to improve access to the engine as repairs are performed (refer to Chapter 11 if necessary). Cover the fenders to prevent damage to the paint. Special pads are available, but an old bedspread or blanket will also work.

If vacuum, exhaust, oil or coolant leaks develop, indicating a need for gasket or seal replacement, the repairs can generally be made with the engine in the vehicle. The intake and exhaust manifold gaskets, oil pan gasket, crankshaft oil seals and cylinder head gasket are all accessible with the engine in place.

Exterior engine components, such as the intake and exhaust manifolds, the oil pan, the oil pump, the water pump, the starter motor, the alternator and the fuel system components can be removed for repair with the engine in place.

Since the camshaft(s) and cylinder head can be removed without pulling the engine, valve component servicing can also be accomplished with the engine in the vehicle. Replacement of the timing chain and sprockets is also possible with the engine in the vehicle.

In extreme cases caused by a lack of necessary equipment, repair or replacement of piston rings, pistons, connecting rods and rod bearings is possible with the engine in the vehicle. However, this practice is not recommended because of the cleaning and preparation work that must be done to the components involved.

3   Top Dead Center (TDC) for number 1 piston - locating

▶ Refer to illustrations 3.8, 3.10, 3.11, 3.12, 3.13a, 3.13b and 3.13c

➡ **Note: You will need two special tools for this procedure: the camshaft positioning tool (303-1565, or equivalent) and the timing pin (303-507).**

1   Relieve the fuel system pressure (see Chapter 4), then disconnect the battery negative cable (see Chapter 5).

2   Remove the passenger's side inner fender splash shield (see Chapter 11).

3   Remove the engine splash shield fasteners and splash shield.

4   Remove the drivebelt (see Chapter 1).

5   Remove the brake vacuum pump (see Chapter 9) and the high-pressure fuel pump (see Chapter 4).

6   Remove the valve cover (see Section 4), and remove the rear intake camshaft bearing cap (see Section 10).

7   Prevent the camshaft from turning by using a wrench on the flats of the intake camshaft, then loosen and remove the brake vacuum pump adapter from the end of the camshaft.

8   Using a wrench or socket on the crankshaft pulley bolt, rotate the crankshaft clockwise until the marked tooth (TDC) on the crankshaft pulley is at the 6 o'clock position (see illustration).

➡ **Note: Counting counterclockwise, the marked tooth is twenty teeth away from the missing tooth on the crankshaft pulley.**

9   Remove the right-side driveaxle and support bracket (see Chapter 8).

10   The TDC timing hole is located near the lower right front corner of the engine block (on the firewall side), hidden behind the driveaxle support bracket; it provides a means of accurately positioning the no. 1 cylinder at TDC. When you locate this hole, remove the timing pin plug bolt (see illustration).

11   Screw in the timing pin (see illustration).

❋ CAUTION:

We don't recommend trying to fabricate a timing pin with a bolt because while you would be able to determine the correct bolt

diameter and thread pitch, it is impossible to determine what the length of the bolt should be. These pins come in several lengths, depending on the engine family. There is no way to determine the correct pin length without comparing it to a factory or aftermarket tool designed to be used with this engine. Using a bolt of the wrong length could damage the engine. Also, never use the timing pin as a means to stop the engine from rotating - tool breakage and/or engine damage can result.

➡ **Note: With the timing pin installed the engine can still be rotated counterclockwise.**

12   Turn the crankshaft slowly clockwise until the crankshaft counterweight comes into contact with the timing pin and the tooth on the crankshaft pulley is in a center line with the Crankshaft Position (CKP) sensor (see illustration) - in this position, the engine is set to TDC on no. 1 cylinder.

3.8 The marked tooth (TDC) on the crankshaft pulley at the 6 o'clock position

3.10 Remove the timing hole plug . . .

3.11 . . . and insert the timing pin tool

3.12 The marked tooth (TDC) aligned with the center line of the Crankshaft Position (CKP) sensor

3.13a Remove the rear intake camshaft cap

3.13b Prevent the camshaft from turning by holding it with a wrench on the hex surface (A), then unscrew the vacuum pump adapter (B)

3.13c When the engine is at TDC for cylinder no. 1, the slots in the ends of the camshafts will be horizontal (and the offset portions will be even with the cylinder head surface). Manufacturer tool no. 303-1565 can then be inserted into the slots

13 The camshafts each have a machined slot at the transaxle end of the engine. Both slots will be completely horizontal, and at the same height as the cylinder head machined surface, when the engine is at TDC on the Number 1 cylinder. Manufacturer service tool 303-1565 is used to check this position, and to positively locate the camshafts in position. The rear intake camshaft cap and the vacuum pump drive adapter will have to be removed from the intake camshaft (see illustrations).

→ Note: The timing slots in the camshafts are offset. If the service tool cannot be installed, remove the timing pin and carefully rotate the crankshaft three fourths of a turn clockwise and repeat Steps 12 and 13 of this procedure.

⁂ CAUTION:

Never use the camshaft alignment tool as a means to stop the engine from rotating - engine damage can result.

14 Before rotating the crankshaft again, make sure that the tools are removed. Do not forget to install the brake vacuum pump adapter and tighten it securely.

15 Once no. 1 cylinder has been positioned at TDC on the compression stroke, TDC for any of the other cylinders can then be located by rotating the crankshaft clockwise 180-degrees at a time and following the firing order (see this Chapter's Specifications).

4   Valve cover - removal and installation

REMOVAL

1   Disconnect the cable from the negative battery terminal (see Chapter 5).

2   Remove the individual ignition coil assemblies from the spark plugs (see Chapter 5).

3   Remove the Charge Air Cooler (CAC) inlet and outlet tubes (see Chapter 4), then remove the CAC bracket fasteners and bracket.

4   Disconnect the electrical connectors for the Variable Camshaft Timing (VCT) solenoids, EVAP canister purge, Fuel Rail Pressure (FRP) sensor and the Manifold Absolute Pressure (MAP) sensor.

5   Disconnect the vacuum lines and retainers.

6   Remove the bracket for the wiring harness on the valve cover stud, then set the harness aside.

7   Remove the engine oil dipstick.

8   Working progressively, unscrew the valve cover retaining fasten-

ers, noting the captive spacer sleeve and rubber seal, then detach the cover.

9   Discard the cover gasket. This must be replaced whenever it is disturbed. Check that the sealing faces are undamaged and that the rubber seal at each bolt hole is serviceable. Replace any worn or damaged spark plug tube seals or Variable Camshaft Timing (VCT) solenoid seals.

INSTALLATION

◆ Refer to illustrations 4.11 and 4.13

10 On installation, clean the cover and cylinder head gasket faces carefully. Install a new gasket onto the valve cover, ensuring that it is located correctly by the rubber seals and spacer sleeves.

11 At the top of the timing chain cover, apply a small bead of RTV

4.11 Apply a bead of RTV sealant to the joints where the timing chain cover meets the cylinder head

4.13 Valve cover bolt tightening sequence

sealant to the joints where the timing chain cover meets the cylinder head (see illustration).

12 Install the cover to the cylinder head, ensuring that the gasket remains seated as the cover is tightened.

13 Tighten the cover bolts, a little at a time in sequence (see illustration), to the torque listed in this Chapter Specifications.

14 Reconnect the battery.

15 Run the engine and check for signs of oil leakage.

5   Valve clearances - check and adjustment

▶ **Refer to illustration 5.4**

1 Disconnect the cable from the negative battery terminal (see Chapter 5).

2 Remove the spark plugs (see Chapter 1), then remove the valve cover (see Section 4).

3 Loosen the right front wheel lug nuts, raise the front of the vehicle and support it securely on jackstands, then remove the wheel. Remove the fender splash shield.

4 Using a wrench or socket on the crankshaft pulley bolt, rotate the crankshaft clockwise and check each lifter when its camshaft lobe is straight up, ensuring that the measurement is between the base circle of the camshaft lobe and the top of the lifter. Use feeler gauges to measure the clearances (see illustration).

5 The clearance must be checked between each camshaft lobe and the lifter it operates. Keep careful notes of the measurements recorded for each lifter.

6 If some measurements fall outside the recommended clearances in this Chapter's Specifications, the camshafts must be removed and the out-of-spec lifters removed (see Section 10). New lifters are available with various thicknesses to correct the valve clearances. Each lifter is marked with a thickness number. Only refer to the numbers after the decimal point. A "0.650" marking refers to an actual thickness of 3.650 mm.

7 To arrive at the desired thickness for new lifters: add the thickness of the original lifter (such as 0.650 mm) to the clearance you measured. Subtract the midrange figure for ideal clearance (see the Specifications) from that number and you have the proper lifter thickness to order. Every

5.4 Check the valve clearances with a feeler gauge of the specified thickness. If the clearance is correct, you should feel a slight drag as the feeler gauge is slid between the lifter and the camshaft

thickness is not available, so choose the closest to your requirement.

8 Refer to Section 10 for installation of the camshafts. Once the camshafts and timing chain have been installed, recheck the valve clearances.

9 The remainder of installation is the reverse of removal. Run the engine and check for oil leaks.

6 Intake manifold - removal and installation

REMOVAL

▶ **Refer to illustrations 6.8 and 6.10**

1   Disconnect the cable from the negative battery terminal (see Chapter 5).

2   Raise the vehicle and support it securely on jackstands.

3   Remove the engine splash shield fasteners and shield.

4   Disconnect the EVAP tube from the Charge Air Cooler (CAC) outlet tube, then loosen the CAC outlet tube clamp and pull the tube off of the throttle body.

5   Disconnect the electrical connectors from the throttle body, Fuel Rail Pressure (FRP) sensor and the Manifold Absolute Pressure (MAP) sensor.

6   Disengage the EVAP line and heater hose retainers underneath of the manifold.

7   Remove the EVAP canister purge valve (see Chapter 6).

8   Release the power brake booster vacuum hose from the intake manifold by depressing the red quick-connect lock ring and pulling the hose outward at the same time (see illustration).

9   Release the harness clips and set aside the wiring harness at the top of the intake manifold.

10 Remove the mounting bolts and pull the intake manifold away from the engine enough to access and disconnect the crankcase vent hose from the oil separator (see illustration). Squeeze the two clips on the vent hose to release it.

INSTALLATION

11 There are individual gaskets for each of the four ports of the intake manifold. Using new manifold gaskets, install the intake manifold. Tighten the bolts a little at a time, working from the center out, to the torque listed in this Chapter's Specifications.

12 Installation is otherwise the reverse of removal.

6.8 Push in on the lock ring while pulling the brake booster vacuum hose from the intake manifold

6.10 Intake manifold fasteners

7 Crankshaft pulley - removal and installation

REMOVAL

❋❋ CAUTION:

Once the crankshaft pulley is loosened, the crankshaft (timing) sprocket will be loosened as well. The engine is considered out-of-time at this point. The installation procedure in this Section must be followed exactly to re-time the engine properly. Severe engine damage may occur otherwise.

➡ **Note: You will need two special tools for this procedure: the camshaft positioning tool (303-1565, or equivalent) and the timing pin (303-507).**

1   Remove the drivebelt (see Chapter 1).

2   Remove the fasteners from the right driveaxle intermediate shaft bracket.

3   Set the engine to TDC using the camshaft and crankshaft positioning tools (see Section 3).

4   The crankshaft must be held to prevent its rotation while the pulley bolt is unscrewed. Use a strap wrench around the crankshaft pulley to hold it. The manufacturer recommends using an 1/2-inch drive air or electric impact gun to remove the pulley bolt.

⁑ CAUTION:

Failure to hold the crankshaft pulley securely while removing the pulley bolt could result in engine damage. NEVER use the timing pin or the camshaft alignment tool as a means of locking the crankshaft - they are designed for calibration only. Engine damage could occur by using these tools for anything other than their intended purpose.

5   Unscrew the pulley bolt.

6   Remove the pulley and the diamond washer behind it. Obtain a new pulley bolt and diamond washer.

INSTALLATION

7   Install a new diamond washer onto the nose of the crankshaft.

8   Lightly coat the crankshaft front seal with clean engine oil, then install the crankshaft pulley.

➡ **Note: If the seal shows signs of leakage, you may want to replace it before installing the crankshaft pulley (see Section 9).**

9   Install the Crankshaft Position (CKP) sensor alignment tool (#303-1521) onto the sensor. Install a new crankshaft pulley bolt and washer, hand tight only, and remove the tool.

10   Using the strap wrench to hold the pulley, tighten the crankshaft pulley bolt in stages, to the torque listed in this Chapter's Specifications.

⁑ CAUTION:

Do not use an impact gun to tighten the crankshaft pulley bolt.

11   Remove the timing pin from the cylinder block.

12   Remove the camshaft alignment tool.

13   Remove the spark plugs and rotate the engine clockwise two complete revolutions by turning the crankshaft pulley bolt with a wrench or large socket.

⁑ CAUTION:

If you feel resistance at any point, stop and find out why. If the valve timing is incorrect, the valves may be contacting the pistons.

14   Rotate the engine again to achieve TDC (see Section 3).

➡ **Note: Rotate the engine in the clockwise direction only.**

15   Install the timing pin into the cylinder block.

16   With the tooth on the crankshaft pulley in a center line with the CKP sensor, install the camshaft alignment tool and check the position of the camshafts. If the tool cannot be installed, the engine timing must be corrected by repeating the TDC procedure (see Section 3).

17   The correct engine timing is achieved when the camshaft alignment tool is in place, the timing pin is inserted, and the crankshaft pulley TDC tooth is in a center line with the CKP sensor, simultaneously.

18   Once correct engine timing is achieved, remove all the alignment tools and bolts and install the timing pin plug.

19   Reinstall all components removed previously.

8   Timing chain cover, timing chain and tensioner - removal and installation

TIMING CHAIN COVER

Removal

1   Relieve the fuel system pressure (see Chapter 4), then disconnect the negative battery cable (see Chapter 5).

2   Loosen the water pump pulley bolts, remove the drivebelt and drivebelt idler pulley (see Chapter 1), then remove the water pump pulley (see Chapter 3).

3   Remove the fuel injection high pressure pump and housing (see Chapter 4).

4   Remove the crankshaft pulley (see Section 7). After this Step, the engine must remain at TDC with the valve cover removed.

5   Disconnect the Crankshaft Position (CKP) sensor electrical connector, then remove the sensor (see Chapter 6).

➡ **Note: Unfortunately with this engine, any time this sensor is removed, a new sensor must be installed. The new sensor is packaged with a special sensor alignment tool that is critical for installation.**

6   Remove the power steering hose bracket fastener and bracket from the bottom of cover.

7   Support the engine from above with an engine support fixture (see Chapter 7A, illustration 5.11). Raise the engine enough to remove the right engine mount (see Section 16).

8   Unbolt and set aside the power steering pump without disconnecting the hoses (see Chapter 10), then remove the pump bracket bolts and bracket.

9   Remove the crankshaft front oil seal (see Section 9).

10   Remove the bolts, stud bolts and the timing chain cover (see illustration 8.11).

Installation

▶ **Refer to illustration 8.11**

11 Installation is the reverse of removal, noting the following:

a) *Clean the mating surfaces of all sealant.*

8.11 Timing chain cover bolt tightening sequence

➡ **Note: Be careful not to gouge or use any abrasives on the mating surfaces.**

b) *Install the engine cover within ten minutes of applying a 2.5 mm bead of RTV sealant.*
c) *Tighten the bolts a little at a time, in sequence (see illustration), to the torque listed in this Chapter's Specifications.*
d) *Install a new crankshaft front oil seal.*
e) *Verify proper crankshaft/camshaft timing (see Section 7).*
f) *Install a new CKP sensor, which includes the necessary alignment tool (see Chapter 6). Do not tighten the sensor mounting bolts until the installation tool is in place.*

TIMING CHAIN AND TENSIONER

Removal

▶ **Refer to illustrations 8.13a and 8.13b**

12 Remove the timing chain cover (see Steps 1 through 10).

13 Compress the timing chain tensioner and place a pin (a drill bit or paper clip will work) into the hole to hold it in the compressed position (see illustration).

➡ **Note: The tensioner contacts the right-hand chain guide.**

> ※ **CAUTION:**
>
> **Compress only the round plunger on the tensioner and not the ratchet mechanism. The ratchet is next to the plunger and has square sides. If the ratchet needs to be reset, perform the following (see illustration):**

a) *Remove the tensioner and place it lightly in a vise, with the jaws contacting the plunger and tensioner housing.*
b) *Place a pick-type tool in the hole closest to the ratchet to relieve the tension on the ratchet mechanism.*
c) *While holding the pick tool in place, move the ratchet back into the tensioner, then install a pin into the other hole to keep the plunger and ratchet compressed.*
d) *Remove the tensioner from the vise.*

14 Remove the two tensioner mounting bolts, then remove the tensioner.

8.13a Compress the tensioner and insert the lock pin

8.13b Timing chain tensioner details

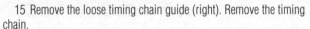

8.18 Use a wrench on the hex portion to hold the camshaft while removing/installing the sprocket bolt

8.22 Compress the tensioner to release the lock pin

15 Remove the loose timing chain guide (right). Remove the timing chain.

16 The left chain guide and camshaft sprockets can now be removed if necessary.

Installation

▶ Refer to illustrations 8.18 and 8.22

17 Remove the camshaft alignment tool (if installed).

18 Loosen both camshaft phaser and sprocket bolts but don't remove them. Use a wrench on the hexagonal area of the camshaft to hold it while turning the camshaft sprocket bolt (see illustration).

❋❋ CAUTION:

Damage to the valves or pistons may occur if the camshafts are rotated during this procedure.

19 Install the left chain guide (if removed).

20 Install the timing chain.

21 Install the right chain guide.

22 Install the timing chain tensioner and tighten the fasteners to the torque listed in this Chapter's Specifications. Remove the pin to release the tensioner to engage the chain guide (see illustration).

23 Install the camshaft alignment tool.

24 Tighten the camshaft sprocket bolts to the torque listed in this Chapter's Specifications while holding the camshafts in place with a wrench on the hex surface of the camshafts.

❋❋ CAUTION:

Do not rely on the camshaft alignment tool to hold the camshafts while tightening the camshaft sprocket bolts. Tool and engine damage may occur.

25 The timing chain cover can now be installed (see Step 11).

26 Install the fuel injection pump housing, making sure the camshaft lobe is at its lowest point on the lobe (see Chapter 4).

27 The remainder of installation is the reverse of removal.

9 Crankshaft front oil seal - replacement

▶ Refer to illustrations 9.5 and 9.6

1 Remove the crankshaft pulley (see Section 7).

2 Use a screwdriver or hook tool to carefully pry out the seal.

➡ **Note: Be careful not to damage the timing chain cover bore where the seal is seated or the nose and sealing surface of the crankshaft.**

3 Another procedure for removing the seal is to drill a small hole on each side of the seal and place a self-tapping screw in each hole. Use these screws as a means of pulling the seal out without having to pry on the seal itself.

4 Wipe the sealing surfaces in the engine cover and on the crankshaft. Clean and coat them with clean engine oil.

5 Start installing the new seal by pressing it into the timing chain cover (see illustration).

9.5 Make certain that the oil seal is kept square as it is placed in the bore

9.6 A socket of the correct size can be used to install the new seal

6 Once started, use a seal driver or a suitable socket of the correct size to carefully drive the seal squarely into place (see illustration).

7 The seal should be flush with the timing chain cover and remain square when installed.

8 Coat the lip of the seal (where it contacts the crankshaft) with clean engine oil.

9 Install the crankshaft pulley (see Section 7).

10 Camshafts and lifters - removal, inspection and installation

➡ **Note:** Whenever the camshafts are to be removed for a procedure, it's a good idea to check the valve clearances before disassembly (see Section 5), so any required new lifters can be ordered from a dealership.

REMOVAL

▶ **Refer to illustrations 10.3 and 10.6**

1 Remove the timing chain (see Section 8).

➡ **Note:** Before removing the timing chain, note the positions of the no. 1 cylinder cam lobes and the slots in the ends of the camshafts (for the alignment tool). When installing the camshafts, the lobes and the slots in the ends of the camshafts must be in the same positions.

2 Remove the camshaft phaser and sprockets.

➡ **Note:** The camshaft phaser and sprockets should be marked with indelible ink so that it can be reinstalled in the same position. When loosening the camshaft sprocket bolts, place a wrench on the hexagonal area of the camshaft to prevent it from turning (see illustration 8.18).

3 Remove the Variable Camshaft Timing (VCT) solenoid fasteners and pull the solenoids out of the front camshaft bearing cap (see illustration).

4 Remove the front camshaft bearing cap bolts and lift the cap from both camshafts.

5 Mark the bearing caps for each position and the direction it faces - the bearing caps must be reinstalled in their original positions.

✳✳ CAUTION:

The camshaft bearing caps must be loosened in order or the camshafts can be damaged.

6 Working in the sequence shown, loosen the camshaft bearing cap bolts progressively by half a turn at a time (see illustration). Work only as described, to release gradually and evenly the pressure of the valve springs on the caps.

7 Withdraw the caps, noting their markings and the presence of the locating dowels, then remove the camshafts. The exhaust camshaft can be identified by the reference lobe for the high pressure fuel pump on the end (and it is longer, as well); therefore, there is no need to mark the camshafts.

10.3 Remove the Variable Camshaft Timing (VCT) solenoid retaining bolts

10.6 Camshaft bearing cap loosening sequence - loosen each pair of bolts on the designated bearing cap in sequence

8   Obtain sixteen small, clean containers, and number them 1 to 16. Using a rubber suction tool (such as a valve-lapping tool), withdraw each lifter in turn and place them in the containers. Do not interchange the lifters.

INSPECTION

▶ **Refer to illustrations 10.10 and 10.13**

9   With the camshafts and lifters removed, check each for signs of obvious wear (scoring, pitting, etc.) and for roundness and replace if necessary.

10 Measure the outside diameter of each lifter - take measurements at the top and bottom of each lifter, then a second set at right-angles to the first; if any measurement is significantly different from the others, the lifter is tapered or oval (as applicable) and must be replaced (see illustration). If the necessary equipment is available, measure the inside diameter of the corresponding cylinder head bore. No manufacturer's specifications were available at the time of writing; if the lifters or the cylinder head bores are excessively worn, new lifters and/or a new cylinder head may be required.

11 If the engine's valve components have sounded noisy, it may be just that the valve clearances need adjusting (see Section 5).

12 Visually examine the camshaft lobes for score marks, pitting, galling (wear due to rubbing) and evidence of overheating (blue, discolored areas). Look for flaking away of the hardened surface layer of each lobe. If any such signs are evident, replace the component concerned.

13 Examine the camshaft bearing journals and the cylinder head bearing surfaces for signs of obvious wear or pitting. If any such signs are evident, consult an automotive machine shop for advice. Also check that the bearing oil ways in the cylinder head are clear (see illustration).

14 Using a micrometer, measure the diameter of each journal at several points. If the diameter of any one journal is less than the specified value, replace the camshaft.

15 To check the bearing journal running clearance, remove the lifters, use a suitable solvent and a clean lint-free rag to carefully clean all bearing surfaces, then install the camshafts and bearing caps with a strand of Plastigage across each journal. Tighten the bearing cap bolts in the proper sequence (see illustration 10.25) to the specified torque setting (do not rotate the camshafts), then remove the bearing caps and use the scale provided to measure the width of the compressed strands. Scrape off the Plastigage with your fingernail or the edge of a credit card - don't scratch or nick the journals or bearing caps.

16 If the running clearance of any bearing is found to be worn to beyond the specified service limits, install a new camshaft and repeat the check; if the clearance is still excessive, the cylinder head must be replaced.

17 To check camshaft endplay, remove the lifters, clean the bearing surfaces carefully and install the camshafts and bearing caps. Tighten the bearing cap bolts to the specified torque wrench setting, then measure the endplay using a dial indicator mounted on the cylinder head so that its tip bears on the camshaft right-hand end.

18 Tap the camshaft fully towards the gauge, zero the gauge, then tap the camshaft fully away from the gauge and note the gauge reading. If the endplay measured is found to be at or beyond the specified service limit, install a new camshaft and repeat the check; if the clearance is still excessive, the cylinder head must be replaced.

INSTALLATION

▶ **Refer to illustration 10.25**

19 Confirm that the crankshaft is still positioned at TDC and that the timing pin is in place.

20 Liberally oil the cylinder head lifter bores and the lifters. Carefully install the lifters to the cylinder head, ensuring that each lifter is replaced to its original bore.

21 Liberally oil the camshaft bearing surfaces in the cylinder head, taking care not to get any on the camshaft cap mating surface.

22 Ensuring that each camshaft is in its original location, install the camshafts, locating each so that lobes for cylinder no. 1 are in the same position as noted in Step 1 and the slot in its left-hand end is parallel to, and just above, the cylinder head mating surface. Check that, as each camshaft is laid in position, the TDC setting tool will fit into the slot.

✷✷ CAUTION:

When the camshaft bearing caps are tightened, it is imperative that the camshafts do not rotate from their TDC positions.

23 Check that all mating surfaces are completely clean, unmarked and free from oil. Apply a 0.039-inch (1 mm) bead of RTV sealant to the

10.10 Measure the lifter outside diameter at several points

10.13 Check that the camshaft bearing oil ways are not blocked with debris

exhaust camshaft rear bearing cap, making sure to keep the sealant out of the oil galleys.

24 Apply a little oil to the camshaft journals and lobes, then install each of the camshaft bearing caps to its previously-noted position,

10.25 Camshaft bearing cap tightening sequence

except the front bearing cap, so that its numbered side faces outwards, to the front (exhaust) or to the rear (intake).

25 Ensuring that each cap is kept square to the cylinder head as it is tightened down and working in the sequence shown, tighten the camshaft bearing cap bolts slowly and by one turn at a time, until each cap touches the cylinder head (see illustration). This is the Step 1 torque.

26 Next, using the same sequence, tighten the bearing cap bolts to the Step 2 torque listed in this Chapter's Specifications.

27 Install the front bearing cap and tighten the cap in tighten the camshaft bearing cap bolts slowly and by one turn at a time, until the cap touches the cylinder head. This is the Step 3 torque then tighten the front bearing cap bolts to the Step 4 torque listed in this Chapter's Specifications.

28 Install the variable camshaft timing (VCT) solenoids into the front camshaft bearing cap and tighten the fasteners to the torque listed in this Chapter's Specifications.

29 Install the phasers and sprockets to the camshafts, tightening the retaining bolts loosely.

30 The remainder of the reassembly procedure, including replacement of the timing chain and setting the valve timing, is as described in Section 8.

31 Before installing the valve cover, check the valve clearances (see Section 5).

11 Cylinder head - removal and installation

⁑ WARNING:

Wait until the engine is completely cool before beginning this procedure.

REMOVAL

1 Relieve the fuel pressure (see Chapter 4).

2 Disconnect the cable from the negative battery terminal (see Chapter 5).

3 Remove the air filter housing and charger air cooler inlet and outlet pipes (see Chapter 4).

4 Remove the power steering pump and bracket (see Chapter 10), and the alternator (see Chapter 5).

5 Drain the cooling system (see Chapter 1).

6 Remove the turbocharger (see Chapter 4).

7 Remove the coolant expansion tank (see Chapter 3).

8 Remove the timing chain (see Section 8).

➡ **Note: Whenever the camshafts are to be removed for a procedure, it's a good idea to check the valve clearances before disassembly, so any required new lifters can be ordered from a dealership.**

9 Disconnect the Camshaft Position (CMP) sensor electrical connector (see Chapter 6).

10 Unbolt and remove the VCT solenoid valves from the front camshaft bearing cap (see Section 10).

11 Remove the camshafts and lifters (see Section 10), keeping the lifters in order.

12 Remove the fuel rail and injectors (see Chapter 4).

13 Disconnect the hoses from the coolant outlet housing.

14 Remove the intake manifold (see Section 6).

15 If an engine support fixture or hoist is being used to hold the engine up and it interferes with removal of the cylinder head, use a floor jack and block of wood to support the engine from below.

16 Loosen the cylinder head bolts progressively and by half a turn at a time, working in the reverse order of the tightening sequence (see illustration 11.30a).

⁑ CAUTION:

The head bolts are torque-to-yield bolts that must be replaced with new ones on installation.

17 Lift the cylinder head from the engine compartment (see illustration).

18 If the head is stuck, be careful how you choose to free it. Remember that the cylinder head is made of aluminum alloy, which is easily damaged. Striking the head with tools carries the risk of damage, and the head is located on two dowels, so its movement will be limited. Do not, under any circumstances, pry the head between the mating surfaces, as this will certainly damage the sealing surfaces for the gasket, leading to leaks. Try rocking the head free, to break the seal, taking care not to damage any of the surrounding components.

19 Once the head has been removed, remove and discard the gasket. Check for the presence of locating dowels in the cylinder block and cylinder head. If dowels are present, make sure they are returned to their original locations after cleaning the components.

11.29 Apply a light coat of oil to the cylinder head bolt threads

11.30a Cylinder head bolt tightening sequence

INSPECTION

20 The mating faces of the cylinder head and cylinder block must be perfectly clean before replacing the head. Use spray-on gasket remover and a hard plastic or wood scraper to remove all traces of gasket and carbon.

21 Take particular care during the cleaning operations, as aluminum alloy is easily damaged. Also, make sure that the carbon is not allowed to enter the oil and water passages - this is particularly important for the lubrication system, as carbon could block the oil supply to the engine's components.

22 To prevent carbon entering the gap between the pistons and bores, smear a little grease in the gap. After cleaning each piston, use a small brush to remove all traces of grease and carbon from the gap, then wipe away the remainder with a clean rag.

23 Check the mating surfaces of the cylinder block and the cylinder head for nicks, deep scratches and other damage. Also check the cylinder head gasket surface and the cylinder block gasket surface with a precision straight-edge and feeler gauges. If either surface exceeds the warpage limit listed in this Chapter's Specifications, the manufacturer states that the component out of specification must be replaced. If the gasket mating surface of your cylinder head or block is out of specification or is severely nicked or scratched, you may want to consult with an automotive machine shop for advice.

INSTALLATION

▶ **Refer to illustrations 11.29, 11.30a and 11.30b**

24 Wipe clean the mating surfaces of the cylinder head and cylinder block. If equipped, install the alignment dowels into their original locations.

25 The cylinder head bolt holes must be free from oil or water. This is most important, because a hydraulic lock in a cylinder head bolt hole can cause a fracture of the block casting when the bolt is tightened. Note the location of the cylinder head alignment dowels in the block.

26 Position a new gasket on the cylinder block surface, so that the "TOP" mark is facing up.

27 As the cylinder head is such a heavy and awkward assembly to

11.30b You can use a torque angle gauge, or you can carefully note the starting and stopping points of the wrench handle

install, it is helpful to make up a pair of guide studs from two 10 mm (thread size) studs approximately 90 mm long, with a screwdriver slot cut in one end - you can use two of the old cylinder head bolts with their heads cut off. Screw these guide studs, screwdriver slot upwards to permit removal, into the bolt holes at diagonally-opposite corners of the cylinder block surface; ensure that approximately 70 mm of stud protrudes above the gasket.

28 Install the cylinder head, sliding it down the guide studs (if used) and locating it on the dowels. Unscrew the guide studs (if used) when the head is in place.

29 Coat the threads with engine oil - do not apply more than a light film of oil (see illustration). Install the *NEW* cylinder head bolts and screw them in by hand only until finger-tight.

➡ **Note: New cylinder head bolts must be used.**

30 Working progressively and in the sequence shown, first tighten all the bolts to the specified Step 1 torque setting listed in this Chapter's Specifications (see illustration). On these engines there are five tightening stages, the final two using the angle torque method (see illustration).

31 Replacement of the other components removed is a reversal of removal.

32 Change the engine oil and filter and refill the cooling system (see Chapter 1).

12 Oil pan - removal and installation

REMOVAL

1 Raise the vehicle and support it securely on jackstands.

2 Drain the engine oil (see Chapter 1), then clean and install the engine oil drain plug, tightening it to the torque listed in the Chapter 1 Specifications. Remove and discard the oil filter, so that it can be replaced with the oil.

3 Remove the engine lower splash shield.

4 Remove the air filter housing (see Chapter 4).

5 The transaxle must be moved slightly back from the engine. Support the engine from above with a support fixture (see Chapter 2C) connected to the left end of the engine, near the transaxle, and support the transaxle with a floor jack. Loosen the upper engine-to-transaxle mounting bolts and back them off about 3/16-inch (5 mm), loosen the left-side engine-to-bellhousing bolts, then loosen the right-side bolts.

⁂ CAUTION:

The transaxle must not be moved back more than 0.19-inch (5 mm) or the transaxle can be damaged.

6 Remove the transaxle roll restrictor mount through bolts and remove the mount (see Chapter 7A).

7 Remove the catalytic converter (see Chapter 4).

8 Remove the three bellhousing-to-pan bolts, and one oil pan-to-bellhousing bolt. Also remove the timing chain cover-to-oil pan fasteners. Remove the power steering hose bracket retaining nut and move the hose away from the oil pan.

9 Remove the a/c compressor and tie the compressor out of the way (see Chapter 3), without disconnecting the compressor lines.

10 Use a screwdriver to pry between the engine and transaxle until the bellhousing has moved away from the block to the limit of the loosened bolts (about 0.20-inch [5 mm]).

11 Progressively unscrew the oil pan retaining bolts evenly until all the bolts are removed. Use a rubber mallet to loosen the oil pan seal, then lower the oil pan, turning it as necessary to clear the exhaust system. Unfortunately, the use of sealant can make removal of the oil pan more difficult. Be careful when prying between the mating surfaces, otherwise they will be damaged, resulting in leaks when finished. With care, a putty knife can be used to cut through the sealant.

INSTALLATION

12 Thoroughly clean and degrease the mating surfaces of the lower engine block/crankcase and oil pan, removing all traces of sealant, then use a clean rag to wipe out the oil pan.

13 Apply a 1/8-inch wide bead of sealant to the oil pan flange so that the bead is approximately 3/16-inch from the outside edge of the flange. Make sure the bead is around the inside edge of the bolt holes. Also apply sealant to the front flange of the oil pan where it meets the timing chain cover.

➡ **Note: The oil pan must be installed within 10 minutes of applying the sealant.**

14 Install the oil pan bolts, only tightening them finger tight at this time.

15 Install the timing chain cover-to-oil pan fasteners and tighten them to the torque listed in this Chapter's Specifications.

16 Tighten the oil pan-to engine block bolts, a little at a time, working from the center outwards in a circular pattern, to the torque listed in this Chapter's Specifications.

17 Tighten the oil pan-to-bellhousing bolts and the transaxle to engine bolts, a little at a time to draw them together evenly, to the torque listed in this Chapter's Specifications.

18 Lower the vehicle to the ground. Before refilling the engine with oil, wait at least 1 hour for the sealant to cure, or whatever time is indicated by the sealant manufacturer. Trim off the excess sealant with a sharp knife. Install a new oil filter (see Chapter 1).

13 Oil pump - removal and installation

▶ **Refer to illustrations 13.6, 13.8 and 13.9**

➡ **Note: The oil pump is serviced as a complete unit without any sub-assembly or internal inspection.**

1 Drain the engine oil and remove the oil filter (see Chapter 1).

2 Support the engine from above with a support fixture (see Chapter 2C).

3 Remove the timing chain cover (see Section 8).

4 Remove the a/c compressor fasteners and tie the compressor out of the way without disconnecting the compressor lines.

5 Remove the oil pan (see Section 12).

6 Remove the oil pick-up tube (see illustration).

7 Use a screwdriver to pry the end of the oil pump drive chain tensioner's spring from under the shouldered bolt. Remove the two bolts and the tensioner.

13.6 The oil pump pick-up tube is held by two mounting bolts (typical)

13.8 Using a holding tool on the oil pump drive sprocket to remove the retaining bolt

13.9 Remove the four mounting bolts for the oil pump

8   Remove the chain from the oil pump sprocket. While holding the oil pump drive sprocket with a suitable tool, remove the sprocket bolt from the oil pump, then remove the sprocket (see illustration).

9   Remove the oil pump mounting bolts, then remove the pump (see illustration).

10   Installation is the reverse of removal, noting the following points:

   a) Replace all gaskets with new ones.

   b) Tighten the oil pump mounting bolts to the torque listed in this Chapter's Specifications in a criss-cross pattern.

   c) After installing the oil pan, install a new oil filter and refill the crankcase with oil (see Chapter 1).

   d) Be certain to check for any oil warning lights in the instrument panel after the vehicle has been started and idling.

14   Driveplate - removal, inspection and installation

REMOVAL

1   Remove the transaxle (see Chapter 7A). Now is a good time to check components such as oil seals and replace them if necessary.

2   Use a center-punch or paint to make alignment marks on the driveplate and crankshaft to make replacement easier - the bolt holes are slightly offset, and will only line up one way, but making a mark eliminates the guesswork.

3   Hold the driveplate stationary and unscrew the bolts. To prevent the driveplate from turning, insert one of the transaxle mounting bolts into the cylinder block and have an assistant engage a wide-bladed screwdriver with the starter ring gear teeth while the driveplate bolts are loosened.

4   Loosen and remove each bolt in turn and ensure that new replacements are obtained for reassembly. These bolts are subjected to severe stresses and so must be replaced, regardless of their apparent condition, whenever they are removed.

5   Remove the driveplate - do not drop it.

INSPECTION

6   Clean the driveplate to remove grease and oil. Check for cracked

and broken ring gear teeth.

7   Clean and inspect the mating surfaces of the flywheel and the crankshaft. If the oil seal is leaking, replace it (see Section 15) before replacing the driveplate. If the engine has high mileage, it may be worth installing a new seal as a matter of course, given the amount of work needed to access it.

INSTALLATION

8   On installation, ensure that the engine/transaxle adapter plate is in place (where necessary), then install the driveplate on the crankshaft so that all bolt holes align - it will fit only one way - check this using the marks made on removal. Install the new bolts, tightening them by hand.

9   Lock the driveplate by the method used on disassembly. Working in a diagonal sequence to tighten them evenly and increasing to the final amount in two or three stages, tighten the new bolts to the torque listed in this Chapter's Specifications.

10   The remainder of reassembly is the reverse of the removal procedure

15   Rear main oil seal - replacement

♦ **Refer to illustration 15.9**

1   The one-piece rear main oil seal is pressed into the rear main oil seal carrier mounted at the rear of the block. Remove the transaxle (see

Chapter 7A) and the driveplate (see Section 14).

2   Remove the oil pan (see Section 12).

3   Unbolt the oil seal and carrier.

15.9 Rear main oil seal carrier tightening sequence

4 Clean the mating surface for the oil seal carrier on the cylinder block and the crankshaft. Carefully remove and polish any burrs or raised edges on the crankshaft that may have caused the seal to fail.

5 Lightly coat the inside lip of the new seal with clean engine oil.

Use a thin (but durable) two-inch wide plastic strip (or a two-liter plastic beverage bottle cut to size) around the inside circumference of the seal to act as a liner for installation. The manufacturer tool (#303-328) for this purpose also works well.

6 With the plastic seal liner or tool in place, carefully move the new carrier (with seal factory-installed) into position by sliding it onto the contact surface of the crankshaft.

7 Install the oil seal carrier bolts and finger tighten them while holding the carrier in place. Align the bottom of the seal carrier precisely with the bottom edge of the engine block to ensure that the surfaces are flush before tightening the carrier mounting bolts.

✳✳ CAUTION:

The oil pan may leak if the two surfaces are not perfectly flush.

8 Carefully remove the plastic liner or tool so that the new seal contacts the crankshaft mating surface correctly.

9 Tighten the oil seal carrier to the torque listed in this Chapter's Specifications using the proper sequence (see illustration).

10 The remainder of installation is the reverse of removal.

16 Engine mount - check and replacement

1 Engine mounts seldom require attention, but broken or deteriorated mounts should be replaced immediately or the added strain placed on the driveline components may cause damage or wear.

CHECK

2 During the check, the engine must be raised slightly to remove the weight from the mounts.

3 Raise the vehicle and support it securely on jackstands, then position a jack under the engine oil pan. Place a large wood block between the jack head and the oil pan to prevent oil pan damage, then carefully raise the engine just enough to take the weight off the mounts.

✳✳ WARNING:

DO NOT place any part of your body under the engine when it's supported only by a jack!

4 Check the mount to see if the rubber is cracked, hardened or separated from the bushing in the center of the mount.

5 Check for relative movement between the mount and the engine or chassis. Use a large screwdriver or prybar to attempt to move the mounts. If movement is noted, lower the engine and tighten the mount fasteners.

REPLACEMENT

✳✳ WARNING:

Wait until the engine is completely cool before beginning this procedure.

➡ **Note: Refer to Chapter 7 for information on the transaxle mount.**

6 Disconnect the cable from the negative terminal of the battery (see Chapter 5).

7 Remove the engine splash shield fasteners and shield.

8 Remove the coolant expansion tank (see Chapter 3).

9 Place a floor jack under the engine with a wood block between the jack head and oil pan, then raise the engine slightly to relieve the weight from the mount.

10 Remove the power steering fluid reservoir nuts and place the reservoir out of the way.

11 Disengage the wiring harness retainer from the valve cover stud and move the harness out of the way.

12 Remove the fasteners and detach the mount from the frame and engine.

✳✳ CAUTION:

Do not disconnect more than one mount at a time, except during engine removal.

13 Installation is the reverse of removal. Use thread-locking compound on the mount bolts and be sure to tighten them securely.

Specifications

General

Engine type	Four-cylinder, in-line, DOHC
Displacement	122 cubic inches (1999 cc)
Engine VIN code	9
Firing order	1-3-4-2
Bore	3.4449 inches (87.5 mm)
Stroke	3.2717 inches (83.1 mm)
Compression ratio	9.3:1
Compression pressure	See Chapter 2C
Oil pressure	See Chapter 2C

FRONT OF VEHICLE

Cylinder locations

Camshafts

Lobe height	
Intake	0.326 inch (8.3 mm)
Exhaust	0.291 inch (7.4 mm)
Bearing journal diameter	0.9827 to 0.9835 inch (24.96 to 24.98 mm)
Runout	0.0012 inch (0.03 mm)

Valve clearances (cold)

Ideal clearance	
Intake	0.0095 inch (0.25 mm)
Exhaust	0.0142 inch (0.36 mm)
Acceptable clearance	
Intake	0.007 to 0.012 inch (0.19 to 0.30 mm)
Exhaust	0.012 to 0.017 inch (0.30 to 0.42 mm)

Warpage limits

Cylinder head gasket surfaces (head and block)	0.0020 inch (0.05 mm)
Exhaust manifold	0.030 inch (0.76 mm)

Torque specifications	Ft-lbs (unless otherwise indicated)	Nm

➡ **Note: One foot-pound (ft-lb) of torque is equivalent to 12 inch-pounds (in-lbs) of torque. Torque values below approximately 15 foot-pounds are expressed in inch-pounds, because most foot-pound torque wrenches are not accurate at these smaller values.**

Camshaft bearing cap bolts (in sequence - see illustration 10.25)		
Step 1, All but front bearing cap	62 in-lbs	7
Step 2, All but front bearing cap	142 in-lbs	16
Step 3, Front bearing cap (3-bolt)	62 in-lbs	7
Step 4, Front bearing cap (3-bolt)	142 in-lbs	16
Camshaft phaser and sprocket bolts		
Step 1	30	40
Step 2	Tighten an additional 60-degrees	
Crankshaft pulley bolt		
Step 1	74	100
Step 2	Tighten an additional 90-degrees	
Cylinder head bolts (in sequence - see illustration 11.30a)		
Step 1	62 in-lbs	7
Step 2	133 in-lbs	15
Step 3	41	55
Step 4	Tighten an additional 90-degrees	
Step 5	Tighten an additional 90-degrees	

Torque specifications	Ft-lbs (unless otherwise indicated)	Nm

➡ **Note: One foot-pound (ft-lb) of torque is equivalent to 12 inch-pounds (in-lbs) of torque. Torque values below approximately 15 foot-pounds are expressed in inch-pounds, because most foot-pound torque wrenches are not accurate at these smaller values.**

Variable Camshaft Timing (VCT) solenoid bolt	89 in-lbs	10
Valve cover bolts (in sequence - see		
illustration 4.13)	89 in-lbs	10
Turbocharger mounting nuts	37	50
Engine mount nuts\bolts	66	90
Driveplate bolts		
Step 1	37	50
Step 2	50	80
Step 3	83	112
Intake manifold bolts	177 in-lbs	20
Crankshaft rear oil seal and retainer	89 in-lbs	10
Oil pan-to-bellhousing bolts	35	48
Timing chain cover-to-oil pan bolts	89 in-lbs	10
Oil pan-to-engine block bolts	177 in-lbs	20
Oil pick-up pipe bolts	89 in-lbs	10
Oil pump-to-cylinder block bolts		
Step 1	89 in-lbs	10
Step 2	177 in-lbs	20
Sprocket bolt	18	25
Oil pump chain tensioner and guide bolts	89 in-lbs	10
Timing chain cover (in sequence - see illustration 8.11)		
8 mm bolts	89 in-lbs	10
13 mm bolts	35	48
Timing chain guide bolts	89 in-lbs	10
Timing chain tensioner bolts	89 in-lbs	10
Transaxle-to-engine bolts	35	48

2B

V6 ENGINES

Section

1   General information

This Part of Chapter 2 covers in-vehicle repairs for the 3.5L and 3.7L Double Overhead Camshaft (DOHC) V6 engines. These engines feature aluminum engine blocks and aluminum cylinder heads with dual overhead camshafts and four valves per cylinder.

All information on engine removal and installation, as well as general overhaul procedures, is in Part C of Chapter 2.

The following repair procedures are based on the assumption that the engine is installed in the vehicle. If the engine has been removed and mounted on a stand, many of the Steps in this Part of Chapter 2 will not apply. Some procedures on the engines do, however, require engine removal.

In this Chapter, "left" and "right" are used to describe locations on the vehicle. These directions are in relation to the vehicle overall from the position of sitting in the driver's seat. However, for simplicity in describing the cylinder banks of the V6 engine, they are termed "front" (closest to the radiator) and "rear" (closest to the firewall).

2   Repair operations possible with the engine in the vehicle

Many major repairs can be done without removing the engine from the vehicle. Clean the engine compartment and the exterior of the engine with a pressure washer or degreaser solvent before doing any work. Cleaning the engine and engine compartment will make repairs easier and help to keep dirt out of the engine.

It may help to remove the hood for better access to the engine. Refer to Chapter 11, if necessary.

If the engine has vacuum, exhaust, oil, or coolant leaks that indicate the need for gasket replacement, repairs can usually be done with the engine in the vehicle. The intake and exhaust manifold gaskets, the timing chain cover gasket, the oil pan gasket, crankshaft oil seals, and cylinder head gaskets are all accessible with the engine in the vehicle.

Exterior engine components, such as the intake and exhaust manifolds, the oil pan, the water pump, the starter motor, the alternator, and many fuel system components also can be serviced with the engine installed. The timing chain cover, timing chain, camshafts and cylinder head procedures must be performed with the engine removed from the vehicle.

3   Valve clearance - check and adjustment

▶ Refer to illustrations 3.5 and 3.8

➡ Note: The engine must be cold before checking the valve clearances.

➡ Note: Checking and, if necessary, adjusting the valve clearance is only necessary after replacement of the camshaft(s) or other valve-related parts, or if the valve train is making excessive noise.

1   Disconnect the cable from the negative terminal of the battery (see Chapter 5).

2   Remove the spark plugs (see Chapter 1).

3   Remove the valve covers (see Section 4).

4   Using a socket and a breaker bar on the crankshaft pulley center bolt, rotate the engine until the cam lobes on the cylinder to be checked are pointing away from the lifters.

5   Measure the clearance of the valves with a feeler gauge (see illustration). Record each measurement and compare your measurements with the desired valve clearance found in this Chapter's Specifications. Note which ones are out of specification, as this data will be used later to determine the required replacement lifters.

3.5 Measure the valve clearance for each valve with a feeler gauge of the specified thickness - if the clearance is correct, you should be able to feel a slight drag on the gauge as you pull it out

6   Repeat Steps 4 and 5 until the clearances for all valves have been measured.

7   If a clearance is out of specification, the lifter must be replaced with a new lifter that has a different thickness head to correct the clearance. Refer to Section 10 and remove the camshafts to access the lifters.

8   Mark the lifters that are to be replaced, and record which valve they came from. Use a micrometer to measure the thickness of the head of the lifter, making sure the measurement is precise and on the center projection on the underside of the lifter (see illustration).

9   To calculate the correct thickness for a replacement lifter that will place the valve clearance within the specified value, use the following formula:

$N = R + (M1 - M2)$
N = thickness of new lifter
R = thickness of old lifter
$M1$ = measured valve clearance
$M2$ = standard valve clearance

10   Lifters are marked on the underside as to their size. A marking of 3.310 on the underside of the lifter indicates a thickness value of 3.31 mm, or 0.13 inch.

3.8 Use a micrometer to measure the thickness of the head of the lifter

11   Mark the new lifters as to their destination, lubricate them with engine assembly lube and install them. After replacing the lifters, reinstall the camshafts and the timing chains (see Sections 9 and 10), then re-check the valve clearances.

---

4   Valve covers - removal and installation

REMOVAL

1   Disconnect the cable from the negative battery terminal (see Chapter 5).

2   Remove the engine cover, if equipped.

3   Remove the ignition coils from the cover to be removed (see Chapter 5).

Front valve cover

▶ **Refer to illustration 4.4**

4   Disconnect the vent tube from the valve cover (see illustration).

5   Disconnect the wiring harness from the valve cover and position it off to the side. Remove the engine oil dipstick.

6   Disconnect the oxygen sensor connector and fuel injector electrical connectors.

Rear valve cover

7   Remove the power steering fluid hose retainers and move the hose out of the way.

8   Disconnect the oxygen sensor (HO2S) and catalyst monitor sensor (CMS) connectors and the fuel injector electrical connectors.

Both valve covers

▶ **Refer to illustrations 4.9 and 4.10**

9   Disconnect the two electrical connectors at the valve cover for the VCT solenoids, being careful not to twist the solenoids (see illustration).

4.4 Detach the vent tube from the valve cover

4.9 Disconnect the electrical connectors from the VCT oil control solenoids in each valve cover

4.10 Valve cover fasteners

4.12 Check the spark plug tube seals, VCT solenoid seals and valve cover gasket. If they are in good condition they can be reused

4.13 Check the bolt seals - replace them if they're not in good condition

4.14 Apply RTV sealant to the seams where the timing chain cover meets the cylinder head

10 Remove the valve cover fasteners, then separate the wiring/clips and remove the valve cover from the cylinder head (see illustration). Use hand-pressure to wiggle the valve cover from the cylinder head.

✳✳ CAUTION:

If that doesn't work, do not use a hammer. Try to slip a flexible putty knife between the cylinder head and cover to break the gasket seal. Don't pry at the cover-to-cylinder head joint or damage to the sealing surfaces may occur (leading to oil leaks in the future).

INSTALLATION

▶ **Refer to illustrations 4.12, 4.13, 4.14 and 4.16**

11 The mating surfaces of each cylinder head and valve cover must be perfectly clean when the covers are installed. Remove all traces of sealant and old gasket material, then clean the mating surfaces with brake cleaner. If there's sealant or oil on the mating surfaces when the cover is installed, oil leaks may develop.

12 Inspect the spark plug seals, the seals for the VCT solenoids and the valve cover gasket (see illustration). Do not replace them unless necessary.

13 Make sure the bolt seals are in good condition (see illustration).

14 Apply a bead of RTV sealant to the joints where the engine front cover meets the cylinder head and install the valve cover within four minutes (see illustration).

15 Carefully position the cover on the cylinder head and install the bolts.

16 Tighten the bolts a little at a time, in the proper sequence (see illustration), to the torque listed in this Chapter's Specifications.

17 The remainder of installation is the reverse of removal.

18 Start the engine and check carefully for oil leaks as the engine warms up.

4.16 Valve cover bolt tightening sequence (left side shown, right side similar)

5 Intake manifolds - removal and installation

UPPER INTAKE MANIFOLD

Removal

1 Disconnect the cable from the negative battery terminal (see Chapter 5).

2 Remove the engine cover.

3 Remove the air filter housing and hoses (see Chapter 4).

4 Disconnect the PCM electrical connectors and move the harnesses out of the way (see Chapter 6).

5 Disconnect the EVAP canister vent solenoid and throttle body electrical connectors.

6 Disconnect the line from the EVAP canister vent solenoid.

7 Disconnect the brake booster vacuum hose and crankcase vent hose from the upper intake manifold.

8 Disengage the coolant tube and wiring harness retainers and move the tube and harness out of the way.

9 Remove the upper intake support bracket fastener from the upper intake.

10 Remove the manifold mounting bolts and detach the manifold from the engine.

➡ **Note: Do not use a hammer. Once the manifold is off, cover the intake ports of the engine with clean shop rags.**

Installation

▶ **Refer to illustration 5.12**

11 Remove the old gaskets from the manifold. Clean the manifold and cylinder head mating surfaces.

12 Install the new manifold gaskets to the grooves in the manifold. Install the manifold and bolts. Tighten the bolts in the indicated sequence (see illustration) to the torque listed in this Chapter's Specifications.

13 The remainder of the installation is the reverse of removal.

LOWER INTAKE MANIFOLD

✳✳ WARNING:

Wait until the engine is completely cool before beginning this procedure.

Removal

14 Remove the upper intake manifold (see Steps 1 through 10).

15 Drain the cooling system (see Chapter 1).

16 Cover the drivebelt with plastic wrap, then remove the thermostat housing (see Chapter 3). Disconnect the heater hose from the manifold.

5.12 Upper intake manifold bolt TIGHTENING sequence

5.22 Lower intake manifold bolt TIGHTENING sequence

17 Detach the fuel line from the fuel rail (see Chapter 4).

18 Disconnect the electrical connectors from the injectors.

19 Loosen the intake manifold mounting bolts in 1/4-turn increments, in the reverse of the tightening sequence (see illustration 5.22), until they can be removed by hand.

Installation

▶ **Refer to illustration 5.22**

20 Remove the gaskets from the grooves in the manifold. Clean the manifold and cylinder head mating surfaces.

21 Install new gaskets into the grooves in the manifold, then carefully set the manifold in place.

22 Install the bolts and tighten them to the torque listed in this Chapter's Specifications, following the recommended sequence (see illustration).

23 The remainder of installation is the reverse of removal.

24 Refill the cooling system (see Chapter 1).

25 Start the engine and check carefully for oil or coolant leaks at the intake manifold joints.

6 Exhaust manifolds - removal and installation

➡ **Note: Before beginning this procedure, allow the engine to cool completely, and apply penetrating oil to the manifold and converter fasteners.**

➡ **Note: On 2011 and later models, the front exhaust manifold and catalytic converter are integrated into one piece.**

FRONT EXHAUST MANIFOLD

▶ **Refer to illustration 6.6**

1 Disconnect the cable from the negative battery terminal (see Chapter 5).

2 Disconnect the electrical connector for the oxygen sensor and the catalytic converter monitor (see Chapter 6).

3 Raise the front of the vehicle and support it securely on jackstands.

4 From below, disconnect the exhaust Y-pipe.

5 Remove the heat shield over the front exhaust manifold.

6 Remove and discard the six nuts securing the exhaust manifold (see illustration). Remove and discard the manifold gasket.

7 Remove the exhaust manifold and converter.

8 Using a stud holding tool (available at auto parts stores) or a pair of nuts tightened together over a stud, extract the exhaust manifold studs and discard them.

9 Using a scraper, remove all old gasket material and carbon deposits from the manifold and cylinder head mating surfaces. If the gasket was leaking, check the manifold for warpage and have it resurfaced if necessary.

✳ CAUTION:

Be very careful when scraping on aluminum engine parts such as the cylinder heads. Aluminum is soft and gouges easily. Severely gouged parts may require replacement.

6.6 Remove the front exhaust mounting nuts from the studs (four of six shown)

10 Install new exhaust manifold studs with light oil on the threads, then install a new manifold gasket over the studs. Install the manifold and new self-locking nuts.

11 Tighten the nuts, starting with the center fasteners and working towards the ends, to the torque listed in this Chapter's Specifications.

12 The remainder of installation is the reverse of removal.

REAR EXHAUST MANIFOLD

13 Disconnect the cable from the negative battery terminal (see Chapter 5).

14 Disconnect the connector to the rear bank oxygen sensor.

15 Raise the vehicle and support it securely on jackstands.

16 Remove the Y-pipe-to-catalytic converter flange nuts and disconnect the Y-pipe. Remove the rear-bank catalytic converter.

17 Remove and discard the six exhaust manifold mounting nuts and remove the manifold from the engine. Remove and discard the manifold gasket.

18 Using a stud holding tool (available at auto parts stores) or a pair of new nuts tightened together over a stud, extract the exhaust manifold studs and discard them.

19 Using a scraper, remove all gasket material and carbon deposits from the exhaust manifold and cylinder head mating surfaces.

⁂ CAUTION:

Be very careful when scraping on aluminum engine parts. Aluminum is soft and gouges easily. Severely gouged parts may require replacement. If the gasket was leaking, check the manifold for warpage and have it resurfaced if necessary.

20 Install new exhaust manifold studs with light oil on the threads, then install a new manifold gasket over the studs. Install the manifold and new self-locking nuts.

21 Tighten the nuts, starting with the center fasteners and working towards the ends, to the torque listed in this Chapter's Specifications.

22 The remainder of installation is the reverse of removal.

7 Crankshaft pulley and front oil seal - removal and installation

REMOVAL

▶ **Refer to illustrations 7.5 and 7.6**

1 Disconnect the cable from the negative battery terminal (see Chapter 5).

2 Loosen the right front wheel lug nuts. Raise the front of the vehicle and support it securely on jackstands, then remove the wheel.

3 Remove the fender splash shield.

4 Remove the drivebelt (see Chapter 1).

5 Use a two-pin spanner to hold the crankshaft pulley while removing the crankshaft pulley retaining bolt (see illustration).

6 Using a three-jaw puller, remove the crankshaft pulley (see illustration).

⁂ CAUTION:

Be sure to use the proper adapter on the end of the crankshaft to prevent damage to the threads or end of the crankshaft. Also, the jaws of the puller must grasp the hub of the pulley, not the outer diameter.

7 Using a seal puller, remove the seal from the timing chain cover. Note the depth at which the seal fits in the front cover and the orientation of the sealing lip so that the new seal will be installed in the same direction and to the same depth.

INSTALLATION

▶ **Refer to illustration 7.10**

8 Inspect the front cover and the pulley seal surface for nicks, burrs, or other roughness that could damage the new seal. Correct as necessary.

9 Lubricate the new seal with clean engine oil and install it in the timing chain cover with a suitable seal driver which draws the seal in slowly. Be sure that the lip of the seal faces inward. If a seal driver is unavailable, carefully tap the seal into place with a large socket and hammer until it's flush with the timing chain cover surface.

10 Align the pulley keyway with the crankshaft key and install the pulley with a suitable pulley installation tool available at auto parts stores (see illustration). Install and tighten the pulley bolt to the torque listed in this Chapter's Specifications.

➡ **Note: The manufacturer suggests that a new pulley bolt be installed.**

11 Reinstall the remaining parts in the reverse order of removal. Tighten the wheel lug nuts to the torque listed in the Chapter 1 Specifications.

12 Reconnect the battery, then start the engine and check for oil leaks.

7.5 Use a two-pin spanner to hold the pulley while removing the bolt

7.6 Remove the crankshaft pulley with a three-jaw puller

7.10 Using a pulley installation tool, turn the nut to drive the pulley onto the nose of the crankshaft

8 Timing chain cover - removal and installation

✴ WARNING:

The air conditioning system is under high pressure. DO NOT loosen any fittings or remove any components until after the system has been discharged. Air conditioning refrigerant must be properly discharged into an EPA-approved container at a dealer service department or an automotive air conditioning repair facility. Always wear eye protection when disconnecting air conditioning system fittings.

✴ WARNING:

Wait until the engine is completely cool before beginning this procedure.

➡ **Note: The timing chain cover can be removed with the engine in the vehicle but it is very difficult to do. It is recommended that the engine be removed to perform this procedure (see Chapter 2C); ignore the steps here which don't apply.**

REMOVAL

1 Have the air conditioning system discharged by a dealer service department or an automotive air conditioning shop before proceeding (see **Warning** above).

2 Relieve the fuel system pressure (see Chapter 4).

3 Disconnect the cable from the negative battery terminal (see Chapter 5).

4 Loosen the right front wheel lug nuts. Raise the front of the vehicle and support it securely on jackstands, then remove the wheel.

5 Remove the engine cover pushpins and remove the cover, if equipped.

6 Remove the drivebelt (see Chapter 1).

7 Remove the drivebelt tensioner and two idler pulleys from the timing chain cover.

8 Remove the valve covers (see Section 4).

9 Remove the alternator (see Chapter 5).

10 Remove the crankshaft pulley (see Section 7).

11 Remove the roll restrictor heat shield fasteners and shield, then remove the roll restrictor (see Chapter 7A).

12 Remove the power steering pump and reservoir (see Chapter 10).

13 Remove the coolant expansion tank (see Chapter 3).

14 Disconnect the Powertrain Control Module (PCM) electrical connector (see Chapter 6) and move the harness out of the way.

15 Disconnect the Crankshaft Position (CKP) sensor. Remove the Camshaft Position (CMP) sensors from the front of each cylinder head.

16 Support the engine from above with a hoist or engine support fixture, using chains fastened to the engine lift brackets (see illustration).

17 Disconnect the electrical connectors at the air conditioning compressor, then remove the compressor mounting bolts and compressor. Remove the compressor bracket from the timing chain cover.

18 Remove or disconnect any remaining wires, hoses, clamps, or brackets that will interfere with timing chain cover removal.

19 Place a floor jack, with a block of wood between the front of the oil pan and the jack then raise the jack enough to slightly support the engine.

20 Remove the transaxle mount through bolt, then remove the mount support brace and mount (see Chapter 7A).

21 Remove the front engine mount (see Section 16).

22 With the floor jack supporting the engine, slowly lower the engine until the lower timing chain cover bolt (M10) just above the crankshaft seal can be removed.

23 Using the floor jack, raise the engine approximately 4 inches, and remove the two upper timing chain cover bolts (M10).

➡ **Note: Take a digital photo or draw a sketch of the timing chain cover and fasteners. Identify the location of all bolts for installation in their original locations.**

24 Loosen the remaining 22 timing chain cover (M8) bolts gradually and evenly, then remove the fasteners. Start with the oil pan-to-cover bolts, then the other bolts. Remove the remaining timing cover bolt (M6) and remove the timing chain cover.

✴ CAUTION:

Make sure all of the timing chain cover bolts are removed before attempting to remove the cover.

25 Remove and discard the cover-to-cylinder block gaskets.

INSTALLATION

▸ **Refer to illustration 8.33**

26 Inspect and clean all sealing surfaces of the timing chain cover and the block.

✴ CAUTION:

Be very careful when scraping on aluminum engine parts. Aluminum is soft and gouges easily. Severely gouged parts may require replacement.

27 Replace the crankshaft seal in the front cover (see Section 7).

28 Apply a 1/8-inch bead of RTV sealant to the mating surface of the cover.

29 Apply a 3/16-inch bead of sealant to the areas where the oil pan and cylinder heads meet the engine block.

30 Install two dowel pins (bolts with heads cut off) into holes 20 and 19 in the engine block (see illustration 8.33).

31 Slide the timing chain cover onto the engine. The dowel pins will position it correctly.

32 Make sure the fasteners are in their original locations. Tighten the fasteners by hand until the cover is contacting the block and cylinder heads around its entire edge.

33 Install bolts 17 through 20 and remove the locating pins. Install the rest of the bolts and tighten in sequence (see illustration) to the torque steps listed in this Chapter's Specifications. Install the engine mount.

34 Install the drivebelt and tensioner. Tighten the tensioner pulley to the torque listed in this Chapter's Specifications.

35 Install the crankshaft pulley (see Section 7).

36 Connect the wiring harness connectors to the CMP and CKP sensors.

37 Install the power steering pump and hoses (see Chapter 10).

38 Reinstall the remaining parts in the reverse order of removal.

39 Have the system evacuated, recharged and leak tested by the shop that discharged it.

8.33 Timing chain cover bolt tightening sequence

9 Timing chain and sprockets - removal and installation

⁂ CAUTION:

These engines are difficult to work on and require some special tools. On any procedure involving the timing chains, the Steps must be read carefully and disassembly must proceed using the special tools, otherwise damage to the engine will result.

⁂ CAUTION:

Because this is an interference engine design, if the timing chain has broken, there will be damage to the valves (and possibly the pistons), requiring removal of the cylinder heads.

⁂ CAUTION:

The timing system is complex. Severe engine damage will occur if you make any mistakes. Do not attempt this procedure unless you are highly experienced with this type of repair. If you are at all unsure of your abilities, consult an expert. Double-check all your work and be sure everything is correct before you attempt to start the engine.

REMOVAL

▶ **Refer to illustration 9.4**

➡ **Note: On 2010 and earlier engines, the procedure can only be done with the engine removed (see Chapter 2C); ignore the steps here which don't apply.**

➡ **Note: Two special camshaft holding tools (manufacturer tool no. 303-1248) are required for this procedure.**

9.4 The position of the intake cam sprocket marks when the engine is set to TDC compression for cylinder no. 1 (upper arrows); lower arrows indicate the VCT assembly mounting bolts (2010 and earlier models)

➡ **Note: Since the water pump on this engine is located behind the timing chain and components, it makes sense to replace the water pump, since it is easily accessed during a timing chain replacement procedure.**

1 Disconnect the cable from the negative battery terminal (see Chapter 5).

2 Remove the valve covers (see Section 4).

3 Remove the timing chain cover (see Section 8).

4 Reinstall the crankshaft sprocket bolt and set the engine to TDC for cylinder number 1 (see illustration).

➡ **Note: At this point the TDC position will be approximate; when the special tools are installed in Step 6 or 14, the TDC position will be exact.**

9.13 Remove three of the camshaft cap bolts to remove the valvetrain oil tubes (2011 and later models)

9.18 Remove the VCT oil control solenoid mounting bolts (A and B) - (C) is the exhaust VCT unit and (D) is the intake VCT unit (2011 and later models)

2010 and earlier models

5   These engines have three timing chains: The long primary chain drives the VCT sprockets (on each intake camshaft) and the water pump, while a smaller chain on each head drives the exhaust camshafts.

6   Install the special camshaft holding tools (manufacturer tool no. 303-1248) on each cylinder head to lock the camshafts in the TDC position.

7   Remove the VCT assembly mounting bolts from the rear cylinder head, then the front cylinder head (see illustration 9.4).

8   Remove the bolts, then remove the primary timing chain tensioner and tensioner arm. Remove the lower chain guide from the front cylinder bank. Mark the chain links opposite the timing marks on the camshafts (if not already marked), and remove the primary timing chain.

9   Remove the upper chain guide from the front cylinder bank. If necessary, remove the crankshaft sprocket.

10   If the secondary timing chains and camshaft sprockets are to be removed for inspection or another procedure, compress the tensioner(s) and insert a pin into the hole in the tensioner to hold it in the retracted position. Unscrew the bolts for the intake (VCT) and exhaust camshaft sprockets, then remove both sprockets and the chain as an assembly.

☀ CAUTION:

Make sure the camshaft holding tool is in place and prevents the camshafts from turning while unscrewing the bolts. Also, new bolts must be used for reassembly.

11   Remove the bolts and the secondary chain tensioners.

→ **Note: The camshaft holding tool must be loosened and tilted (toward the flywheel end of the engine) to access the rearmost bolt of the tensioner.**

2011 and later models

▶ **Refer to illustrations 9.13 and 9.18**

12   Turn the engine clockwise until the VCT units (camshaft sprockets) on each intake camshaft are positioned at 90-degrees (12 o'clock) in relation to the top surface of the cylinder heads.

13   Remove the bolts that secure the valve train oil tubes to each cyl-

inder head (see illustration).

14   Install the special camshaft locking tools (303-1248), with the tools holding the flats on each camshaft.

15   If you can't see the timing marks on the timing chain, add a paint dot to align with the marks on the VCT units and the crankshaft timing sprocket.

16   Remove the two bolts and the primary timing chain tensioner arm, then unbolt and remove the two tensioners.

17   Remove the mounting bolts and remove the lower left chain guide, then the lower right chain guide.

18   Remove the bolts securing the VCT solenoids to the cylinder heads (see illustration). You may have to twist or wiggle the solenoids to disengage them.

→ **Note: The intake solenoids are white, the exhaust solenoids are black.**

19   Keep the VCT solenoids in clean plastic sandwich bags, marked with their location.

20   Remove the primary timing chain.

21   The two camshafts on each cylinder head are jointly driven by a smaller secondary timing chain.

22   Depress and lock the secondary chain tensioner on each bank, using the factory tool (303-1530) inserted in the large hole at the first camshaft bearing cap, or use a length of threaded rod and nuts to hold the tensioner down, by pushing from the camshaft bearing cap.

23   With the camshafts still locked at TDC, remove the mounting bolts from the VCT units (camshaft sprockets), then remove the sprockets and secondary timing chains from the camshafts.

24   If the primary timing chain sprocket (at the center of the front of the block) is to be replaced, remove the nine bolts securing the plate that mounts the gear to the front of the block.

INSTALLATION

2010 and earlier models

▶ **Refer to illustration 9.27**

25   Install the primary timing chain guide for the rear (right) cylinder bank and tighten the bolts to the torque listed in this Chapter's Specifications.

26 Tilt the rear (right) cylinder bank camshaft holding tool to the rear and install the secondary timing chain tensioner, tightening the bolts to the torque listed in this Chapter's Specifications. Don't remove the lock pin from the tensioner yet.

27 Install the secondary timing chains onto the camshaft sprockets. The colored links on the chain must align with the marks/camshaft keyway slots in the sprockets (see illustration).

28 Install the sprockets/VCT actuator (phaser)/secondary timing chain onto the rear camshafts. When installing the camshaft sprocket bolts, NEW bolts must be used. Tighten the bolts to the torque listed in this Chapter's Specifications.

29 Tilt the front (left) cylinder bank camshaft holding tool to the rear and install the secondary timing chain tensioner, tightening the bolts to the torque listed in this Chapter's Specifications. Don't remove the lock pin from the tensioner yet.

30 Install the sprockets/VCT actuator (phaser)/secondary timing chain (with the marks aligned as shown in illustration 9.27) onto the front camshafts. When installing the camshaft sprocket bolts, NEW bolts must be used. Tighten the bolts to the torque listed in this Chapter's Specifications. Remove the lock pin from the tensioner.

31 Install the crankshaft sprocket.

32 Install the primary timing chain onto the crankshaft sprocket and the VCT sprockets, making sure the colored links (or marks) on the chain align with the marks on the sprockets.

➡ **Note: At TDC compression for cylinder no. 1, the crankshaft sprocket keyway will be in approximately the 11 o'clock position and the timing mark on the crankshaft sprocket will be in approximately the 4 o'clock position.**

33 Install the upper chain guide on the front (left) cylinder bank, tightening the bolts to the torque listed in this Chapter's Specifications.

34 Install the lower chain guide for the front cylinder bank, tightening the bolts to the torque listed in this Chapter's Specifications.

35 Install the primary timing chain tensioner arm to the rear cylinder bank. Place the timing chain tensioner in a soft-jawed vise, with the jaws bearing on the tensioner body and the plunger. Swing the lever on the tensioner counterclockwise, then tighten the vise until the tensioner plunger has been retracted. Swing the lever clockwise, aligning the hole in the lever with the hole in the tensioner body, then install a lock pin made of heavy wire, or a drill bit or small Allen wrench. Remove the tensioner from the vise.

36 Install the primary timing chain tensioner, tightening the bolts to the torque listed in this Chapter's Specifications. Remove the lock pin from the tensioner.

➡ **Note: It might be necessary to rotate the crankshaft slightly to create a little slack in the chain to enable the tensioner to be installed.**

37 Recheck the timing marks to make sure they are all in proper alignment.

38 Check the seals on the VCT housing, replacing them if necessary.

39 Install the VCT housings, making sure the dowels engage completely with their corresponding holes in the cylinder head. Install the bolts and tighten them a little at a time to the torque listed in this Chapter's Specifications.

40 Remove the camshaft holding tools, then rotate the engine by hand at least two revolutions and verify that there is no binding.

❊❊❊ **CAUTION:**

If any resistance is felt, STOP; double-check your work and find out why.

9.27 Align the secondary timing chain colored links with the keyways of the sprockets (2010 and earlier models)

9.46 Align the colored links of the secondary timing chain with the marks on the back of the sprockets (VCT units) – 2011 and later models

41 Install the timing chain cover (see Section 8).

42 Reinstall the engine/transaxle. Refill the engine with oil (install a new filter) and coolant (see Chapter 1).

2011 and later models

▶ **Refer to illustrations 9.46 and 9.48**

43 If the primary chain gear and its plate were removed, clean the mounting surface and the block, then install the sprocket and plate with a new gasket. Prepare the primary chain tensioners by pushing in the release button and compressing the plunger until a nail or large paper clip can be inserted to hold the plunger.

44 If the secondary timing chain tensioners were removed, they cannot be reused. New tensioners must be installed.

❊❊❊ **WARNING:**

Do not remove the plastic clip that is keeping the new tensioner compressed.

45 The tensioner is installed to the correct depth when you hear a snap. Install the tensioner shoe. The plastic clip can now be removed with pliers.

46 Align the colored links with the marks on the VCT units and install the chain on the backside of the VCT units (see illustration). Align the two VCT units with the dowel pins on the front of the camshafts.

9.48 Align the colored links on the primary timing chain with the marks on the crankshaft and camshaft sprockets (VCT units) – 2011 and later models

47 New bolts must be used to install the VCT units. Tighten the bolts to the torque listed in this Chapter's Specifications.

48 When the secondary chains and VCT units are installed and aligned, install the primary timing chain, aligning the colored links with the marks on the sprockets (see illustration). When all components are installed and aligned, pull the pins holding back the two primary chain tensioners.

49 Reinstall the remaining parts in the reverse order of removal.

50 Carefully rotate the crankshaft by hand through at least two full revolutions (use a socket and breaker bar on the crankshaft pulley center bolt).

✳ CAUTION:

If you feel any resistance, STOP! There is something wrong - most likely, valves are contacting the pistons. You must find the problem before proceeding.

51 Install a new oil filter, then add engine oil and coolant (see Chapter 1).

52 Run the engine and check for leaks.

10 Camshafts and lifters - removal inspection, and installation

✳ CAUTION:

These engines are difficult to work on and require some special tools. On any procedure involving the timing chains, the Steps must be read carefully and disassembly must proceed using the special tools, otherwise damage to the engine will result.

✳ CAUTION:

Because this is an interference engine design, if the timing chain has broken, there will be damage to the valves (and possibly the pistons) and will require removal of the cylinder heads.

10.2 Front (left) bank camshaft timing marks (keyways) in the neutral position – 2010 and earlier engines

✳ CAUTION:

The timing system is complex. Severe engine damage will occur if you make any mistakes. Do not attempt this procedure unless you are highly experienced with this type of repair. If you are at all unsure of your abilities, consult an expert. Double-check all your work and be sure everything is correct before you attempt to start the engine.

➡ **Note: This procedure can only be done with the engine removed (see Chapter 2C).**

➡ **Note: Two special camshaft holding tools (manufacturer tool no. 303-1248) are required for this procedure.**

REMOVAL

1 Before removing the camshafts, check the valve clearances (see Section 3).

2010 and earlier models

▸ **Refer to illustrations 10.2 and 10.5**

2 Remove the primary timing chain and the front (left) cylinder bank VCT assembly/camshaft sprockets/secondary timing chain (see Section 9), then remove the camshaft holding tool from the front (left) cylinder bank camshafts. Confirm that the camshafts are in the neutral positions after the holding tool has been removed (see illustration).

3 Note the location of each camshaft cap. Use a marker on each cap or notes on paper or cardboard if they're not marked.

10.5 Rear (right) bank camshaft timing marks (keyways) in the neutral position – 2010 and earlier engines

10.13a Lobe lift can be obtained by measuring camshaft lobe height . . .

4   Working in the order opposite that of the tightening sequence (see illustration 10.19), remove the camshaft bearing cap bolts. Remove the caps, then lift the camshafts from the cylinder head. Lay all of the parts out in order to prevent mixing them up.

5   Remove the primary timing chain and the rear (right) cylinder bank VCT assembly/camshaft sprockets/secondary timing chain (see Section 9), then remove the camshaft holding tool from the rear (right) cylinder bank camshafts. Confirm that the camshafts are in their neutral positions after the holding tool has been removed (see illustration).

6   Note the location of each camshaft cap. Use a marker on each cap, or make notes on paper or cardboard, if they're not marked.

7   Working in the order opposite that of the tightening sequence (see illustration 10.21), remove the camshaft bearing cap bolts. Remove the caps, then lift the camshafts from the cylinder head. Lay all of the parts out in order to prevent mixing them up.

2011 and later models

8   Remove the primary timing chain and camshaft VCT units (see Section 9).

9   Loosen the camshaft cap and mega-cap mounting bolts and remove the caps.

✳ CAUTION:

Keep the caps in order and don't mix them up.

Remove the camshafts from the cylinder head.

All models

10 With the camshafts removed, the lifters can be removed using a magnet.

✳ CAUTION:

They must be stored in an egg carton or other divided and marked container, so they can be restored to their original locations during reassembly.

10.13b . . . and by measuring the camshaft base circle - the difference between the two measurements equals lobe lift

INSPECTION

▶ **Refer to illustrations 10.13a and 10.13b**

11 After the camshafts have been removed, clean them with solvent, then inspect the bearing journals for uneven wear and pitting. If the journals are damaged, the bearing saddles in the cylinder heads and caps are probably damaged as well. The head and camshaft caps will have to be replaced.

12 Measure the bearing journals with a micrometer and compare to the Specifications in this Chapter to determine whether they are excessively worn or out-of-round.

13 Measure the camshaft lobe height and the base circle (see illustrations). The difference between the two measurements is the lobe lift (lobe height - base circle = lobe lift). Record this figure for future reference and repeat the check on the remaining camshaft lobes. Compare the results to the values listed in this Chapter's Specifications.

10.19 Front (left) bank camshaft bearing cap tightening sequence – 2010 and earlier engines

10.21 Rear (right) bank camshaft bearing cap tightening sequence – 2010 and earlier engines

14 Inspect the camshaft lobes for heat discoloration, score marks, chipped areas, pitting and uneven wear. If the lobes are in good condition and if the lobe lift measurements are as specified, you can reuse the camshafts.

INSTALLATION

15 Rotate the crankshaft counterclockwise and position the keyway in the 9 o'clock position (this is the neutral position).

✻✻ CAUTION:

The crankshaft must remain in this position until the camshafts are installed and the valve clearances are checked and, if necessary, adjusted.

16 Lubricate the lifters with clean engine oil and reinstall them in their original locations. If any valve clearances were out-of-specification, replace the lifter(s) with new ones of the proper thickness to achieve the desired clearance.

17 At the front of each camshaft, there are two grooves to hold seals. Obtain new seals and install them in the camshaft grooves.

2010 and earlier models

▶ Refer to illustrations 10.19 and 10.21

18 Lubricate the camshafts and bearing saddles in the cylinder head for the front (left) cylinder bank with clean engine oil or camshaft installation lube. Set the camshafts in the cylinder head, making sure they are in their neutral positions (see illustration 10.2).

19 Lubricate the friction surfaces of the front bank camshaft bearing caps with clean engine oil or camshaft installation lube and install them in their proper positions. Install the bolts and tighten them, in the proper sequence (see illustration), to the torque listed in this Chapter's Specifications.

20 Lubricate the camshafts and bearing saddles in the cylinder head for the rear (right) cylinder bank with clean engine oil or camshaft

installation lube. Set the camshafts in the cylinder head, making sure they are in their neutral positions (see illustration 10.5).

21 Lubricate the friction surfaces of the rear bank camshaft bearing caps with clean engine oil or camshaft installation lube and install them in their proper positions. Install the bolts and tighten them, in the proper sequence (see illustration), to the torque listed in this Chapter's Specifications.

22 Check and if necessary, adjust the valve clearances (see Chapter 2A).

➡ Note: Since the crankshaft is in its neutral position, the camshafts can be turned without the danger of the valves contacting the pistons. Insert a bolt into the front of the camshaft to turn it.

23 Return the camshafts to their positions shown in illustrations 10.2 and 10.5, then install the camshaft holding tools.

2011 and later models

▶ Refer to illustrations 10.25a, 10.25b, 10.26, 10.29a and 10.29b

➡ Note: The split where the ends of each seal come together must face UP (12 o'clock position) on the camshafts when they are installed.

24 Lubricate the camshaft bearing journals and cam lobes with moly-based grease or camshaft installation lubricant.

25 Position the camshafts in the cylinder head in their neutral positions (see illustrations).

26 Install the camshaft bearing caps (in their original locations), and tighten the bolts, in sequence (see illustration), to the torque listed in this Chapter's Specifications.

27 Recheck the valve clearances (see Section 3). Since the crankshaft is in the neutral position, the camshafts can be turned without the valves contacting the pistons.

28 Remove the camshaft cap bolts that secure the valve train oil tubes. Remove the oil tubes.

29 Rotate the camshafts to position the dowel pins in their proper positions for installing the VCT units and secondary timing chains (see illustrations). Install the camshaft holding tools.

10.25a When installing the rear (right) bank cylinder head camshafts, position the dowel pins like this - 2011 and later models

10.25b When installing the left (front) bank cylinder head camshafts, position the dowel pins like this - 2011 and later models

All models

30 Install the VCT units (see Section 9).

31 Rotate the crankshaft clockwise to position the keyway in the 11 o'clock position.

32 Install the primary timing chain (see Section 9).

33 Reinstall the valve train oil tubes and tighten the bearing cap bolts to the torque listed in this Chapter's Specifications.

34 The remainder of installation is the reverse of removal.

35 Before starting and running the engine, refill the cooling system, change the oil and install a new oil filter (see Chapter 1).

10.26 Camshaft bearing cap tightening sequence – 2011 and later models

10.29a Rotate the left (front) bank cylinder head camshafts so the dowel pins are positioned like this (TDC position), then install the camshaft holding tool – 2011 and later models

10.29b Rotate the right (rear) bank cylinder head camshafts so the dowel pins are positioned like this (TDC position), then install the camshaft holding tool – 2011 and later models

11 Cylinder heads - removal and installation

✻✻ WARNING:

Wait until the engine is completely cool before beginning this procedure.

➡ **Note: This procedure can only be done with the engine removed (see Chapter 2C).**

REMOVAL

1 Relieve the fuel system pressure (see Chapter 4), then disconnect the cable from the negative battery terminal (see Chapter 5).

2 Drain the cooling system (see Chapter 1).

3 Remove the engine (see Chapter 2C).

4 Remove the intake manifold(s) (see Section 5) and the exhaust manifolds (see Section 6).

5 Remove the valve covers (see Section 4).

6 Remove the camshafts and lifters (see Section 10).

7 Remove the drivebelt and the drivebelt tensioner (see Chapter 1).

8 Remove the two Camshaft Position (CMP) sensors at the rear of each cylinder head. Disconnect any other electrical connectors from the cylinder head and mark them with tape for correct reassembly.

9 Loosen the cylinder head bolts in 1/4-turn increments until they can be removed by hand. Work from bolt-to-bolt in the reverse of the tightening sequence (see illustration 11.18a).

➡ **Note: Remove the bolts and discard them - new bolts must be used when installing the cylinder head(s).**

10 Lift the cylinder head(s) off the engine. If resistance is felt, DO NOT pry between the cylinder head and engine block as damage to the mating surfaces will result. To dislodge the cylinder head, place a wood block against the end of it and strike the wood block with a hammer or pry against a casting protrusion. Store the cylinder heads on blocks of wood to prevent damage to the gasket sealing surfaces.

11.13 Check the cylinder head and block surfaces for flatness with a straightedge

11 Cylinder head disassembly and inspection procedures should be performed by a qualified automotive machine shop.

INSTALLATION

▶ **Refer to illustrations 11.13, 11.18a and 11.18b**

12 The mating surfaces of the cylinder heads and engine block must be perfectly clean when the cylinder heads are installed. Cover all openings with shop rags to keep debris out of the engine. Use a vacuum cleaner to remove any debris that falls into the valley or intake ports.

✻✻ CAUTION:

Do not use a scraper of any kind or abrasive discs to remove old gasket material, as the block, heads and intake manifold(s) are aluminum.

13 Check the engine block and cylinder head mating surfaces for nicks, deep scratches and other damage. If damage is slight, it can be removed with a file - if it's excessive, machining may be the only alternative. Use a straightedge and feeler gauges to check for warpage (see illustration). If the warpage is beyond Specifications, have the head machined at an automotive machine shop.

14 Use a tap of the correct size to chase the threads in the block head bolt holes. Dirt, corrosion, sealant and damaged threads will affect torque readings.

15 Position the new gasket(s) over the dowel pins in the engine block. Make sure it's facing the right way. If the cylinder head is to be replaced, a new secondary timing chain tensioner will be required.

16 Carefully position the cylinder head(s) on the engine block without disturbing the gasket(s).

17 Lightly oil the new cylinder head bolts and turn down by hand until snug.

✻✻ CAUTION:

The cylinder head bolts are the torque-to-yield type and are stretched during tightening. Therefore, the original bolts must be discarded and new bolts installed during assembly.

18 Tighten the bolts, in the recommended sequence, to the torque and angle of rotation listed in this Chapter's Specifications (see illustrations).

➡ **Note: The method used for the cylinder head bolt tightening procedure is referred to as the "torque angle" or "torque-to-yield" method; follow the procedure exactly. Tighten the bolts using a torque wrench, then use a breaker bar and a special torque angle adapter (available at auto parts stores) to tighten the bolts the required angle.**

19 The remainder of installation is the reverse of removal.

20 Change the engine oil and filter and refill the cooling system (see Chapter 1), then start the engine and check carefully for oil and coolant leaks.

11.18a Cylinder head bolt tightening sequence

11.18b An angle gauge takes the guesswork out of tightening the torque-to-yield cylinder head bolts

12 Oil pan - removal and installation

REMOVAL

1   Raise the vehicle and support it securely on jackstands (see "Jacking and towing" at the front of this manual).

2   Drain the engine oil (see Chapter 1), then clean and install the engine oil drain plug, tightening it to the torque listed in the Chapter 1 Specifications. Remove and discard the oil filter, so that it can be replaced with the oil.

3   Remove the lower engine splash shield.

4   Remove the air filter housing (see Chapter 4).

5   Remove the crossover and Y-pipe and converter assembly from the vehicle (see Chapter 4).

6   Remove the nut and stud from the alternator.

7   The transaxle must be moved slightly back from the engine. Support the engine from above with a support fixture (see Chapter 2C) connected to the left end of the engine, near the transaxle, and support the transaxle with a floor jack. Loosen the upper engine-to-transaxle mounting bolts and back them off about 0.19-inch (5 mm), loosen the left-side engine-to-bellhousing bolts, then loosen the right-side bolts.

✳✳ CAUTION:

The transaxle must not be moved back more than 0.19-inch (5 mm) or the transaxle can be damaged.

8   Remove the transaxle roll restrictor mount through bolts and remove the mount (see Chapter 7A).

9   Remove the catalytic converter (see Chapter 4).

10 On AWD models, remove the transfer case support brackets.

11 Remove the a/c compressor and tie the compressor out of the way (see Chapter 3), without disconnecting the compressor lines.

12 Remove the driveplate inspection cover fasteners and cover.

13 Remove the three upper bellhousing-to-engine bolts, the three side bellhousing-to-engine bolts, the one engine-to-bellhousing bolt and four oil pan-to-bellhousing bolts. Also remove the timing chain

cover-to-oil pan fasteners.

14 Use a screwdriver to pry between the engine and transaxle until the bellhousing has moved away from the block to the limit of the loosened bolts (about 0.20-inch [5 mm]).

15 Remove the sixteen oil pan fasteners and remove the oil pan.

16 There are notches at the top rear corners of the oil pan where a large screwdriver can safely be used to pry the pan loose, if necessary.

17 Thoroughly clean surfaces of the pan, the engine, timing chain cover and transaxle of all traces of RTV sealant using lacquer thinner or acetone. The surfaces must be free of any residue that will keep the sealant from adhering properly. Clean the oil pan inside and out with solvent and dry with compressed air. Use RTV sealant remover rather than scraping the pan or block surfaces.

INSTALLATION

18 Apply a 7/32-inch (5.5 mm) bead of RTV sealant at the junctures of the rear main seal housing and the block, and also where the pan meets the front cover.

19 Apply a 1/8-inch (3 mm) bead of RTV sealant around the inner perimeter of the oil pan's mounting surface and install the oil pan. Install the four corner bolts within four minutes of applying the RTV sealant. Install and tighten the remaining bolts within an hour.

20 When all of the pan-to-engine bolts are started, tighten the bolts, in sequence, to the torque listed in this Chapter's Specifications. After the pan-to-engine bolts are tightened, install and tighten the pan-to-transmission bolts, and all fasteners loosened in Step 13.

21 The remainder of installation is the reverse of removal, noting the following items:

a) *Tighten all fasteners to the torque values listed in this Chapter's Specifications.*

b) *Always replace any self-locking nuts disturbed on removal.*

c) *Refer to Chapter 1 and fill the engine with fresh engine oil. Install a new oil filter.*

d) *Start the engine and check for leaks.*

13 Oil pump - removal and installation

1 Drain the oil and remove the oil filter (see Chapter 1).
2 Remove the timing chain cover (see Section 8).
3 Remove the oil pan (see Section 12).
4 Remove the primary timing chain (see Section 9).
5 Slide the crankshaft sprocket from the crankshaft.
6 Remove the two fasteners and remove the oil pump pickup and screen assembly.
7 Remove the three oil pump mounting bolts and remove the oil pump.

8 Install the oil pump, then reinstall the oil pump pickup tube and screen with a new O-ring.
9 The remainder of installation is the reverse of removal.
10 Fill the engine with fresh engine oil and install a new oil filter (see Chapter 1).
11 Start the engine and check for leaks.

14 Rear main oil seal - replacement

➡ **Note: The one-piece rear main oil seal is pressed into a carrier mounted at the rear of the block.**

1 Remove the transaxle (see Chapter 7A).
2 Remove the driveplate (see Section 15) and the crankshaft sensor ring.
3 Remove the Crankshaft Position (CKP) sensor (see Chapter 6).
4 The old seal can be removed by prying it out with a screwdriver or by making one or two small holes in the seal flange with a sharp pick, then using a screw-in type slide-hammer puller. Note how far the seal is recessed into the bore before removing it; the new seal will have to be recessed an equal amount.

✳✳ CAUTION:

Be very careful not to scratch or otherwise damage the crankshaft or the bore in the housing, or oil leaks could develop!

5 The seal installation can be performed more easily by unbolting and removing the seal retainer plate. Remove all the mounting bolts, then use two of the retainer-to-oil pan bolts and start them into the two threaded holes in the retainer plate. Tightening these two bolts alternately will push the retainer from the engine. Remove all traces of RTV sealant. Apply a 3/16-inch bead of RTV where the block and oil pan flanges meet.
6 Install the retainer to the engine and install all the bolts within 10 minutes of applying the sealant.
7 Make sure the bore is clean, then apply a film of clean engine oil to the outer edge and the lips of the new seal. The seal must be pressed squarely into the bore; a special seal installation tool (#303-1250 and 205-153) should be used. Hammering it into place is not recommended.
8 Install the CKP sensor (see Chapter 6).
9 Reinstall the driveplate, making sure the crankshaft sensor ring is between the crankshaft and the driveplate.
10 Reinstall the transaxle (see Chapter 7A).

15 Driveplate - removal and installation

1 Raise the vehicle and support it securely on jackstands, then remove the transaxle (see Chapter 7A). If it's leaking, now would be a very good time to replace the front pump seal/O-ring.
2 Look for factory paint marks that indicate driveplate-to-crankshaft alignment. If they aren't there, use a center-punch or paint to make alignment marks on the driveplate and crankshaft to ensure correct alignment during reinstallation.
3 Remove the bolts that secure the driveplate to the crankshaft. If the crankshaft turns, use a flywheel holding tool or wedge a screwdriver in the ring gear teeth to jam the driveplate.
4 Remove the driveplate from the crankshaft.
5 Check for cracked and broken ring gear teeth.

6 Clean and inspect the mating surfaces of the driveplate and the crankshaft. If the crankshaft rear seal is leaking, replace it before reinstalling the driveplate (see Section 14).
7 Position the driveplate against the crankshaft, but make sure the crankshaft sensor ring is positioned between the driveplate and the engine. Align the marks made during removal. Note that some engines have an alignment dowel or staggered bolt holes to ensure correct installation.
8 Tighten the bolts to the torque listed in this Chapter's Specifications.
9 The remainder of installation is the reverse of removal.

16 Engine mounts - inspection and replacement

▶ **Refer to illustrations 16.1a and 16.1b**

This procedure is essentially the same as for the four-cylinder engine. The engine must be fully supported when removing/installing engine mounts. Refer to Chapter 2, Part A and follow the procedure outlined there, but refer to the illustrations for this Section.

16.1a Remove the two bolts (A) and the roll restrictor (B) from the frame bracket

16.1b Remove the engine mount bracket nuts (A) and the bracket-to-mount bolt (B)

Specifications

General

3.5L V6 engine

Engine type	Double overhead cam (DOHC) V6
Displacement	214 cubic inches
Engine VIN code	C
Bore	3.64 inches (92.5 mm)
Stroke	3.41 inches (86.7 mm)
Compression ratio	10.8:1
Compression pressure	See Chapter 2C
Firing order	1-4-2-5-3-6
Oil pressure	See Chapter 2C

3.7L V6 engine

Engine type	Double overhead cam (DOHC) V6
Displacement	226 cubic inches
Engine VIN code	K
Bore	3.75 inches (95.5 mm)
Stroke	3.41 inches (86.7 mm)
Compression ratio	10.5:1
Compression pressure	See Chapter 2C
Firing order	1-4-2-5-3-6
Oil pressure	See Chapter 2C

1-4-2-5-3-6

36075-B-SPECS HAYNES

Cylinder location diagram

Camshafts

Lobe lift	
Intake	0.394 inch (10.0 mm)
Exhaust	0.38 inch (9.65 mm)
Journal diameter	
First journal	1.537 to 1.538 inches (39.0398 to 39.0652 mm)
Others	1.023 to 1.024 inches (25.9842 to 26.01 mm)
Bearing outside diameter	
First journal	1.535 to 1.536 inches (38.99 to 39.01 mm)
Others	1.021 to 1.022 inches (25.933 to 25.959 mm)
Journal-to-bearing oil clearance (maximum)	
First journal	0.0029 inch (0.0737 mm)
Others	0.0030 inch (0.0762 mm)
Endplay	
Standard	0.0012 to 0.0066 inch (0.03 to 0.17 mm)
Service limit	0.0075 inch (0.190 mm)

Valve clearances - engine cold

Intake	0.006 to 0.010 inch (0.15 to 0.25 mm)
Exhaust	0.014 to 0.018 inch (0.36 to 0.46 mm)

Warpage limits

Head gasket surface warpage limit	
End-to-end	0.003 inch (0.08 mm)
Side-to-side	0.002 inch (0.05 mm)

Torque specifications*	Ft-lbs (unless otherwise indicated)	Nm

➡ **Note: One foot-pound (ft-lb) of torque is equivalent to 12 inch-pounds (in-lbs) of torque. Torque values below approximately 15 foot-pounds are expressed in inch-pounds, because most foot-pound torque wrenches are not accurate at these smaller values.**

Camshaft bearing cap bolts (in sequence - see illustrations 10.19 and 10.21 or 10.26)		
Step 1	71 in-lbs	8
Step 2	Tighten an additional 45-degrees	
Camshaft sprocket and Variable Camshaft Timing (VCT) bolt		
Step 1	30	40
Step 2	Loosen one turn	
Step 3	18	25
Step 4	Tighten an additional 180-degrees	
Crankshaft pulley bolt		
Step 1	89	121
Step 2	Loosen one full turn (360-degrees)	
Step 3	37	50
Step 4	Tighten an additional 90-degrees	
Cylinder head bolts		
Main bolts (in sequence - see illustration 11.18a)		
Step 1	177 in-lbs	20
Step 2	26	35
Step 3	Tighten an additional 90-degrees	
Step 4	Tighten an additional 90-degrees	
Step 5	Tighten an additional 90-degrees	
M6 bolt (at front of cylinder head)	89 in-lbs	10
Drivebelt tensioner bolt	18	25
Driveplate-to-crankshaft bolts	59	80
Exhaust manifold/catalytic converter nuts		
Step 1	15	20
Step 2	18	25
Intake manifold assembly (in sequence - see illustrations 5.12 and 5.22)		
Upper intake manifold bolts		
Step 1	89 in-lbs	10
Step 2	Tighten an additional 45-degrees	
Lower intake manifold bolts	89 in-lbs	10
Oil pan bolts		
Step 1, bolts 10 ,11, 13, 14	Hand tighten	
Step 2	Align oil pan with rear of transaxle	
Step 3	Install the oil pan-to-bellhousing bolts (hand tight)	
Step 4, bolts 10 ,11, 13, 14	27 in-lbs	3
Step 5	Install the front cover-to-oil pan bolts (hand tight)	
Step 6, install remaining bolts	Hand tighten	
Step 7, bolts 1 through 9 and 11 through 14	177 in-lbs	20
Step 8, bolts 15 and 16	89 in-lbs	10
Step 9, bolt 10	177 in-lbs	20
Oil pump screen cover and tube bolts	89 in-lbs	10
Oil pump-to-engine block bolts	89 in-lbs	10

* Refer to Chapter 2, Part C for additional torque specifications

Torque specifications* (continued)   Ft-lbs (unless otherwise indicated)   Nm

➡ Note: One foot-pound (ft-lb) of torque is equivalent to 12 inch-pounds (in-lbs) of torque. Torque values below approximately 15 foot-pounds are expressed in inch-pounds, because most foot-pound torque wrenches are not accurate at these smaller values.

Timing chain cover bolts (in sequence - see illustration 8.33)		
Step 1, bolts 7, 8, 15, 17, 18, 21 and 22	27 in-lbs	3
Step 2, install remaining bolts	Hand tighten	
Step 3, bolts 1 through 22	89 in-lbs	10
Step 4, bolts 23 through 25	133 in-lbs	15
Step 5, bolt 26	89 in-lbs	10
Step 6, bolt 26	Loosen one full turn	
Step 7, bolts 23 through 25	22	30
Step 8, bolts 23 through 25	Tighten an additional 90-degrees	
Step 9, bolts 1 through 22	177 in-lbs	20
Step 10, bolts 1 through 22	Tighten an additional 45-degrees	
Step 11, bolt 26	89 in-lbs	10
Step 12, bolt 26	Tighten an additional 45-degrees	
Timing chain guides	89 in-lbs	10
Timing chain tensioner bolts	89 in-lbs	10
Valve cover bolts		
(in sequence - see illustration 4.16)	89 in-lbs	10
Variable Camshaft Timing (VCT) oil control solenoid		
Step 1	71 in-lbs	8
Step 2	Tighten an additional 20-degrees	

* Refer to Chapter 2, Part C for additional torque specifications

Section

Reference to other Chapters

CHECK ENGINE light on - See Chapter 6

1 General information - engine overhaul

▶ Refer to illustrations 1.1, 1.2, 1.3, 1.4, 1.5 and 1.6

Included in this portion of Chapter 2 are general information and diagnostic testing procedures for determining the overall mechanical condition of your engine.

The information ranges from advice concerning preparation for an overhaul and the purchase of replacement parts and/or components to detailed, step-by-step procedures covering removal and installation.

The following Sections have been written to help you determine whether your engine needs to be overhauled and how to remove and install it once you've determined it needs to be rebuilt. For information concerning in-vehicle engine repair, see Chapter 2A or 2B.

It's not always easy to determine when, or if, an engine should be completely overhauled, because a number of factors must be considered.

High mileage is not necessarily an indication that an overhaul is needed, while low mileage doesn't preclude the need for an overhaul. Frequency of servicing is probably the most important consideration. An engine that's had regular and frequent oil and filter changes, as well as other required maintenance, will most likely give many thousands of miles of reliable service. Conversely, a neglected engine may require an overhaul very early in its service life.

Excessive oil consumption is an indication that piston rings, valve seals and/or valve guides are in need of attention. Make sure that oil leaks aren't responsible before deciding that the rings and/or guides are bad. Perform a cylinder compression check to determine the extent of the work required (see Section 3). Also check the vacuum readings under various conditions (see Section 4).

Check the oil pressure with a gauge installed in place of the oil pressure sending unit and compare it to this Chapter's Specifications (see Section 2). If it's extremely low, the bearings and/or oil pump are probably worn out.

Loss of power, rough running, knocking or metallic engine noises, excessive valve train noise and high fuel consumption rates may also point to the need for an overhaul, especially if they're all present at the same time. If a complete tune-up doesn't remedy the situation, major mechanical work is the only solution.

An engine overhaul involves restoring the internal parts to the specifications of a new engine. During an overhaul, the piston rings are replaced and the cylinder walls are reconditioned (rebored and/or honed) (see illustrations 1.1 and 1.2). If a rebore is done by an automotive machine shop, new oversize pistons will also be installed. The main bearings and connecting rod bearings are generally replaced with new ones and, if necessary, the crankshaft may be reground to restore the journals (see illustration 1.3). Generally, the valves are serviced as well, since they're usually in less-than-perfect condition at this point. While the engine is being overhauled, other components, such as the starter and alternator, can be rebuilt as well. The end result should be a like-new engine that will give many trouble-free miles.

➡ Note: Critical cooling system components such as the hoses, drivebelts, thermostat and water pump should be replaced with new parts when an engine is overhauled. The radiator should be checked carefully to ensure that it isn't clogged or leaking (see Chapter 3). If you purchase a rebuilt engine or short block, some rebuilders will not warranty their engines unless the radiator has been professionally flushed. Also, we don't recommend overhauling the oil pump - always install a new one when an engine is rebuilt.

1.1 An engine block being bored. An engine rebuilder will use special machinery to recondition the cylinder bores

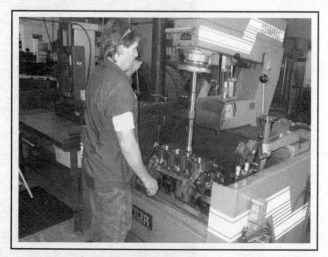

1.2 If the cylinders are bored, the machine shop will normally hone the engine on a machine like this

1.3 A crankshaft having a main bearing journal ground

1.4 A machinist checks for a bent connecting rod, using specialized equipment

1.5 A bore gauge being used to check the main bearing bore

1.6 Uneven piston wear like this indicates a bent connecting rod

Overhauling the internal components on today's engines is a difficult and time-consuming task that requires a significant amount of specialty tools and is best left to a professional engine rebuilder (see illustrations 1.4, 1.5 and 1.6). A competent engine rebuilder will handle the inspection of your old parts and offer advice concerning the reconditioning or replacement of the original engine. Never purchase parts or have machine work done on other components until the block has been thoroughly inspected by a professional machine shop. As a general rule, time is the primary cost of an overhaul, especially since the vehicle may be tied up for a minimum of two weeks or more. Be aware that some engine builders only have the capability to rebuild the engine you bring them while other rebuilders have a large inventory of rebuilt exchange engines in stock. Also be aware that many machine shops could take as much as two weeks time to completely rebuild your engine depending on shop workload. Sometimes it makes more sense to simply exchange your engine for another engine that's already rebuilt to save time.

2 Oil pressure check

▶ **Refer to illustrations 2.2 and 2.3**

1   Low engine oil pressure can be a sign of an engine in need of rebuilding. A low oil pressure indicator (often called an "idiot light") is not a test of the oiling system. Such indicators only come on when the oil pressure is dangerously low. Even a factory oil pressure gauge in the instrument panel is only a relative indication, although much better for driver information than a warning light. A better test is with a mechanical (not electrical) oil pressure gauge.

2   Locate the oil pressure sending unit:

   a) *On four-cylinder engines, the oil pressure sending unit is located on the front of the engine, threaded into the oil filter adapter (see illustration).*

   b) *On V6 engines, the sending unit is located on the front side of the block.*

3   Unscrew the oil pressure sending unit and screw in the hose for your oil pressure gauge (see illustration). If necessary, install an adapter fitting. Use Teflon tape or thread sealant on the threads of the adapter and/or the fitting on the end of your gauge's hose.

4   Connect an accurate tachometer to the engine, according to the tachometer manufacturer's instructions.

5   Check the oil pressure with the engine running (normal operating temperature) at the specified engine speed, and compare it to this Chapter's Specifications. If it's extremely low, the bearings and/or oil pump are probably worn out.

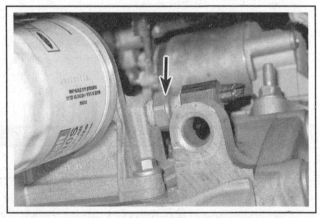

2.2 The oil pressure sending unit is located on the oil filter adapter (four-cylinder enfine shown)

2.3 The oil pressure can be checked by removing the sending unit and installing a pressure gauge in its place

3 Cylinder compression check

♦ **Refer to illustration 3.6**

1   A compression check will tell you what mechanical condition the upper end of your engine (pistons, rings, valves, head gaskets) is in. Specifically, it can tell you if the compression is down due to leakage caused by worn piston rings, defective valves and seats or a blown head gasket.

➡ **Note: The engine must be at normal operating temperature and the battery must be fully charged for this check.**

2   Begin by cleaning the area around the ignition coils before you remove them (compressed air should be used, if available). The idea is to prevent dirt from getting into the cylinders as the compression check is being done.

3   Remove all of the spark plugs from the engine (see Chapter 1).

4   Remove the air intake duct from the throttle body, then block the throttle wide open.

5   Disable the fuel pump (see Chapter 4, Section 3).

6   Install a compression gauge in the spark plug hole (see illustration).

7   Crank the engine over at least seven compression strokes and watch the gauge. The compression should build up quickly in a healthy engine. Low compression on the first stroke, followed by gradually increasing pressure on successive strokes, indicates worn piston rings. A low compression reading on the first stroke, which doesn't build up during successive strokes, indicates leaking valves or a blown head gasket (a cracked head could also be the cause). Deposits on the undersides of the valve heads can also cause low compression. Record the highest gauge reading obtained.

8   Repeat the procedure for the remaining cylinders and compare the results to this Chapter's Specifications.

9   Add some engine oil (about three squirts from a plunger-type oil can) to each cylinder, through the spark plug hole, and repeat the test.

10 If the compression increases after the oil is added, the piston rings are definitely worn. If the compression doesn't increase significantly, the leakage is occurring at the valves or head gasket. Leakage past the valves may be caused by burned valve seats and/or faces or warped, cracked or bent valves.

3.6 Use a compression gauge with a threaded fitting for the spark plug hole, not the type that requires hand pressure to maintain the seal

11 If two adjacent cylinders have equally low compression, there's a strong possibility that the head gasket between them is blown. The appearance of coolant in the combustion chambers or the crankcase would verify this condition.

12 If one cylinder is slightly lower than the others, and the engine has a slightly rough idle, a worn lobe on the camshaft could be the cause.

13 If the compression is unusually high, the combustion chambers are probably coated with carbon deposits. If that's the case, the cylinder head(s) should be removed and decarbonized.

14 If compression is way down or varies greatly between cylinders, it would be a good idea to have a leak-down test performed by an automotive repair shop. This test will pinpoint exactly where the leakage is occurring and how severe it is.

15 After performing the test, don't forget to unblock the throttle plate.

4 Vacuum gauge diagnostic checks

♦ **Refer to illustrations 4.4 and 4.6**

1   A vacuum gauge provides inexpensive but valuable information about what is going on in the engine. You can check for worn rings or cylinder walls, leaking head or intake manifold gaskets, incorrect carburetor adjustments, restricted exhaust, stuck or burned valves, weak valve springs, improper ignition or valve timing and ignition problems.

2   Unfortunately, vacuum gauge readings are easy to misinterpret, so they should be used in conjunction with other tests to confirm the diagnosis.

3   Both the absolute readings and the rate of needle movement are important for accurate interpretation. Most gauges measure vacuum in inches of mercury (in-Hg). The following references to vacuum assume the diagnosis is being performed at sea level. As elevation increases (or atmospheric pressure decreases), the reading will decrease. For every 1,000 foot increase in elevation above approximately 2,000 feet, the

gauge readings will decrease about one inch of mercury.

4   Connect the vacuum gauge directly to the intake manifold vacuum, not to ported (throttle body) vacuum (see illustration). Be sure no hoses are left disconnected during the test or false readings will result.

5   Before you begin the test, allow the engine to warm up completely. Block the wheels and set the parking brake. With the transaxle in Park, start the engine and allow it to run at normal idle speed.

❊❊ **WARNING:**

Keep your hands and the vacuum gauge clear of the fans.

6   Read the vacuum gauge; an average, healthy engine should normally produce about 17 to 22 in-Hg with a fairly steady needle (see illustration). Refer to the following vacuum gauge readings and what they indicate about the engine's condition:

7   A low steady reading usually indicates a leaking gasket between the intake manifold and cylinder head(s) or throttle body, a leaky vacuum hose, late ignition timing or incorrect camshaft timing. Check ignition timing with a timing light and eliminate all other possible causes, utilizing the tests provided in this Chapter before you remove the timing chain cover to check the timing marks.

8   If the reading is three to eight inches below normal and it fluctuates at that low reading, suspect an intake manifold gasket leak at an intake port or a faulty fuel injector.

9   If the needle has regular drops of about two-to-four inches at a steady rate, the valves are probably leaking. Perform a compression check or leak-down test to confirm this.

10   An irregular drop or down-flick of the needle can be caused by a sticking valve or an ignition misfire. Perform a compression check or leak-down test and read the spark plugs.

11   A rapid vibration of about four in-Hg vibration at idle combined with exhaust smoke indicates worn valve guides. Perform a leak-down test to confirm this. If the rapid vibration occurs with an increase in engine speed, check for a leaking intake manifold gasket or head gasket, weak valve springs, burned valves or ignition misfire.

12   A slight fluctuation, say one inch up and down, may mean ignition problems. Check all the usual tune-up items and, if necessary, run

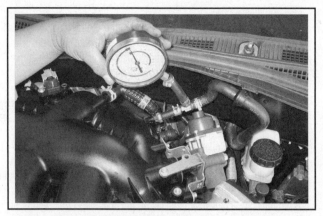

4.4 A simple vacuum gauge can be handy in diagnosing engine condition and performance

the engine on an ignition analyzer.

13   If there is a large fluctuation, perform a compression or leak-down test to look for a weak or dead cylinder or a blown head gasket.

14   If the needle moves slowly through a wide range, check for a clogged PCV system, incorrect idle fuel mixture, throttle body or intake

4.6 Typical vacuum gauge readings

manifold gasket leaks.

15 Check for a slow return after revving the engine by quickly snapping the throttle open until the engine reaches about 2,500 rpm and let it shut. Normally the reading should drop to near zero, rise above normal idle reading (about 5 in-Hg over) and then return to the previous idle reading. If the vacuum returns slowly and doesn't peak when the throttle is snapped shut, the rings may be worn. If there is a long delay, look for a restricted exhaust system (often the muffler or catalytic converter). An easy way to check this is to temporarily disconnect the exhaust ahead of the suspected part and redo the test.

5 Engine rebuilding alternatives

The do-it-yourselfer is faced with a number of options when purchasing a rebuilt engine. The major considerations are cost, warranty, parts availability and the time required for the rebuilder to complete the project. The decision to replace the engine block, piston/connecting rod assemblies and crankshaft depends on the final inspection results of your engine. Only then can you make a cost effective decision whether to have your engine overhauled or simply purchase an exchange engine for your vehicle.

Some of the rebuilding alternatives include:

Individual parts - If the inspection procedures reveal that the engine block and most engine components are in reusable condition, purchasing individual parts and having a rebuilder rebuild your engine may be the most economical alternative. The block, crankshaft and piston/connecting rod assemblies should all be inspected carefully by a machine shop first.

Short block - A short block consists of an engine block with a crankshaft and piston/connecting rod assemblies already installed. All new bearings are incorporated and all clearances will be correct. The existing camshafts, valve train components, cylinder head and external

parts can be bolted to the short block with little or no machine shop work necessary.

Long block - A long block consists of a short block plus an oil pump, oil pan, cylinder head, valve cover, camshaft and valve train components, timing sprockets and chain or gears and timing cover. All components are installed with new bearings, seals and gaskets incorporated throughout. The installation of manifolds and external parts is all that's necessary.

Low mileage used engines - Some companies now offer low mileage used engines which are a very cost effective way to get your vehicle up and running again. These engines often come from vehicles which have been totaled in accidents or come from other countries which have a higher vehicle turn over rate. A low mileage used engine also usually has a similar warranty like the newly remanufactured engines.

Give careful thought to which alternative is best for you and discuss the situation with local automotive machine shops, auto parts dealers and experienced rebuilders before ordering or purchasing replacement parts.

6 Engine removal - methods and precautions

◗ **Refer to illustrations 6.1, 6.2 and 6.3**

If you've decided that an engine must be removed for overhaul or major repair work, several preliminary steps should be taken. Read all removal and installation procedures carefully prior to committing to this job. These engines are removed by lowering the engine to the floor, along with the transmission, and then raising the vehicle sufficiently to slide the assembly out; this will require a vehicle hoist as well as an engine hoist. Make sure the engine hoist is rated in excess of the combined weight of the engine and transmission. A transmission jack

is also very helpful. Safety is of primary importance, considering the potential hazards involved in removing the engine from the vehicle.

Locating a suitable place to work is extremely important. Adequate work space, along with storage space for the vehicle, will be needed. If a shop or garage isn't available, at the very least a flat, level, clean work surface made of concrete or asphalt is required.

Cleaning the engine compartment and engine before beginning the removal procedure will help keep tools clean and organized (see illustrations 6.1 and 6.2).

If you're a novice at engine removal, get at least one helper. One

6.1 After tightly wrapping water-vulnerable components, use a spray cleaner on everything, with particular concentration on the greasiest areas, usually around the valve cover and lower edges of the block. If one section dries out, apply more cleaner

6.2 Depending on how dirty the engine is, let the cleaner soak in according to the directions and then hose off the grime and cleaner. Get the rinse water down into every area you can get at; then dry important components with a hair dryer or paper towels

person cannot easily do all the things you need to do to remove a big heavy engine and transmission assembly from the engine compartment. Also helpful is to seek advice and assistance from someone who's experienced in engine removal.

Plan the operation ahead of time. Arrange for or obtain all of the tools and equipment you'll need prior to beginning the job (see illustration 6.3). Some of the equipment necessary to perform engine removal and installation safely and with relative ease are (in addition to a vehicle hoist and an engine hoist) a heavy duty floor jack (preferably fitted with a transmission jack head adapter), complete sets of wrenches and sockets as described in the front of this manual, wooden blocks, plenty of rags and cleaning solvent for mopping up spilled oil, coolant and gasoline.

Plan for the vehicle to be out of use for quite a while. A machine shop can do the work that is beyond the scope of the home mechanic. Machine shops often have a busy schedule, so before removing the engine, consult the shop for an estimate of how long it will take to rebuild or repair the components that may need work.

6.3 Get an engine stand sturdy enough to firmly support the engine while you're working on it. Stay away from three-wheeled models; they have a tendency to tip over more easily, so get a four-wheeled unit

7   Engine - removal and installation

✷✷ WARNING:

The models covered by this manual are equipped with Supplemental Restraint systems (SRS), more commonly known as airbags. Always disable the airbag system before working in the vicinity of airbag system components to avoid the possibility of accidental deployment of the airbag, which could cause personal injury (see Chapter 12).

✷✷ WARNING:

Gasoline is extremely flammable, so take extra precautions when you work on any part of the fuel system. Don't smoke or allow open flames or bare light bulbs near the work area, and don't work in a garage where a gas-type appliance (such as a water heater or clothes dryer) is present. Since gasoline is carcinogenic, wear fuel-resistant gloves when there's a possibility of being exposed to fuel, and, if you spill any fuel on your skin, rinse it off immediately with soap and water. Mop up any spills immediately and do not store fuel-soaked rags where they could ignite. The fuel system is under constant pressure, so, if any fuel lines are to be disconnected, the fuel pressure in the system must be relieved first (see Chapter 4 for more information). When you perform any kind of work on the fuel system, wear safety glasses and have a Class B type fire extinguisher on hand.

✷✷ WARNING:

The engine must be completely cool before beginning this procedure.

✷✷ WARNING:

The air conditioning system is under high pressure. DO NOT loosen any fittings or remove any components until after the system has been discharged. Air conditioning refrigerant should be properly discharged into an EPA-approved container at a dealership service department or an automotive air conditioning repair facility. Always wear eye protection when disconnecting air conditioning system fittings.

➡ Note: Engine removal on these models is a difficult job, especially for the do-it-yourself mechanic working at home. Because of the vehicle's design, the manufacturer states that the engine and transaxle have to be removed as a unit from the bottom of the vehicle, not the top. With a floor jack and jackstands the vehicle can't be raised high enough and supported safely enough for the engine/transaxle assembly to slide out from underneath. The manufacturer recommends that removal of the engine/transaxle assembly only be performed on a vehicle hoist.

REMOVAL

1 Have the air conditioning system discharged by an automotive air conditioning technician.

2 Park the vehicle on a frame-contact type vehicle hoist. The pads of the hoist arms must contact the body welt along each side of the vehicle.

3 Relieve the fuel system pressure (see Chapter 4), then disconnect the negative cable from the battery.

4 Place protective covers on the fenders and cowl and remove the hood (see Chapter 11).

5 Remove the air filter housing (see Chapter 4).

6 Remove the cowl panels (see Chapter 11).

7 Remove the battery and battery tray (see Chapter 5).

8 Loosen the front wheel lug nuts and the driveaxle/hub nuts, then raise the vehicle on the hoist. Drain the cooling system and engine oil and remove the drivebelt (see Chapter 1).

9 Clearly label, then disconnect all vacuum lines, coolant and emissions hoses, wiring harness connectors, ground straps and fuel lines. Masking tape and/or a touch up paint applicator work well for marking items. Take instant photos or sketch the locations of components and brackets.

10 On V6 models, remove the upper intake manifold (see Chapter 2B).

11 On four-cylinder models, disconnect the high pressure fuel pump quick disconnect line (see Chapter 4).

12 Remove the alternator and the starter (see Chapter 5).

13 Remove the power steering pump and all hose retainers (see Chapter 10).

14 Remove the heater hoses and radiator hoses (see Chapter 3).

15 On four-cylinder models, disconnect and remove the charge air cooler inlet and outlet pipes (see Chapter 4).

16 Remove the coolant expansion tank, engine cooling fan and radiator (see Chapter 3).

➡ **Note: This step is not absolutely necessary, but it will help avoid damage to the cooling fans and radiator as the engine is lowered out of the vehicle. If the radiator is not taken out it will still be necessary to detach the transaxle oil cooler lines from the bottom of the radiator.**

17 Disconnect the shift cable(s) from the transaxle (see Chapter 7A).

18 Disconnect any wiring harness connectors from the transaxle.

19 Remove the air conditioning compressor (see Chapter 3), and cap all the lines to prevent dirt and moisture from entering the system.

20 Place the wheels in a straight position, then lock the steering wheel in place and detach the steering column shaft from the steering gear (see Chapter 10).

➡ **Note: It may be necessary to use a steering wheel holding tool to prevent the wheel from moving.**

21 Disconnect the PCM harness connectors and place the connectors out of the way (see Chapter 6).

22 On four-cylinder models, disconnect the Transmission Control Module (TCM) electrical connector and harness retainers, then place the harness out of the way.

23 Detach the exhaust pipe(s) from the exhaust manifold(s) (see Chapter 4).

24 Detach all wiring harnesses and hoses from between the engine/transaxle and the chassis. Be sure to mark all connectors to facilitate reassembly.

25 Remove the wheels, then remove the brake calipers. Tie the calipers out of the way with a piece of wire (see Chapter 9).

26 Remove the driveaxles (see Chapter 8). On AWD vehicles, remove the rear driveshaft.

27 Disconnect the EVAP line quick disconnect connectors at the rear of the subframe.

28 Detach the stabilizer bar links from the bar and separate the lower control arms from the steering knuckles. Also detach the tie-rod ends from the steering knuckles (see Chapter 10).

29 Mark the relationship of the torque converter to the driveplate, then remove the torque converter-to-driveplate nuts (see Chapter 7A).

30 Remove the roll restrictor between the lower rear part of the engine and the subframe.

31 Remove the subframe-to-bumper nuts and separate the bumper from the subframe.

32 Remove the subframe brace bolts and remove the brace.

33 Attach a lifting sling or chain to the engine. Position an engine hoist and connect the sling to it. If no lifting hooks or brackets are present, you'll have to fasten the chains or slings to some substantial part of the engine - ones that are strong enough to take the weight, but in locations that will provide good balance. Take up the slack until there is slight tension on the sling or chain. Position the chain on the hoist so it balances the engine and the transaxle level with the vehicle.

34 Mark the position of each corner of the subframe to the chassis. Support the subframe with two floor jacks, then remove the fasteners and lower the subframe. Remove it from underneath the vehicle.

35 Remove the transaxle mount (see Chapter 7A) and the right-side engine mount (see Chapter 2A).

36 Recheck to be sure nothing is still connecting the engine or transaxle to the vehicle. Disconnect and label anything still remaining.

37 Slowly lower the engine/transaxle from the vehicle.

➡ **Note: Placing a sheet of hardboard or paneling between the engine and the floor makes moving the powertrain easier.**

38 Once the powertrain is on the floor, disconnect the engine lifting hoist and raise the vehicle hoist until the powertrain can be slid out from underneath.

➡ **Note: A helper will be needed to move the powertrain.**

39 Reconnect the chain or sling and raise the engine/transaxle with the hoist. Support the transmission with a jack (preferably one with a transmission jack head adapter). Separate the engine from the transaxle (see Chapter 7A).

40 Remove the driveplate and the crankshaft sensor ring, then mount the engine on a stand.

INSTALLATION

➡ **Note: The manufacturer recommends replacing all subframe and suspension fasteners with new ones whenever they are loosened or removed.**

41 Installation is the reverse of removal, noting the following points:

a) *Check the engine/transaxle mounts. If they're worn or damaged, replace them.*

b) *Attach the transaxle to the engine following the procedure described in Chapter 7A.*

c) *Add coolant, oil, power steering and transmission fluids as needed (see Chapter 1).*

d) *Align the subframe reference marks before tightening the bolts.*

e) *Tighten the subframe mounting fasteners to the torque listed in the Chapter 10 Specifications.*

f) *Reconnect the negative battery cable (see Chapter 5).*

g) *Run the engine and check for proper operation and leaks. Shut off the engine and recheck fluid levels.*

h) *Have the air conditioning system re-charged and leak tested by the shop that discharged it.*

8 Engine overhaul - disassembly sequence

1 It's much easier to remove the external components if it's mounted on a portable engine stand. A stand can often be rented quite cheaply from an equipment rental yard. Before the engine is mounted on a stand, the driveplate should be removed from the engine.

2 If a stand isn't available, it's possible to remove the external engine components with it blocked up on the floor. Be extra careful not to tip or drop the engine when working without a stand.

3 If you're going to obtain a rebuilt engine, all external components must come off first, to be transferred to the replacement engine. These components include:

Turbocharger
Driveplate
Emissions-related components
Engine mounts and mount brackets
Intake/exhaust manifolds
Fuel injection components

Oil filter
Ignition coils and spark plugs
Thermostat and housing assembly
Water pump

→ **Note: When removing the external components from the engine, pay close attention to details that may be helpful or important during installation. Note the installed position of gaskets, seals, spacers, pins, brackets, washers, bolts and other small items.**

4 If you're going to obtain a short block (assembled engine block, crankshaft, pistons and connecting rods), remove the timing chain, cylinder head, oil pan, oil pump pick-up tube, oil pump and water pump from your engine so that you can turn in your old short block to the rebuilder as a core. See "Engine rebuilding alternatives" for additional information regarding the different possibilities to be considered.

9 Pistons and connecting rods - removal and installation

REMOVAL

▶ **Refer to illustrations 9.1, 9.3 and 9.4**

→ **Note: Prior to removing the piston/connecting rod assemblies, remove the cylinder head and oil pan (see Chapter 2A or 2B).**

1 Use your fingernail to feel if a ridge has formed at the upper limit of ring travel (about 1/4-inch down from the top of each cylinder). If carbon deposits or cylinder wear have produced ridges, they must be completely removed with a special tool (see illustration). Follow the manufacturer's instructions provided with the tool. Failure to remove the ridges before attempting to remove the piston/connecting rod assemblies may result in piston breakage.

2 After the cylinder ridges have been removed, turn the engine so

the crankshaft is facing up. On four-cylinder engines, remove the balance shaft assembly (see Section 13). On V6 engines, remove the main bearing cap support brace.

3 Before the main bearing caps or main-bearing support bridge and connecting rods are removed, check the connecting rod endplay with feeler gauges. Slide them between the first connecting rod and the crankshaft throw until the play is removed (see illustration). Repeat this procedure for each connecting rod. The endplay is equal to the thickness of the feeler gauge(s). Check with an automotive machine shop for the endplay service limit (a typical end play limit should measure between 0.005 to 0.015 inch [0.127 to 0.381 mm]). If the play exceeds the service limit, new connecting rods will be required. If new rods (or a new crankshaft) are installed, the endplay may fall under the minimum allowable. If it does, the rods will have to be machined to restore it. If necessary, consult an automotive machine shop for advice.

9.1 Before you try to remove the pistons, use a ridge reamer to remove the raised material (ridge) from the top of the cylinders

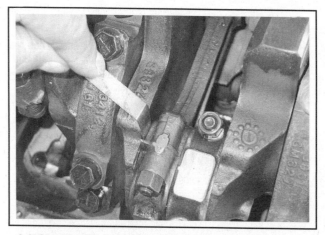

9.3 Checking the connecting rod endplay (side clearance)

9.4 If the connecting rods and caps are not marked, use permanent ink or paint to mark the caps to the rods by cylinder number (for example, this would be the No. 4 connecting rod)

9.14 With the ring square in the cylinder, measure the ring end gap with a feeler gauge

4   Check the connecting rods and caps for identification marks. If they aren't plainly marked, use paint or marker to clearly identify each rod and cap (1, 2, 3, etc., depending on the cylinder they're associated with) (see illustration).

5   Loosen each of the connecting rod cap bolts 1/2-turn at a time until they can be removed by hand.

➡ **Note: New connecting rod cap bolts must be used when reassembling the engine, but save the old bolts for use when checking the connecting rod bearing oil clearance.**

6   Remove the number one connecting rod cap and bearing insert. Don't drop the bearing insert out of the cap.

7   Remove the bearing insert and push the connecting rod/piston assembly out through the top of the engine. Use a wooden or plastic hammer handle to push on the upper bearing surface in the connecting rod. If resistance is felt, double-check to make sure that all of the ridge was removed from the cylinder.

8   Repeat the procedure for the remaining cylinders.

9   After removal, reassemble the connecting rod caps and bearing inserts in their respective connecting rods and install the cap bolts finger tight. Leaving the old bearing inserts in place until reassembly will help prevent the connecting rod bearing surfaces from being accidentally nicked or gouged.

10   The pistons and connecting rods are now ready for inspection and overhaul at an automotive machine shop.

9.13 Install the piston ring into the cylinder then push it down into position using a piston so the ring will be square in the cylinder

PISTON RING INSTALLATION

▶ **Refer to illustrations 9.13, 9.14, 9.15, 9.19a, 9.19b and 9.22**

11   Before installing the new piston rings, the ring end gaps must be checked. It's assumed that the piston ring side clearance has been checked and verified correct.

12   Lay out the piston/connecting rod assemblies and the new ring sets so the ring sets will be matched with the same piston and cylinder during the end gap measurement and engine assembly.

13   Insert the top (number one) ring into the first cylinder and square it up with the cylinder walls by pushing it in with the top of the piston (see illustration). The ring should be near the bottom of the cylinder, at the lower limit of ring travel.

14   To measure the end gap, slip feeler gauges between the ends of the ring until a gauge equal to the gap width is found (see illustration). The feeler gauge should slide between the ring ends with a slight amount of drag. A typical ring gap should fall between 0.010 and 0.020 inch (0.25 to 0.50 mm) for compression rings and up to 0.030 inch (0.76 mm) for the oil ring steel rails. If the gap is larger or smaller than specified, double-check to make sure you have the correct rings before proceeding.

15   If the gap is too small, it must be enlarged or the ring ends may come in contact with each other during engine operation, which can cause serious damage to the engine. If necessary, increase the end gaps by filing the ring ends very carefully with a fine file. Mount the file in a vise equipped with soft jaws, slip the ring over the file with the ends contacting the file face and slowly move the ring to remove material from the ends. When performing this operation, file only by pushing the ring from the outside end of the file towards the vise (see illustration).

16   Excess end gap isn't critical unless it's greater than 0.040 inch (1.01 mm). Again, double-check to make sure you have the correct ring type.

17   Repeat the procedure for each ring that will be installed in the first cylinder and for each ring in the remaining cylinders. Remember to keep rings, pistons and cylinders matched up.

18   Once the ring end gaps have been checked/corrected, the rings can be installed on the pistons.

19   The oil control ring (lowest one on the piston) is usually installed first. It's composed of three separate components. Slip the spacer/expander into the groove (see illustration). If an anti-rotation tang is used, make sure it's inserted into the drilled hole in the ring groove. Next, install the upper side rail in the same manner (see illustration).

9.15 If the ring end gap is too small, clamp a file in a vise as shown and file the piston ring ends - be sure to remove all raised material

9.19a Installing the spacer/expander in the oil ring groove

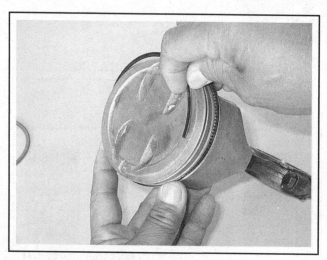

9.19b DO NOT use a piston ring installation tool when installing the oil control side rails

9.22 Use a piston ring installation tool to install the number 2 and the number 1 (top) rings - be sure the directional mark on the piston ring(s) is facing toward the top of the piston

Don't use a piston ring installation tool on the oil ring side rails, as they may be damaged. Instead, place one end of the side rail into the groove between the spacer/expander and the ring land, hold it firmly in place and slide a finger around the piston while pushing the rail into the groove. Finally, install the lower side rail.

20 After the three oil ring components have been installed, check to make sure that both the upper and lower side rails can be rotated smoothly inside the ring grooves.

21 The number two (middle) ring is installed next. It's usually stamped with a mark which must face up, toward the top of the piston. Do not mix up the top and middle rings, as they have different cross-sections.

➡ **Note: Always follow the instructions printed on the ring package or box - different manufacturers may require different approaches.**

22 Use a piston ring installation tool and make sure the identification mark is facing the top of the piston, then slip the ring into the middle groove on the piston (see illustration). Don't expand the ring any more than necessary to slide it over the piston.

23 Install the number one (top) ring in the same manner. Make sure the mark is facing up. Be careful not to confuse the number one and number two rings.

24 Repeat the procedure for the remaining pistons and rings.

INSTALLATION

25 Before installing the piston/connecting rod assemblies, the cylinder walls must be perfectly clean, the top edge of each cylinder bore must be chamfered, and the crankshaft must be in place.

26 Remove the cap from the end of the number one connecting rod (refer to the marks made during removal). Remove the original bearing inserts and wipe the bearing surfaces of the connecting rod and cap with a clean, lint-free cloth. They must be kept spotlessly clean.

Connecting rod bearing oil clearance check

▶ **Refer to illustrations 9.30, 9.35, 9.37 and 9.41**

27 Clean the back side of the new upper bearing insert, then lay it in

ENGINE BEARING ANALYSIS

Debris

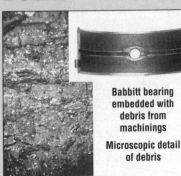

Babbitt bearing embedded with debris from machinings

Microscopic detail of debris

Microscopic detail of gouges

Overplated copper alloy bearing gouged by cast iron debris

Aluminum bearing embedded with glass beads

Microscopic detail of glass beads

Damaged lining caused by dirt left on the bearing back

Misassembly

Result of a lower half assembled as an upper - blocking the oil flow

Excessive oil clearance is indicated by a short contact arc

Polished and oil-stained backs are a result of a poor fit in the housing bore

Result of a wrong, reversed, or shifted cap

Overloading

Damage from excessive idling which resulted in an oil film unable to support the load imposed

Damaged upper connecting rod bearings caused by engine lugging; the lower main bearings (not shown) were similarly affected

The damage shown in these upper and lower connecting rod bearings was caused by engine operation at a higher-than-rated speed under load

Misalignment

A warped crankshaft caused this pattern of severe wear in the center, diminishing toward the ends

A poorly finished crankshaft caused the equally spaced scoring shown

A tapered housing bore caused the damage along one edge of this pair

A bent connecting rod led to the damage in the "V" pattern

Lubrication

Result of dry start: The bearings on the left, farthest from the oil pump, show more damage

Result of a low oil supply or oil starvation

Severe wear as a result of inadequate oil clearance

Corrosion

Microscopic detail of corrosion

Corrosion is an acid attack on the bearing lining generally caused by inadequate maintenance, extremely hot or cold operation, or inferior oils or fuels

Microscopic detail of cavitation

Example of cavitation - a surface erosion caused by pressure changes in the oil film

Damage from excessive thrust or insufficient axial clearance

Bearing affected by oil dilution caused by excessive blow-by or a rich mixture

place in the connecting rod.

28 Make sure the tab on the bearing fits into the recess in the rod. Don't hammer the bearing insert into place and be very careful not to nick or gouge the bearing face. Don't lubricate the bearing at this time.

29 Clean the back side of the other bearing insert and install it in the rod cap. Again, make sure the tab on the bearing fits into the recess in the cap, and don't apply any lubricant. It's critically important that the mating surfaces of the bearing and connecting rod are perfectly clean and oil free when they're assembled.

30 Position the piston ring gaps at 90-degree intervals around the piston as shown (see illustration).

31 Lubricate the piston and rings with clean engine oil and attach a piston ring compressor to the piston. Leave the skirt protruding about 1/4-inch to guide the piston into the cylinder. The rings must be compressed until they're flush with the piston.

32 Rotate the crankshaft until the number one connecting rod journal is at BDC (bottom dead center) and apply a liberal coat of engine oil to the cylinder walls.

33 With the mark on top of the piston facing the front (timing belt or chain end) of the engine, gently insert the piston/connecting rod assem-

bly into the number one cylinder bore and rest the bottom edge of the ring compressor on the engine block.

34 Tap the top edge of the ring compressor to make sure it's contacting the block around its entire circumference.

35 Gently tap on the top of the piston with the end of a wooden or plastic hammer handle (see illustration) while guiding the end of the connecting rod into place on the crankshaft journal. The piston rings may try to pop out of the ring compressor just before entering the cylinder bore, so keep some downward pressure on the ring compressor. Work slowly, and if any resistance is felt as the piston enters the cylinder, stop immediately. Find out what's hanging up and fix it before proceeding. Do not, for any reason, force the piston into the cylinder - you might break a ring and/or the piston.

36 Once the piston/connecting rod assembly is installed, the connecting rod bearing oil clearance must be checked before the rod cap is permanently installed.

37 Cut a piece of the appropriate size Plastigage slightly shorter than the width of the connecting rod bearing and lay it in place on the number one connecting rod journal, parallel with the journal axis (see illustration).

38 Clean the connecting rod cap bearing face and install the rod cap. Make sure the mating mark on the cap is on the same side as the mark on the connecting rod (see illustration 9.4).

39 Install the old rod bolts, at this time, and tighten them to the torque listed in this Chapter's Specifications.

➡ **Note: Use a thin-wall socket to avoid erroneous torque readings that can result if the socket is wedged between the rod cap and the bolt head. If the socket tends to wedge itself between the fastener and the cap, lift up on it slightly until it no longer contacts the cap. DO NOT rotate the crankshaft at any time during this operation.**

40 Remove the fasteners and detach the rod cap, being very careful not to disturb the Plastigage.

41 Compare the width of the crushed Plastigage to the scale printed on the Plastigage envelope to obtain the oil clearance (see illustration). The connecting rod oil clearance is usually about 0.001 to 0.002 inch (0.025 to 0.05 mm). Consult an automotive machine shop for the clearance specified for the rod bearings on your engine. One the covered vehicles, code numbers on the block and crankshaft are used to select the proper bearings, using a chart at a dealership service/parts department.

9.30 Position the piston ring end gaps as shown

9.35 Use a plastic or wooden hammer handle to push the piston into the cylinder

9.37 Place Plastigage on each connecting rod bearing journal parallel to the crankshaft centerline

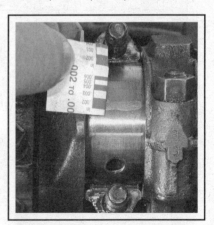

9.41 Use the scale on the Plastigage package to determine the bearing oil clearance - be sure to measure the widest part of the Plastigage and use the correct scale; it comes with both standard and metric scales

42 If the clearance is not as specified, the bearing inserts may be the wrong size (which means different ones will be required). Before deciding that different inserts are needed, make sure that no dirt or oil was between the bearing inserts and the connecting rod or cap when the clearance was measured. Also, recheck the journal diameter. If the Plastigage was wider at one end than the other, the journal may be tapered. If the clearance still exceeds the limit specified, the bearing will have to be replaced with an undersize bearing.

✸✸ **CAUTION:**

When installing a new crankshaft always use a standard size bearing.

Final installation

43 Carefully scrape all traces of the Plastigage material off the rod journal and/or bearing face. Be very careful not to scratch the bearing - use your fingernail or the edge of a plastic card.

44 Make sure the bearing faces are perfectly clean, then apply a uniform layer of clean moly-base grease or engine assembly lube to both of them. You'll have to push the piston into the cylinder to expose the face of the bearing insert in the connecting rod.

45 Slide the connecting rod back into place on the journal, install the rod cap, install the new bolts and tighten them to the torque listed in this Chapter's Specifications.

✸✸ **CAUTION:**

Install new connecting rod cap bolts. Do NOT reuse old bolts - they have stretched and cannot be reused. Again, work up to the torque in three steps.

46 Repeat the entire procedure for the remaining pistons/connecting rods.

47 The important points to remember are:
a) *Keep the back sides of the bearing inserts and the insides of the connecting rods and caps perfectly clean when assembling them.*
b) *Make sure you have the correct piston/rod assembly for each cylinder.*
c) *The mark on the piston must face the front (timing chain) of the engine.*
d) *Lubricate the cylinder walls liberally with clean oil.*
e) *Lubricate the bearing faces when installing the rod caps after the oil clearance has been checked.*

48 After all the piston/connecting rod assemblies have been correctly installed, rotate the crankshaft a number of times by hand to check for any obvious binding.

49 As a final step, check the connecting rod endplay, as described in Step 3. If it was correct before disassembly and the original crankshaft and rods were reinstalled, it should still be correct. If new rods or a new crankshaft were installed, the endplay may be inadequate. If so, the rods will have to be removed and taken to an automotive machine shop for resizing.

10 Crankshaft - removal and installation

REMOVAL

▶ **Refer to illustrations 10.1 and 10.3**

➡ **Note: The crankshaft can be removed only after the engine has been removed from the vehicle. It's assumed that the driveplate, crankshaft pulley, timing chain, oil pan, oil pump body, oil filter and piston/connecting rod assemblies have already been removed. The rear main oil seal retainer must be unbolted and separated from the block before proceeding with crankshaft removal.**

1 Before the crankshaft is removed, measure the endplay. Mount a dial indicator with the indicator in line with the crankshaft and just touching the end of the crankshaft as shown (see illustration).

2 Pry the crankshaft all the way to the rear and zero the dial indicator. Next, pry the crankshaft to the front as far as possible and check the reading on the dial indicator. The distance traveled is the endplay. A typical crankshaft endplay will fall between 0.003 to 0.010 inch (0.076 to 0.254 mm). If it is greater than that, check the crankshaft thrust surfaces for wear after it's removed. If no wear is evident, new main bearings should correct the endplay.

3 If a dial indicator isn't available, feeler gauges can be used. Gently pry the crankshaft all the way to the front of the engine. Slip feeler gauges between the crankshaft and the front face of the thrust bearing or washer to determine the clearance (see illustration).

4 Loosen the main bearing cap beam bolts (four-cylinder engines)

10.1 Checking crankshaft endplay with a dial indicator

10.3 Checking the crankshaft endplay with feeler gauges at the thrust bearing journal

10.17 Place the Plastigage onto the crankshaft bearing journal as shown

10.19a Main bearing cap beam bolt tightening sequence (four-cylinder engines)

or main bearing cap support brace and main bearing cap bolts (V6 engines) 1/4-turn at a time each, until they can be removed by hand. Loosen the bolts in the reverse of the tightening sequence (see illustration(s) 10.19a or 10.19b and 10.19c).

➡ **Note: New main bearing cap bolts must be used when reassembling the engine, but save the old bolts for use when checking the main bearing oil clearance.**

5   If you're working on a four-cylinder engine, remove the main bearing cap support beam. If you're working on a V6 engine, remove the main bearing caps. Try not to drop the bearing inserts if they come out with the assembly.

6   Carefully lift the crankshaft out of the engine. It may be a good idea to have an assistant available, since the crankshaft is quite heavy and awkward to handle. With the bearing inserts in place inside the engine block and main bearing caps or lower cylinder block, reinstall the main bearing caps or lower cylinder block onto the engine block and tighten the bolts finger tight.

INSTALLATION

7   Crankshaft installation is the first step in engine reassembly. It's assumed at this point that the engine block and crankshaft have been cleaned, inspected and repaired or reconditioned.

8   Position the engine block with the bottom facing up.

9   Remove the bolts and lift off the support beam, main bearing caps or lower cylinder block, as applicable.

10 If they're still in place, remove the original bearing inserts. Wipe the bearing surfaces of the block and main bearing cap assembly with a clean, lint-free cloth. They must be kept spotlessly clean. This is critical for determining the correct bearing oil clearance.

Main bearing oil clearance check

▶ **Refer to illustrations 10.17, 10.19a, 10.19b, 10.19c and 10.21**

11 Without mixing them up, clean the back sides of the new upper main bearing inserts (with grooves and oil holes) and lay one in each main bearing saddle in the engine block. Each upper bearing (engine block) has an oil groove and oil hole in it.

✷✷ CAUTION:

The oil holes in the block must line up with the oil holes in the upper bearing inserts.

➡ **Note: The thrust bearing on the four-cylinder engine is located on the engine block number 3 (center) journal. The thrust washers on the V6 engines are located on the 4th journal (two upper on each side of the main saddle, one lower on the rear of the main bearing cap). The grooves on shim-type thrust washers must face the crankshaft (not the main bearing saddle). Clean the back sides of the lower main bearing inserts and lay them in the corresponding location in the main bearing caps or the lower cylinder block. Make sure the tab on the bearing insert fits into its corresponding recess.**

✷✷ CAUTION:

Do not hammer the bearing insert into place and don't nick or gouge the bearing faces. DO NOT apply any lubrication at this time.

12 Clean the faces of the bearing inserts in the block and the crankshaft main bearing journals with a clean, lint-free cloth.

13 Check or clean the oil holes in the crankshaft, as any dirt here can go only one way - straight through the new bearings.

14 Once you're certain the crankshaft is clean, carefully lay it in position in the cylinder block.

15 Before the crankshaft can be permanently installed, the main bearing oil clearance must be checked.

16 Cut several strips of the appropriate size of Plastigage. They must be slightly shorter than the width of the main bearing journal.

17 Place one piece on each crankshaft main bearing journal, parallel with the journal axis as shown (see illustration).

18 Clean the faces of the bearing inserts in the main bearing caps or the lower cylinder block. Hold the bearing inserts in place and install the caps or the lower cylinder block onto the crankshaft and cylinder block. DO NOT disturb the Plastigage.

19 Apply clean engine oil to all bolt threads prior to installation, then install all bolts finger-tight.

➡ **Note: Use the old bolts at this time.**

Tighten the bolts in the sequence shown (see illustrations) progressing in steps, to the torque listed in this Chapter's Specifications. DO NOT rotate the crankshaft at any time during this operation.

20 Remove the bolts in the reverse order of the tightening sequence and carefully lift the caps or the lower cylinder block straight up and off the block. Do not disturb the Plastigage or rotate the crankshaft.

10.19b Main bearing cap bolt tightening sequence (V6 engines)

10.19c Main bearing cap support brace, bolt tightening sequence (V6 engines)

21 Compare the width of the crushed Plastigage on each journal to the scale printed on the Plastigage envelope to determine the main bearing oil clearance (see illustration). Check with an automotive machine shop for the oil clearance for your engine.

22 If the clearance is not as specified, the bearing inserts may be the wrong size (which means different ones will be required). Before deciding if different inserts are needed, make sure that no dirt or oil was between the bearing inserts and the cap assembly or block when the clearance was measured. If the Plastigage was wider at one end than the other, the crankshaft journal may be tapered. If the clearance still exceeds the limit specified, the bearing insert(s) will have to be replaced with an undersize bearing insert(s).

> ❄ **CAUTION:**
>
> **When installing a new crankshaft always install a standard bearing insert set.**

23 Carefully scrape all traces of the Plastigage material off the main bearing journals and/or the bearing insert faces. Be sure to remove all residue from the oil holes. Use your fingernail or the edge of a plastic card - don't nick or scratch the bearing faces.

Final installation

24 Carefully lift the crankshaft out of the cylinder block.

25 Clean the bearing insert faces in the cylinder block, then apply a thin, uniform layer of moly-base grease or engine assembly lube to each of the bearing surfaces. Be sure to coat the thrust faces as well as the journal face of the thrust bearing.

26 Make sure the crankshaft journals are clean, then lay the crankshaft back in place in the cylinder block.

27 Clean the bearing insert faces and apply the same lubricant to them. Clean the engine block and the bearing caps/lower cylinder block thoroughly. The surfaces must be free of oil residue.

28 On V6 engines, install the lower cylinder block onto the crankshaft and cylinder block. If you're working on a four-cylinder engine, install the main bearing caps in their proper locations, with the arrows on the caps facing the front of the engine.

10.21 Use the scale on the Plastigage package to determine the bearing oil clearance - be sure to measure the widest part of the Plastigage and use the correct scale; it comes with both standard and metric scales

29 Prior to installation, apply clean engine oil to all of the NEW bolt threads, wiping off any excess, then install all bolts finger-tight.

30 Tighten the support beam (four-cylinder engine) or caps (V6 engines), following the correct torque sequence (see illustration 10.19a or 10.19b). Torque the bolts to the Specifications listed in this Chapter. On V6 engines, install the main bearing cap support brace, tightening the bolts to the torque listed in this Chapter's Specifications in the proper sequence (see illustration 10.19c).

31 Recheck the crankshaft endplay with a feeler gauge or a dial indicator. The endplay should be correct if the crankshaft thrust faces aren't worn or damaged and if new bearings have been installed.

32 Rotate the crankshaft a number of times by hand to check for any obvious binding. It should rotate with a running torque of 50 in-lbs or less. If the running torque is too high, correct the problem at this time.

33 Install a new rear main oil seal (see Chapter 2A or 2B).

11 Engine overhaul - reassembly sequence

1   Before beginning engine reassembly, make sure you have all the necessary new parts, gaskets and seals as well as the following items on hand:

>   Common hand tools
>   A 1/2-inch drive torque wrench
>   New engine oil
>   Gasket sealant
>   Thread locking compound

2   If you obtained a short block it will be necessary to install the cylinder head, the oil pump and pick-up tube, the oil pan, the water pump, the timing belt and timing cover, and the valve cover (see Chapter 2A or 2B). In order to save time and avoid problems, the external components must be installed in the following general order:

>   Thermostat and housing cover
>   Water pump
>   Intake and exhaust manifolds
>   Turbocharger (four-cylinder models)
>   Fuel injection components
>   Emission control components
>   Spark plugs
>   Ignition coils
>   Oil filter
>   Engine mounts and mount brackets
>   Driveplate

12 Initial start-up and break-in after overhaul

❋❋ WARNING:

Have a fire extinguisher handy when starting the engine for the first time.

1   Once the engine has been installed in the vehicle, double-check the engine oil and coolant levels.

2   With the spark plugs out of the engine and the fuel pump disabled (see Chapter 4, Section 3), crank the engine until oil pressure registers on the gauge or the light goes out.

3   Install the spark plugs, and restore the ignition system and fuel pump functions.

4   Start the engine. It may take a few moments for the fuel system to build up pressure, but the engine should start without a great deal of effort.

5   After the engine starts, it should be allowed to warm up to normal operating temperature. While the engine is warming up, make a thorough check for fuel, oil and coolant leaks.

6   Shut the engine off and recheck the engine oil and coolant levels.

7   Drive the vehicle to an area with minimum traffic, accelerate from 30 to 50 mph, then allow the vehicle to slow to 30 mph with the throttle closed. Repeat the procedure 10 or 12 times. This will load the piston rings and cause them to seat properly against the cylinder walls. Check again for oil and coolant leaks.

8   Drive the vehicle gently for the first 500 miles (no sustained high speeds) and keep a constant check on the oil level. It is not unusual for an engine to use oil during the break-in period.

9   At approximately 500 to 600 miles, change the oil and filter.

10   For the next few hundred miles, drive the vehicle normally. Do not pamper it or abuse it.

11   After 2,000 miles, change the oil and filter again and consider the engine broken in.

13 Balance shaft assembly (four-cylinder engine) - removal and installation

1   The balance shaft assembly is bolted to the crankshaft main bearing support beam. A gear on the crankshaft meshes with a gear on the balance shaft assembly. When the engine is operating, the assembly smoothes engine vibrations.

2   The balancer is a precision-machined assembly, there are no serviceable parts inside and it should not be disassembled. If the backlash is out of Specification (see Steps 5 through 8), the assembly must be replaced as a complete unit.

REMOVAL

3   Position the crankshaft at TDC (see Chapter 2A). Remove the four mounting bolts.

4   With the engine turned crankshaft side up on the engine stand, lift the assembly straight up from the engine.

13.6 Method of checking the backlash in the balancer assembly

13.9 Remove/install the balance shaft assembly bolts only when the crank is at TDC and these balancer dots align

INSPECTION

▶ **Refer to illustration 13.6**

5   When the balance shaft assembly is in place, the backlash between the drive gear (on the crankshaft) and the driven gear on the assembly can be checked. Remove the timing peg.

6   Attach a 5 mm Allen wrench to the top of the driveshaft with the long end of the wrench pointing straight up. Secure a dial-indicator fixture to the engine so that the tip of the indicator is against the top of the wrench (see illustration).

7   Use a pry tool against the crankshaft front counterweight to apply thrust pressure, while turning the crankshaft back-and-forth. Record the measurements of the dial-indicator. Measurements should be taken at the following degrees of engine rotation: 10, 30, 100, 190 and 210 degrees. Compare your results with the allowable range of backlash given in this Chapter's Specifications.

8   If the backlash is out of range, the assembly must be replaced.

INSTALLATION

▶ **Refer to illustration 13.9**

9   When installing the balance shaft assembly, the engine must set to TDC for cylinder number 1. Before installing the assembly, rotate it to align the timing marks on both shafts of the assembly (see illustration). Bolt the assembly to the engine and recheck that the timing marks are still aligned and that the crankshaft has not moved. Tighten the bolts in a criss-cross pattern to the torque listed in this Chapter's Specifications.

10   The crankshaft timing peg should remain installed to keep the engine at TDC until installation of the timing chain and sprockets is completed.

Specifications

General

Cylinder compression	Lowest cylinder must be within 75% of the highest cylinder
Oil pressure	
Four-cylinder engines, hot, at 2000 rpm	29 to 39 psi (200 to 268 kPa)
V6 engine, at 1500 rpm	30 psi (206 kPa)
Balance shaft assembly backlash	
(four-cylinder engines)	0.0008 to 0.0047 inch (0.020 to 0.120 mm)

Torque specifications	Ft-lbs (unless otherwise indicated)	Nm

➡ **Note: One foot-pound (ft-lb) of torque is equivalent to 12 inch-pounds (in-lbs) of torque. Torque values below approximately 15 foot-pounds are expressed in inch-pounds, because most foot-pound torque wrenches are not accurate at these smaller values.**

	Ft-lbs (unless otherwise indicated)	Nm
Balance shaft assembly mounting bolts (four-cylinder engines)		
Step 1	18	25
Step 2	31	42
Connecting rod bolts*		
Four-cylinder engines		
Step 1	89 in-lbs	10
Step 2	21	29
Step 3	Tighten an additional 90 degrees	
V6 engines		
Step 1	17	23
Step 2	32	43
Step 3	Tighten an additional 90 degrees	
Main bearing bolts*		
Four-cylinder engines		
Step 1	44 in-lbs	5
Step 2	18	25
Step 3	Tighten an additional 90 degrees	
V6 engines		
Step 1, bolts 1 through 8	44	60
Step 2, bolts 1 through 8	Tighten an additional 90 degrees	
Step 3, side bolts 10 through 16	33	45
Step 4, side bolts 10 through 16	Tighten an additional 90 degrees	
Main bearing cap support brace (V6 engines)		
Step 1	177 in-lbs	20
Step 2	Tighten an additional 90-degrees	

Use new bolts

Section

Reference to other Chapters

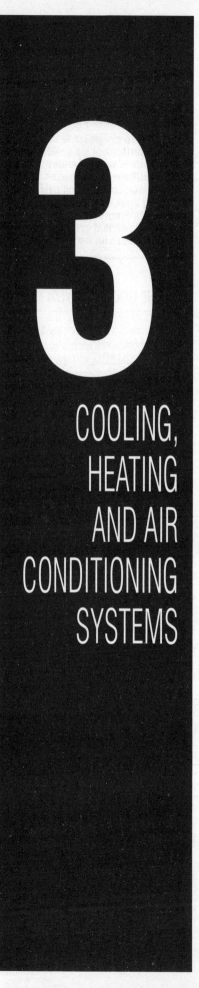

3

COOLING, HEATING AND AIR CONDITIONING SYSTEMS

1 General information

ENGINE COOLING SYSTEM

All modern vehicles employ a pressurized engine cooling system with thermostatically controlled coolant circulation. The cooling system consists of a radiator, an expansion tank or coolant reservoir, a pressure cap (located on the expansion tank or radiator), a thermostat, a cooling fan, and a water pump.

The water pump circulates coolant through the engine. The coolant flows around each cylinder and around the intake and exhaust ports, near the spark plug areas and in close proximity to the exhaust valve guides.

A thermostat controls engine coolant temperature. During warm up, the closed thermostat prevents coolant from circulating through the radiator. As the engine nears normal operating temperature, the thermo-stat opens and allows hot coolant to travel through the radiator, where it's cooled before returning to the engine.

HEATING SYSTEM

The heating system consists of a blower fan and heater core located in a housing under the dash, the hoses connecting the heater core to the engine cooling system and the heater/air conditioning control head on the dashboard. Hot engine coolant is circulated through the heater core. When the heater mode is activated, a flap door in the housing opens to expose the heater core to the passenger compartment through air ducts. A fan switch on the control head activates the blower motor, which forces air through the core, heating the air.

AIR CONDITIONING SYSTEM

The air conditioning system consists of a condenser mounted in front of the radiator, an evaporator mounted adjacent to the heater core, a compressor mounted on the engine, a receiver-drier or accumulator and the plumbing connecting all of the above components.

A blower fan forces the warmer air of the passenger compartment through the evaporator core (sort of a radiator-in-reverse), transferring the heat from the air to the refrigerant. The liquid refrigerant boils off into low pressure vapor, taking the heat with it when it leaves the evaporator.

2 Troubleshooting

COOLANT LEAKS

▶ **Refer to illustration 2.2**

1 A coolant leak can develop anywhere in the cooling system, but the most common causes are:

  a) *A loose or weak hose clamp*
  b) *A defective hose*
  c) *A faulty pressure cap*
  d) *A damaged radiator*
  e) *A bad heater core*
  f) *A faulty water pump*
  g) *A leaking gasket at any joint that carries coolant*

2 Coolant leaks aren't always easy to find. Sometimes they can only be detected when the cooling system is under pressure. Here's where a cooling system pressure tester comes in handy. After the engine has cooled completely, the tester is attached in place of the pressure cap, then pumped up to the pressure value equal to that of the pressure cap rating (see illustration). Now, leaks that only exist when the engine is fully warmed up will become apparent. The tester can be left connected to locate a nagging slow leak.

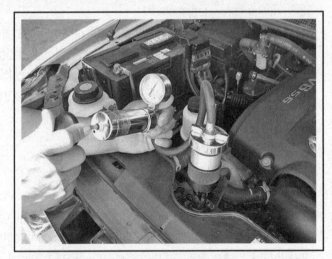

2.2 The cooling system pressure tester is connected in place of the pressure cap, then pumped up to pressurize the system

2.5a The combustion leak detector consists of a bulb, syringe and test fluid

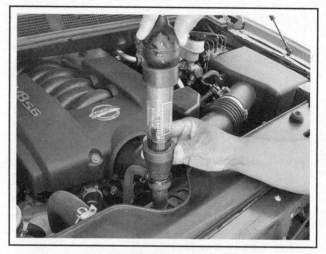

2.5b Place the tester over the cooling system filler neck and use the bulb to draw a sample into the tester

COOLANT LEVEL DROPS, BUT NO EXTERNAL LEAKS

▶ **Refer to illustrations 2.5a and 2.5b**

3   If you find it necessary to keep adding coolant, but there are no external leaks, the probable causes include:

a) A blown head gasket
b) A leaking intake manifold gasket (only on engines that have coolant passages in the manifold)
c) A cracked cylinder head or cylinder block

4   Any of the above problems will also usually result in contamination of the engine oil, which will cause it to take on a milkshake-like appearance. A bad head gasket or cracked head or block can also result in engine oil contaminating the cooling system.

5   Combustion leak detectors (also known as block testers) are available at most auto parts stores. These work by detecting exhaust gases in the cooling system, which indicates a compression leak from a cylinder into the coolant. The tester consists of a large bulb-type syringe and bottle of test fluid (see illustration). A measured amount of the fluid is added to the syringe. The syringe is placed over the cooling system filler neck and, with the engine running, the bulb is squeezed and a sample of the gases present in the cooling system are drawn up through the test fluid (see illustration). If any combustion gases are present in the sample taken, the test fluid will change color.

6   If the test indicates combustion gas is present in the cooling system, you can be sure that the engine has a blown head gasket or a crack in the cylinder head or block, and will require disassembly to repair.

PRESSURE CAP

▶ **Refer to illustration 2.8**

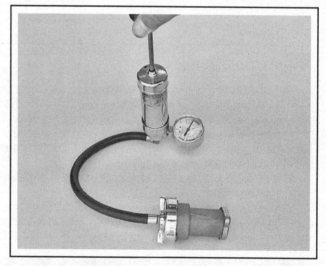

2.8 Checking the cooling system pressure cap with a cooling system pressure tester

7   The cooling system is sealed by a spring-loaded cap, which raises the boiling point of the coolant. If the cap's seal or spring are worn out, the coolant can boil and escape past the cap. With the engine completely cool, remove the cap and check the seal; if it's cracked, hardened or deteriorated in any way, replace it with a new one.

8   Even if the seal is good, the spring might not be; this can be checked with a cooling system pressure tester (see illustration). If the cap can't hold a pressure within approximately 1-1/2 lbs of its rated pressure (which is marked on the cap), replace it with a new one.

9   The cap is also equipped with a vacuum relief spring. When the engine cools off, a vacuum is created in the cooling system. The vacuum relief spring allows air back into the system, which will equalize the pressure and prevent damage to the radiator (the radiator tanks could collapse if the vacuum is great enough). If, after turning the engine off and allowing it to cool down you notice any of the cooling system hoses collapsing, replace the pressure cap with a new one.

2.10 Typical thermostat:

1	Flange	5	Valve seat
2	Piston	6	Valve
3	Jiggle valve	7	Frame
4	Main coil spring	8	Secondary coil spring

THERMOSTAT

▶ Refer to illustration 2.10

10 Before assuming the thermostat (see illustration) is responsible for a cooling system problem, check the coolant level (see Chapter 1), drive-belt tension (see Chapter 1) and temperature gauge (or light) operation.

11 If the engine takes a long time to warm up (as indicated by the temperature gauge or heater operation), the thermostat is probably stuck open. Replace the thermostat with a new one.

12 If the engine runs hot or overheats, a thorough test of the thermostat should be performed.

13 Definitive testing of the thermostat can only be made when it is removed from the vehicle. If the thermostat is stuck in the open position at room temperature, it is faulty and must be replaced.

✳✳ CAUTION:

Do not drive the vehicle without a thermostat. The computer may stay in open loop and emissions and fuel economy will suffer.

14 To test a thermostat, suspend the (closed) thermostat on a length of string or wire in a pot of cold water.

15 Heat the water on a stove while observing thermostat. The thermostat should fully open before the water boils.

16 If the thermostat doesn't open and close as specified, or sticks in any position, replace it.

COOLING FAN

Electric cooling fan

17 If the engine is overheating and the cooling fan is not coming on when the engine temperature rises to an excessive level, unplug the fan motor electrical connector(s) and connect the motor directly to the battery with fused jumper wires. If the fan motor doesn't come on, replace the motor.

18 If the fan motor is okay, but it isn't coming on when the engine

2.28 The water pump weep hole is generally located on the underside of the pump

gets hot, the cooling fan control module or the Powertrain Control Module (PCM) might be defective.

19 These control circuits are fairly complex, and checking them should be left to a qualified automotive technician.

20 Check all wiring and connections to the fan motor. Refer to the wiring diagrams at the end of Chapter 12.

21 If no obvious problems are found, the problem could be the Cylinder Head Temperature (CHT) sensor or the Powertrain Control Module (PCM). Have the cooling fan system and circuit diagnosed by a dealer service department or repair shop with the proper diagnostic equipment.

Belt-driven cooling fan

22 Disconnect the cable from the negative terminal of the battery and rock the fan back and forth by hand to check for excessive bearing play.

23 With the engine cold (and not running), turn the fan blades by hand. The fan should turn freely.

24 Visually inspect for substantial fluid leakage from the clutch assembly. If problems are noted, replace the clutch assembly.

25 With the engine completely warmed up, turn off the ignition switch and disconnect the negative battery cable from the battery. Turn the fan by hand. Some drag should be evident. If the fan turns easily, replace the fan clutch.

WATER PUMP

26 A failure in the water pump can cause serious engine damage due to overheating.

Drivebelt-driven water pump

▶ Refer to illustration 2.28

27 There are two ways to check the operation of the water pump while it's installed on the engine. If the pump is found to be defective, it should be replaced with a new or rebuilt unit.

28 Water pumps are equipped with weep (or vent) holes (see illustration). If a failure occurs in the pump seal, coolant will leak from the hole.

29 If the water pump shaft bearings fail, there may be a howling sound at the pump while it's running. Shaft wear can be felt with the drivebelt removed if the water pump pulley is rocked up and down (with the engine off). Don't mistake drivebelt slippage, which causes a squealing sound, for water pump bearing failure.

Timing chain or timing belt-driven water pump

30 Water pumps driven by the timing chain or timing belt are located underneath the timing chain or timing belt cover.

31 Checking the water pump is limited because of where it is located. However, some basic checks can be made before deciding to remove the water pump. If the pump is found to be defective, it should be replaced with a new or rebuilt unit.

32 One sign that the water pump may be failing is that the heater (climate control) may not work well. Warm the engine to normal operating temperature, confirm that the coolant level is correct, then run the heater and check for hot air coming from the ducts.

33 Check for noises coming from the water pump area. If the water pump impeller shaft or bearings are failing, there may be a howling sound at the pump while the engine is running.

➡ **Note: Be careful not to mistake drivebelt noise (squealing) for water pump bearing or shaft failure.**

34 It you suspect water pump failure due to noise, wear can be confirmed by feeling for play at the pump shaft. This can be done by rocking the drive sprocket on the pump shaft up and down. To do this you will need to remove the tension on the timing chain or belt as well as access the water pump.

All water pumps

35 In rare cases or on high-mileage vehicles, another sign of water pump failure may be the presence of coolant in the engine oil. This condition will adversely affect the engine in varying degrees.

➡ **Note: Finding coolant in the engine oil could indicate other serious issues besides a failed water pump, such as a blown head gasket or a cracked cylinder head or block.**

36 Even a pump that exhibits no outward signs of a problem, such as noise or leakage, can still be due for replacement. Removal for close examination is the only sure way to tell. Sometimes the fins on the back of the impeller can corrode to the point that cooling efficiency is diminished significantly.

HEATER SYSTEM

37 Little can go wrong with a heater. If the fan motor will run at all speeds, the electrical part of the system is okay. The three basic heater problems fall into the following general categories:

a) *Not enough heat*
b) *Heat all the time*
c) *No heat*

38 If there's not enough heat, the control valve or door is stuck in a partially open position, the coolant coming from the engine isn't hot enough, or the heater core is restricted. If the coolant isn't hot enough, the thermostat in the engine cooling system is stuck open, allowing coolant to pass through the engine so rapidly that it doesn't heat up quickly enough. If the vehicle is equipped with a temperature gauge instead of a warning light, watch to see if the engine temperature rises to the normal operating range after driving for a reasonable distance.

39 If there's heat all the time, the control valve or the door is stuck wide open.

40 If there's no heat, coolant is probably not reaching the heater core, or the heater core is plugged. The likely cause is a collapsed or plugged hose, core, or a frozen heater control valve. If the heater is the type that flows coolant all the time, the cause is a stuck door or a broken or kinked control cable.

AIR CONDITIONING SYSTEM

41 If the cool air output is inadequate:

a) *Inspect the condenser coils and fins to make sure they're clear*
b) *Check the compressor clutch for slippage.*
c) *Check the blower motor for proper operation.*
d) *Inspect the blower discharge passage for obstructions.*
e) *Check the system air intake filter for clogging.*

42 If the system provides intermittent cooling air:

a) *Check the circuit breaker, blower switch and blower motor for a malfunction.*
b) *Make sure the compressor clutch isn't slipping.*
c) *Inspect the plenum door to make sure it's operating properly.*
d) *Inspect the evaporator to make sure it isn't clogged.*
e) *If the unit is icing up, it may be caused by excessive moisture in the system, incorrect super heat switch adjustment or low thermostat adjustment.*

43 If the system provides no cooling air:

a) *Inspect the compressor drivebelt. Make sure it's not loose or broken.*
b) *Make sure the compressor clutch engages. If it doesn't, check for a blown fuse.*
c) *Inspect the wire harness for broken or disconnected wires.*
d) *If the compressor clutch doesn't engage, bridge the terminals of the A/C pressure switch(es) with a jumper wire; if the clutch now engages, and the system is properly charged, the pressure switch is bad.*
e) *Make sure the blower motor is not disconnected or burned out.*
f) *Make sure the compressor isn't partially or completely seized.*
g) *Inspect the refrigerant lines for leaks.*
h) *Check the components for leaks.*
i) *Inspect the receiver-drier/accumulator or expansion valve/tube for clogged screens.*

44 If the system is noisy:

a) *Look for loose panels in the passenger compartment.*
b) *Inspect the compressor drivebelt. It may be loose or worn.*
c) *Check the compressor mounting bolts. They should be tight.*
d) *Listen carefully to the compressor. It may be worn out.*
e) *Listen to the idler pulley and bearing and the clutch. Either may be defective.*
f) *The winding in the compressor clutch coil or solenoid may be defective.*
g) *The compressor oil level may be low.*
h) *The blower motor fan bushing or the motor itself may be worn out.*
i) *If there is an excessive charge in the system, you'll hear a rumbling noise in the high pressure line, a thumping noise in the compressor, or see bubbles or cloudiness in the sight glass.*
j) *If there's a low charge in the system, you might hear hissing in the evaporator case at the expansion valve, or see bubbles or cloudiness in the sight glass.*

3 Air conditioning and heating system - check and maintenance

AIR CONDITIONING SYSTEM

※※ WARNING:

The air conditioning system is under high pressure. Do not loosen any hose fittings or remove any components until after the system has been discharged. Air conditioning refrigerant should be properly discharged into an EPA-approved recovery/recycling unit at a dealer service department or an automotive air conditioning repair facility. Always wear eye protection when disconnecting air conditioning system fittings.

※※ CAUTION:

All models covered by this manual use environmentally friendly R-134a. This refrigerant (and its appropriate refrigerant oils) are not compatible with R-12 refrigerant system components and must never be mixed or the components will be damaged.

※※ CAUTION:

When replacing entire components, additional refrigerant oil should be added equal to the amount that is removed with the component being replaced. Read the can before adding any oil to the system, to make sure it is compatible with the R-134a system.

1   The following maintenance checks should be performed on a regular basis to ensure that the air conditioning continues to operate at peak efficiency.
    a) *Inspect the condition of the compressor drivebelt. If it is worn or deteriorated, replace it (see Chapter 1).*
    b) *Check the drivebelt tension (see Chapter 1).*

3.9 Insert a thermometer in the center vent, turn on the air conditioning system and wait for it to cool down; depending on the humidity, the output air should be 35 to 40 degrees cooler than the ambient air temperature

    c) *Inspect the system hoses. Look for cracks, bubbles, hardening and deterioration. Inspect the hoses and all fittings for oil bubbles or seepage. If there is any evidence of wear, damage or leakage, replace the hose(s).*
    d) *Inspect the condenser fins for leaves, bugs and any other foreign material that may have embedded itself in the fins. Use a fin comb or compressed air to remove debris from the condenser.*
    e) *Make sure the system has the correct refrigerant charge.*

2   It's a good idea to operate the system for about ten minutes at least once a month. This is particularly important during the winter months because long term non-use can cause hardening, and subsequent failure, of the seals. Note that using the Defrost function operates the compressor.

3   If the air conditioning system is not working properly, proceed to Step 6 and perform the general checks outlined below.

4   Because of the complexity of the air conditioning system and the special equipment necessary to service it, in-depth troubleshooting and repairs beyond checking the refrigerant charge and the compressor clutch operation are not included in this manual. However, simple checks and component replacement procedures are provided in this Chapter.

5   The most common cause of poor cooling is simply a low system refrigerant charge. If a noticeable drop in system cooling ability occurs, one of the following quick checks will help you determine if the refrigerant level is low.

Checking the refrigerant charge

▶ **Refer to illustration 3.9**

6   Warm the engine up to normal operating temperature.

7   Place the air conditioning temperature selector at the coldest setting and put the blower at the highest setting.

8   After the system reaches operating temperature, feel the larger pipe exiting the evaporator at the firewall. The outlet pipe should be cold (the tubing that leads back to the compressor). If the evaporator outlet pipe is warm, the system probably needs a charge.

9   Insert a thermometer in the center air distribution duct (see illustration) while operating the air conditioning system at its maximum setting - the temperature of the output air should be 35 to 40 degrees F below the ambient air temperature (down to approximately 40 degrees F). If the ambient (outside) air temperature is very high, say 110 degrees F, the duct air temperature may be as high as 60 degrees F, but generally the air conditioning is 35 to 40 degrees F cooler than the ambient air.

10   Further inspection or testing of the system requires special tools and techniques and is beyond the scope of the home mechanic.

Adding refrigerant

▶ **Refer to illustrations 3.11 and 3.13**

※※ CAUTION:

Make sure any refrigerant, refrigerant oil or replacement component you purchase is designated as compatible with R-134a systems.

11 Purchase an R-134a automotive charging kit at an auto parts store (see illustration). A charging kit includes a can of refrigerant, a tap

valve and a short section of hose that can be attached between the tap valve and the system low side service valve.

✳✳ CAUTION:

Never add more than one can of refrigerant to the system. If more refrigerant than that is required, the system should be evacuated and leak tested.

12 Back off the valve handle on the charging kit and screw the kit onto the refrigerant can, making sure first that the O-ring or rubber seal inside the threaded portion of the kit is in place.

✳✳ WARNING:

Wear protective eyewear when dealing with pressurized refrigerant cans.

13 Remove the dust cap from the low-side charging port and attach the hose's quick-connect fitting to the port (see illustration).

✳✳ WARNING:

DO NOT hook the charging kit hose to the system high side! The fittings on the charging kit are designed to fit only on the low side of the system.

14 Warm up the engine and turn On the air conditioning. Keep the charging kit hose away from the fan and other moving parts.

➡ **Note: The charging process requires the compressor to be running. If the clutch cycles off, you can put the air conditioning switch on High and leave the car doors open to keep the clutch on and compressor working. The compressor can be kept on during the charging by removing the connector from the pressure switch and bridging it with a paper clip or jumper wire during the procedure.**

15 Turn the valve handle on the kit until the stem pierces the can, then back the handle out to release the refrigerant. You should be able to hear the rush of gas. Keep the can upright at all times, but shake it occasionally. Allow stabilization time between each addition.

➡ **Note: The charging process will go faster if you wrap the can with a hot-water-soaked rag to keep the can from freezing up.**

16 If you have an accurate thermometer, you can place it in the center air conditioning duct inside the vehicle and keep track of the output air temperature. A charged system that is working properly should cool down to approximately 40 degrees F. If the ambient (outside) air temperature is very high, say 110 degrees F, the duct air temperature may be as high as 60 degrees F, but generally the air conditioning is 35 to 40 degrees F cooler than the ambient air.

17 When the can is empty, turn the valve handle to the closed position and release the connection from the low-side port. Reinstall the dust cap.

18 Remove the charging kit from the can and store the kit for future use with the piercing valve in the UP position, to prevent inadvertently piercing the can on the next use.

HEATING SYSTEMS

19 If the carpet under the heater core is damp, or if antifreeze vapor or steam is coming through the vents, the heater core is leaking. Remove it (see Section 12) and install a new unit (most radiator shops will not repair a leaking heater core).

20 If the air coming out of the heater vents isn't hot, the problem could stem from any of the following causes:

  a) *The thermostat is stuck open, preventing the engine coolant from warming up enough to carry heat to the heater core. Replace the thermostat (see Section 4).*
  b) *There is a blockage in the system, preventing the flow of coolant through the heater core. Feel both heater hoses at the firewall. They should be hot. If one of them is cold, there is an obstruction in one of the hoses or in the heater core, or the heater control valve is shut. Detach the hoses and back flush the heater core with a water hose. If the heater core is clear but circulation is impeded, remove the two hoses and flush them out with a water hose.*
  c) *If flushing fails to remove the blockage from the heater core, the core must be replaced (see Section 12).*

ELIMINATING AIR CONDITIONING ODORS

▶ **Refer to illustration 3.24**

21 Unpleasant odors that often develop in air conditioning systems are caused by the growth of a fungus, usually on the surface of the

3.11 R-134a automotive air conditioning charging kit

3.13 The low-side charging port is located in the evaporator outlet line at the right-rear corner of the engine compartment

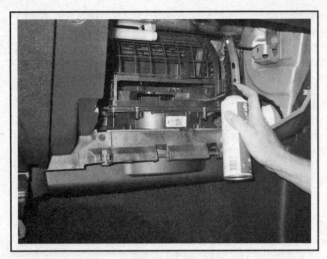

3.24 Insert the nozzle of the disinfectant can into the return-air intake behind the glove box

evaporator core. The warm, humid environment there is a perfect breeding ground for mildew to develop.

22 The evaporator core on most vehicles is difficult to access, and factory dealerships have a lengthy, expensive process for eliminating the fungus by opening up the evaporator case and using a powerful disinfectant and rinse on the core until the fungus is gone. You can service your own system at home, but it takes something much stronger than

basic household germ-killers or deodorizers.

23 Aerosol disinfectants for automotive air conditioning systems are available in most auto parts stores, but remember when shopping for them that the most effective treatments are also the most expensive. The basic procedure for using these sprays is to start by running the system in the RECIRC mode for ten minutes with the blower on its highest speed. Use the highest heat mode to dry out the system and keep the compressor from engaging by disconnecting the wiring connector at the compressor.

24 The disinfectant can usually comes with a long spray hose. Insert the nozzle into an intake port inside the cabin, and spray according to the manufacturer's recommendations (see illustration). Try to cover the whole surface of the evaporator core, by aiming the spray up, down and sideways. Follow the manufacturer's recommendations for the length of spray and waiting time between applications.

AUTOMATIC HEATING AND AIR CONDITIONING SYSTEMS

25 Some vehicles are equipped with an optional automatic climate control system. This system has its own computer that receives inputs from various sensors in the heating and air conditioning system. This computer, like the PCM, has self-diagnostic capabilities to help pinpoint problems or faults within the system. Vehicles equipped with automatic heating and air conditioning systems are very complex and considered beyond the scope of the home mechanic. Vehicles equipped with automatic heating and air conditioning systems should be taken to dealer service department or other qualified facility for repair.

4   Thermostat - replacement

✳ WARNING:

Wait until the engine is completely cool before performing this procedure.

REMOVAL

➡ **Note: The thermostat and thermostat housing on four-cylinder models are replaced as an assembly.**

1   Disconnect the cable from the negative battery terminal (see Chapter 5).

2   Drain the cooling system (see Chapter 1). If the coolant is relatively new and still in good condition, save it and reuse it.

3   Follow the lower radiator hose to the engine to locate the thermostat housing.

4   Loosen the hose clamp, then detach the hose from the fitting. If it's stuck, grasp it near the end with a pair of adjustable pliers and twist it to break the seal, then pull it off. If the hose is old or if it has deteriorated, cut it off and install a new one.

5   If the outer surface of the thermostat housing cover, which mates with the hose, is already corroded, pitted, or otherwise deteriorated, it might be damaged even more by hose removal. If it is, replace the thermostat housing cover.

Four-cylinder models

▶ **Refer to illustration 4.7**

6   Disconnect the heater hose from the thermostat housing or quick-connect fitting.

7   Remove the thermostat housing bolts (see illustration), then detach the housing from the engine.

4.7 Remove the thermostat housing bolts and housing - four-cylinder engine

V6 models

Thermostat

8 Remove the air filter housing and duct (see Chapter 4).

9 Remove the two bolts and detach the coolant inlet cover. If the cover is stuck, tap it with a soft-face hammer to jar it loose. Be prepared for some coolant to spill as the gasket seal is broken.

10 Note how it's installed, which end is facing up, or out, then remove the thermostat and O-ring.

Thermostat housing

11 Remove the air filter housing and duct (see Chapter 4).

12 Disconnect and remove the upper and lower radiator hoses, heater hoses and expansion tank hose.

13 Remove the mounting bolts and separate the housing from the coolant tube.

❉❉ CAUTION:

The other end of the coolant tube is a slip fit into the engine block; if the tube is pulled when separating the thermostat housing it may come out of the block.

INSTALLATION

14 Clean the sealing surfaces. Also inspect the hoses, replacing them as necessary.

Four-cylinder models

15 Install the thermostat housing, using a new gasket. Tighten the

bolts to the torque listed in this Chapter's Specifications. Reconnect the radiator hose and heater hose.

V6 models

Thermostat

16 Install a new rubber O-ring on the thermostat, then install the thermostat in the housing, spring-end first. Make sure that you install the thermostat with the jiggle valve at 12 o'clock.

17 Install the thermostat housing cover and bolts, then tighten the bolts to the torque listed in this Chapter's Specifications.

18 Reattach the lower radiator hose to the coolant inlet cover. Make sure that the hose clamp is still tight. If it isn't, replace it.

Thermostat housing

19 Install a new thermostat-to-coolant pipe rubber O-ring, then lubricate the O-ring with clean coolant.

20 Install a new thermostat gasket on the thermostat housing, then install the housing.

21 Install the thermostat housing cover and bolts, then tighten the bolts to the torque listed in this Chapter's Specifications.

22 Reattach the radiator hoses, heater hoses and expansion tank hose to the thermostat housing. Make sure that the hose clamp is still tight. If it isn't, replace it.

All models

23 Refill the cooling system and bleed the air from the system (see Chapter 1).

24 Start the engine and allow it to reach normal operating temperature, then check for leaks and proper thermostat operation.

5   Engine cooling fans - replacement

❉❉ WARNING:

To avoid possible injury or damage, DO NOT operate the engine with a damaged fan. Do not attempt to repair fan blades - replace a damaged fan with a new one.

➡ **Note: Always be sure to check for blown fuses before attempting to diagnose an electrical circuit problem.**

➡ **Note: Four-cylinder models are equipped with a single fan motor, while V6 models are equipped with two fan motors. Both types are controlled by a fan module controlled by the PCM.**

1 If the engine is overheating and the cooling fan is not coming on when the engine temperature rises to an excessive level, see Section 2. Check the fuses in the underhood fuse/relay box.

2 If the fuses are okay, check all wiring and connections to the fan motor. Refer to the wiring diagrams at the end of Chapter 12. If no obvious problems are found, the problem could be the Cylinder Head Temperature (CHT) sensor, the cooling fan control module or the Powertrain Control Module (PCM). Have the cooling fan system and circuit diagnosed by a dealer service department or repair shop with the proper diagnostic equipment.

REPLACEMENT

▶ **Refer to illustration 5.5**

❉❉ WARNING:

Wait until the engine is completely cool before performing this procedure.

❉❉ WARNING:

These models have an airbag sensor mounted near the radiator support bracket. It will be necessary to disarm the system prior to performing any work around the radiator, fans or other components in this area (see Chapter 12).

3 Disconnect the cable from the negative battery terminal (see Chapter 5).

4 Drain the cooling system (see Chapter 1). If the coolant is relatively new and still in good condition, save it and reuse it. Detach the

5.5 Radiator splash shield fastener locations

5.8 Remove the cooler line support bracket bolt (A), then remove the fan shroud lower fastener (B) (left side shown) - four-cylinder models

5.14 Fan shroud upper fastener locations – four-cylinder models

upper radiator hose from the radiator and position it aside.

5   Raise the vehicle and secure it on jackstands. Remove the lower splash shield under the radiator (see illustration).

6   Remove the air filter housing and duct (see Chapter 4).

Four-cylinder models

▸ **Refer to illustration 5.8 and 5.14**

7   Raise the vehicle and support it on jack stands.

8   Remove the transaxle cooling lines support bracket bolt and lower the cooling lines (see illustration).

9   Remove the lower fan shroud fasteners (see illustration 5.8).

10 Disconnect the charge air cooler tubes from the cooler and the throttle body (see Chapter 4).

11 Disconnect the Manifold Absolute Pressure (MAP) sensor electrical connector (see Chapter 6) and the cooling fan electrical connector.

12 Disconnect the upper radiator hose clamps and remove the hose.

13 Unclip the transaxle fluid lines from the retaining clips, remove the transaxle cooler fastener and move the cooler out of the way.

14 Remove the upper fan shroud fasteners (see illustration) and lift the fan shroud assembly out of the vehicle.

V6 models

15 Disconnect the block heater harness from the top of the fan shroud, if equipped.

16 Disconnect the upper radiator hose and move it out of the way.

17 Disconnect the fan motor electrical connector.

18 Remove the fan shroud mounting bolts and lift the fan shroud assembly out of the vehicle.

All models

19 To detach the fan blade from the motor, remove the fan blade fasteners and the fan blade from the motor.

20 To detach the motor from the shroud, remove the retaining fasteners.

21 Installation is the reverse of removal.

➡ **Note: When reinstalling the fan assembly, make sure the rubber air shields around the shroud are still in place - without them, the cooling system may not work efficiently.**

22 Reconnect the battery, refill the cooling system and bleed the air from the system (see Chapter 1).

23 Start the engine and allow it to reach normal operating temperature, then check for leaks and proper operation.

6 Coolant expansion tank - removal and installation

▶ Refer to illustration 6.2

✳ WARNING:

Wait until the engine is completely cool before beginning this procedure.

1 Drain the cooling system (see Chapter 1).
2 Remove the fasteners securing the expansion tank to the fender (see illustration).
3 Lift the tank up enough to disconnect the hoses (see illustration 6.2).
4 Clean out the tank with soapy water and a brush to remove any deposits inside. Inspect the reservoir carefully for cracks. If you find a crack, replace the reservoir.
5 Installation is the reverse of removal.

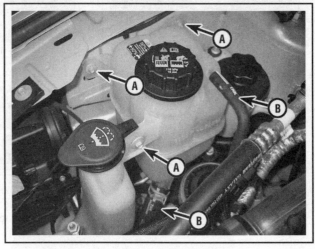

6.2 Remove the expansion tank fasteners (A), then disconnect the hoses (B)

7 Radiator - removal and installation

✳ WARNING:

Wait until the engine is completely cool before beginning this procedure.

✳ WARNING:

These models have an airbag sensor mounted near the radiator support. It will be necessary to disarm the airbag system prior to performing any work around the radiator, fans or other components in this area (see Chapter 12).

REMOVAL

▶ Refer to illustration 7.8

1 Disconnect the cable from the negative battery terminal (see Chapter 5).
2 Raise the vehicle and place it securely on jackstands. Remove the lower splash shield.
3 Drain the cooling system (see Chapter 1). If the coolant is relatively new and in good condition, save it and reuse it. Detach the radiator hose from the bottom of the radiator.
4 Disconnect the expansion tank hose from the radiator.
5 Remove the cooling fan/shroud assembly from the radiator (see Section 5).

7.8 Remove the A/C line bracket bolt and bracket from the top of the radiator

6 Remove the upper and lower radiator hoses.
7 Remove the front bumper cover (see Chapter 11).
8 Remove the a/c line bracket bolt from the top of the radiator (see illustration) and the radiator support.

7.10 Unclip and remove the air deflector from the top of the radiator

7.11 Disconnect the front impact sensor connector (A) then disengage the harness retainers (B)

7.13 Use quick disconnect tool #307-569 to release the cooler lines

7.14 Remove the radiator bracket mounting bolts from the front

Four-cylinder models

▶ Refer to illustrations 7.10, 7.11, 7.13 and 7.14

9   Remove the charge air cooler (see Chapter 4).

10 Unclip the air deflector from the top of the radiator (see illustration), then remove it.

11 Disconnect the front impact sensor connector then disengage the harness retainers (see illustration) and move the harness out of the way.

12 Remove the transaxle cooler line bracket fastener, then push the secondary latches off of the line connection. Use a drip pan to catch spilled fluid and plug the lines and fittings.

13 Using a quick disconnect tool or special tool #307-569, release the cooler lines from the radiator (see illustration).

14 Remove the radiator bracket bolts (see illustration).

15 Remove the a/c condenser bolts (see Section 14) and move the condenser out of the way.

16 Unclip the air deflector from the bottom of the radiator.

17 Carefully lift out the radiator. Don't spill coolant on the vehicle or scratch the paint. Make sure the rubber radiator insulators that fit on the bottom and top of the radiator and into the sockets in the body remain in place in the body for proper reinstallation of the radiator.

V6 models

18 Remove the radiator support bracket bolts, then pull the radiator towards the engine and remove the upper brackets.

19 Disengage the a/c line push pin type retainers from the side of the radiator.

20 Remove the condenser-to-radiator mounting bolts and separate the condenser from the radiator.

21 On 2010 and earlier models, lift then remove the tabs from the radiator support and lean the radiator towards the engine. Disengage the pin-type retainers from the radiator.

22 Carefully lift out the radiator. Don't spill coolant on the vehicle or scratch the paint. Make sure the rubber radiator insulators that fit on the bottom of the radiator and into the sockets in the body remain in place in the body for proper reinstallation of the radiator.

INSTALLATION

23 Remove bugs and dirt from the radiator with compressed air and a soft brush. Don't bend the cooling fins. Inspect the radiator for leaks and damage. If it needs repair, have a radiator shop or a dealer service department do the work.

24 Inspect the rubber insulators in the lower crossmember for cracks and deterioration. Make sure that they're free of dirt and gravel. When installing the radiator, make sure that it's correctly seated on the insulators before fastening the top brackets.

25 Installation is otherwise the reverse of the removal procedure. After installation, fill the cooling system with the correct mixture of antifreeze and water (see Chapter 1).

26 Start the engine and check for leaks. Allow the engine to reach normal operating temperature, indicated by the upper radiator hose becoming hot. Recheck the coolant level and add more if required.

27 If you're working on an automatic transaxle-equipped vehicle, check and add fluid as needed.

8   Water pump - replacement

REMOVAL

1   Disconnect the cable from the negative battery terminal (see Chapter 5).

2   Drain the cooling system (see Chapter 1).

3   Loosen the water pump pulley bolts on four-cylinder engines, then, on all models, remove the drivebelt.

Four-cylinder models

▶ **Refer to illustrations 8.6 and 8.7**

4   Loosen the right front wheel lug nuts. Raise the vehicle and secure it on jackstands.

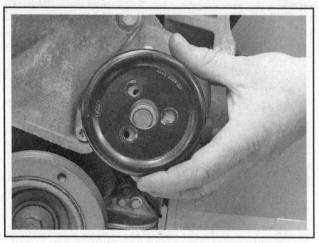

8.6 Remove the bolts and separate the water pump pulley from the pump

8.7 Remove the water pump bolts - four-cylinder engines

5   Remove the right front wheel and the inner fender splash shield (see Chapter 11).

6   Remove the water pump pulley (see illustration).

7   Remove the bolts attaching the water pump to the engine block and remove the pump from the engine (see illustration). If the water pump is stuck, gently tap it with a soft-faced hammer to break the seal.

8   Clean the bolt threads and the threaded holes in the engine and remove all corrosion and sealant. Remove all traces of old gasket material from the sealing surfaces.

V6 models

▶ **Refer to illustration 8.9**

9   On V6 engines, the water pump is mounted to the front of the block but is driven by the timing chain and thus not accessible without removing the timing chain (see Chapter 2B). Remove the pump mounting bolts (see illustration).

INSTALLATION

10 Compare the new pump to the old one to make sure that they're identical.

11 Apply a thin film of RTV sealant to hold the new gasket in place during installation. O-rings should be coated with clean coolant.

12 Carefully mate the pump to the water pump housing.

13 Install the water pump bolts (four-cylinder models, see illustration 8.7; V6 models see illustration 8.9) and tighten them to the torque listed in this Chapter's Specifications.

14 The remainder of installation is the reverse of removal. Refill and bleed the cooling system (see Chapter 1).

15 Operate the engine to check for leaks.

8.9 Water pump bolt locations and tightening sequence - V6 engines

9 Engine Coolant Temperature (ECT) sensor - replacement

▶ Refer to illustration 9.2

✳ WARNING:

Wait until the engine is completely cool before beginning this procedure.

➡ Note: Four-cylinder models are equipped with an Engine Coolant Temperature (ECT) sensor; it functions as the coolant temperature sending unit for the temperature gauge.

1 Drain the cooling system (see Chapter 1).
2 The ECT sensor is located on the left rear corner of the cylinder head (see illustration).
3 Disconnect the electrical connector to the sensor.
4 Remove the retaining clip.
5 Remove the sensor and discard the O-ring

9.2 ECT sensor location (four-cylinder models)

6 Installation is the reverse of removal. Use a new O-ring.
7 Refill the cooling system (see Chapter 1).

10 Blower motor resistor and blower motor - replacement

✳ WARNING:

The models covered by this manual are equipped with Supplemental Restraint Systems (SRS), more commonly known as airbags. Always disable the airbag system before working in the vicinity of any airbag system component to avoid the possibility of accidental deployment of the airbag, which could cause personal injury (see Chapter 12).

BLOWER MOTOR RESISTOR

▶ Refer to illustration 10.2

➡ Note: The blower motor resistor also called the blower motor speed control works in conjunction with the HVAC module to vary the speed of the blower motor.

1 Remove the glovebox (see Chapter 11).

2 Disconnect the electrical connector from the blower motor resistor (see illustration).
3 Remove the blower motor resistor mounting screws and remove the resistor from the evaporator housing.
4 Installation is the reverse of removal.

BLOWER MOTOR

▶ Refer to illustration 10.6

5 Remove the lower trim panel from below the glovebox (see Chapter 11).
6 Disconnect the blower motor electrical connector (see illustration).
7 Remove the blower motor mounting screws and remove the blower motor.
8 Installation is the reverse of removal.

10.2 Unplug the blower motor resistor connector, then remove the mounting screws

10.6 Location of the blower motor electrical connector (A) and the blower motor mounting screws (B)

11 Heater/air conditioner control assembly - removal and installation

✳ WARNING:

The models covered by this manual are equipped with Supplemental Restraint Systems (SRS), more commonly known as airbags. Always disable the airbag system before working in the vicinity of any airbag system component to avoid the possibility of accidental deployment of the airbag, which could cause personal injury (see Chapter 12).

➡ Note: The heater/air conditioner control assembly is incorporated in the Front Controls Interface Module (FCIM); if there is a problem, the entire module must be replaced.

1 Disconnect the cable from the negative battery terminal (see Chapter 5).
2 Remove the left and right floor console upper trim panels (see Chapter 11).

EDGE MODELS

▶ **Refer to illustration 11.5**

3 Place the shift lever in the neutral position.
4 Remove the floor console trim screws and slide the panel back (see Chapter 11).
5 Remove the FCIM retaining screws (see illustration) and remove the module.

MKX MODELS

6 Remove the screws from the lower corners of the FCIM.

11.5 Front Controls Interface Module (FCIM) retaining screws

7 Using a plastic trim tool, start from the bottom of the panel and work your way to the top, disengaging the retaining clips.
8 Remove the FCIM from the instrument panel.

ALL MODELS

9 Disconnect the electrical connectors at the module.
10 Installation is the reverse of removal.

12 Heater core - replacement

▶ **Refer to illustrations 12.3 and 12.5**

✳ WARNING:

The models covered by this manual are equipped with Supplemental Restraint Systems (SRS), more commonly known as airbags. Always disarm the airbag system before working in the vicinity of any airbag system component to avoid the possibility of accidental deployment of the airbag, which could cause personal injury (see Chapter 12).

✳ WARNING:

The air conditioning system is under high pressure. DO NOT loosen any fittings or remove any components until after the system has been discharged. Air conditioning refrigerant must be properly discharged into an EPA-approved container at a dealer service department or an automotive air conditioning

repair facility. Always wear eye protection when disconnecting air conditioning system fittings.

✳ WARNING:

Wait until the engine is completely cool before beginning this procedure.

➡ Note: This is a difficult procedure for the home mechanic, involving numerous hard-to-find fasteners, clips and electrical connectors.

1 Have the air conditioning system recovered by a dealer service department or by an automotive air conditioning shop before proceeding (see **Warning** above).
2 Disconnect the cable from the negative battery terminal (see Chapter 5).

12.3 Disconnect the two heater core hoses then remove the hoses retaining clamp (B)

12.5 Remove the nuts securing the HVAC housing to the firewall (not all fasteners visible here)

3   Drain the cooling system (see Chapter 1). Disconnect the heater hoses from the heater core inlet and outlet pipes at the firewall (see illustration), then disconnect the thermostatic expansion valve and the two refrigerant pipes.

4   Remove the instrument panel (see Chapter 11). On V6 models, remove the lower cowl grille panel to access some HVAC unit fasteners.

5   Tag and disconnect the cables (if equipped) and electrical connectors from the HVAC unit. Remove the housing-to-firewall nuts (see illustration).

6   The heater core is in the center of the HVAC unit, to the left of the blower motor housing. Remove the heater core cover screws and pull the heater core out of the housing.

7   Installation is the reverse of removal. Reconnect the heater core inlet and outlet hoses at the firewall. Use a new gasket where the two air conditioning pipes meet the expansion valve at the firewall.

8   Refill and bleed the cooling system (see Chapter 1). Have the system evacuated, recharged and leak-tested by the shop that discharged it.

13 Air conditioning compressor - removal and installation

❄ WARNING:

The air conditioning system is under high pressure. DO NOT loosen any fittings or remove any components until after the system has been discharged. Air conditioning refrigerant must be properly discharged into an EPA-approved container at a dealer service department or an automotive air conditioning repair facility. Always wear eye protection when disconnecting air conditioning system fittings.

❄ CAUTION:

If the compressor is being replaced due to failure, the rest of the system should be flushed by a technician to remove particles or contaminants.

REMOVAL

1   Have the air conditioning system recovered by a dealer service department or by an automotive air conditioning shop before proceeding (see **Warning** above).

2   Loosen the right front wheel lug nuts. Raise the vehicle and secure it on jackstands. Remove the right front wheel.

3   Remove the right front fender splash shield and the engine splash shield.

4   Remove the drivebelt (see Chapter 1).

Four-cylinder models

▶ Refer to illustration 13.6

5   Remove the mounting nut from the rear of the compressor, then remove the stud.

6   Disconnect the electrical connector from the compressor clutch field coil (see illustration).

7   Disconnect the inlet and outlet lines from the compressor (see illustration 13.6). Remove and discard the old O-rings.

8   Remove the compressor mounting bolts (see illustration 13.6) and remove the compressor.

V6 models

9   Remove the mounting nut from the rear of the compressor, then remove the stud.

10 Disconnect the electrical connector from the compressor clutch field coil (see illustration 13.6).

11 Remove the compressor mounting bolts and lower the compres-

sor until the inlet and outlet lines to the compressor can be reached.

12 Disconnect the inlet and outlet lines from the compressor. Remove and discard the old O-rings.

13 Remove the compressor from the vehicle.

INSTALLATION

14 If a new compressor is being installed, follow the directions that came with the compressor regarding the draining of excess oil prior to installation.

15 The clutch may have to be transferred from the original to the new compressor.

16 Before reconnecting the inlet and outlet lines to the compressor, replace all O-rings and lubricate them with refrigerant oil.

17 Installation is otherwise the reverse of removal.

18 Have the system evacuated, recharged and leak-tested by the shop that discharged it.

13.6 Compressor details (four-cylinder engine shown, V6 engines similar)

1   Compressor clutch field coil electrical connector
2   Compressor inlet and outlet lines
3   Mounting stud/nut
4   Mounting bolts

14 Air conditioning condenser - removal and installation

❄ WARNING:

The air conditioning system is under high pressure. DO NOT loosen any fittings or remove any components until after the system has been discharged. Air conditioning refrigerant must be properly discharged into an EPA-approved container at a dealer service department or an automotive air conditioning repair facility. Always wear eye protection when disconnecting air conditioning system fittings.

➡ **Note: The air conditioning condenser has an integrated receiver/drier, equipped with a receiver/drier desiccant bag. The receiver/drier desiccant bag may be removed and replaced with a new one (available from the dealer).**

1   Have the air conditioning system discharged by a dealer service department or an automotive air conditioning shop before proceeding (see **Warning** above).

2   Remove the radiator (see Section 7).

FOUR-CYLINDER MODELS

3   Disconnect the refrigerant inlet and outlet pipes from the condenser. Remove the bolt or nut securing the pipes to the block that is part of the condenser. Cap the lines to prevent contamination.

V6 MODELS

4   Disconnect the refrigerant inlet and outlet pipes from the condenser. Remove the bolt or nut securing the pipes to the block that is part of the condenser. Cap the lines to prevent contamination. The refrigerant pipe block is retained by a bolt and a rivet that must be drilled out.

5   Remove the transaxle cooler outlet line secondary latch covering the fitting.

6   Using quick disconnect special tool #307-569, disconnect and remove the transaxle cooler line.

ALL MODELS

7   Remove the condenser. If reinstalling the same condenser, store it with the line fittings facing up to prevent oil from draining out.

8   If installing a new condenser, pour one ounce of refrigerant oil of the correct type into it prior to installation.

9   Before reconnecting the refrigerant lines to the condenser, coat a pair of new O-rings with refrigerant oil, install them in the refrigerant line fittings and tighten the condenser inlet and outlet nuts to the torque listed in this Chapter's Specifications.

10 Installation is otherwise the reverse of removal.

11 Have the system evacuated, recharged and leak tested by the shop that discharged it.

Receiver/drier desiccant bag

12 Remove the condenser as previously described in this Section.

13 Remove the threaded plug at the bottom left of the condenser.

14 Using needle nose pliers, pull the desiccant bag out of the receiver drier.

15 Insert a new bag into the receiver drier.

16 Install the plug and tighten it to the torque listed in this Chapter's Specifications.

15 Air conditioning pressure cycling switch - replacement

▶ **Refer to illustration 15.3**

15.3 Disconnect the pressure cycling switch (pressure transducer) electrical connector

❋❋ WARNING:

The air conditioning system is under high pressure. DO NOT loosen any fittings or remove any components until after the system has been discharged. Air conditioning refrigerant must be properly discharged into an EPA-approved container at a dealer service department or an automotive air conditioning repair facility. Always wear eye protection when disconnecting air conditioning system fittings.

1   The pressure cycling switch is located on top of the hard line from the condenser to the air conditioning thermostatic expansion valve (TXV). The pressure cycling switch detects low refrigerant line pressure, and switches the A/C system off, then back on again to provide higher pressure. If the pressure increases too high, the pressure cut-off switch (located in the high-pressure side of the system) shuts the system off.

2   Have the air conditioning system recovered by a dealer service department or by an automotive air conditioning shop before proceeding (see **Warning** above).

3   Unplug the electrical connector from the pressure cycling switch (see illustration).

4   Unscrew the pressure cycling switch.

5   Lubricate the switch O-ring with clean refrigerant oil of the correct type.

6   Screw the new switch into place until hand tight, then tighten it securely.

7   Reconnect the electrical connector.

8   Have the system evacuated, recharged and leak tested by the shop that discharged it.

16 Air conditioning thermostatic expansion valve (TXV) - general information

❋❋ WARNING:

The air conditioning system is under high pressure. DO NOT loosen any hose fittings or remove any components until the system has been discharged. Air conditioning refrigerant must be properly discharged into an EPA-approved recovery/recycling unit by a dealer service department or an automotive air conditioning repair facility. Always wear eye protection when disconnecting air conditioning system fittings.

There are several ways that air conditioning systems convert the high-pressure liquid refrigerant from the compressor to lower-pressure vapor. The conversion takes place at the air conditioning evaporator; the evaporator is chilled as the refrigerant passes through, cooling the airflow through the evaporator for delivery to the vents. The conversion is usually accomplished by a sudden change in the tubing size. Many vehicles have a removable controlled orifice in one of the AC pipes at the firewall.

The models covered by this manual use a thermostatic expansion valve (TXV) that accomplishes the same purpose as a controlled orifice. To remove the TXV, have the air conditioning system discharged by a licensed air conditioning technician, then disconnect the refrigerant lines from the TXV at the firewall, remove the two bolts securing the valve, then remove the valve.

Specifications

General

Expansion tank cap pressure rating	14 to 18 psi (95 to 124 kPa)
Cooling system capacity	See Chapter 1
Refrigerant type	R-134a
Refrigerant capacity	Refer to HVAC specification tag

Torque specifications

➡ **Note: One foot-pound (ft-lb) of torque is equivalent to 12 inch-pounds (in-lbs) of torque. Torque values below approximately 15 foot-pounds are expressed in inch-pounds, because most foot-pound torque wrenches are not accurate at these smaller values.**

Condenser inlet and outlet nuts	80 in-lbs	9 Nm
Receiver drier plug	27 in-lbs	3 Nm
Thermostat housing bolts	89 in-lbs	10 Nm
Water pump fasteners		
Four-cylinder engines	89 in-lbs	10 Nm
V6 engines		
2010 and earlier models	89 in-lbs	
2011 and later models		
Step 1	89 in-lbs	
Step 2	Tighten an additional 45 degrees	
Water pump pulley bolts (2.0L)	177 in-lbs	20 Nm

Notes

4

FUEL AND EXHAUST SYSTEMS

1   General information

FUEL SYSTEM WARNINGS

Gasoline is extremely flammable and repairing fuel system components can be dangerous. Consider your automotive repair knowledge and experience before attempting repairs which may be better suited for a professional mechanic.

- *Don't smoke or allow open flames or bare light bulbs near the work area*
- *Don't work in a garage with a gas-type appliance (water heater, clothes dryer)*
- *Use fuel-resistant gloves. If any fuel spills on your skin, wash it off immediately with soap and water*
- *Clean up spills immediately*
- *Do not store fuel-soaked rags where they could ignite*
- *Prior to disconnecting any fuel line, you must relieve the fuel pressure (see Section 3)*
- *Wear safety glasses*
- *Have a proper fire extinguisher on hand*

FUEL SYSTEM

The fuel system consists of the fuel tank, electric fuel pump/fuel level sending unit (located in the fuel tank), fuel rail, fuel injectors and, on four-cylinder models, a high pressure fuel pump mounted to the end of the cylinder head. The fuel injection system is a multi-port system; multi-port fuel injection uses timed impulses to inject the fuel directly into the intake port of each cylinder. The Powertrain Control Module (PCM) controls the injectors. The PCM monitors various engine parameters and delivers the exact amount of fuel required into the intake ports.

Fuel is circulated from the fuel pump to the fuel rail through fuel lines running along the underside of the vehicle. Various sections of the fuel line are either rigid metal or nylon, or flexible fuel hose. The various sections of the fuel hose are connected either by quick-connect fittings or threaded metal fittings.

EXHAUST SYSTEM

The exhaust system consists of the exhaust manifold(s), catalytic converter(s), muffler(s), tailpipe and all connecting pipes, flanges and clamps. The catalytic converters are an emission control device added to the exhaust system to reduce pollutants.

2   Troubleshooting

ELECTRIC FUEL PUMP

▶ **Refer to illustrations 2.2 and 2.4**

1   The electric fuel pump is located inside the fuel tank. Sit inside the vehicle with the windows closed, turn the ignition key to ON (not START) and listen for the sound of the fuel pump as it's briefly activated. You will only hear the sound for a second or two, but that sound tells you that the pump is working. Alternatively, have an assistant listen at the fuel filler cap.

2   On 2010 and earlier models, if the pump does not come on, make sure that the inertia switch (see illustration) has not opened the fuel pump circuit. The inertia switch is a resettable circuit breaker that automatically opens the fuel pump circuit in the event of an accident. To access it, remove the left rear quarter trim panel (see Chapter 11).

3   On 2011 and later models, a fuel-cut off system is used in case of an accident. If there has been an accident, the restraint system sends a signal to the Fuel Pump Control Module (FPCM) and shuts the module off. To reset the FPCM, turn the ignition key to the "OFF" position, then to the "ON" position and start the engine.

➡ **Note: This may take a few attempts.**

2.2 The fuel pump inertia switch is located behind the left rear quarter panel. To reset it, push the button on top (2010 and earlier models)

4   Check the fuel pump fuse and relay (see illustration). If the fuse and relay are okay, check the wiring back to the fuel pump. If the fuse, relay, wiring and inertia switch are okay, the fuel pump is probably defective. If the pump runs continuously with the ignition key in the ON position, the Powertrain Control Module (PCM) is probably defective. Have the PCM checked by a professional mechanic.

FUEL INJECTION SYSTEM

➡ **Note: The following procedure is based on the assumption that the fuel pump is working and the fuel pressure is adequate (see Section 4).**

5   Check all electrical connectors that are related to the system. Check the ground wire connections for tightness. Verify that the battery is fully charged (see Chapter 5).
6   Inspect the air filter element (see Chapter 1).
7   Check all fuses related to the fuel system (see Chapter 12).
8   Check the air induction system between the throttle body and the intake manifold for air leaks. Also inspect the condition of all vacuum hoses connected to the intake manifold and to the throttle body.
9   Remove the air intake duct from the throttle body and look for dirt, carbon, varnish, or other residue in the throttle body, particularly around the throttle plate. If it's dirty, clean it with carb cleaner, a tooth-brush and a clean shop towel.
10 Check to see if any trouble codes are stored in the PCM (see Chapter 6).

2.4 The fuel pump fuse (A) is located in the engine compartment fuse box; (B) is the fuel pump relay (this is a 2012 model; the location of the fuse and relay varies with model and year - refer to the guide in your owner's manual)

3   Fuel pressure relief procedure

✳ **WARNING:**

Gasoline is extremely flammable. See Fuel system warnings in Section 1.

2007 MODELS

1   Disconnect the cable from the negative terminal of the battery (see Chapter 5).
2   Locate the Schrader valve test port on the left (driver's) end of the fuel rail for the front cylinder bank.
3   Connect a fuel pressure gauge (equipped with a bleed-off hose) to the Schrader valve.
4   Direct the bleed-off hose into an approved fuel container, then open the bleed-off valve. When the flow of fuel ceases, the pressure is relieved.

2008 THROUGH 2010 MODELS

5   Disconnect the electrical connector from the fuel pump inertia switch (see illustration 2.2).
6   Start the engine an allow it to run until it dies.
7   After the engine stalls, crank it over for a few more seconds to make sure the pressure has been relieved.
8   Disconnect the cable from the negative terminal of the battery before working on the fuel system (see Chapter 5).

2011 AND LATER MODELS

▶ **Refer to illustration 3.10**

9   Raise the rear of the vehicle and support it securely on jackstands. Remove the undervehicle panel from in front of the left rear wheel.
10 Disconnect the Fuel Pump Control Module (FPCM) electrical connector (see illustration).

3.10 Disconnect the Fuel Pump Control Module (FPCM) electrical connector (2011 and later models)

3.14 Loosen the high pressure fuel tube with a flare-nut wrench while covering it with a shop towel

11 Start the engine and allow to idle until the engine stalls, then crank the engine a few times to make sure all the pressure is released.

12 Disconnect the cable from the negative terminal of the battery

before working on the fuel system (see Chapter 5).

✳ CAUTION:

On four-cylinder models, the fuel pressure must also be released from the high pressure fuel pump prior to disconnecting any fuel lines in the delivery or low pressure system (see Steps 13 through 15).

HIGH PRESSURE FUEL PUMP PRESSURE RELEASE (FOUR-CYLINDER MODELS ONLY)

▶ **Refer to illustration 3.14**

13 Relieve the fuel system pressure (see Steps 9 through 12).

14 Place a flare nut wrench on the high pressure fuel tube (see illustration), then wrap the wrench and nut with a shop towel to absorb any remaining fuel pressure while loosening the nut.

15 Loosen the high pressure fuel tube-to-fuel injection pump flare nut and release the remaining pressure.

4 Fuel pressure - check

▶ **Refer to illustrations 4.1 and 4.3**

✳ WARNING:

Gasoline is extremely flammable. See Fuel system warnings in Section 1.

➡ **Note: The following procedure assumes that the fuel pump is receiving voltage and runs.**

1 A fuel pressure gauge, with the proper adapter(s) and capable of

reading fuel pressures within the range listed in this Chapter's Specifications, will be required (see illustration).

2 On 2007 models, locate the fuel pressure test port on the fuel rail, unscrew the cap and connect a fuel pressure gauge.

3 On 2008 and later models, relieve the fuel system pressure (see Section 3), detach the fuel feed line from the fuel rail (V6 models) or from the high-pressure fuel pump (four-cylinder models) (see illustration) and tee-in the fuel pressure gauge using the proper adapters.

4 Start the engine and allow it to idle. Note the gauge reading as soon as the pressure stabilizes, and compare it with the pressure listed in this Chapter's Specifications.

4.1 This fuel pressure testing kit contains all the necessary fittings and adapters, along with the fuel pressure gauge, to test most automotive systems

4.3 On four-cylinder models, detach the fuel feed line from the high-pressure fuel pump and connect a fuel pressure gauge between the line and the pump

5   If the fuel pressure is not within specifications:
  a) *Check for a restriction in the fuel system (kinked fuel line, plugged fuel pump inlet strainer or clogged fuel filter). If no restrictions are found, replace the fuel pump module (see Section 7).*
  b) *If the fuel pressure is higher than specified, replace the fuel pump module (see Section 7).*

6   Turn off the engine. Fuel pressure should not fall more than 8 psi over five minutes. If it does, the problem could be a leaky fuel injector, fuel line leak, or faulty fuel pump module.
7   Relieve the fuel system pressure (2008 and later models). Disconnect the fuel pressure gauge. Wipe up any spilled gasoline.

5   Fuel lines and fittings - general information and disconnection

✳ WARNING:

Gasoline is extremely flammable. See Fuel system warnings in Section 1.

1   Relieve the fuel pressure before servicing fuel lines or fittings (see Section 3), then disconnect the cable from the negative battery terminal (see Chapter 5) before proceeding.
2   The fuel supply line connects the fuel pump in the fuel tank to the fuel rail on the engine. The Evaporative emission (EVAP) system lines connect the fuel tank to the EVAP canister and connect the canister to the intake manifold.
3   Whenever you're working under the vehicle, be sure to inspect all fuel and evaporative emission lines for leaks, kinks, dents and other damage. Always replace a damaged fuel or EVAP line immediately.
4   If you find signs of dirt in the lines during disassembly, disconnect all lines and blow them out with compressed air. Inspect the fuel strainer on the fuel pump pick-up unit for damage and deterioration.

STEEL TUBING

5   It is critical that the fuel lines be replaced with lines of equivalent type and specification.
6   Some steel fuel lines have threaded fittings. When loosening these fittings, hold the stationary fitting with a wrench while turning the tube nut.

PLASTIC TUBING

7   When replacing fuel system plastic tubing, use only original equipment replacement plastic tubing.

✳ CAUTION:

When removing or installing plastic fuel line tubing, be careful not to bend or twist it too much, which can damage it. Also, plastic fuel tubing is NOT heat resistant, so keep it away from excessive heat.

FLEXIBLE HOSES

8   When replacing fuel system flexible hoses, use only original equipment replacements.
9   Don't route fuel hoses (or metal lines) within four inches of the exhaust system or within ten inches of the catalytic converter. Make sure that no rubber hoses are installed directly against the vehicle, particularly in places where there is any vibration. If allowed to touch some vibrating part of the vehicle, a hose can easily become chafed and it might start leaking. A good rule of thumb is to maintain a minimum of 1/4-inch clearance around a hose (or metal line) to prevent contact with the vehicle underbody.

Disconnecting Fuel Line Fittings

Two-tab type fitting; depress both tabs with your fingers, then pull the fuel line and the fitting apart

On this type of fitting, depress the two buttons on opposite sides of the fitting, then pull it off the fuel line

Threaded fuel line fitting; hold the stationary portion of the line or component (A) while loosening the tube nut (B) with a flare-nut wrench

Plastic collar-type fitting; rotate the outer part of the fitting

Metal collar quick-connect fitting; pull the end of the retainer off the fuel line, and disengage the other end from the female side of the fitting . . .

. . . insert a fuel line separator tool into the female side of the fitting, push it into the fitting until it releases the locking tabs inside the fitting, and pull the two halves of the fitting apart

Hairpin-type clip; spread the two legs of the clip apart . . .

. . . pull the clip out and detach the coupling from the component (fitting detached for clarity)

Spring-lock coupling; remove the safety cover . . .

. . . install a coupling release tool and close the clamshell halves of the tool around the coupling . . .

. . . push the tool into the fitting, then pull the two lines apart

6 Exhaust system servicing - general information

▶ Refer to illustration 6.1

✳ WARNING:

Allow exhaust system components to cool before inspection or repair. Also, when working under the vehicle, make sure it is securely supported on jackstands.

1   The exhaust system consists of the exhaust manifolds, catalytic converter, muffler, tailpipe and all connecting pipes, flanges and clamps. The exhaust system is isolated from the vehicle body and from chassis components by a series of rubber hangers (see illustration). Periodically inspect these hangers for cracks or other signs of deterioration, replacing them as necessary.

➡ **Note: On 2011 and later V6 models, the front manifold and front catalytic converter have been combined into a single unit.**

2   Conduct regular inspections of the exhaust system to keep it safe and quiet. Look for any damaged or bent parts, open seams, holes, loose connections, excessive corrosion or other defects which could allow exhaust fumes to enter the vehicle. Do not repair deteriorated exhaust system components; replace them with new parts.

3   If the exhaust system components are extremely corroded, or rusted together, a cutting torch is the most convenient tool for removal. Consult a properly-equipped repair shop. If a cutting torch is not available, you can use a hacksaw, or if you have compressed air, there are special pneumatic cutting chisels that can also be used. Wear safety goggles to protect your eyes from metal chips and wear work gloves to protect your hands.

4   Here are some simple guidelines to follow when repairing the exhaust system:

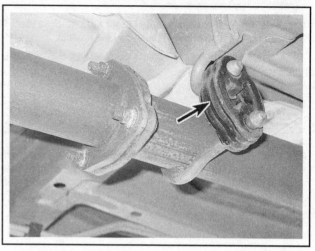

6.1 A typical exhaust system hanger. Inspect regularly and replace at the first sign of damage or deterioration

a) Work from the back to the front when removing exhaust system components.
b) Apply penetrating oil to the exhaust system component fasteners to make them easier to remove.
c) Use new gaskets, hangers and clamps.
d) Apply anti-seize compound to the threads of all exhaust system fasteners during reassembly.
e) Be sure to allow sufficient clearance between newly installed parts and all points on the underbody to avoid overheating the floor pan and possibly damaging the interior carpet and insulation. Pay particularly close attention to the catalytic converter and heat shield.

7 Fuel pump module - removal and installation

✳ WARNING:

Gasoline is extremely flammable. See Fuel system warnings in Section 1.

FUEL PUMP MODULE

▶ Refer to illustration 7.3

➡ **Note: The fuel pump module includes the fuel pump, the fuel level sending unit and a fuel filter. The fuel level sending unit is the only item that can be serviced separately.**

➡ **Note: On AWD models, a fuel level sending unit is mounted on the fuel pump module in the driver's side of the fuel tank, and a separate fuel level sensor is located in the passenger's side of the fuel tank.**

1   Relieve the fuel system pressure (see Section 3). Disconnect the cable from the negative battery terminal (see Chapter 5).
2   Remove the fuel tank (see Section 8).
3   Remove the pump module lock ring using a lock ring removal

7.3 Using a brass punch and a hammer to unscrew the fuel pump module lock ring

tool (manufacturer tool no. 310-123, or equivalent) or tap the fuel pump module lock ring counterclockwise with a hammer and brass punch (to avoid sparks) (see illustration).

4   Carefully pull the fuel pump module out of the tank enough to

disconnect the fuel vapor hose quick-connect fitting, and separate the hose. Lift the module out of tank completely, angling it as necessary to protect the fuel level sensor float arm.

➡ **Note: On AWD models, the fuel vapor hose quick connect fitting and line are located at the base of the module.**

5 Inspect the O-ring and replace it if it shows any sign of deterioration.

6 Installation is the reverse of removal.

FUEL LEVEL SENDING UNIT

➡ **Note: On AWD models, two fuel level sensors are used; one is mounted on the fuel pump module in the driver's side of the fuel tank, and a separate fuel level sensor is located in the passenger's side of the fuel tank.**

7 Remove the fuel pump module (see Steps 1 through 4).

8 Press the locking tab inwards and slide the fuel level sender up and off of the sensor.

9 Installation is the reverse of removal.

FUEL LEVEL SENSOR (AWD MODELS)

10 Remove the fuel tank (see Section 8).

11 Remove the lock ring using a lock ring removal tool (#310-123) or tap the lock ring counterclockwise with a hammer and brass punch (to avoid sparks) (see illustration 7.3).

12 Pull the fuel level sensor out of the tank, disconnect the fuel hose quick-connect fitting, and separate the hose. Lift the module out of tank completely, angling it as necessary to protect the fuel level sensor float arm.

13 Inspect the O-ring and replace it if it shows any sign of deterioration.

14 Installation is the reverse of removal.

8 Fuel tank - removal and installation

▶ **Refer to illustrations 8.7, 8.8 and 8.9**

✳✳ **WARNING:**

Gasoline is extremely flammable. See Fuel system warnings in Section 1.

➡ **Note: The following procedure is much easier to perform if the fuel tank is empty.**

1 Remove the fuel tank filler cap to relieve fuel tank pressure.

2 Relieve the fuel system pressure (see Section 3).

3 Disconnect the cable from the negative battery terminal (see Chapter 5).

4 Raise the rear of the vehicle and support it securely on jackstands.

5 On AWD models, remove the driveshaft (see Chapter 8).

6 Remove the rear portion of the exhaust system.

7 Disconnect the EVAP and fuel supply line quick-connect fittings (see illustration).

8 Loosen the hose clamp and disconnect the fuel filler neck hose from the tank (see illustration). Also disconnect the fuel pump module electrical connector.

9 Support the fuel tank securely, then remove the fuel tank retaining strap bolts (see illustration). Remove the straps and carefully lower the fuel tank.

➡ **Note: On AWD models, the fuel tank must be moved forward as it is lowered to clear the rear differential.**

10 Installation is the reverse of removal. Tighten the fuel tank strap bolts securely.

11 Reconnect the cable to the negative battery terminal (see Chapter 5), then start the engine and check for fuel leaks.

8.7 Fuel supply line (A) and EVAP hose (B) quick-connect fittings

8.8 EVAP vapor hose quick-connect fitting (A) and fuel tank filler neck hose clamp (B)

8.9 Fuel tank strap bolts

9 Air filter housing - removal and installation

AIR INTAKE DUCT

1   Disconnect the PCV fresh air hose from the air intake duct.
2   On four-cylinder models, loosen the clamp at the air intake duct and the charge air cooler inlet tube and remove the intake duct.
3   On V6 models, loosen the clamps at the air filter housing and the throttle body and remove the air intake duct.
4   Installation is the reverse of removal.

AIR FILTER HOUSING

5   Remove the air intake duct.
6   Disconnect the electrical connector from the MAF sensor (see Chapter 6).
7   Remove the air filter housing cover and filter element.
8   Pull up on the housing to detach the locating pins from the grommets.
9   Inspect the condition of the filter housing mounting grommets. If they're cracked, torn or deteriorated, replace them.
10 Installation is the reverse of removal.

10 Throttle body - removal and installation

▶ **Refer to illustrations 10.3 and 10.6**

✳ WARNING:

Wait until the engine is completely cool before beginning this procedure.

1   Disconnect the cable from the negative battery terminal (see Chapter 5).
2   Remove the air intake duct (see Section 9).
3   On four-cylinder models, loosen the clamp and remove the charge air cooler pipe from the throttle body (see illustration).
4   Disconnect the electrical connector from the throttle body.
5   On V6 models, disconnect the fuel vapor line retainer from the side of the throttle body.
6   Remove the throttle body mounting fasteners and detach the throttle body from the intake manifold (see illustration). Discard the gasket; it should be replaced with a new one. Cover the intake manifold opening with a clean shop towel.
7   Installation is the reverse of removal. Use a new gasket and tighten the throttle body fasteners to the torque listed in this Chapter's Specifications.

10.3 Loosen the charge air cooler pipe clamp (four-cylinder model)

10.6 Throttle body mounting fasteners (four-cylinder model shown) - manifold removed for clarity

11 Fuel rail and injectors - removal and installation

✳ WARNING:

Gasoline is extremely flammable. See Fuel system warnings in Section 1.

1   Relieve the fuel system pressure (see Section 3).
2   Disconnect the cable from the negative battery terminal (see Chapter 5).

FOUR-CYLINDER MODELS

▶ **Refer to illustrations 11.7, 11.10, 11.15, 11.16, 11.17a, 11.17b and 11.18**

3   Remove the intake manifold (see Chapter 2A). Remove the drive-belt, then unbolt the power steering pump and position it aside (don't disconnect the hoses) (see Chapter 10).
4   Disconnect the high pressure fuel lines from the fuel pump and fuel rail (see Section 12).

➡ **Note: The manufacturer recommends replacing the fuel lines anytime they are removed.**

5   Disconnect the electrical connectors for all wiring that shares the harness with the fuel injectors, then disconnect the four fuel injector electrical connectors. Using a trim removal tool, disengage the two pin-type retainers that secure the wiring harness and harness insulator from the fuel rail, then push the harness aside.
6   Clean the area around each injector using compressed air.
7   Remove the fuel rail mounting fasteners (see illustration) and discard them, then remove the fuel rail and injectors. Make sure to use new fuel rail bolts on installation.

➡ **Note: The fuel injectors may remain in the fuel rails when the rail is removed, but normally they remain in the cylinder heads and require the use of a removal tool.**

8   Remove each fuel injector retaining clip with a pair of needle-nose pliers, then remove the injector from its bore in the fuel rail. Remove and discard the upper injector O-rings. Repeat this procedure for each injector.

➡ **Note: Even if you only removed the fuel rail assembly to replace a single injector or a leaking O-ring, replace all of the fuel injector retaining clips and O-rings.**

9   If any injectors stick in the cylinder head, use special tool #310-206 attached to a slide hammer to remove the injector(s).
10   Remove the old combustion chamber Teflon sealing ring, upper O-ring and support ring from each injector (see illustration).

✳ CAUTION:

Be extremely careful not to damage the groove for the seal or the rib in the floor of the groove. If you damage the groove or the rib, you must replace the injector.

11   Before installing the new Teflon seal on each injector, thoroughly clean the groove for the seal and the injector shaft. Remove all combustion residue and varnish with a clean shop rag.

Teflon seal installation using the special tools

12   The manufacturer recommends that you use the tools included in the special injector tool set to install the Teflon lower seals on the injectors: Install the special seal assembly cone on the injector, install the special sleeve on the injector and use the sleeve to push on the assembly cone, which pushes the Teflon seal into place on its groove. Do NOT use any lubricants to do so.
13   Pushing the Teflon seal into place in its groove expands it slightly. There are three sizing sleeves in the special tool set with progressively smaller inside diameters. Using a clockwise rotating motion of about 180 degrees, install the slightly larger sleeve onto the injector and over the Teflon seal until the sleeve hits its stop, then carefully turn the sleeve counterclockwise as you pull it off the injector. Use the slightly smaller sizing sleeve the same way, followed by the smallest sizing ring. The seal is now sized. Repeat this step for each injector.

Teflon seal installation without special tools

14   If you don't have the special injector tool set, the Teflon seal can be installed using this method: First, find a socket that is equal or very close in diameter to the diameter of the end of the fuel injector.

11.7 Fuel rail mounting bolts (four-cylinder models)

11.10 To remove the Teflon sealing ring, cut it off with a hobby knife (be careful not to scratch the injector groove)

15 Work the new Teflon seal onto the end of the socket (see illustration).

16 Place the socket against the end of the injector (see illustration) and slide the seal from the socket onto the injector. Do NOT use any lubricants to do so. Continue pushing the seal onto the injector until it seats into its mounting groove.

17 Because the inside diameter of the seal has to be stretched open to fit over the bore of the socket and the injector, its outside diameter is now slightly too large - it is no longer flush with the surface of the injector. It must be shrunk back to its original size. To do so, push a piece of plastic tubing with an interference fit onto the end of the socket; a plastic straw that fits tightly on the injector will work. After pushing the plastic tubing onto the socket about an inch, snip off the rest of the tubing, then use the socket to push the tubing onto the end of the injector (see illustration), sliding it onto the injector until it completely covers the new seal (see illustration). Leave the tubing on for a few hours, then remove it. The seal should now be shrunk back its original outside diameter, or close to it.

Injector and fuel rail installation

18 Install a new support ring on the top of the injector, then lubricate the new upper O-ring with clean engine oil and install it on the injector. Do NOT oil the new Teflon seal. Note that the O-ring is installed above the support ring (see illustration).

19 Thoroughly clean the injector bores with a small nylon brush.

20 Insert each injector into its bore in the fuel rail. Install the new retaining clips on the injectors.

21 Install the injectors and fuel rail assembly on the cylinder head. Tighten the fuel rail mounting fasteners to the torque listed in this Chapter's Specifications, starting with the center bolt and working outwards.

22 The remainder of installation is the reverse of removal.

23 If removed, install a new fuel rail pressure sensor (see Chapter 6).

V6 MODELS

▶ **Refer to illustrations 11.29 and 11.30**

24 Remove the upper intake manifold (see Chapter 2B).

25 Disconnect the fuel supply line at the fuel rail (see "Disconnecting Fuel Line Fittings").

26 Disconnect the electrical connector from each fuel injector.

11.15 Slide the new Teflon seal onto the end of a socket that's the same diameter as the end of the fuel injector . . .

11.16 . . . align the socket with the end of the injector and slide the seal onto the injector and into its mounting groove

11.17a Use the socket to push a short section of plastic tubing onto the end of the injector and over the new seal . . .

11.17b . . . then leave the plastic tubing in place for several hours to compress the new seal

11.18 Note that the upper O-ring (1) is installed *above* the support ring (2)

11.29 Before removing the injector retaining clips, note how they're installed to ensure that they're correctly reinstalled

11.30 Injector O-rings

27 Detach the three pin-type retainers from the fuel rail, push the wiring harness aside and remove the other three injector electrical connectors.

28 Remove the four fuel rail mounting bolts, then remove the fuel rail and injectors as a single assembly.

29 Release the fuel injector retaining clip (see illustration) and remove each injector from its bore in the fuel rail.

30 Remove and discard the upper and lower injector O-rings (see illustration) from each injector.

➡ Note: Even if you only removed the fuel rail assembly to replace a single injector or a leaking O-ring, it's a good idea to remove all of the injectors from the fuel rail and replace all of the O-rings at the same time.

31 Coat the new upper O-rings with clean engine oil and slide them into place on each of the fuel injectors. Coat the new lower O-rings with clean engine oil and install them on the lower ends of the injectors.

32 Coat the outside surface of each upper O-ring with clean engine oil, then insert each injector into its bore in the fuel rail. Secure the injectors to the fuel rail with the injector retaining clips.

33 On all models, tighten the fuel rail bolts securely. The remainder of installation is the reverse of removal.

34 Reconnect the cable to the negative battery terminal (see Chapter 5), then turn the ignition switch to ON (but don't operate the starter). This activates the fuel pump for about two seconds, which builds up fuel pressure in the fuel lines and the fuel rail. Repeat this step two or three times, then check the fuel lines, fuel rails and injectors for fuel leaks.

12 High-pressure fuel pump (four-cylinder engine) – removal and installation

✳✳ WARNING:

Gasoline is extremely flammable. See Fuel system warnings in Section 1.

REMOVAL

▶ Refer to illustrations 12.4 and 12.9

1 Relieve the fuel system pressure (see Section 3).

2 Disconnect the cable from the negative battery terminal (see Chapter 5).

3 Remove the air filter housing intake duct.

4 Disconnect the fuel injection pump electrical connector (see illustration).

5 Carefully remove the pump insulator from around the outside of the pump (see illustration 12.4).

6 Disconnect the quick disconnect line and remove the fuel line to the fuel pump.

12.4 Disconnect the electrical connector (A), then remove the insulator (B) from the high-pressure fuel pump

12.9 High-pressure fuel pump details

1   Fuel feed line
2   High-pressure fuel line
3   Fuel pump mounting bolts

12.11 Check the high-pressure fuel pump tappet for wear (A). Install a new O-ring (B) on the pump

12.13 The cam lobe (and tappet) must be at its lowest point before installing the pump

7   Loosen then remove the fuel lines using a flare nut wrench.

➡ **Note: The manufacturer recommends replacing the fuel line anytime they are removed.**

8   Slide the heater hose clip forward then up to expose the fuel pump shield bolts. Remove the shield bolts and shield.

9   Loosen the fuel pump bolts (see illustration), alternating one turn at a time until the bolts and pump can be removed. The bolts must be replaced after they have be removed.

❈ **CAUTION:**

The fuel pump is under extreme pressure - if the bolts are not loosened evenly and one complete turn at a time the pump or housing will be damaged.

10 Remove and discard the fuel pump O-ring.

INSTALLATION

▶ **Refer to illustrations 12.11 and 12.13**

11 Before installing the fuel injection pump, check the pump tappet in the pump body for wear or damage (see illustration).

12 Install a new O-ring on the pump, then apply clean oil to the pump tappet and the O-ring.

13 Rotate the engine until the cam lobe for the fuel injection pump is on the lowest point or Bottom Dead Center (BDC) (see illustration). The pump tappet will be as low as it can go.

14 Set the pump in the housing, then install the *new* bolts hand tight.

15 Tighten the bolts in even stages, alternating between the bolts, to the torque listed in this Chapter's Specifications.

16 The remainder of installation is the reverse of removal.

13 Charge air cooler - removal and installation

▶ **Refer to illustrations 13.3a, 13.3b and 13.4**

❈ **CAUTION:**

Whenever the turbocharger, charge air cooler or cooler tubes are removed always cover any opening to prevent debris from falling in. The system is easily damaged, so carefully clean all openings before reassembling.

1   Remove the cooling fan shroud (see Chapter 3).

2   Remove the Manifold Absolute Pressure Temperature (MAPT) sensor (see Chapter 6).

3   Loosen the clamps securing the inlet and outlet tubes to the charge air cooler (see illustrations), then disconnect the tubes.

4   Remove the charge air cooler bolts (see illustration). Slide the cooler to the left while pulling the left side out and carefully remove the cooler from the vehicle.

5   Installation is the reverse of removal.

13.3a Disconnect the charge air cooler inlet tube . . .

13.3b . . . and the outlet tube clamps

13.4 The charge air cooler is secured by two bolts on each end (left side shown)

14 Turbocharger - removal and installation

✳✳ WARNING:

Wait until the engine is completely cool before beginning this procedure.

✳✳ CAUTION:

Do not disassemble the turbocharger or try to adjust the wastgate actuator. The turbocharger or possibly even the engine could be damaged.

✳✳ CAUTION:

Whenever the turbocharger, charge air cooler or cooler tubes are removed, always cover any opening to prevent debris from falling in. The system is easily damaged, so carefully clean all openings before reassembling.

▶ Refer to illustrations 14.5, 14.6a, 14.6b, 14.7a, 14.7b, 14.8, 14.10 and 14.11

REMOVAL

1   Raise the vehicle and support it securely on jackstands.
2   Remove the catalytic converter (see Chapter 6).

14.5 Remove the turbocharger heat shield mounting bolts

3   Remove the charge air cooler inlet tube (see Section 13) and the turbocharger ivnlet pipe.
4   Drain the cooling system (see Chapter 1).
5   Remove the turbocharger heat shield mounting bolts and remove the shield (see illustration).
6   From above, squeeze and slide back the hose clamps on the coolant line (see illustration). From below, remove the coolant outlet

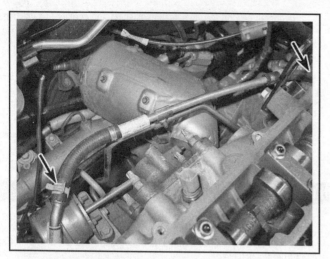

14.6a Detach the hoses at each end of the coolant pipe

14.6b Disconnect the coolant outlet line from the turbocharger and the engine block

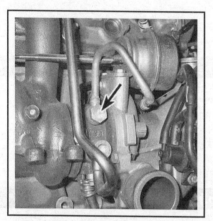

14.7a Remove the oil supply line banjo bolt and detach the line from the turbocharger . . .

14.7b . . . then remove this banjo bolt (A) from the other end of the oil line. Detach the line from the block, then pull out the filter and install a new one. (B) are coolant lines

14.10 Turbocharger oil drain tube bolts

line banjo bolt and disconnect the line from the turbocharger (see illustration).

➡ **Note: Always replace the linked sealing washers to the banjo bolts and coolant lines.**

7   Remove the oil supply line banjo bolts and discard the sealing washers (see illustrations), then pull the inline oil supply filter out of the engine block and replace it with a new one.

8   Disconnect the vacuum lines and electrical connectors to the turbocharger.

9   Detach the coolant lines from the right end of the turbocharger (see illustration 14.6b).

10   Remove the oil drain tube mounting bolts and drain tube, then discard the gasket and drain tube (see illustration).

➡ **Note: The factory requires the oil drain tube be replaced whenever it is removed.**

11   Remove and discard the turbocharger mounting nuts (see illustration), then carefully maneuver the turbocharger from the vehicle.

12   Use a stud removal tool (available from most auto parts stores) to remove the turbocharger studs from the cylinder head. Discard the studs.

14.11 Remove the turbocharger mounting nuts

INSTALLATION

13 Install the four new studs in the cylinder head.

14 Install the turbocharger and tighten the new nuts to the torque listed in this Chapter's Specifications.

15 Install the new oil drain tube and new drain tube gaskets, then install and tighten the bolts to the torque listed in this Chapter's Specifications.

16 Install new oil feed line sealing washers and coolant line washers. Tighten the banjo bolts to the torque listed in this Chapter's Specifications.

17 The remainder of installation is the reverse of removal.

18 Refill the cooling system and change the engine oil and filter (see Chapter 1).

15 Fuel pump control module - removal and installation

1 Raise the rear of the vehicle and support it securely on jackstands. Remove the undervehicle panel from in front of the left rear wheel.

2 Disconnect the electrical connector from the fuel pump control module (see illustration 3.10).

3 Remove the control module mounting bolts and detach the module from the vehicle.

4 Installation is the reverse of removal.

Specifications

General

Fuel system pressure (approximate, while running)	
2.0L engine	55 to 75 psi (380 to 520 kPa)
3.5L and 3.7L engines	65 psi (450 kPa)

Torque specifications	Ft-lbs (unless otherwise indicated)	Nm

➡ **Note: One foot-pound (ft-lb) of torque is equivalent to 12 inch-pounds (in-lbs) of torque. Torque values below approximately 15 ft-lbs are expressed in inch-pounds, since most foot-pound torque wrenches are not accurate at these smaller values.**

Throttle body mounting fasteners	89 in-lbs	10
Fuel rail mounting bolts		
Four-cylinder models		
Step 1	71 in-lbs	8
Step 2	Tighten an additional 26-degrees	
V6 models	89 in-lbs	10
High-pressure fuel pump mounting bolts (four-cylinder)		
Step 1	44 in-lbs	5
Step 2	Tighten an additional 55-degrees	
High-pressure fuel tube flare nuts (four-cylinder)		
Step 1	133 in-lbs	15
Step 2	Tighten an additional 30-degrees	
High-pressure fuel tube bracket bolts (four-cylinder)	89 in-lbs	10
Turbocharger		
Coolant line banjo bolts	21	28
Oil line banjo bolts	18	25
Oil drain tube bolts	89 in-lbs	10
Turbocharger mounting studs	150 in-lbs	17
Turbocharger mounting nuts	37	50

Section

5

ENGINE ELECTRICAL SYSTEMS

1 General information and precautions

GENERAL INFORMATION

Ignition system

The electronic ignition system consists of the Crankshaft Position (CKP) sensor, the Camshaft Position (CMP) sensor, the Knock Sensor (KS), the Powertrain Control Module (PCM), the ignition switch, the battery, the individual ignition coils, and the spark plugs. For more information on the CKP, CMP and KS sensors, as well as the PCM, refer to Chapter 6.

Charging system

The charging system includes the alternator (with an integral voltage regulator), the Powertrain Control Module (PCM), the Body Control Module (BCM), a charge indicator light on the dash, the battery, a fuse or fusible link and the wiring connecting all of these components. The charging system supplies electrical power for the ignition system, the lights, the radio, etc. The alternator is driven by a drivebelt.

Starting system

The starting system consists of the battery, the ignition switch, the starter relay, the Powertrain Control Module (PCM), the Body Control Module (BCM), the Transmission Range (TR) switch, the starter motor and solenoid assembly, and the wiring connecting all of the components.

PRECAUTIONS

Always observe the following precautions when working on the electrical system:

a) *Be extremely careful when servicing engine electrical components. They are easily damaged if checked, connected or handled improperly.*
b) *Never leave the ignition switched on for long periods of time when the engine is not running.*
c) *Never disconnect the battery cables while the engine is running.*
d) *Maintain correct polarity when connecting battery cables from another vehicle during jump starting - see the "Booster battery (jump) starting" Section at the front of this manual.*
e) *Always disconnect the cable from the negative battery terminal before working on the electrical system, but read the battery disconnection procedure first (see Section 3).*

It's also a good idea to review the safety-related information regarding the engine electrical systems located in the "Safety first!" Section at the front of this manual before beginning any operation included in this Chapter.

2 Troubleshooting

IGNITION SYSTEM

1   If a malfunction occurs in the ignition system, do not immediately assume that any particular part is causing the problem. First, check the following items:

a) *Make sure that the cable clamps at the battery terminals are clean and tight.*
b) *Test the condition of the battery (see Steps 21 through 24). If it doesn't pass all the tests, replace it.*

c) *Check the ignition coil or coil pack connections.*
d) *Check any relevant fuses in the engine compartment fuse and relay box (see Chapter 12). If they're burned, determine the cause and repair the circuit.*

Check

▶ **Refer to illustration 2.3**

❊❊ WARNING:

Because of the high voltage generated by the ignition system, use extreme care when performing a procedure involving ignition components.

➡ **Note 1: The ignition system components on these vehicles are difficult to diagnose. In the event of ignition system failure that you can't diagnose, have the vehicle tested at a dealer service department or other qualified auto repair facility.**

➡ **Note 2: You'll need a spark tester for the following test. Spark testers are available at most auto supply stores.**

2   If the engine turns over but won't start, verify that there is sufficient ignition voltage to fire the spark plugs as follows.

3   On models with a coil-over-plug type ignition system, remove a coil and install the tester between the boot at the lower end of the coil and the spark plug (see illustration). On models with spark plug wires, disconnect a spark plug wire from a spark plug and install the tester between the spark plug wire boot and the spark plug.

2.3 Spark tester

4 Crank the engine and note whether or not the tester flashes.

> ☀☀ **CAUTION:**
>
> **Do NOT crank the engine or allow it to run for more than five seconds; running the engine for more than five seconds may set a Diagnostic Trouble Code (DTC) for a cylinder misfire.**

Models with a coil-over-plug type ignition system

5 If the tester flashes during cranking, the coil is delivering sufficient voltage to the spark plug to fire it. Repeat this test for each cylinder to verify that the other coils are OK.

6 If the tester doesn't flash, remove a coil from another cylinder and swap it for the one being tested. If the tester now flashes, you know that the original coil is bad. If the tester still doesn't flash, the PCM or wiring harness is probably defective. Have the PCM checked out by a dealer service department or other qualified repair shop (testing the PCM is beyond the scope of the do-it-yourselfer because it requires expensive special tools).

7 If the tester flashes during cranking but a misfire code (related to the cylinder being tested) has been stored, the spark plug could be fouled or defective.

Models with spark plug wires

8 If the tester flashes during cranking, sufficient voltage is reaching the spark plug to fire it.

9 Repeat this test on the remaining cylinders.

10 Proceed on this basis until you have verified that there's a good spark from each spark plug wire. If there is, then you have verified that the coils in the coil pack are functioning correctly and that the spark plug wires are OK.

11 If there is no spark from a spark plug wire, then either the coil is bad, the plug wire is bad or a connection at one end of the plug wire is loose. Assuming that you're using new plug wires or known good wires, then the coil is probably defective. Also inspect the coil pack electrical connector. Make sure that it's clean, tight and in good condition.

12 If all the coils are firing correctly, but the engine misfires, then one or more of the plugs might be fouled. Remove and check the spark plugs or install new ones (see Chapter 1).

13 No further testing of the ignition system is possible without special tools. If the problem persists, have the ignition system tested by a dealer service department or other qualified repair shop.

CHARGING SYSTEM

14 If a malfunction occurs in the charging system, do not automatically assume the alternator is causing the problem. First check the following items:

a) *Check the drivebelt tension and condition, as described in Chapter 1. Replace it if it's worn or deteriorated.*

b) *Make sure the alternator mounting bolts are tight.*

c) *Inspect the alternator wiring harness and the connectors at the alternator and voltage regulator. They must be in good condition, tight and have no corrosion.*

d) *Check the fusible link (if equipped) or main fuse in the underhood fuse/relay box. If it is burned, determine the cause, repair the circuit and replace the link or fuse (the vehicle will not start and/or the accessories will not work if the fusible link or main fuse is blown).*

e) *Start the engine and check the alternator for abnormal noises (a shrieking or squealing sound indicates a bad bearing).*

f) *Check the battery. Make sure it's fully charged and in good condition (one bad cell in a battery can cause overcharging by the alternator).*

g) *Disconnect the battery cables (negative first, then positive). Inspect the battery posts and the cable clamps for corrosion. Clean them thoroughly if necessary (see Chapter 1). Reconnect the cables (positive first, negative last).*

Alternator - check

15 Use a voltmeter to check the battery voltage with the engine off. It should be at least 12.6 volts (see illustration 2.21).

16 Start the engine and check the battery voltage again. It should now be approximately 13.5 to 15 volts.

17 If the voltage reading is more or less than the specified charging voltage, the voltage regulator is probably defective, which will require replacement of the alternator (the voltage regulator is not replaceable separately). Remove the alternator and have it bench tested (most auto parts stores will do this for you).

18 The charging system (battery) light on the instrument cluster lights up when the ignition key is turned to ON, but it should go out when the engine starts.

19 If the charging system light stays on after the engine has been started, there is a problem with the charging system. Before replacing the alternator, check the battery condition, alternator belt tension and electrical cable connections.

20 If replacing the alternator doesn't restore voltage to the specified range, have the charging system tested by a dealer service department or other qualified repair shop.

Battery - check

◆ **Refer to illustrations 2.21 and 2.23**

21 Check the battery state of charge. Visually inspect the indicator eye on the top of the battery (if equipped with one); if the indicator eye is black in color, charge the battery as described in Chapter 1. Next perform an open circuit voltage test using a digital voltmeter.

➡ **Note: The battery's surface charge must be removed before accurate voltage measurements can be made. Turn on the high beams for ten seconds, then turn them off and let the vehicle stand for two minutes.**

2.21 To test the open circuit voltage of the battery, touch the black probe of the voltmeter to the negative terminal and the red probe to the positive terminal of the battery; a fully charged battery should be at least 12.6 volts

With the engine and all accessories Off, touch the negative probe of the voltmeter to the negative terminal of the battery and the positive probe to the positive terminal of the battery (see illustration). The battery voltage should be 12.6 volts or slightly above. If the battery is less than the specified voltage, charge the battery before proceeding to the next test. Do not proceed with the battery load test unless the battery charge is correct.

22 Disconnect the negative battery cable, then the positive cable from the battery.

23 Perform a battery load test. An accurate check of the battery condition can only be performed with a load tester (see illustration). This test evaluates the ability of the battery to operate the starter and other accessories during periods of high current draw. Connect the load tester to the battery terminals. Load test the battery according to the tool manufacturer's instructions. This tool increases the load demand (current draw) on the battery.

24 Maintain the load on the battery for 15 seconds and observe that the battery voltage does not drop below 9.6 volts. If the battery condition is weak or defective, the tool will indicate this condition immediately.

➡ Note: Cold temperatures will cause the minimum voltage reading to drop slightly. Follow the chart given in the manufacturer's instructions to compensate for cold climates. Minimum load voltage for freezing temperatures (32 degrees F) should be approximately 9.1 volts.

STARTING SYSTEM

The starter rotates, but the engine doesn't

25 Remove the starter (see Section 8). Check the overrunning clutch and bench test the starter to make sure the drive mechanism extends fully for proper engagement with the flywheel ring gear. If it doesn't, replace the starter.

26 Check the flywheel ring gear for missing teeth and other damage. With the ignition turned off, rotate the flywheel so you can check the entire ring gear.

The starter is noisy

27 If the solenoid is making a chattering noise, first check the battery (see Steps 21 through 24). If the battery is okay, check the cables and connections.

28 If you hear a grinding, crashing metallic sound when you turn the key to Start, check for loose starter mounting bolts. If they're tight, remove the starter and inspect the teeth on the starter pinion gear and flywheel ring gear. Look for missing or damaged teeth.

29 If the starter sounds fine when you first turn the key to Start, but then stops rotating the engine and emits a zinging sound, the problem is probably a defective starter drive that's not staying engaged with the

2.23 Connect a battery load tester to the battery and check the battery condition under load following the tool manufacturer's instructions

ring gear. Replace the starter.

The starter rotates slowly

30 Check the battery (see Steps 21 through 24).

31 If the battery is okay, verify all connections (at the battery, the starter solenoid and motor) are clean, corrosion-free and tight. Make sure the cables aren't frayed or damaged.

32 Check that the starter mounting bolts are tight so it grounds properly. Also check the pinion gear and flywheel ring gear for evidence of a mechanical bind (galling, deformed gear teeth or other damage).

The starter does not rotate at all

33 Check the battery (see Steps 21 through 24).

34 If the battery is okay, verify all connections (at the battery, the starter solenoid and motor) are clean, corrosion-free and tight. Make sure the cables aren't frayed or damaged.

35 Check all of the fuses in the underhood fuse/relay box.

36 Check that the starter mounting bolts are tight so it grounds properly.

37 Check for voltage at the starter solenoid "S" terminal when the ignition key is turned to the start position. If voltage is present, replace the starter/solenoid assembly. If no voltage is present, the problem could be the starter relay, the Transmission Range (TR) switch (see Chapter 6), or with an electrical connector somewhere in the circuit (see the wiring diagrams at the end of Chapter 12). Also, on many modern vehicles, the Powertrain Control Module (PCM) and the Body Control Module (BCM) control the voltage signal to the starter solenoid; on such vehicles a special scan tool is required for diagnosis.

3   Battery - disconnection

✳✳ CAUTION:

Always disconnect the cable from the negative battery terminal FIRST and hook it up LAST or the battery may be shorted by the tool being used to loosen the cable clamps.

Some systems on the vehicle require battery power to be available at all times, either to maintain continuous operation (alarm system, power door locks, etc.), or to maintain control unit memory (radio station presets, Powertrain Control Module (PCM) and other control units). When the battery is disconnected, the power that maintains these systems is cut. So, before you disconnect the battery, please note that on a vehicle with power door locks, it's a wise precaution to remove the key from the ignition and to keep it with you, so that it does not get locked inside if the power door locks should engage accidentally when the battery is reconnected!

Devices known as "memory-savers" can be used to avoid some of these problems. Precise details vary according to the device used. The typical memory saver is plugged into the cigarette lighter and is connected to a spare battery. Then the vehicle battery can be disconnected from the electrical system. The memory saver will provide sufficient current to maintain audio unit security codes, PCM memory, etc. and will provide power to always hot circuits such as the clock and radio memory circuits.

☀ WARNING 1:

Some memory savers deliver a considerable amount of current in order to keep vehicle systems operational after the main bat-

tery is disconnected. If you're using a memory saver, make sure that the circuit concerned is actually open before servicing it.

☀ WARNING 2:

If you're going to work near any of the airbag system components, the battery MUST be disconnected and a memory saver must NOT be used. If a memory saver is used, power will be supplied to the airbag, which means that it could accidentally deploy and cause serious personal injury.

To disconnect the battery for service procedures requiring power to be cut from the vehicle, loosen the cable end bolt and disconnect the cable from the negative battery terminal. Isolate the cable end to prevent it from coming into accidental contact with the battery terminal.

4 Battery and battery tray - removal and installation

▶ **Refer to illustrations 4.1 and 4.5**

1   Disconnect the cable from the negative battery terminal first, then disconnect the cable from the positive battery terminal (see illustration).
2   Remove the battery hold-down clamp.
3   Lift out the battery. Be careful - it's heavy.

➡ **Note: Battery straps and handlers are available at most auto parts stores for reasonable prices. They make it easier to remove and carry the battery.**

4   If you are replacing the battery, make sure you get one that's identical, with the same dimensions, amperage rating, cold cranking rating, etc. Also, if the battery was equipped with a heat shield, remove it from the old battery and install it on the new one.
5   If necessary for access to other components, remove the battery tray (see illustration).
6   Installation is the reverse of removal. Connect the positive cable first and the negative cable last.

4.1 Battery details - four-cylinder model shown, V6 models similar

1   *Negative battery terminal (cable already disconnected)*
2   *Positive battery cable clamp nut*
3   *Hold-down bolt and wedge*

4.5 Battery tray mounting bolts

5   Battery cables - replacement

1   When removing the cables, always disconnect the cable from the negative battery terminal first and hook it up last, or you might accidentally short out the battery with the tool you're using to loosen the cable clamps. Even if you're only replacing the cable for the positive terminal, be sure to disconnect the negative cable from the battery first.

2   Disconnect the old cables from the battery, then trace each of them to their opposite ends and disconnect them. Note the routing of each cable before disconnecting it to ensure correct installation.

3   If you are replacing any of the old cables, take them with you when buying new cables. It is vitally important that you replace the cables with identical parts.

4   Clean the threads of the solenoid or ground connection with a wire brush to remove rust and corrosion. Apply a light coat of battery terminal corrosion inhibitor or petroleum jelly to the threads to prevent future corrosion.

5   Attach the cable to the solenoid or ground connection and tighten the mounting nut/bolt securely.

6   Before connecting a new cable to the battery, make sure that it reaches the battery post without having to be stretched.

7   Connect the cable to the positive battery terminal first, then connect the ground cable to the negative battery terminal.

6   Ignition coils - replacement

▶ Refer to illustration 6.4 and 6.6

1   Disconnect the cable from the negative battery terminal (see Section 3).

2   On four-cylinder models, remove the air filter outlet duct, then remove the EVAP canister purge valve fastener and move the valve out of the way.

3   On V6 models, remove the upper intake manifold to access the rear (right) bank ignition coils.

4   Disconnect the electrical connector from the ignition coil (see illustration).

5   Remove the mounting fasteners from the ignition coil.

6   Grasp the coil firmly and pull it off the spark plug (see illustration).

7   Installation is the reverse of removal.

6.4 Ignition coil details (four-cylinder engine shown, other engines similar)

1   Electrical connector   *2   Mounting fasteners*

6.6 Grasp the top of the coil and twist the coil while pulling it up and off of the spark plug

7   Alternator - removal and installation

1   Disconnect the cable from the negative battery terminal (see Section 3).

2   Remove the drivebelt (see Chapter 1).

FOUR-CYLINDER MODELS

▶ Refer to illustration 7.5

3   Remove the Charge Air Cooler (CAC) upper pipe (see Chapter 4).

4   Remove the power steering pump mounting bolts (see Chapter 10) and move the pump out of the way.

5   Pull back the protective cover from the alternator's battery terminal, remove the nut and disconnect the battery cable from the alternator (see illustration). Set the battery cable aside. Disconnect the electrical connector from the alternator.

6   Remove the alternator mounting fasteners (see illustration).

V6 MODELS

7   Remove the cooling fan (see Chapter 3).

8   Push back the protective cover from the alternator's battery terminal, remove the nut and disconnect the battery cable from the alternator. Disconnect the electrical connector from the alternator.

9   Remove the alternator upper mounting stud nut.

10   Remove the alternator lower mounting bolt and remove the alternator.

ALL MODELS

11   If you're replacing the alternator, take the old one with you when purchasing the replacement unit. Make sure that the new/rebuilt unit looks identical to the old alternator. Look at the electrical terminals on the backside of the alternator. They should be the same in number, size and location as the terminals on the old alternator. Finally, look at the identification numbers. They will be stamped into the housing or printed on a tag attached to the housing. Make sure that the ID numbers are the same on both alternators.

12   Many new/rebuilt alternators DO NOT have a pulley installed, so you might have to swap the pulley from the old unit to the new/rebuilt one. When buying an alternator, find out the store's policy regarding pulley swaps. Some stores perform this service free of charge. If your local auto parts store doesn't offer this service, you'll have to purchase a puller for removing the pulley and do it yourself.

7.5 Alternator mounting details (four-cylinder models)

1   B+ terminal   3   Mounting bolts
2   Electrical connector

13   Installation is the reverse of removal. Tighten the alternator mounting bolts securely.

14   Reconnect the cable to the negative terminal of the battery. Check the charging voltage (see Section 2) to verify that the alternator is operating correctly.

8   Starter motor - removal and installation

FOUR-CYLINDER MODELS

▶ **Refer to illustration 8.3**

1   Detach the cable from the negative terminal of the battery (see Section 3).

2   Raise the vehicle and support it securely on jackstands. Remove the underbody cover.

3   Disconnect the starter motor solenoid wire nut and the starter motor battery cable nut, and disconnect both wires from the starter (see illustration).

4   Remove the nut that secures the ground wire to the starter mounting stud and disconnect the ground wire from the stud. Remove the mounting stud bolts and remove the starter.

5   Installation is the reverse of removal. Tighten the starter mounting stud bolts securely.

8.3 Starter motor details - four-cylinder models

1   Starter motor battery   3   Mounting stud bolts
     terminal
2   Starter solenoid terminal

8.8 Starter motor details - V6 models

1   *Starter motor battery terminal*
2   *Starter solenoid terminal*

**8.9 Starter motor mounting bolt (other bolt not visible) -
V6 models**

V6 MODELS

▶ **Refer to illustrations 8.8 and 8.9**

6   Remove the air filter housing (see Chapter 4).
7   Disconnect the transaxle shift cable, then remove the transaxle
shift lever nut and lever (see Chapter 7A).

8   Remove the starter motor solenoid wire nut and the starter motor
battery cable nut, then disconnect both wires from the starter motor (see
illustration).
9   Remove the starter motor mounting fasteners (see illustration)
and remove the starter motor.
10 Installation is the reverse of removal.

6

EMISSIONS AND ENGINE CONTROL SYSTEMS

Section

To prevent pollution of the atmosphere from incompletely burned and evaporating gases, and to maintain good driveability and fuel economy, a number of emission control systems are incorporated. They include the:

CATALYTIC CONVERTER

A catalytic converter is an emission control device in the exhaust system that reduces certain pollutants in the exhaust gas stream. There are two types of converters: oxidation converters and reduction converters.

Oxidation converters contain a monolithic substrate (a ceramic honeycomb) coated with the semi-precious metals platinum and palladium. An oxidation catalyst reduces unburned hydrocarbons (HC) and carbon monoxide (CO) by adding oxygen to the exhaust stream as it passes through the substrate, which, in the presence of high temperature and the catalyst materials, converts the HC and CO to water vapor (H_2O) and carbon dioxide (CO_2).

Reduction converters contain a monolithic substrate coated with platinum and rhodium. A reduction catalyst reduces oxides of nitrogen (NOx) by removing oxygen, which in the presence of high temperature and the catalyst material produces nitrogen (N) and carbon dioxide (CO_2).

Catalytic converters that combine both types of catalysts in one assembly are known as three-way catalysts or TWCs. A TWC can reduce all three pollutants.

EVAPORATIVE EMISSIONS CONTROL (EVAP) SYSTEM

The Evaporative Emissions Control (EVAP) system prevents fuel system vapors (which contain unburned hydrocarbons) from escaping into the atmosphere. On warm days, vapors trapped inside the fuel tank expand until the pressure reaches a certain threshold. Then the fuel vapors are routed from the fuel tank through the fuel vapor vent valve and the fuel vapor control valve to the EVAP canister, where they're stored temporarily until the next time the vehicle is operated. When the conditions are right (engine warmed up, vehicle up to speed, moderate or heavy load on the engine, etc.) the PCM opens the canister purge valve, which allows fuel vapors to be drawn from the canister into the intake manifold. Once in the intake manifold, the fuel vapors mix with incoming air before being drawn through the intake ports into the combustion chambers where they're burned up with the rest of the air/fuel mixture. The EVAP system is complex and virtually impossible to troubleshoot without the right tools and training.

POWERTRAIN CONTROL MODULE (PCM)

The Powertrain Control Module (PCM) is the brain of the engine management system. It also controls a wide variety of other vehicle systems. In order to program the new PCM, the dealer needs the vehicle as well as the new PCM. If you're planning to replace the PCM with a new one, there is no point in trying to do so at home because you won't be able to program it yourself.

POSITIVE CRANKCASE VENTILATION (PCV) SYSTEM

The Positive Crankcase Ventilation (PCV) system reduces hydrocarbon emissions by scavenging crankcase vapors, which are rich in unburned hydrocarbons. A PCV valve or orifice regulates the flow of gases into the intake manifold in proportion to the amount of intake vacuum available.

The PCV system generally consists of the fresh air inlet hose, the PCV valve or orifice and the crankcase ventilation hose (or PCV hose). The fresh air inlet hose connects the air intake duct to a pipe on the valve cover. The crankcase ventilation hose (or PCV hose) connects the PCV valve or orifice in the valve cover or crankcase vent oil separator to the intake manifold.

Emissions and engine control components (four-cylinder engine shown):

1   Accelerator Pedal Position (APP) sensor (at the top of accelerator pedal assembly)
2   Exhaust Camshaft Position (CMP) sensor (Top, rear of valve cover, above exhaust camshaft)
3   Intake Camshaft Position (CMP) sensor (Top, rear of valve cover, above intake camshaft)
4   Transmission Control Module (TCM)

5   Mass Air Flow/Intake Air Temperature (MAF/IAT) sensor
6   Manifold Absolute Pressure Temperature (MAPT) sensor
7   Knock sensors (on front side of engine block)
8   Positive Crankcase Ventilation (PCV) vent oil separator (on side of the engine block)

9   Fuel Rail Pressure (FRP) sensor (near the end of the fuel rail)
10 EVAP canister purge solenoid valve (top of engine compartment, above valve cover)
11 Crankshaft Position (CKP) sensor (lower right rear corner of block, near crankshaft pulley)
12 Powertrain Control Module (PCM) (right side of the engine cowl)

Information Sensors

Accelerator Pedal Position (APP) sensor - as you press the accelerator pedal, the APP sensor alters its voltage signal to the PCM in proportion to the angle of the pedal, and the PCM commands a motor inside the throttle body to open or close the throttle plate accordingly

Camshaft Position (CMP) sensor - produces a signal that the PCM uses to identify the number 1 cylinder and to time the firing sequence of the fuel injectors

Crankshaft Position (CKP) sensor - produces a signal that the PCM uses to calculate engine speed and crankshaft position, which enables it to synchronize ignition timing with fuel injector timing, and to detect misfires

Engine Coolant Temperature (ECT) sensor - a thermistor (temperature-sensitive variable resistor) that sends a voltage signal to the PCM, which uses this data to determine the temperature of the engine coolant

Fuel tank pressure sensor - measures the fuel tank pressure and controls fuel tank pressure by signaling the EVAP system to purge the fuel tank vapors when the pressure becomes excessive

Intake Air Temperature (IAT) sensor - monitors the temperature of the air entering the engine and sends a signal to the PCM to determine injector pulse-width (the duration of each injector's on-time) and to adjust spark timing (to prevent spark knock)

Knock sensor - a piezoelectric crystal that oscillates in proportion to engine vibration which produces a voltage output that is monitored by the PCM. This retards the ignition timing when the oscillation exceeds a certain threshold

Manifold Absolute Pressure (MAP) sensor - monitors the pressure or vacuum inside the intake manifold. The PCM uses this data to determine engine load so that it can alter the ignition advance and fuel enrichment

Mass Air Flow (MAF) sensor - measures the amount of intake air drawn into the engine. It uses a hot-wire sensing element to measure the amount of air entering the engine

Oxygen sensors - generates a small variable voltage signal in proportion to the difference between the oxygen content in the exhaust stream and the oxygen content in the ambient air. The PCM uses this information to maintain the proper air/fuel ratio. A second oxygen sensor monitors the efficiency of the catalytic converter

Throttle Position (TP) sensor - a potentiometer that generates a voltage signal that varies in relation to the opening angle of the throttle plate inside the throttle body. Works with the PCM and other sensors to calculate injector pulse width (the duration of each injector's on-time)

Photos courtesy of Wells Manufacturing, except APP and MAF sensors.

2 On Board Diagnosis (OBD) system

GENERAL DESCRIPTION

1 All models are equipped with the second generation OBD-II system. This system consists of an on-board computer known as the Powertrain Control Module (PCM), and information sensors, which monitor various functions of the engine and send data to the PCM. This system incorporates a series of diagnostic monitors that detect and identify fuel injection and emissions control system faults and store the information in the computer memory. This system also tests sensors and output actuators, diagnoses drive cycles, freezes data and clears codes.

2 The PCM is the brain of the electronically controlled fuel and emissions system. It receives data from a number of sensors and other electronic components (switches, relays, etc.). Based on the information it receives, the PCM generates output signals to control various relays, solenoids (fuel injectors) and other actuators. The PCM is specifically calibrated to optimize the emissions, fuel economy and driveability of the vehicle.

3 It isn't a good idea to attempt diagnosis or replacement of the PCM or emission control components at home while the vehicle is under warranty. Because of a federally-mandated warranty which covers the emissions system components and because any owner-induced damage to the PCM, the sensors and/or the control devices may void this warranty, take the vehicle to a dealer service department if the PCM or a system component malfunctions.

SCAN TOOL INFORMATION

▶ **Refer to illustrations 2.4a and 2.4b**

4 Because extracting the Diagnostic Trouble Codes (DTCs) from an engine management system is now the first step in troubleshooting many computer-controlled systems and components, a code reader, at the very least, will be required (see illustration). More powerful scan tools can also perform many of the diagnostics once associated with expensive factory scan tools (see illustration). If you're planning to obtain a generic scan tool for your vehicle, make sure that it's compatible with OBD-II systems. If you don't plan to purchase a code reader or scan tool and don't have access to one, you can have the codes extracted by a dealer service department or an independent repair shop.

➡ **Note: Some auto parts stores even provide this service.**

2.4a Simple code readers are an economical way to extract trouble codes when the CHECK ENGINE light comes on

2.4b Hand-held scan tools like these can extract computer codes and also perform diagnostics

3   Obtaining and clearing Diagnostic Trouble Codes (DTCs)

All models covered by this manual are equipped with on-board diagnostics. When the PCM recognizes a malfunction in a monitored emission or engine control system, component or circuit, it turns on the Malfunction Indicator Light (MIL) on the dash. The PCM will continue to display the MIL until the problem is fixed and the Diagnostic Trouble Code (DTC) is cleared from the PCM's memory. You'll need a scan tool to access any DTCs stored in the PCM.

Before outputting any DTCs stored in the PCM, thoroughly inspect ALL electrical connectors and hoses. Make sure that all electrical connections are tight, clean and free of corrosion. And make sure that all hoses are correctly connected, fit tightly and are in good condition (no cracks or tears).

3.1 The Data Link Connector (DLC) is located below the steering column

ACCESSING THE DTCS

▶ **Refer to illustration 3.1**

1   The Diagnostic Trouble Codes (DTCs) can only be accessed with a code reader or scan tool. Professional scan tools are expensive, but relatively inexpensive generic code readers or scan tools (see illustrations 2.4a and 2.4b) are available at most auto parts stores. Simply plug the connector of the scan tool into the diagnostic connector (see illustration). Then follow the instructions included with the scan tool to extract the DTCs.

2   Once you have outputted all of the stored DTCs, look them up on the accompanying DTC chart.

3   After troubleshooting the source of each DTC, make any necessary repairs or replace the defective component(s).

Clearing the DTCs

4   Clear the DTCs with the code reader or scan tool in accordance with the instructions provided by the tool's manufacturer.

DIAGNOSTIC TROUBLE CODES

5   The accompanying tables are a list of the Diagnostic Trouble Codes (DTCs) that can be accessed by a do-it-yourselfer working at home (there are many, many more DTCs available to professional mechanics with proprietary scan tools and software, but those codes cannot be accessed by a generic scan tool). If, after you have checked and repaired the connectors, wire harness and vacuum hoses (if applicable) for an emission-related system, component or circuit, the problem persists, have the vehicle checked by a dealer service department or other qualified repair shop.

OBD-II TROUBLE CODES

Code	Probable cause
P0010	Intake camshaft position actuator, open circuit (Bank 1)
P0011	Intake camshaft position timing over-advanced (Bank 1)
P0012	Intake camshaft position timing, over-retarded (Bank 1)
P0016	Crankshaft position-to-camshaft position correlation (Bank 1)
P0018	Crankshaft position-to-camshaft position correlation (Bank 2)
P0020	Intake camshaft position actuator, open circuit (Bank 2)
P0021	Intake camshaft position timing over-advanced (Bank 2)
P0022	Intake camshaft position timing over-retarded (Bank 2)
P0030	Oxygen sensor heater control circuit (Bank 1, Sensor 1)

Code	Probable cause
P0040	Oxygen sensor signals swapped (Bank 1, Sensor 1/Bank 2, Sensor 1)
P0041	Oxygen sensor signals swapped (Bank 1, Sensor 2/Bank 2, Sensor 2)
P0050	Oxygen sensor heater control circuit (Bank 2, Sensor 1)
P0053	Oxygen sensor heater resistance (Bank 1, Sensor 1)
P0054	Oxygen sensor heater resistance (Bank 1, Sensor 2)
P0055	Oxygen sensor heater resistance (Bank 1, Sensor 3)
P0059	Oxygen sensor heater resistance (Bank 2, Sensor 1)
P0060	Oxygen sensor heater resistance (Bank 2, Sensor 2)
P0068	Manifold Absolute Pressure (MAP) sensor/Mass Air Flow (MAF) sensor-to-throttle position correlation
P0097	Intake Air Temperature (IAT) sensor 2 circuit, low voltage
P0098	Intake Air Temperature (IAT) sensor 2 circuit, high voltage
P0102	Mass or volume air flow A circuit, low voltage
P0103	Mass or volume air flow A circuit, high voltage
P0104	Mass Air Flow (MAF) sensor A circuit, intermittent or erratic signal
P0106	Manifold Absolute Pressure (MAP) sensor circuit, range or performance problem
P0107	Manifold Absolute Pressure (MAP) sensor circuit, low voltage
P0108	Manifold Absolute Pressure (MAP) sensor circuit, high voltage
P0109	Manifold Absolute Pressure (MAP) sensor circuit, intermittent signal
P0111	Intake Air Temperature (IAT) sensor circuit, range or performance problem
P0112	Intake Air Temperature (IAT) sensor circuit, low voltage
P0113	Intake Air Temperature (IAT) sensor circuit, high voltage
P0114	Intake Air Temperature (IAT) sensor circuit, intermittent or erratic signal
P0116	Engine Coolant Temperature (ECT) sensor circuit, range or performance problem
P0117	Engine Coolant Temperature (ECT) sensor circuit, low voltage
P0118	Engine Coolant Temperature (ECT) sensor circuit, high voltage
P0119	Engine Coolant Temperature (ECT) sensor circuit, intermittent or erratic signal
P0121	Throttle Position (TP) sensor A circuit, range or performance problem

OBD-II TROUBLE CODES (CONTINUED)

Code	Probable cause
P0122	Throttle Position (TP) sensor A circuit, low voltage
P0123	Throttle Position (TP) sensor A circuit, high voltage
P0125	Insufficient coolant temperature for closed loop fuel control
P0128	Coolant temperature below coolant thermostat's regulating temperature
P0130	Oxygen sensor circuit malfunction (Bank 1, Sensor 1)
P0132	Oxygen sensor circuit, high voltage (Bank 1, Sensor 1)
P0133	Oxygen sensor circuit, slow response (Bank 1, Sensor 1)
P0134	Oxygen sensor circuit, no activity detected (Bank 1, Sensor 1)
P0135	Oxygen sensor heater circuit malfunction (Bank 1, Sensor 1)
P0138	Oxygen sensor circuit, high voltage (Bank 1, Sensor 2)
P0139	Oxygen sensor circuit, slow response (Bank 1, Sensor 2)
P013A	Oxygen sensor slow response, rich to lean (Bank 1, Sensor 2)
P013C	Oxygen sensor slow response, rich to lean (Bank 2, Sensor 2)
P013E	Oxygen sensor delayed response, rich to lean (Bank 1, Sensor 2)
P0144	Oxygen sensor circuit, high voltage (Bank 1, Sensor 3)
P0147	Oxygen sensor heater circuit malfunction (Bank 1, Sensor 3)
P0148	Fuel delivery error
P014A	Oxygen sensor delayed response, rich to lean (Bank 2, Sensor 2)
P0150	Oxygen sensor circuit malfunction (Bank 2, Sensor 1)
P0152	Oxygen sensor circuit, high voltage (Bank 2, Sensor 1)
P0153	Oxygen sensor circuit, slow response (Bank 2, Sensor 1)
P0154	Oxygen sensor circuit, no activity detected (Bank 2, Sensor 1)
P0155	Oxygen sensor heater circuit malfunction (Bank 2, Sensor 1)
P0158	Oxygen sensor circuit, high voltage (Bank 2, Sensor 2)
P0159	Oxygen sensor circuit, slow response (Bank 2, Sensor 2)

Code	Probable cause
P0161	Oxygen sensor heater circuit malfunction (Bank 2, Sensor 2)
P0171	System too lean (Bank 1)
P0172	System too rich (Bank 1)
P0174	System too lean (Bank 2)
P0175	System too rich (Bank 2)
P0180	Fuel temperature sensor circuit malfunction
P0181	Fuel temperature sensor circuit, range or performance problem
P0182	Fuel temperature sensor circuit, low voltage
P0183	Fuel temperature sensor circuit, high voltage
P0191	Fuel rail pressure sensor circuit, range or performance problem
P0192	Fuel rail pressure sensor circuit, low voltage
P0193	Fuel rail pressure sensor circuit, high voltage
P0196	Engine Oil Temperature (EOT) sensor circuit, range or performance problem
P0197	Engine Oil Temperature (EOT) sensor circuit, low voltage
P0198	Engine Oil Temperature (EOT) sensor circuit, high voltage
P0201	Injector open circuit, cylinder 1
P0202	Injector open circuit, cylinder 2
P0203	Injector open circuit, cylinder 3
P0204	Injector open circuit, cylinder 4
P0205	Injector open circuit, cylinder 5
P0206	Injector open circuit, cylinder 6
P0217	Engine coolant over-temperature condition
P0218	Transaxle fluid temperature over-temperature condition
P0219	Engine over-speed condition
P0221	Throttle Position (TP) sensor circuit, range or performance problem
P0222	Throttle Position (TP) sensor circuit, low voltage
P0223	Throttle Position (TP) sensor circuit, high voltage

OBD-II TROUBLE CODES (CONTINUED)

Code	Probable cause
P0230	Fuel pump primary circuit malfunction
P0231	Fuel pump secondary circuit, low voltage
P0232	Fuel pump secondary circuit, high voltage
P025A	Fuel pump module control circuit open
P025B	Fuel pump module control circuit range or performance problem
P0297	Vehicle over-speed condition
P0298	Engine oil over-temperature condition
P0300	Random misfire detected
P0301	Cylinder 1 misfire
P0302	Cylinder 2 misfire
P0303	Cylinder 3 misfire
P0304	Cylinder 4 misfire
P0305	Cylinder 5 misfire
P0306	Cylinder 6 misfire
P0315	Crankshaft position system variation not learned
P0316	Misfire detected on start-up (first 1000 revolutions)
P0320	Ignition/distributor engine speed input circuit
P0325	Knock sensor 1 circuit malfunction (Bank 1)
P0326	Knock sensor 1 circuit, range or performance problem (Bank 1)
P0330	Knock sensor 2 circuit malfunction (Bank 2)
P0331	Knock sensor 2 circuit, range or performance problem (Bank 2)
P0340	Camshaft Position (CMP) sensor circuit malfunction (Bank 1 or single sensor)
P0341	Camshaft Position (CMP) sensor circuit, range or performance problem (Bank 1 or single sensor)
P0344	Camshaft Position (CMP) sensor circuit, intermittent signal (Bank 1 or single sensor)
P0345	Camshaft Position (CMP) sensor circuit malfunction (Bank 2)

Code	Probable cause
P0346	Camshaft Position (CMP) sensor circuit, range or performance problem (Bank 2)
P0349	Camshaft Position (CMP) sensor circuit, intermittent signal (Bank 2)
P0350	Ignition coil primary/secondary circuit malfunction
P0351	Ignition coil A primary/secondary circuit malfunction
P0352	Ignition coil B primary/secondary circuit malfunction
P0353	Ignition coil C primary/secondary circuit malfunction
P0354	Ignition coil D primary/secondary circuit malfunction
P0355	Ignition coil E primary/secondary circuit malfunction
P0356	Ignition coil F primary/secondary circuit malfunction
P0420	Catalyst system efficiency below threshold (Bank 1)
P0430	Catalyst system efficiency below threshold (Bank 2)
P0442	Evaporative Emission (EVAP) system, small leak detected
P0443	Evaporative Emission (EVAP) system, purge control valve circuit malfunction
P0446	Evaporative Emission (EVAP) system, vent control circuit malfunction
P0451	Evaporative Emission (EVAP) system, pressure sensor range or performance problem
P0452	Evaporative Emission (EVAP) system, pressure sensor, low voltage
P0453	Evaporative Emission (EVAP) system, pressure sensor, high voltage
P0454	Evaporative Emission (EVAP) system, pressure sensor, intermittent signal
P0455	Evaporative Emission (EVAP) system, gross leak detected/no flow
P0456	Evaporative Emission (EVAP) system, very small leak detected
P0457	Evaporative Emission (EVAP) system, leak detected (fuel cap loose or off)
P0460	Fuel level sensor circuit malfunction
P0461	Fuel level sensor circuit, range or performance problem
P0462	Fuel level sensor circuit, low voltage
P0463	Fuel level sensor circuit, high voltage
P0480	Fan 1 control circuit malfunction
P0481	Fan 2 control circuit malfunction

OBD-II TROUBLE CODES (CONTINUED)

Code	Probable cause
P0483	Fan performance
P0491	Secondary Air Injection (AIR) system, insufficient flow (Bank 1)
P0500	Vehicle Speed Sensor (VSS)
P0503	Vehicle Speed Sensor (VSS), intermittent, erratic or high signal
P0505	Idle Air Control (IAC) system
P0506	Idle Air Control (IAC) system, rpm lower than expected
P0507	Idle Air Control (IAC) system, rpm higher than expected
P050A	Cold start idle air control performance
P050B	Cold start ignition timing performance
P050E	Cold start engine exhaust temperature out of range
P0511	Idle Air Control (IAC) system circuit malfunction
P0512	Starter request circuit malfunction
P0528	Fan speed sensor circuit, no signal
P052A	Cold start camshaft position timing over-advanced (Bank 1)
P052B	Cold start camshaft position timing over-retarded (Bank 1)
P052C	Cold start camshaft position timing over-advanced (Bank 2)
P052D	Cold start camshaft position timing over-retarded (Bank 2)
P0532	Air conditioning refrigerant pressure sensor circuit, low voltage
P0533	Air conditioning refrigerant pressure sensor circuit, high voltage
P0534	Air conditioning refrigerant charge loss
P0537	Air conditioning evaporator temperature sensor circuit, low voltage
P0538	A/C evaporator temperature sensor circuit, high voltage
P053A	Positive Crankcase Ventilation (PCV) heater control circuit open
P0552	Power Steering Pressure (PSP) sensor circuit, low voltage
P0553	Power Steering Pressure (PSP) sensor circuit, high voltage

Code	Probable cause
P0562	System voltage low
P0563	System voltage high
P0571	Brake switch circuit malfunction
P0572	Brake switch circuit, low voltage
P0573	Brake switch circuit, high voltage
P0579	Cruise control multifunction input circuit, ranger or performance problem
P0581	Cruise control multifunction input circuit, high voltage
P0600	Serial communication link
P0601	Powertrain Control Module (PCM), memory checksum error
P0602	Powertrain Control Module (PCM) programming error
P0603	Powertrain Control Module (PCM), Keep Alive Memory (KAM) error
P0604	Powertrain Control Module (PCM), Random Access Memory (RAM) error
P0605	Powertrain Control Module (PCM), Read Only Memory (ROM) error
P0606	Powertrain Control Module (PCM) processor
P0607	Powertrain Control Module (PCM) performance
P060A	Internal control module monitoring processor performance
P060B	Internal control module analog/digital processing performance
P060C	Internal control module main processor performance
P060D	Internal control module accelerator pedal position performance
P0610	Powertrain Control Module (PCM) options error
P061B	Internal control module torque calculation performance
P061C	Internal control module engine rpm performance
P061D	Internal control module engine air mass performance
P061F	Internal control module throttle actuator controller performance
P0620	Alternator control circuit malfunction
P0622	Alternator field terminal, circuit malfunction
P0625	Alternator field terminal, low circuit voltage

OBD-II TROUBLE CODES (CONTINUED)

Code	Probable cause
P0626	Alternator field terminal, high circuit voltage
P0627	Fuel pump, open control circuit
P062C	Internal control module vehicle speed performance
P062F	Internal control module EEPROM error
P0642	Sensor reference voltage (VREF) circuit below VREF minimum voltage
P0643	Sensor reference voltage (VREF) circuit, high voltage
P0645	Air conditioning clutch relay control circuit malfunction
P064D	Internal control module oxygen sensor processor performance (Bank 1)
P064E	Internal control module oxygen sensor processor performance (Bank 2)
P0657	Actuator supply voltage, open circuit
P065B	Alternator control circuit range or performance problem
P065B	Alternator control circuit range or performance problem
P0660	Intake Manifold Tuning Valve (IMTV) control circuit, open circuit (Bank 1)
P0663	Intake Manifold Tuning Valve (IMTV) control circuit, open circuit (Bank 2)
P0685	Powertrain Control Module (PCM) power relay control circuit open
P0689	Powertrain Control Module (PCM) power relay sense circuit, low voltage
P0690	Powertrain Control Module (PCM) power relay sense circuit, high voltage
P06B8	Internal control module Non-volatile random access memory (NVRAM) error
P0703	Brake switch input circuit malfunction
P0704	Clutch switch input circuit malfunction
P0705	Transmission Range (TR) sensor circuit (PRNDL) input problem
P0706	Transmission Range (TR) sensor circuit, range or performance problem
P0707	Transmission Range (TR) sensor circuit, low voltage
P0708	Transmission range sensor circuit, high voltage
P0711	Transmission fluid temperature sensor circuit, range or performance problem

Code	Probable cause
P0712	Transmission fluid temperature sensor circuit, low input
P0713	Transmission fluid temperature sensor circuit, high input
P0715	Input/turbine speed sensor circuit malfunction
P0716	Input/turbine speed sensor circuit, range or performance problem
P0717	Input/turbine speed sensor circuit, no signal
P0720	Output Shaft Speed (OSS) sensor circuit malfunction
P0721	Output Shaft Speed (OSS) sensor circuit, range or performance problem
P0722	No signal from Output Shaft Speed (OSS) sensor
P0723	Output Shaft Speed (OSS) sensor circuit, intermittent signal
P0729	Gear 6 incorrect ratio
P072C	Stuck in Gear 1
P072E	Stuck in Gear 3
P072F	Stuck in Gear 4
P0730	Incorrect gear ratio
P0731	Incorrect gear ratio, first gear
P0732	Incorrect gear ratio, second gear
P0733	Incorrect gear ratio, third gear
P0734	Incorrect gear ratio, fourth gear
P0735	Incorrect gear ratio, fifth gear
P0736	Incorrect gear ratio, reverse gear
P0740	Torque converter clutch solenoid circuit, open
P0741	Torque converter clutch, circuit performance problem or stuck in Off position
P0742	Torque converter clutch circuit, stuck in On position
P0743	Torque converter clutch solenoid circuit, electrical malfunction
P0744	Torque converter clutch circuit, intermittent
P0745	Pressure control solenoid A electrical malfunction

OBD-II TROUBLE CODES (CONTINUED)

Code	Probable cause
P0748	Pressure control solenoid malfunction
P0750	Shift solenoid A, performance problem
P0751	Shift solenoid A, performance problem or stuck in Off position
P0752	Shift solenoid A, stuck in On position
P0753	Shift solenoid A, electrical problem
P0755	Shift solenoid B, performance problem
P0756	Shift solenoid B, performance problem or stuck in Off position
P0757	Shift solenoid B, stuck in On position
P0758	Shift solenoid B, electrical problem
P0760	Shift solenoid C, performance problem
P0761	Shift solenoid C, performance problem or stuck in Off position
P0762	Shift solenoid C, stuck in On position
P0763	Shift solenoid C, electrical problem
P0765	Shift solenoid D, performance problem
P0766	Shift solenoid D, performance problem or stuck in Off position
P0767	Shift solenoid D, stuck in On position
P0768	Shift solenoid D, electrical problem
P0770	Shift solenoid E, performance problem
P0771	Shift solenoid E, performance problem or stuck in Off position
P0772	Shift solenoid E, stuck in On position
P0773	Shift solenoid E, electrical problem
P0774	Shift solenoid E, intermittent electrical problem
P0777	Pressure control solenoid "B" stuck On
P0778	Pressure control solenoid "B" electrical
P0780	Shift malfunction

Code	Probable cause
P0791	Intermediate shaft speed sensor circuit malfunction
P0812	Reverse input circuit malfunction
P0815	Upshift switch circuit malfunction
P0816	Downshift switch circuit malfunction
P0817	Starter disable circuit malfunction
P0830	Clutch pedal switch circuit malfunction
P0840	Transmission fluid pressure sensor circuit malfunction
P0841	Transmission fluid pressure sensor/switch "A" circuit range/performance problem
P0850	Park/neutral switch input circuit malfunction
P0882	Transmission control module (TCM) power input signal low
P0894	Transmission component slipping
P0960	Pressure control (PC) solenoid A - control circuit open
P0961	Pressure control (PC) solenoid A - control circuit range/performance problem
P0962	Pressure control (PC) solenoid A - control circuit low
P0963	Pressure control (PC) solenoid A - control circuit high
P0973	Shift solenoid (SS) A - control circuit low
P0974	Shift solenoid (SS) A - control circuit high
P0976	Shift solenoid (SS) B - control circuit low
P0977	Shift solenoid (SS) B - control circuit high
P0978	Shift solenoid (SS) C - control circuit range/performance problem
P0979	Shift solenoid (SS) C - control circuit low
P0980	Shift solenoid (SS) C - control circuit high
P0981	Shift solenoid (SS) D - control circuit range/performance problem
P0982	Shift solenoid (SS) D - control circuit low
P0983	Shift solenoid (SS) D - control circuit high
P0984	Shift solenoid (SS) E - control circuit range/performance problem

OBD-II TROUBLE CODES (CONTINUED)

Code	Probable cause
P0985	Shift solenoid (SS) E - control circuit low
P0986	Shift solenoid (SS) E - control circuit high
P0997	Shift solenoid (SS) F - control circuit range/performance problem
P0998	Shift solenoid (SS) F - control circuit low
P0999	Shift solenoid (SS) F - control circuit high

4 Accelerator Pedal Position (APP) sensor - replacement

▶ **Refer to illustration 4.1**

1 Disconnect the electrical connector from the upper end of the APP sensor assembly (see illustration).

2 Remove the accelerator pedal/APP sensor assembly mounting nuts and remove the assembly.

3 Installation is the reverse of removal.

4.1 Disconnect the APP sensor electrical connector (A) and remove the mounting nuts (B)

5 Camshaft Position (CMP) sensor – replacement

1 Disconnect the cable from the negative battery terminal (see Chapter 5).

FOUR-CYLINDER MODELS

▶ **Refer to illustration 5.2**

➥ **Note: The CMP sensors are located at the top corners of the valve cover, above the left end of the intake and exhaust camshaft.**

2 Disconnect the CMP sensor electrical connector (see illustration).

3 Remove the CMP sensor mounting bolt and remove the sensor from the valve cover.

4 Inspect the condition of the CMP sensor O-ring. If it's cracked, torn or deteriorated, replace it.

5 Installation is the reverse of removal.

5.2 The intake CMP sensor (A) and the exhaust CMP sensor (B) are located on the top of the valve cover (four-cylinder engine)

V6 MODELS

➡ **Note: There are four CMP sensors, two on the end of each cylinder head.**

6   Remove the air filter housing and air intake duct (see Chapter 4).
7   Disconnect the CMP sensor electrical connector.

8   Remove the CMP sensor mounting bolt and remove the CMP sensor from the cylinder head.
9   Remove the CMP sensor O-ring and inspect its condition. If it's cracked, torn or otherwise deteriorated, replace it.
10 Lubricate the sensor O-ring with clean engine oil. Installation is otherwise the reverse of removal.

6   Crankshaft Position (CKP) sensor - replacement

➡ **Note: Replacing the CKP sensor might set a Diagnostic Trouble Code (DTC). If it does, and you have a generic scan tool that can clear codes, erase the code and see if it reappears. If it does, drive the vehicle to a dealer service department to perform a Misfire Monitor Neutral Profile Correction procedure with a factory scan tool.**

1   Disconnect the cable from the negative battery terminal (see Chapter 5).
2   If you're working on a four-cylinder model, loosen the right front wheel lug nuts. Raise the front of the vehicle and place it securely on jackstands. Remove the right front wheel, then remove the inner fender splash shield (see Chapter 11). On all models, remove the engine under-cover.

FOUR-CYLINDER MODELS

Removal

▶ **Refer to illustration 6.4**

➡ **Note: The CKP sensor is located at the lower front corner of the timing chain cover.**

3   Put the No. 1 cylinder at Top Dead Center (TDC) (see Chapter 2A).
4   Disconnect the electrical connector from the CKP sensor (see illustration).
5   Unscrew the CKP sensor mounting bolts and remove the sensor.

Installation

▶ **Refer to illustration 6.8**

➡ **Note: If you're installing a new CKP sensor, the new sensor comes with a special alignment jig (#303-1521) that, according to the manufacturer, is available only with a new sensor. However, you might be able to find an aftermarket tool that does the same thing. If you removed the CKP sensor simply to access some other component, like the timing chain, use the alternate method of aligning the CKP sensor included here.**

6   Install the CKP sensor but don't tighten the sensor mounting bolts.
7   If you're installing a new CKP sensor, align the sensor with the special alignment jig (included with the new sensor) in accordance with the manufacturer's instructions. With the alignment jig in place, tighten the CKP sensor bolts securely, then remove the alignment jig.
8   If you're installing the old CKP sensor, look at the sensor trigger wheel, or timing plate, that's mounted on the backside of the crankshaft pulley. Note the small teeth that stick out from the circumference of the timing plate. There is a blank spot on the edge of the timing plate, where there are no teeth. From this blank area, count 20 teeth in a counterclockwise direction, then use a straightedge to draw a straight line from the center of the 20th tooth through the center of the crankshaft pulley (see illustration). Position the centerline of the CKP sensor with the line that you made, then tighten the sensor bolts securely.
9   Installation is otherwise the reverse of removal.

6.4 CKP sensor details (four-cylinder models):

1   *Electrical connector*   3   *CKP sensor*
2   *Mounting bolts*

6.8 CKP sensor alignment details (four-cylinder models)

V6 MODELS

➡ **Note: The CKP sensor is located on the left front side of the engine block, near the transaxle.**

10 Remove the upstream and downstream oxygen sensors from the catalytic converter for the front cylinder head (see Section 12), then

remove the catalyst for the front cylinder head (see Section 19).
11 Remove the CKP sensor heat shield mounting bolt and nut, then remove the heat shield.
12 Remove the rubber grommet cover.
13 Disconnect the CKP sensor electrical connector.
14 Remove the CKP sensor mounting bolt and remove the sensor.
15 Installation is the reverse of removal.

7   Cylinder Head Temperature (CHT) sensor - replacement

✳✳ WARNING:

Wait until the engine has cooled completely before beginning this procedure.

FOUR-CYLINDER MODELS

♦ **Refer to illustration 7.3**

1 Disconnect the cable from the negative battery terminal (see Chapter 5).
2 Remove the air filter outlet duct, then disconnevct the charge air cooler inlet pipe (see Chapter 4).
3 Pull back the rubber weather cover from the CHT sensor electrical connector and disconnect the connector (see illustration).
4 Unscrew the CHT sensor from the cylinder head.
5 When installing the CHT sensor, tighten it to the torque listed in this Chapter's Specifications. Installation is the reverse of removal.

V6 MODELS

➡ **Note: The CHT sensor is screwed into the rear cylinder head below the lower intake manifold.**

6 Disconnect the cable from the negative battery terminal (see Chapter 5).

7.3 The CHT sensor is located on the back side of the cylinder head (four-cylinder engine)

7 Remove the lower intake manifold (see Chapter 2B).
8 Disconnect the CHT sensor electrical connector.
9 Unscrew and remove the CHT sensor.
10 When installing the CHT sensor, tighten it to the torque listed in this Chapter's Specifications. Installation is otherwise the reverse of removal.

8   Engine Coolant Temperature (ECT) sensor - replacement

The ECT sensor is used only on four cylinder engines and is located on the driver's side of the cylinder head on the water outlet housing. It

is the sending unit for the coolant temperature indicator.
For replacement of the ECT sensor, refer to Chapter 3.

9   Knock sensors - replacement

1 Disconnect the cable from the negative battery terminal (see Chapter 5).

FOUR-CYLINDER MODELS

♦ **Refer to illustration 9.4**

➡ **Note: The knock sensors are located on the front side of the block, behind the intake manifold.**

2 Remove the intake manifold (see Chapter 2A).
3 Disconnect the electrical connector from the knock sensor.
4 Remove the knock sensor bolt and remove the knock sensor (see illustration).

➡ **Note: The right hand knock sensor must be installed with the wire end of the sensor pointing towards the 6 o'clock position and the left side knock sensor must be installed with the wire end pointing towards the 3 o'clock position.**

5 Installation is the reverse of removal. Tighten the knock sensor bolt to the torque listed in this Chapter's Specifications.

V6 MODELS

➡ **Note: The knock sensors are located in the valley between the cylinder heads.**

6   Remove the upper and lower intake manifold (see Chapter 2B).
7   Remove the thermostat housing and coolant tube (see Chapter 3).
8   Disconnect the knock sensor electrical connector(s).
9   Remove the knock sensor bolt(s) and remove the knock sensor(s).
10   Installation is the reverse of removal.

9.4 The right hand knock sensor (A), must be installed with the wire end of the sensor pointing towards the 6 o'clock position and the left side knock sensor (B not visible) must be installed with the wire end pointing towards the 3 o'clock position (four-cylinder models)

10 Manifold Absolute Pressure Temperature (MAPT) sensor (four-cylinder models only) - replacement

▸ **Refer to illustration 10.2**

➡ **Note: The MAPT sensor is located on the front left side of the charge air cooler.**

1   Disconnect the cable from the negative battery terminal (see Chapter 5).
2   Disconnect the electrical connector from the MAPT sensor (see illustration).
3   Remove the MAPT sensor retaining bolt (see illustration 10.2) and remove the sensor from the charge air cooler.
4   Installation is the reverse of removal.

10.2 The MAPT sensor is located on top of the charge air cooler (four-cylinder engine)

11 Mass Air Flow/Intake Air Temperature (MAF/IAT) sensor - replacement

▸ **Refer to illustration 11.2**

1   Remove the air intake duct (see Chapter 4).
2   Disconnect the electrical connector from the MAF/IAT sensor (see illustration).
3   Remove the MAF/IAT sensor mounting fasteners and remove the sensor from the air filter housing.
4   Installation is the reverse of removal.

11.2 The MAF/IAT sensor is located on the air filter housing cover (four-cylinder engine shown, other engines similar)

12 Oxygen sensors - replacement

➡ **Note: Because it is installed in the exhaust manifold or pipe, both of which contract when cool, an oxygen sensor might be very difficult to loosen when the engine is cold. Rather than risk damage to the sensor or its mounting threads, start and run the engine for a minute or two, then shut it off. Be careful not to burn yourself during the following procedure.**

1   Be particularly careful when servicing an oxygen sensor:

a) *Oxygen sensors have a permanently attached pigtail and an electrical connector that cannot be removed. Damaging or removing the pigtail or electrical connector will render the sensor useless.*

b) *Keep grease, dirt and other contaminants away from the electrical connector and the louvered end of the sensor.*

c) *Do not use cleaning solvents of any kind on an oxygen sensor.*

d) *Oxygen sensors are extremely delicate. Do not drop a sensor or handle it roughly.*

e) *Make sure that the silicone boot on the sensor is installed in the correct position. Otherwise, the boot might melt and it might prevent the sensor from operating correctly.*

REPLACEMENT

2   Disconnect the cable from the negative battery terminal (see Chapter 5).

3   To access downstream sensors on all models, and the upstream sensor on the exhaust manifold for the rear cylinder head on V6 models, raise the front of the vehicle and place it securely on jackstands. Remove the engine under-cover.

Upstream oxygen sensor

▶ **Refer to illustration 12.4**

➡ **Note: On 2010 and earlier models, there is an upstream sensor in each exhaust manifold. On 2011 and later models, the upstream sensor is installed in the upper part of the integral exhaust manifold/catalytic converter assembly.**

4   Locate the upstream oxygen sensor (see illustration), then trace the sensor's electrical lead to its electrical connector and disconnect the connector. Disengage any harness clips.

5   Using a wrench or an oxygen sensor socket, unscrew the upstream oxygen sensor.

6   If you're going to install the old sensor, apply anti-seize compound to the threads of the sensor to facilitate future removal. If you're going to install a new oxygen sensor, it's not necessary to apply anti-seize compound to the threads; the threads on new sensors already have anti-seize compound on them.

7   Installation is the reverse of removal. Tighten the oxygen sensor to the torque listed in this Chapter's Specifications.

Downstream oxygen sensor (catalyst monitor sensor)

▶ **Refer to illustration 12.8**

➡ **Note: The downstream oxygen sensor is located in the lower end of the exhaust manifold/catalytic converter assembly or on the short section of exhaust pipe, just below the catalyst. There is a downstream oxygen sensor in each exhaust pipe on V6 models.**

8   Locate the downstream oxygen sensor (see illustration), then trace the lead up to the electrical connector and disconnect the connector. Disengage any harness clips.

9   Using a wrench or an oxygen sensor socket, unscrew the downstream oxygen sensor.

10 If you're going to install the old sensor, apply anti-seize compound to the threads of the sensor to facilitate future removal. If you're going to install a new oxygen sensor, it's not necessary to apply anti-seize compound to the threads. The threads on new sensors already have anti-seize compound on them.

11 Installation is the reverse of removal. Tighten the oxygen sensor to the torque listed in this Chapter's Specifications.

12.4 Upstream oxygen sensor location on the exhaust manifold (four-cylinder engine shown, other engines similar)

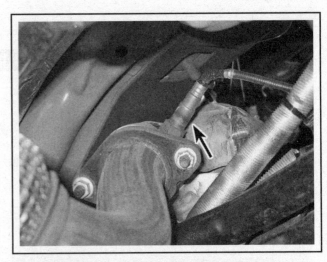

12.8 Downstream oxygen sensor location on the bottom of the catalyst (four-cylinder engine shown, other engines similar)

13 Power Steering Pressure (PSP) switch (2010 and earlier models) - replacement

➡ **Note: The PSP switch is located on top of the power steering pump.**

1 Disconnect the electrical connector from the PSP switch.

2 Using a deep socket, unscrew the PSP switch.
3 Installation is the reverse of removal.

14 Throttle Position (TP) sensor - replacement

The TP sensor is an integral component of the electronic throttle body, and is not separately serviceable. If you need to replace the TP sensor, you must replace the throttle body (see Chapter 4).

15 Transmission Range (TR) sensor - removal and installation

The TR sensor is located in the valve body and repair is beyond the scope of the home mechanic. If you need to replace the TR sensor, we recommend taking the vehicle to your local dealer or other qualified repair shop for repair.

16 Turbine Shaft Speed (TSS) sensor - replacement

➡ **Note: There are two speed sensors: the Turbine Shaft Speed (TSS) sensor and the Output Shaft Speed (OSS) sensor. The TSS sensor is located on top of the transaxle. The OSS sensor is located in the valve body of the transaxle and should be taken to your local dealer or other qualified repair shop for repair.**

1 Raise the vehicle and place it securely on jackstands. Remove the

engine under-cover.
2 Disconnect the electrical connector from the sensor.
3 Remove the sensor mounting bolt and remove the sensor.
4 Remove and discard the old sensor O-ring.
5 When installing the sensor, use a new O-ring. Installation is otherwise the reverse of removal.

17 Transmission Control Module (TCM) - removal and installation

▶ **Refer to illustration 17.3**

※ **CAUTION:**

To avoid electrostatic discharge damage to the TCM, handle the TCM only by its case. Do not touch the electrical terminals during removal and installation. If available, ground yourself to the vehicle with an anti-static ground strap, available at computer supply stores.

17.3 Depress the red tab, then slide the locking tab downward to disconnect the electrical connector from the Transmission Control Module (TCM)

➡ **Note: This procedure applies only to disconnecting, removing and installing the TCM that is already installed in your vehicle. If the TCM is defective and has to be replaced, it must be programmed with new software and calibrations. This procedure requires the use of Vehicle Communication Module (VCM) and Integrated Diagnostic System (IDS) software with appropriate hardware, or equivalent scan tool, so you WILL NOT BE ABLE TO REPLACE THE TCM AT HOME.**

1 Disconnect the cable from the negative battery terminal (see Chapter 5).
2 Remove the air filter outlet duct (see Chapter 4).

3 Disconnect the electrical connectors from the PCM (see illustration).
4 Remove the TCM mounting nuts and remove the TCM from the bracket.
5 Installation is the reverse of removal.

18 Powertrain Control Module (PCM) - removal and installation

♦ **Refer to illustration 18.2**

18.2 Powertrain Control Module (PCM) details: (cowl panel removed for clarity)v

1 *Electrical connectors*
2 *PCM mounting nut*

❊❊ CAUTION:

To avoid electrostatic discharge damage to the PCM, handle the PCM only by its case. Do not touch the electrical terminals during removal and installation. If available, ground yourself to the vehicle with an anti-static ground strap, available at computer supply stores.

➥ **Note:** This procedure applies only to disconnecting, removing and installing the PCM that is already installed in your vehicle. If the PCM is defective and has to be replaced, it must be programmed with new software and calibrations. This procedure requires the use of Vehicle Communication Module (VCM) and Integrated Diagnostic System (IDS) software with appropriate hardware, or equivalent scan tool, so you WILL NOT BE ABLE TO REPLACE THE PCM AT HOME.

1   Disconnect the cable from the negative battery terminal (see Chapter 5).
2   Rotate the red locks towards the center and disconnect the electrical connectors from the PCM (see illustration).
3   Remove the PCM mounting nuts and remove the PCM.
4   Installation is the reverse of removal.

19 Catalytic converter - replacement

❊❊ WARNING:

Wait until the engine has cooled completely before beginning this procedure.

FOUR-CYLINDER ENGINES

1   Raise the vehicle and place it securely on jackstands.
2   Locate the downstream oxygen sensor on the upper central part of the catalyst, trace the sensor to its electrical connector and disconnect it. Unscrew and remove the downstream oxygen sensor/catalyst sensor from the catalyst (see Section 12).
3   Loosen the fasteners on the clamp that secures the front end of the catalyst to the turbocharger. If the threads are severely damaged or rusted, apply some penetrant to the threads and wait awhile before loosening them.
4   Remove the nuts and bolts that secure the flange at the rear end of the catalyst to the exhaust pipe. If the threads are severely damaged or rusted, apply some penetrant to the threads and wait awhile before loosening them.
5   Remove the catalytic converter.
6   Remove and discard the old gasket between the exhaust down pipe and the catalyst mounting flange.

7   Installation is the reverse of removal. Use a new gasket and, if necessary, new fasteners.

V6 ENGINES

➥ **Note:** On all 2011 and later V6 engines, the left (front) catalytic converter is an integral component of the exhaust manifold and cannot be serviced separately (see Chapter 2B).

8   Raise the front of the vehicle and place it securely on jackstands. Remove the engine under-cover.
9   Locate the upstream and downstream oxygen sensors, trace their electrical leads to their respective connectors and disconnect them. Remove both oxygen sensors (see Section 12).
10 If the catalyst and/or exhaust manifold is equipped with a heat shield, remove the heat shield bolts and remove the heat shield from the exhaust manifold. On some models, there is another heat shield protecting the steering gear assembly. If necessary, remove this heat shield as well.
11 Remove the fasteners that secure the heat shield mounting bracket and remove the bracket.
12 Remove the fasteners that secure the catalyst's upper mounting flange to the exhaust manifold. If the threads are severely damaged or rusted, apply some penetrant to the threads and wait awhile before loosening them.

13 Remove the fasteners that secure the lower mounting flange to the exhaust pipe. If the threads are severely damaged or rusted, apply some penetrant to the threads and wait awhile before loosening them.

14 Pull the exhaust pipe down far enough to clear the lower end of the catalyst.

15 Remove the catalyst from the exhaust manifold.

16 Remove and discard the old gaskets between the exhaust manifold flange and the upper catalyst flange and, if equipped, between the lower catalyst flange and the exhaust pipe flange.

17 Installation is the reverse of removal. Use new flange gaskets.

20 Evaporative Emissions Control (EVAP) system - component replacement

EVAP CANISTER PURGE VALVE

Four-cylinder engine

♦ Refer to illustration 20.2

1 Disconnect the cable from the negative battery terminal (see Chapter 5).

2 Disconnect the electrical connector from the canister purge valve (see illustration).

3 Disconnect the EVAP line quick-connect fittings (see Chapter 4 for information on quick-connect fittings).

4 Remove the purge valve mounting stud-bolt and remove the assembly.

5 Installation is the reverse of removal.

V6 engines

6 Disconnect the cable from the negative battery terminal (see Chapter 5).

7 Disconnect the electrical connector from the canister purge valve.

8 Disconnect the EVAP line quick-connect fitting (see Chapter 4 for information on quick-connect fittings).

9 Remove the purge valve mounting bolts and remove the purge valve.

10 Installation is the reverse of removal; use a new O-ring.

EVAP CANISTER

♦ Refer to illustrations 20.13 and 20.15

➡ Note: The EVAP canister is located under the vehicle, towards the rear.

11 Disconnect the cable from the negative battery terminal (see Chapter 5).

12 Raise the vehicle and support it securely on jackstands.

13 Remove the splash shield fasteners and shield, if equipped (see illustration).

14 Disconnect the electrical connector and the vapor hose from the EVAP canister vent solenoid dust separator.

15 Disconnect the two EVAP line quick-connect fittings (see illustration) from the EVAP canister (see Chapter 4 for information on quick-connect fittings).

16 Remove the mounting fasteners that secure the canister and remove the canister.

17 Installation is the reverse of removal.

20.2 The EVAP canister purge valve is located above the valve cover on four-cylinder models

20.13 Remove the EVAP splash shield fasteners

20.15 Disconnect the two EVAP line quick-connect fittings

EVAP CANISTER VENT SOLENOID AND DUST SEPARATOR ASSEMBLY

→ **Note: The EVAP canister vent solenoid is mounted on the EVAP canister.**

18 Remove the EVAP canister (see Steps 11 through 16).

19 Release the two lock tabs and remove the EVAP canister vent solenoid heat shield from the canister by pushing it straight down.

20 Disconnect the fuel vapor hose from the vent solenoid.

21 Release the lock tab and detach the vent solenoid and dust separator assembly from the EVAP canister.

22 Installation is the reverse of removal.

---

21 Fuel Rail Pressure (FRP) sensor (four-cylinder models) - replacement

♦ **Refer to illustration 21.5**

1 Relieve the fuel system pressure (see Chapter 4).

2 Remove the charge air cooler inlet and middle tubes (see Chapter 4).

3 Remove the drivebelt (see Chapter 1).

4 Remove the power steering pump and set it out of the way.

5 Disconnect the FRP sensor electrical connector (see illustration).

6 Unscrew and remove the FRP sensor.

7 Installation is the reverse of removal, tightening the sensor to the torque listed in this Chapter's Specifications.

21.5 Location of the Fuel Rail Pressure (FRP) sensor - manifold removed for clarity

---

22 Positive Crankcase Ventilation (PCV) valve - replacement

FOUR-CYLINDER MODELS

♦ **Refer to illustration 22.2**

→ **Note: The PCV valve is an integral part of the crankcase vent oil separator, which is located on the front side of the engine block.**

1 Remove the intake manifold (see Chapter 2A).

2 Remove the oil vent separator mounting bolts (see illustration) and gasket.

3 Clean the engine block and install a new gasket to the separator.

4 Installation is the reverse of removal, tightening the oil vent separator bolts securely.

22.2 Location of the vent oil separator (four-cylinder engine)

V6 MODELS

➡ **Note: The PCV valve is located on the rear valve cover. According to the manufacturer, the PCV valve must be replaced if it's removed.**

5   Remove the upper intake manifold (see Chapter 2B).
6   Turn the PCV valve counterclockwise and remove it from the valve cover.

7   You must discard the PCV valve every time that you remove it and replace it with a new unit, because the locking mechanism of the PCV valve is damaged by removal.
8   When installing the new PCV valve, make sure that the new valve is oriented correctly before screwing it into place, so that the terminal faces toward the wiring harness. If you install the new PCV valve so that it's facing in the wrong direction, you will have to unscrew it and once you do that, you must replace it again.

23 Variable Valve Timing (VVT) system - description

1   The VVT system controls intake valve timing to increase engine torque in the low and mid-speed range and to increase horsepower in the high-speed range.
2   The VVT system consists of the PCM-controlled Oil Control Valve (OCV), which is mounted on top of the cylinder head, and the VVT actuator, which is mounted on the front end of the camshafts.
3   The PCM-controlled OCV varies the oil pressure in the VVT actuator, which continually varies the timing of both cams.

Torque specifications	Ft-lbs (unless otherwise indicated)	Nm

➡ Note: One foot-pound (ft-lb) of torque is equivalent to 12 inch-pounds (in-lbs) of torque. Torque values below approximately 15 ft-lbs are expressed in inch-pounds, since most foot-pound torque wrenches are not accurate at these smaller values.

Cylinder Head Temperature (CHT) sensor		
Four-cylinder engine	35 in-lbs	4
V6 engines	177 in-lbs	20
Fuel Rail Pressure (FRP) sensor (four-cylinder engine)		
Step 1	53 in-lbs	6
Step 2	Tighten an additional 5-degrees	
Step 3	Loosen 90-degrees	
Step 4	53 in-lbs	6
Step 5	Tighten an additional 21-degrees	
Knock sensor mounting bolt	177 in-lbs	20
Oxygen sensor/catalyst monitor sensor	35	48

7A

AUTOMATIC TRANSAXLE

1   General information

All information on the automatic transaxle is included in this Part of Chapter 7. The transfer case portion of the transaxle is covered in Chapter 7B.

Because of the complexity of the automatic transaxles and the specialized equipment necessary to perform most service operations, this Chapter contains only those procedures related to general diagnosis, routine maintenance, adjustment and removal and installation.

If the transaxle requires major repair work, it should be left to a dealer service department or an automotive or transmission repair shop. Once properly diagnosed you can, however, remove and install the transaxle yourself and save the expense, even if the repair work is done by a transmission shop.

2   Diagnosis - general

1   Automatic transaxle malfunctions may be caused by five general conditions:

   a) *Poor engine performance*
   b) *Improper adjustments*
   c) *Hydraulic malfunctions*
   d) *Mechanical malfunctions*
   e) *Malfunctions in the computer or its signal network*

2   Diagnosis of these problems should always begin with a check of the easily repaired items: fluid level and condition (see Chapter 1), shift cable adjustment and shift lever installation. Next, perform a road test to determine if the problem has been corrected or if more diagnosis is necessary. If the problem persists after the preliminary tests and corrections are completed, additional diagnosis should be performed by a dealer service department or other qualified transmission repair shop. On modern electronically-controlled automatic transaxles, a scan tool is helpful in retrieving trouble codes relating to the transaxle. Refer to the "Troubleshooting" Section at the front of this manual for information on symptoms of transaxle problems.

PRELIMINARY CHECKS

3   Drive the vehicle to warm the transaxle to normal operating temperature.

4   Check the fluid level as described in Chapter 1:

   a) *If the fluid level is unusually low, add enough fluid to bring the level within the designated area of the dipstick, then check for external leaks (see following).*
   b) *If the fluid level is abnormally high, drain off the excess, then check the drained fluid for contamination by coolant. The presence of engine coolant in the automatic transmission fluid indicates that a failure has occurred in the internal radiator oil cooler walls that separate the coolant from the transmission fluid (see Chapter 3).*
   c) *If the fluid is foaming, drain it and refill the transaxle, then check for coolant in the fluid, or a high fluid level.*

5   Check the engine idle speed.

➡ **Note: If the engine is malfunctioning, do not proceed with the preliminary checks until it has been repaired and runs normally.**

6   Check and adjust the shift cable, if necessary (see Section 4).

7   If hard shifting is experienced, inspect the shift cable under the steering column and at the manual lever on the transaxle (see Section 4).

FLUID LEAK DIAGNOSIS

8   Most fluid leaks are easy to locate visually. Repair usually consists of replacing a seal or gasket. If a leak is difficult to find, the following procedure may help.

9   Identify the fluid. Make sure it's transmission fluid and not engine oil or brake fluid (automatic transmission fluid is a deep red color).

10 Try to pinpoint the source of the leak. Drive the vehicle several miles, then park it over a large sheet of cardboard. After a minute or two, you should be able to locate the leak by determining the source of the fluid dripping onto the cardboard.

11 Make a careful visual inspection of the suspected component and the area immediately around it. Pay particular attention to gasket mating surfaces. A mirror is often helpful for finding leaks in areas that are hard to see.

12 If the leak still cannot be found, clean the suspected area thoroughly with a degreaser or solvent, then dry it thoroughly.

13 Drive the vehicle for several miles at normal operating temperature and varying speeds. After driving the vehicle, visually inspect the suspected component again.

14 Once the leak has been located, the cause must be determined before it can be properly repaired. If a gasket is replaced but the sealing flange is bent, the new gasket will not stop the leak. The bent flange must be straightened.

15 Before attempting to repair a leak, check to make sure that the following conditions are corrected or they may cause another leak.

➡ **Note: Some of the following conditions cannot be fixed without highly specialized tools and expertise. Such problems must be referred to a qualified transmission shop or a dealer service department.**

Gasket leaks

16 Check the pan periodically. Make sure the bolts are tight, no bolts are missing, the gasket is in good condition and the pan is flat (dents in the pan may indicate damage to the valve body inside).

17 If the pan gasket is leaking, the fluid level or the fluid pressure may be too high, the vent may be plugged, the pan bolts may be too tight, the pan sealing flange may be warped, the sealing surface of the transaxle housing may be damaged, the gasket may be damaged or the transaxle casting may be cracked or porous. If sealant instead of gasket material has been used to form a seal between the pan and the transaxle housing, it may be the wrong type of sealant.

Seal leaks

18 If a transaxle seal is leaking, the fluid level or pressure may be too high, the vent may be plugged, the seal bore may be damaged, the seal itself may be damaged or improperly installed, the surface of the shaft protruding through the seal may be damaged or a loose bearing may be causing excessive shaft movement.

19 Make sure the dipstick tube seal is in good condition and the tube is properly seated. Periodically check the area around the sensors for leakage. If transmission fluid is evident, check the seals for damage.

Case leaks

20 If the case itself appears to be leaking, the casting is porous and will have to be repaired or replaced.

21 Make sure the oil cooler hose fittings are tight and in good condition.

Fluid comes out vent pipe or fill tube

22 If this condition occurs the possible causes are: the transaxle is overfilled; there is coolant in the fluid; the case is porous; the dipstick is incorrect; the vent is plugged or the drain-back holes are plugged.

3 Shift lever - replacement

✳✳ WARNING:

These models are equipped with a Supplemental Restraint System (SRS), more commonly known as airbags. Always disable the airbag system before working in the vicinity of any airbag system component to avoid the possibility of accidental deployment of the airbag(s), which could cause personal injury (see Chapter 12).

✳✳ WARNING:

Do not use a memory saving device to preserve the PCM or radio memory when working on or near airbag system components.

SHIFT KNOB

▶ **Refer to illustration 3.6**

1   Remove the upper bezel of the floor console around the shifter (see Chapter 11).

2010 and earlier models

2   Disconnect the Transmission Control Switch (TCS) electrical connector.

3   Pry the shift lever covers apart from the top and bottom.

➡ **Note: The covers will need to be replaced once they have been separated.**

4   Remove the two screws in the knob assembly, then remove the knob while pulling the TCS harness out.

5   Installation is the reverse of the removal procedure.

2011 and later models

6   Pull the shift knob boot up and disconnect the electrical connector. Remove the two screws and pull the knob off the shaft (see illustration).

7   Installation is the reverse of the removal procedure.

SHIFT LEVER ASSEMBLY

▶ **Refer to illustrations 3.12, 3.13 and 3.15**

8   Disconnect the cable from the negative battery terminal (see Chapter 5). Wait at least two minutes before proceeding.

9   Remove the floor console center trim cover (see Chapter 11).

10   On 2010 and earlier models, remove the power outlet trim panel fasteners and move the panel out of the way.

11   On 2011 and later MKX models, remove the shift lever trim panel; it is held in place by four screws on each side of the panel.

➡ **Note: On models equipped with an ambient light, unclip the wiring harness and rotate the light counterclockwise to remove it.**

12   Use a trim tool to pry the cable eye from the ballstud on the shifter (see illustration).

13   Release the tabs on the sides of the shift cable and detach it from the console (see illustration).

14   Disconnect any electrical connectors at the shifter assembly.

3.6 **Lift the boot up, disconnect the electrical connector (A) and remove the shift lever mounting screws (B) - 2011 and later Edge models**

3.12 **Pry the cable end from the ballstud on the shifter**

3.13 **Pry the tabs forward to release the cable retainer from the console**

3.15 To remove the shifter assembly, remove the four mounting bolts

15 Remove the mounting bolts and remove the shifter assembly from the floor (see illustration).

16 Installation is the reverse of removal. The shift cable should be adjusted any time it has been disconnected (see Section 4).

PADDLE SHIFTER

17 Disconnect the cable from the negative battery terminal (see Chapter 5). Wait at least two minutes before proceeding.

18 Remove the airbag module from the steering wheel (see Chapter 10, Section 14).

19 Remove the steering wheel switch trim panel screws.

20 Disconnect the electrical connectors from the switch trim panel, then remove the trim panel.

21 Disconnect the electrical connectors to the paddle shifter.

22 Remove the two mounting screws and remove the paddle shifter.

23 Installation is the reverse of removal.

4 Shift cable - replacement and adjustment

※※ WARNING:

The models covered by this manual are equipped with Supplemental Restraint Systems (SRS), more commonly known as airbags. Always disarm the airbag system before working in the vicinity of any airbag system component to avoid the possibility of accidental deployment of the airbag, which could cause personal injury (see Chapter 12). Do not use a memory saving device to preserve the PCM or radio memory when working on or near airbag system components.

➡ Note: This is a difficult procedure for the home mechanic, since replacement of the cables requires removal of the instrument panel and the HVAC housing under the instrument panel.

REPLACEMENT

▶ Refer to illustrations 4.8 and 4.11

1 If the vehicle has just been driven, wait several hours to allow the engine to cool down before beginning this procedure. Disconnect both the negative and positive cables from the battery (see Chapter 5). Wait at least two minutes before proceeding.

2 Remove the air filter housing (see Chapter 4).

3 On V6 models, loosen the hose clamp and disconnect the intake duct from the throttle body.

4 Remove the battery and battery tray (see Chapter 5).

5 Detach the shift cable from the shift lever and console, then remove the center console (see Chapter 11).

6 Disconnect the cable from the shift assembly on the floor (see Section 3).

7 Remove the insulation from the floor area under the center of the instrument panel to access the fasteners securing the cable grommet to the floorpan. Remove the fasteners securing the transaxle cable plate/grommet.

8 To disconnect the shift cable at the transaxle control lever, pop the cable end off of the lever ballstud (see illustration).

9 Squeeze the retaining tabs and detach the cable housing from the mounting bracket on the transaxle.

10 Disconnect any cable retainers along the length of the cable.

11 Remove the grommet plate nuts from the floorpan studs below the HVAC housing (see illustration).

4.8 Pry the cable end from the ballstud on the shift control lever (A), then squeeze the tabs (B) and slide the cable housing out of the bracket

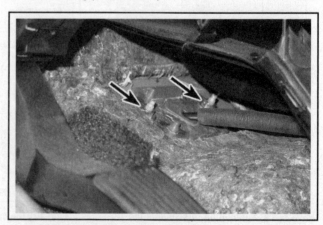

4.11 Shift cable grommet plate nuts

12 Pull the shift cable through the floor from the inside, passing it under and to the left of the air duct that leads to the rear seats.

→ **Note: The grommet is integral to the cable assembly.**

13 Installation is the reverse of removal. Adjust the new cable after installation.

ADJUSTMENT

▶ **Refer to illustration 4.21**

→ **Note: The transmission end of the shift cable is equipped with an adjuster mechanism.**

14 Set the parking brake, then disconnect the cable from the negative battery terminal (see Chapter 5).
15 Remove the air filter housing (see Chapter 4).
16 Place the shifter in Drive.
17 Remove the cable eye from the control arm on the transaxle.
18 Manually move the shift arm at the transaxle clockwise until it stops, then rotate the lever counterclockwise one click (on 2010 and earlier models) or three clicks (on 2011 and later models).
19 On 2011 and later models, remove the Transaxle Control Module (TCM) electrical connector, then remove the TCM bracket fasteners and bracket.
20 On 2010 and earlier models, pry the latch up, then slide the lock tab to the side.
21 On 2011 and later models, carefully pry the adjuster lock tabs out (see illustration). While the tabs are held out, slide the lock forward to unlock the cable.

4.21 Pry the adjuster lock tabs out (A) and slide the lock forward (B) to unlock the cable

22 Slide the shift lever cable end until the cable is aligned with the control lever.
23 Connect the cable end back onto the manual lever ballstud, with the lock still released.
24 Lock the adjuster, then slide the lock tab back on the adjuster.

→ **Note: Make sure the adjuster is locked and the cable is securely seated onto the ball stud.**

25 After installing any remaining components, apply the parking brake, start the engine and shift into each range to verify the adjustment is correct.

5 Automatic transaxle - removal and installation

REMOVAL

▶ **Refer to illustrations 5.11 and 5.32**

1 Disconnect the cables from the battery and remove the battery and battery tray (see Chapter 5).
2 Drain the cooling system (see Chapter 1), then remove the radiator hoses.
3 On four-cylinder models, remove the charge air cooler pipes (see Chapter 4).
4 Remove the air filter housing and duct (see Chapter 4), then remove the housing bracket bolts and bracket.
5 Loosen the hose clamp and remove the duct or pipe to the throttle body.
6 On 2010 and earlier models, remove the nut securing the transaxle fill tube. Rotate the filler tube counterclockwise 90-degrees and pull the tube from the transaxle, if equipped.
7 Disconnect the Transaxle Control Module (TCM) harness electrical connector at the transmission range sensor. Also disconnect the ground straps and remove the bolts holding the electrical harness to the transaxle.
8 Disconnect the shift cable from the transaxle shift control arm (see Section 4). Remove the two bolts securing the transaxle cable mount.
9 Remove the transaxle front and rear wire harness brackets from the transaxle.
10 Disconnect the electrical connectors for the Vehicle Speed Sensor

5.11 Use an overhead support fixture to secure the engine while the transaxle is removed

(VSS) and the TCM (see Chapter 6).
11 Attach an engine support fixture to the lifting hook at the transaxle end of the engine (see illustration). If no hook is provided, use a bolt of the proper size and thread pitch to attach the support fixture chain to a hole at the end of the cylinder head.

→ **Note: Engine support fixtures can be obtained at most equipment rental yards and some auto parts stores.**

On 2010 and earlier V6 engines, the upper intake manifold must be removed first (see Chapter 2B).

5.32 Mark the relationship of the torque converter to the driveplate starting with the slotted hole on the flexplate first

12 Remove the four upper engine-to-transmission mounting bolts.

13 Loosen the driveaxle/hub nuts and the wheel lug nuts, raise the front of the vehicle and support it securely on jackstands or a lift. Remove the wheels.

14 Disconnect the shift cable from the transaxle, and remove the bolts securing the shift cable brackets.

15 Unbolt the power steering hose bracket and retainers.

16 Disconnect the flexible exhaust pipe sections and the Y-pipe. Remove the right-side exhaust heat shield and remove the catalytic converter (see Chapter 4).

17 Remove the heat shield over the roll restrictor, then unbolt the roll restrictor.

18 Remove the driveaxles (see Chapter 8).

19 Remove the splash shields from the left and right fenderwells.

20 Place a block of wood above the lower control arm to protect the outer CV joint on the left side. Remove the left steering knuckle (see Chapter 10).

21 Remove the starter (see Chapter 5).

22 On AWD models, remove the rear driveshaft and wire it aside.

23 Drain the transaxle lubricant (see Chapter 1). Disconnect and plug the transmission fluid hoses.

24 Remove the bolts securing the transaxle support insulator brackets, then remove the brackets.

25 If you're working on an AWD model, remove the transfer case (see Chapter 7B).

26 Support the subframe, then remove the subframe-to-lower bumper nuts from each side.

27 Remove the stabilizer bar-to-subframe bolts and steering gear-to-subframe bolts (see Chapter 10).

28 Remove the subframe support brackets bolts and brackets.

29 Remove the front suspension subframe (see Chapter 10, Section 4).

30 Support the transaxle with a jack - preferably a transmission jack made for this purpose (available at most tool rental yards). Safety chains will help steady the transaxle on the jack.

31 Disconnect the oxygen sensors (see Chapter 6).

32 Remove the torque converter cover and mark the relationship of the torque converter to the driveplate (see illustration). Remove the converter mounting nuts working through the starter opening.

33 Remove the remaining bolts securing the transaxle to the engine.

34 Move the transaxle away from the engine to disengage it from the engine block dowel pins. Carefully lower the transmission jack to the floor and remove the transaxle.

INSTALLATION

35 Installation is the reverse of removal, but note the following points:

a) *As the torque converter is reinstalled, ensure that the drive tangs at the center of the torque converter hub engage with the recesses in the automatic transaxle fluid pump inner gear. This can be confirmed by turning the torque converter while pushing it towards the transaxle. If it isn't fully engaged, it will clunk into place.*

b) *When installing the transaxle, make sure the matchmarks you made on the torque converter and driveplate line up.*

c) *Install all of the driveplate-to-torque converter nuts before tightening any of them.*

d) *Tighten the driveplate-to-torque converter nuts to the specified torque.*

e) *Tighten the transaxle mounting bolts to the specified torque.*

f) *Tighten the suspension crossmember mounting bolts to the torque values listed in this Chapter's Specifications.*

g) *Tighten the driveaxle/hub nuts to the torque value listed in the Chapter 8 Specifications.*

h) *Tighten the wheel lug nuts to the torque listed in the Chapter 1 Specifications.*

i) *Fill the transaxle with the correct type and amount of automatic transmission fluid (see Chapter 1).*

j) *On completion, adjust the shift cable (see Section 4).*

6 Automatic transaxle overhaul - general information

In the event of a problem occurring, it will be necessary to establish whether the fault is electrical, mechanical or hydraulic in nature, before repair work can be contemplated. Diagnosis requires detailed knowledge of the transaxle's operation and construction, as well as access to specialized test equipment, and so is deemed to be beyond the scope of this manual. It is therefore essential that problems with the automatic transaxle are referred to a dealer service department or other qualified repair facility for assessment.

Note that a faulty transaxle should not be removed before the vehicle has been diagnosed by a knowledgeable technician equipped with the proper tools, as troubleshooting must be performed with the transaxle installed in the vehicle.

7   Driveaxle oil seals - replacement

1   Oil leaks frequently occur due to wear of the driveaxle oil seals. Replacement of these seals is relatively easy, since the repair can be performed without removing the transaxle from the vehicle.

2   Driveaxle oil seals are located at the sides of the transaxle, where the driveaxles are attached. If leakage at the seal is suspected, raise the vehicle and support it securely on jackstands. If the seal is leaking, lubricant will be found on the sides of the transaxle, below the seals.

3   Remove the driveaxles (see Chapter 8).

4   Use a screwdriver or prybar to carefully pry the oil seal out of the transaxle bore.

5   If the oil seal cannot be removed with a screwdriver or prybar, a special oil seal removal tool (available at auto parts stores) will be required.

6   Using a large section of pipe or a large deep socket (slightly smaller than the outside diameter of the seal) as a drift, install the new oil seal. Drive it into the bore squarely and make sure it's completely seated. Coat the seal lip with transaxle lubricant.

7   Install the driveaxle(s). Be careful not to damage the lip of the new seal with the inboard splines of the driveaxle.

8   Transaxle mount - replacement

♦ **Refer to illustration 8.5**

1   Insert a large screwdriver or prybar between the mount and the transaxle and pry up.

2   The transaxle should not move excessively away from the mount. If it does, replace the mount.

3   Remove the battery and battery tray (see Chapter 5).

4   Remove the air filter housing (see Chapter 4)

5   Supporting the transaxle with a floor jack, remove the through-bolt nut and bolt and the mount-to-chassis bolts, then remove the mount (see illustration). It may be necessary to raise the transaxle slightly to provide enough clearance to remove the mount.

6   Remove the remaining mount bolts.

7   Installation is the reverse of removal.

➡ **Note: Install all of the mount fasteners before tightening any of them.**

8.5 Transaxle mount details

1	Through-bolt/nut	3	Mount bracket-to-transaxle
2	Mount-to-chassis bolts		nuts

Specifications

General

Fluid type and capacity	See Chapter 1

Torque specifications	Ft-lbs (unless otherwise indicated)	Nm

➡ **Note: One foot-pound (ft-lb) of torque is equivalent to 12 inch-pounds (in-lbs) of torque. Torque values below approximately 15 foot-pounds are expressed in inch-pounds, because most foot-pound torque wrenches are not accurate at these smaller values.**

Torque specifications	Ft-lbs (unless otherwise indicated)	Nm
Crossmember mounting nuts	115	156
Crossmember bracket bolts	76	103
Driveshaft bolts (AWD)	52	72
Fluid pan bolts	80 in-lbs	9
Torque converter-to-driveplate bolts (slotted hole first)	41	55
Transaxle-to-engine mounting bolts	35	48

7B

TRANSFER CASE

Section

Reference to other Chapters

1 General information

Models equipped with V6 engines are offered with optional All Wheel Drive (AWD). The transfer case sends power through a driveshaft that delivers the torque to a rear differential and two rear driveaxles. The AWD control module will shift into AWD when the PCM initiates the need due to differences in wheelslip speed between the front and rear wheels. The system requires no driver input to operate, thus there is no select button on the instrument panel.

Due to the complexity of the transfer case covered in this manual and the need for specialized equipment to perform most service operations, this Chapter contains only routine maintenance and removal and installation procedures.

If the transfer case requires major repair work, it must be replaced as a unit.

2 Transfer case rear output shaft oil seal - removal and installation

▶ **Refer to illustration 2.11**

1 Raise the vehicle and support it securely on jackstands.
2 Drain the transfer case lubricant (see Chapter 1).
3 Remove the driveshaft (see Chapter 8).
4 Mark the relative positions of the pinion, nut and flange.
5 Use a beam- or dial-type inch-pound torque wrench to determine the torque required to rotate the pinion (vehicle in Neutral). Record it for use later.

6 Count the number of threads visible between the end of the nut and the end of the pinion shaft and record it for use later.

7 Remove the flange mounting nut using a two-pin spanner to hold the pinion flange while loosening the locknut.

8 Remove the companion flange, using a puller whose bolt-holes can be attached to two, three or all four of the flange's driveshaft bolt holes. Tighten the puller center bolt to press the flange off the shaft.

9 Pry out the seal with a screwdriver or a seal removal tool. Don't damage the seal bore.

10 Remove the seal deflector, then use a seal-puller to remove the pinion seal.

11 With the seal removed, remove the collapsible bearing spacer (see illustration).

12 Install a new collapsible spacer.

13 Lubricate the lips of the new seal with multi-purpose grease and tap it evenly into position with a seal installation tool or a large socket. Make sure it enters the housing squarely and is tapped in to its full depth.

14 Align the mating marks made before disassembly and install the companion flange. If necessary, tighten the pinion nut to draw the flange into place.

15 Tighten the NEW nut carefully until the original number of threads are exposed and the marks are aligned.

16 Measure the torque required to rotate the pinion and tighten the nut in small increments until it matches the figure recorded in Step 5.

2.11 Rear output shaft seal details

A   Collapsible bearing spacer
B   Output shaft seal
C   Seal deflector
D   Driveshaft companion flange

> ❋❋ **CAUTION:**
>
> **If you exceed the original torque reading by more than 3 in-lbs, the assembly will need to be taken apart again to install a new collapsible spacer.**

17 Connect the driveshaft (see Chapter 8), add the specified lubricant to the transfer case (see Chapter 1) and lower the vehicle.

> ❋❋ **CAUTION:**
>
> **All driveshaft flange and support bearing bolts must be replaced with New fasteners.**

3   Transfer case driveaxle oil seal (right side) - removal and installation

1   Remove the wheel cover or hub cap on the right side. Break the hub nut loose with a socket and large breaker bar.

2   Loosen the wheel lug nuts, raise the vehicle and support it securely on jackstands. Remove the right wheel and the splash panel from the right fenderwell.

3   Remove the right driveaxle and intermediate shaft (see Chapter 8).

4   Remove the transfer case (see Section 4).

5   Carefully remove the seal (there is a non-serviceable bearing behind it). There are several types of seal removal tools. The manufacturer recommends using a slide-hammer tool with an internal-expanding type of seal-puller. Using a long, threaded extension on the slide-hammer allows the seal to be removed without removing the exhaust system.

6   Using a seal installer or a large deep socket as a drift, install the new oil seal. Drive it into the bore squarely and make sure it's completely seated.

7   Lubricate the lip of the new seal with multi-purpose grease, then install a new dust shield.

8   Install the intermediate shaft and driveaxle (see Chapter 8).

9   The remainder of installation is the reverse of removal. Check the transfer case lubricant level and add some, if necessary, to bring it to the appropriate level (see Chapter 1).

4   Transfer case - removal and installation

1   Models equipped with V6 engines are offered with optional All Wheel Drive (AWD). The transfer case sends power to the rear differential and rear driveaxles.

2   Remove the wheel cover or hub cap. Break the hub nut loose with a socket and large breaker bar. Loosen the wheel lug nuts.

3   Raise the front of the vehicle and support it securely on jackstands. Remove the right wheel.

4   Unbolt the front portion of the driveshaft (see Chapter 8) and suspend it from a piece of wire (don't let it hang from the center support bearing).

5   Remove the right driveaxle and intermediate shaft (see Chapter 8). Remove the right-side catalytic converter (see Chapter 6).

6   Remove the roll-restrictor mount fasteners and mount (see Chapter 10, illustration 4.12).

7   Remove the two bolts securing the transfer case to the support bracket.

8   Remove the three bolts securing the transfer case support bracket to the engine.

9   Support the transfer case with a suitable jack.

10 Working on the right side of the transfer case, remove the three transfer case-to-transaxle mounting bolts.

11 Working on the left side, remove the final two mounting bolts (bellhousing-to-transfer case).

12 To remove the transfer case from the vehicle, rock the transfer case until it comes free of the transaxle.

13 Installation is the reverse of removal, noting the following points:

   a) *Install a new compression seal to the case.*
   b) *Tighten the exhaust system fasteners to the torque listed in the Chapter 4 Specifications.*
   c) *Tighten the NEW driveshaft fasteners to the torque listed in the Chapter 8 Specifications.*
   d) *Tighten the transfer case fasteners to the torque listed in this Chapter's Specifications.*
   e) *Refill the transfer case with the proper type and amount of fluid (see Chapter 1).*
   f) *Tighten the wheel lug nuts to the torque listed in the Chapter 1 Specifications.*

Torque specifications*	Ft-lbs (unless otherwise indicated)	Nm

➡ **Note: One foot-pound (ft-lb) of torque is equivalent to 12 inch-pounds (in-lbs) of torque. Torque values below approximately 15 foot-pounds are expressed in inch-pounds, because most foot-pound torque wrenches are not accurate at these smaller values.**

Transfer case-to-transaxle bolts	66	90
Transfer case support bracket-to-engine block mounting bolts	52	70
Transfer case support bracket-to-transfer case mounting bolts	52	70
Roll-restrictor bolts	85	115
Roll-restrictor heat bolts	80-in-lbs	9

8

DRIVELINE

Section

Reference to other Chapters

1   General information

The information in this Chapter deals with the components from the rear of the engine to the drive wheels, except for the transaxle, which is dealt with in the previous Chapter.

Since nearly all the procedures covered in this Chapter involve working under the vehicle, make sure it's securely supported on sturdy jackstands or on a hoist where the vehicle can be easily raised and lowered.

2   Driveaxles - removal and installation

☀☀ WARNING:

Wait until the engine is completely cool before beginning this procedure.

FRONT

Removal

▶ **Refer to illustrations 2.5, 2.7a and 2.7b**

1   Loosen the wheel lug nuts, raise the vehicle and support it securely on jackstands. Remove the wheel. Remove the pushpins securing the splash shield in the fenderwell.

2   With the brakes applied to keep the driveaxle from turning, remove the driveaxle/hub nut but do not discard it yet.

3   Disconnect the brake hose bracket and the wheel speed sensor wiring harness from the shock absorber.

4   Remove the nut and bolt from the lower balljoint (see Chapter 10) and separate the lower control arm from the steering knuckle.

5   Use a drive hub remover or other suitable puller to separate the driveaxle from the hub (see illustration).

6   Swing the knuckle/hub assembly out (away from the vehicle) until the end of the driveaxle is free of the hub. Use a length of wire to secure the knuckle out of the way to the rear. Support the outer end of the driveaxle with a piece of wire to avoid unnecessary strain on the inner CV joint.

7   If you are removing the right side driveaxle, use a brass drift to strike the inner face of the inner CV joint to separate it from the intermediate shaft (see illustration). If you are removing the left side driveaxle, use a driveaxle remover and slide hammer to remove the driveaxle from the transaxle. If a removal tool is not available, pry the inner CV joint out of the transaxle using a large screwdriver or pry bar positioned between the transaxle and the CV joint housing (see illustration). Be careful not to damage the differential seal.

8   Support the CV joints and carefully remove the driveaxle from the vehicle.

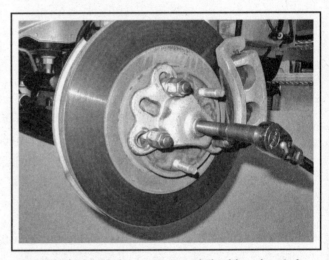

2.5 Using a drive hub remover to push the driveaxle out of the hub splines

2.7a Use a hammer and brass drift to separate the right-side driveaxle from the intermediate shaft

2.7b Carefully pry the inner end of the left-side driveaxle from the transaxle

Installation

9   Pry the old spring clip from the inner end of the driveaxle (left side) or outer end of the intermediate shaft (right side) and install a new one.

10   Lubricate the differential or intermediate shaft seal with multi-purpose grease and raise the driveaxle into position while supporting the CV joints.

➡ **Note: Position the spring clip with the opening facing down; this will ease insertion of the driveaxle and prevent damage to the clip.**

11   Push the splined end of the inner CV joint into the differential side gear (left side) or onto the intermediate shaft (right side) and make sure the spring clip locks in its groove.

✷✷ CAUTION:

Be careful to not let the sharp edges on the left side driveaxle splines cut or damage the oil seal when inserting the driveaxle.

Check that the spring clip has engaged by tugging outward on the inboard CV joint housing.

➡ **Note: To make insertion of the left-side driveaxle easier, position the gap in the spring clip in the 6 o-clock position.**

12   Apply a light coat of multi-purpose grease to the outer CV joint splines, pull out on the steering knuckle assembly and install the stub axle into the hub.

13   Reconnect the lower control arm to the steering knuckle and tighten all fasteners to the torque listed in the Chapter 10 Specifications.

14   Seat the driveaxle using the **old** driveaxle/hub nut. Apply the brake to prevent the driveaxle from rotating, tighten the old driveaxle/hub nut to the specified torque, then remove and discard the old nut. Install a new nut and retighten to the specified torque.

✷✷ CAUTION:

The driveaxle/hub nut must be tightened before lowering the vehicle or damage to the wheel bearings may occur.

➡ **Note: The driveaxle/hub nut is coated with a one-use locking chemical and cannot be re-used for final assembly. The locking chemical is activated by heat created during tightening. The nut must be tightened to the specified torque within five minutes of starting it on the threads or the locking chemical will not activate properly.**

15   Install the wheel and lug nuts, then lower the vehicle.

16   Tighten the lug nuts to the torque listed in the Chapter 1 Specifications.

INTERMEDIATE SHAFT

Removal

▶ **Refer to illustrations 2.20a and 2.20b**

17   Loosen the wheel lug nuts, raise the vehicle and support it securely on jackstands. Remove the wheel.

18   Follow Steps 1 through 8 and remove the right side driveaxle.

19   On front wheel drive models, remove the bolts and nuts securing the catalytic converter support bracket.

20   Remove the bearing-support mounting bolts or nuts (see illustrations) and slide the intermediate shaft out of the transaxle (transfer case on AWD models). Be careful not to damage the seal when pulling the shaft out.

21   Check the support bearing for smooth operation by turning the shaft while holding the bearing. If you feel any roughness, take the intermediate shaft to an automotive machine shop or other qualified repair facility to have a new bearing installed.

Installation

22   Remove the retainer clip from the outboard end of the intermediate shaft and replace it with a new one.

23   If you're working on an AWD model, replace the seal in the transfer case before installing the intermediate shaft.

24   Lubricate the lips of the transaxle seal with multi-purpose grease. Carefully guide the intermediate shaft into the transaxle side gear (transfer case on AWD models) engaging the splines. Ensure that the clip has locked into the gear, then install the mounting fasteners for the bearing support.

2.20a   Intermediate shaft bearing support bolts - early FWD V6 model; later V6 models use three bolts

2.20b   Intermediate shaft bearing support nuts - FWD four-cylinder model (AWD models similar, except use bolts instead of nuts)

2.35 Carefully pry the inner end of the driveaxle from the differential

25 Tighten the fasteners to the torque listed in this Chapter's Specifications.

➡ **Note: On FWD models, it may help to loosely install the bearing support bracket and catalytic converter bracket onto the block then tighten the fasteners once everything is in place.**

26 The remainder of installation is the reverse of removal.

REAR (AWD MODELS)

※ **WARNING:**

The manufacturer recommends replacing all suspension fasteners with new ones during installation.

Removal

▶ **Refer to illustration 2.35**

27 Block the front wheels to prevent the vehicle from rolling. Loosen the wheel lug nuts, raise the rear of the vehicle and support it securely on jackstands. Remove the wheel.

28 Remove the wheel speed sensor and brake line bracket from the wheel knuckle, then remove the brake caliper and brake disc (see Chapter 9). Hang the caliper with a length of wire and do not disconnect the brake hose.

29 Remove the driveaxle/hub nut(s) but do not discard them yet.

➡ **Note: 2011 and later models only have one driveaxle/hub nut.**

30 Use a drive hub remover to separate the driveaxle from the wheel hub (see illustration 2.5).

2011 and later models

31 Remove the hub and bearing assembly (see Chapter 10) then proceed to Step 35

2010 and earlier models

32 While supporting the lower control arm with a jack, unbolt the upper arm and the shock absorber lower bolt from the rear knuckle (see Chapter 10).

33 Disconnect the outer toe link and upper stabilizer bar link.

34 Support the wheel knuckle and remove the nut and bolt to dis-

connect the lower arm from the knuckle.

All models

35 Pry the inner end of the driveaxle out of the differential (see illustration). On 2010 and earlier models, remove it from the vehicle by passing the outer end of the shaft up through the opening in the wheel knuckle. On 2011 and later models, pull the driveaxle out through the hole in the wheel knuckle.

Installation

36 Pry the old spring clip from the inner end of the driveaxle and install a new one.

37 Apply a light film of grease to the area on the inner CV joint stub shaft where the seal rides, then insert the splined end of the inner CV joint into the differential. Make sure the spring clip locks in its groove.

※※ **CAUTION:**

Take care not to damage the differential seal with the driveaxle splines. It is recommended to use a plastic seal protector (manufacturer tool #205-816).

2010 and earlier models

38 Apply a light film of grease to the outer CV joint splines, pass the driveaxle down through the opening in the knuckle and insert the outer end of the driveaxle into the hub.

39 Seat the driveaxle using the **old** driveaxle/hub nut. With the brake applied to prevent the driveaxle from rotating, tighten the **old** driveaxle/hub nut to the specified torque, then remove and discard the old nut.

40 Install the bolts to connect the upper and lower control arms to the wheel knuckle and tighten them to the torque listed in the Chapter 10 Specifications.

2011 and later models

41 Re-attach the wheel speed sensor.

42 Apply a light film of grease to the outer CV joint splines, then install the hub and bearing assembly and tighten the bolts to the torque listed in the Chapter 10 Specifications.

43 Seat the driveaxle using the **old** driveaxle/hub nut. With the brake applied to prevent the driveaxle from rotating, tighten the **old** driveaxle/hub nut to the specified torque, then remove and discard the old nut.

All models

➡ **Note: The new driveaxle/hub nut(s) must be tightened before lowering the vehicle or damage to the wheel bearings may occur.**

➡ **Note: The driveaxle/hub nuts are coated with a one-use locking chemical and cannot be re-used for final assembly. The locking chemical is activated by heat created during tightening. The nut must be tightened to the specified torque within five minutes of starting it on the threads or the locking chemical will not activate properly.**

44 Install **new** inner and outer driveaxle/hub nut(s) (2011 and later models have only one driveaxle/hub nut). With the brake applied to keep the driveaxle from turning, tighten the nut(s) to the specified torque.

45 The remainder of installation is the reverse of removal. Be sure to use new fasteners and tighten them to the specified torque.

46 Install the wheel and lug nuts, then lower the vehicle. Tighten the lug nuts to the torque listed in the Chapter 1 Specifications.

3 Driveaxle boot - replacement

➡ **Note: If the CV joints are worn, indicating the need for an overhaul (usually due to torn boots), explore all options before beginning the job. Complete rebuilt driveaxles are available on an exchange basis, which eliminates much time and work.**

➡ **Note: The driveaxles are equipped with ABS sensor rings on the outer CV joints. Be sure to inspect the sensor rings for chipped or missing teeth.**

1 Remove the driveaxle from the vehicle (see Section 2).

2 Mount the driveaxle in a vise. The jaws of the vise should be lined with wood or rags to prevent damage to the driveaxle.

FRONT

➡ **Note: The outboard CV joint is not removable. The outboard boot can only be replaced if the inboard CV joint is disassembled.**

Removal

3 Remove and discard the boot clamps.

4 Remove the retainer clip and pull the boot back from the inner CV joint. Mark the relationship of the tri-pod to the outer housing.

5 Be careful not to let the bearings slide off the tri-pod as you separate the joint housing from the driveaxle.

6 Remove the retaining clip and use a puller to remove the tri-pod from the shaft.

7 Slide the old inboard boot off the shaft.

8 The outer CV joint boot can now be removed by removing the two boot clamps and sliding the outer boot off at the inboard end of the shaft.

Inspection

9 Clean the old grease from the outer race and the tri-pod bearing

assembly. Carefully disassemble each section of the tri-pod assembly, one at a time so as not to mix up the parts. Clean the needle bearings with solvent.

10 Inspect the rollers, tri-pod, bearings and outer race for scoring, pitting or other signs of abnormal wear, which will warrant the replacement of the inner CV joint.

Reassembly

▶ **Refer to illustrations 3.19, 3.20a, 3.20b, 3.20c, 3.20d and 3.20e**

11 If you are replacing the outboard CV joint boot, slide a new boot onto the shaft. Pack half the grease provided in the sealing boot kit into the outboard CV joint and spread the remaining grease in the sealing boot.

12 Seat the small end of the outboard boot into the groove in the axleshaft and tighten the boot clamps.

13 Slide a new inboard boot clamp (small end), then the inboard sealing boot onto the axleshaft.

14 Slide the tri-pod with the roller bearings onto the axle shaft and install a new snap ring. Again, be careful to not let the bearings fall off the tri-pod.

15 Pack the bearing with half the grease provided in the kit and spread the remaining grease inside the boot.

16 Slide the outer housing over the bearing assembly and install the outer bearing retaining ring.

17 Seat the large end of the boot into the groove in the outer housing.

18 Place the two boot clamps in position on the boot but do not tighten them yet.

19 Position the CV joint mid-way through its travel, then equalize the air pressure in the boot (see illustration).

20 Tighten the boot clamps (see illustrations).

21 Install the driveaxle as outlined in Section 2.

3.19 Equalize the pressure inside the boot by inserting a small, dull screwdriver between the boot and the outer race

3.20a To install new fold-over type clamps, bend the tang down . . .

3.20b . . . and flatten the tabs to hold it in place

3.20c To install band-type clamps you'll need a special tool; install the band with its end pointing in the direction of axle rotation and tighten it securely, then pivot the tool up 90-degrees and tap the center of the clip with a center punch . . .

3.20d . . . then bend the end of the clamp back over the clip and cut off the excess

3.20e If you're installing crimp-type boot clamps, you'll need a pair of special crimping pliers (available at most auto parts stores)

REAR (AWD MODELS)

➡ **Note: The outboard CV joint is not removable. The outboard boot can only be replaced if the inboard CV joint is disassembled.**

Removal

22 Remove the driveaxle from the vehicle (see Section 2).

23 Mount the driveaxle in a vise. The jaws of the vise should be lined with wood or rags to prevent damage to the driveaxle.

24 Remove the two clamps from the inboard boot.

25 With the boot cover pulled back from the CV joint housing, remove and discard the retaining ring from the outer housing and remove the balls and bearing cage.

26 Remove the retaining clip from the axle splines.

27 Remove the inner bearing race and slide the boot off the axle.

28 The outer CV joint boot can now be removed by removing the two boot clamps and sliding the outer boot off at the inboard end of the shaft.

Inspection

29 Thoroughly clean all components with solvent until the old grease is completely removed. Inspect the bearing surfaces of the inner races and housings for cracks, pitting, scoring, and other signs of wear. If any part of the CV joint is worn, you must replace the entire driveaxle assembly (inner CV joint, axleshaft and outer CV joint).

Reassembly

30 If you are replacing the outboard CV joint boot, slide a new boot onto the shaft. Pack half the grease provided in the sealing boot kit into the outboard CV joint and spread the remaining grease in the sealing boot.

31 Seat the outboard boot into the groove in the outboard CV joint housing and tighten the boot clamps.

32 Slide a new inboard boot clamp (small end), then the inboard sealing boot onto the axleshaft.

33 Slide the inner race onto the axle shaft and install a new snap-ring.

34 Place the bearing cage and the eight balls onto the inner race.

35 Pack the bearing with half the grease provided in the kit and spread the remaining grease inside the boot.

36 Slide the outer housing over the bearing assembly and install the outer bearing retaining ring.

37 Seat the large end of the boot into the groove in the outer housing.

38 Place the two boot clamps in position on the boot but do not tighten them yet.

39 Position the CV joint mid-way through its travel, then equalize the air pressure in the boot (see illustration 3.19).

40 Tighten the boot clamps (see illustrations 3.20a through 3.20e).

41 Be sure to replace the retaining clip on the inboard end of the assembly where it engages the transaxle gear.

42 Install the driveaxle as outlined in Section 2.

4 Driveshaft (AWD models) - removal and installation

✳ CAUTION:

The manufacturer recommends replacing driveshaft fasteners with new ones when installing the driveshaft.

1 Raise the vehicle and support it securely on jackstands. Place the shift lever in Neutral.

2 Use chalk or a scribe to mark the relationship of the driveshaft flange to the differential pinion yoke. Do the same at the front U-joint flange where it bolts to the transfer case yoke. This ensures correct

alignment when the driveshaft is reinstalled.

3 Working at the front of the driveshaft, remove the bolts securing the driveshaft to the transfer case.

4 Remove the bolts securing the universal joint flange to the differential pinion yoke.

5 Remove the nuts securing the center support bearing.

➡ **Note: 2007 and 2008 models have two center support bearings.**

6 With help from an assistant, carefully remove the driveshaft from the vehicle.

7 Installation is the reverse of removal. Use your index marks to keep the U-joints in alignment and make sure the mating surfaces are clean so the universal joint flanges seat properly in the yokes. Tighten the fasteners to the torque listed in this Chapter's Specifications.

5   Rear driveaxle oil seals (AWD models) - replacement

1 Raise the rear of the vehicle and support it securely on jackstands. Place the transaxle in Neutral with the parking brake off. Block the front wheels to prevent the vehicle from rolling.

2 Remove the driveaxle(s) (see Section 2).

3 Carefully pry out the driveaxle oil seal with a seal removal tool or a large screwdriver. Be careful not to damage or scratch the seal bore or the bearing inside the case.

4 Using a seal installer or a large deep socket as a drift, install the new oil seal. Drive it into the bore squarely and make sure it's completely seated.

5 Lubricate the lip of the new seal with multi-purpose grease, then install the driveaxle. Be careful not to damage the lip of the new seal.

6 Check the differential lubricant level and add some, if necessary, to bring it to the appropriate level (see Chapter 1).

6   Differential (AWD models) - removal and installation

➡ **Note: On AWD models, the manufacturer uses an Active Torque Control Coupling (ATCC) to manage power distribution to the front and rear wheels. Normally, the front wheels receive the majority of the torque produced by the engine. When the ATCC system senses wheel slip, it automatically increases the torque to the rear wheels. The system is always active, continuously monitoring vehicle conditions and adjusting the torque being delivered to the rear wheels by controlling the current sent to an electric clutch device inside the rear axle. The ATCC system has no mode selector nor does it require any driver input. The ATCC solenoid in the rear axle is not repairable and must be replaced with the rear axle assembly as a unit.**

1 Raise the rear of the vehicle and support it securely on jackstands. Block the front wheels to prevent the vehicle from rolling.

2 Remove the driveshaft (see Section 4).

3 Remove the driveaxles (see Section 2).

4 Remove the rear stabilizer bar (see Chapter 10)

5 Support the rear axle housing with a floor jack.

6 Disconnect the electrical connector on the crossmember.

7 There are four rear differential mounting brackets securing the differential to the subframe, one at either side at the top-front of the assembly and two at the top-rear. Remove the four bolts (two each side) securing the differential to each front bracket.

8 Loosen the two front mounting brackets from the subframe and swing the brackets out to allow clearance to lower the rear differential.

9 Remove the five bolts securing the differential to the rear mounting brackets.

10 Lower the differential with the floor jack.

11 Installation is the reverse of removal. Tighten all fasteners to the torque listed in this Chapter's Specifications.

6   Differential pinion oil seal - replacement

1 Loosen the wheel lug nuts. Raise the rear of the vehicle and support it securely on jackstands. Block the opposite set of wheels to keep the vehicle from rolling off the stands. Remove the wheels.

2 Disconnect the driveshaft from the differential companion flange and fasten it out of the way (see Section 4).

3 Mark the relationship of the pinion flange to the shaft, then count and write down the number of exposed threads on the shaft.

4 A flange holding tool will be required to keep the companion flange from moving while the self-locking pinion nut is loosened. A chain wrench will also work.

5 Remove the pinion nut.

6 Withdraw the flange. It may be necessary to use a two-jaw puller engaged behind the flange to draw it off. Do not attempt to pry or ham-

mer behind the flange or hammer on the end of the pinion shaft.

7 Pry out the old seal and discard it.

8 Inspect the seal bore to ensure it is clean and smooth.

9 Lubricate the lips of the new seal and fill the space between the seal lips with wheel bearing grease, then tap it evenly into position with a seal installation tool or a large socket. Make sure it enters the housing squarely and is tapped in to its full depth.

10 Install the pinion flange, lining up the marks made in Step 3. If necessary, tighten the pinion nut to draw the flange into place. Do not try to hammer the flange into position.

11 Install a new pinion nut, then tighten it to the torque listed in this Chapter's Specifications.

12 The remainder of installation is the reverse of removal.

Torque specifications	Ft-lbs (unless otherwise indicated)	Nm

➡ Note: One foot-pound (ft-lb) of torque is equivalent to 12 inch-pounds (in-lbs) of torque. Torque values below approximately 15 foot-pounds are expressed in inch-pounds, because most foot-pound torque wrenches are not accurate at these smaller values.

Driveaxles

Brake hose-to-knuckle bolt	177 in-lbs	20
Driveaxle/hub nut		
Front driveaxle	258	350
Rear driveaxle (AWD models)	188	255
2010 and earlier models		
Inner nut	203	275
Outer nut	129	175
2011 and later models (one nut)	258	350
Intermediate shaft bearing support bracket		
Bolts (V6 and AWD models)	30	40
Nuts (four-cylinder models)	18	25
Catalytic converter bracket bolts	177 in-lbs	20

Driveshaft (AWD models)

Driveshaft flange bolts at transfer case	52	70
Driveshaft center support bearing nuts	30	40
Rear driveshaft-to-differential pinion flange bolts	52	70

Rear differential (AWD models)

Differential-to-front insulator bracket bolts	66	90
Differential-to-side insulator bracket bolts	66	90
Differential insulator bracket-to-subframe	66	90
Filler plug	21	29
Differential pinion nut	180	244

9

BRAKES

Section

Reference to other Chapters

1 General information

The vehicles covered by this manual are equipped with hydraulically operated front and rear brake systems. The front and rear brakes are disc type. Both the front and rear brakes are self adjusting. The disc brakes automatically compensate for pad wear.

HYDRAULIC SYSTEM

The hydraulic system consists of two separate circuits. The master cylinder has separate reservoirs for the two circuits, and, in the event of a leak or failure in one hydraulic circuit, the other circuit will remain operative. A dual proportioning valve on the firewall provides brake balance between the front and rear brakes.

POWER BRAKE BOOSTER

The power brake booster, utilizing engine manifold vacuum and atmospheric pressure to provide assistance to the hydraulically operated brakes, is mounted on the firewall in the engine compartment.

PARKING BRAKE

The parking brake operates the rear brakes only, through cable actuation. It's activated by a pedal in the driver's foot well. On 2010 and earlier models, a single horseshoe-type parking brake shoe is used inside the drum portion of the brake disc. On 2011 and later models, the parking brake cables are connected to levers on the rear brake calipers which mechanically actuate the rear caliper pistons.

SERVICE

After completing any operation involving disassembly of any part of the brake system, always test drive the vehicle to check for proper braking performance before resuming normal driving. When testing the brakes, perform the tests on a clean, dry, flat surface. Conditions other than these can lead to inaccurate test results.

Test the brakes at various speeds with both light and heavy pedal pressure. The vehicle should stop evenly without pulling to one side or the other. Avoid locking the brakes, because this slides the tires and diminishes braking efficiency and control of the vehicle.

Tires, vehicle load and wheel alignment are factors which also affect braking performance.

PRECAUTIONS

There are some general cautions and warnings involving the brake system on this vehicle:

a) *Use only brake fluid conforming to DOT 3 specifications.*

b) *The brake pads contain fibers which are hazardous to your health if inhaled. Whenever you work on brake system components, clean all parts with brake system cleaner. Do not allow the fine dust to become airborne. Also, wear an approved filtering mask.*

c) *Safety should be paramount whenever any servicing of the brake components is performed. Do not use parts or fasteners which are not in perfect condition, and be sure that all clearances and torque specifications are adhered to. If you are at all unsure about a certain procedure, seek professional advice. Upon completion of any brake system work, test the brakes carefully in a controlled area before putting the vehicle into normal service. If a problem is suspected in the brake system, don't drive the vehicle until it's fixed.*

2 Troubleshooting

PROBABLE CAUSE | **CORRECTIVE ACTION**

No brakes - pedal travels to floor

1 Low fluid level 2 Air in system	1 and 2 Low fluid level and air in the system are symptoms of another problem a leak somewhere in the hydraulic system. Locate and repair the leak
3 Defective seals in master cylinder	3 Replace master cylinder
4 Fluid overheated and vaporized due to heavy braking	4 Bleed hydraulic system (temporary fix). Replace brake fluid (proper fix)

Brake pedal slowly travels to floor under braking or at a stop

1 Defective seals in master cylinder	1 Replace master cylinder
2 Leak in a hose, line, caliper or wheel cylinder	2 Locate and repair leak
3 Air in hydraulic system	3 Bleed the system, inspect system for a leak

PROBABLE CAUSE	CORRECTIVE ACTION

Brake pedal feels spongy when depressed

1 Air in hydraulic system	1 Bleed the system, inspect system for a leak
2 Master cylinder or power booster loose	2 Tighten fasteners
3 Brake fluid overheated (beginning to boil)	3 Bleed the system (temporary fix). Replace the brake fluid (proper fix)
4 Deteriorated brake hoses (ballooning under pressure)	4 Inspect hoses, replace as necessary (it's a good idea to replace all of them if one hose shows signs of deterioration)

Brake pedal feels hard when depressed and/or excessive effort required to stop vehicle

1 Power booster faulty	1 Replace booster
2 Engine not producing sufficient vacuum, or hose to booster clogged, collapsed or cracked	2 Check vacuum to booster with a vacuum gauge. Replace hose if cracked or clogged, repair engine if vacuum is extremely low
3 Brake linings contaminated by grease or brake fluid	3 Locate and repair source of contamination, replace brake pads or shoes
4 Brake linings glazed	4 Replace brake pads or shoes, check discs and drums for glazing, service as necessary
5 Caliper piston(s) or wheel cylinder(s) binding or frozen	5 Replace calipers or wheel cylinders
6 Brakes wet	6 Apply pedal to boil-off water (this should only be a momentary problem)
7 Kinked, clogged or internally split brake hose or line	7 Inspect lines and hoses, replace as necessary

Excessive brake pedal travel (but will pump up)

1 Drum brakes out of adjustment	1 Adjust brakes
2 Air in hydraulic system	2 Bleed system, inspect system for a leak

Excessive brake pedal travel (but will not pump up)

1 Master cylinder pushrod misadjusted	1 Adjust pushrod
2 Master cylinder seals defective	2 Replace master cylinder
3 Brake linings worn out	3 Inspect brakes, replace pads and/or shoes
4 Hydraulic system leak	4 Locate and repair leak

Brake pedal doesn't return

1 Brake pedal binding	1 Inspect pivot bushing and pushrod, repair or lubricate
2 Defective master cylinder	2 Replace master cylinder

Brake pedal pulsates during brake application

1 Brake drums out-of-round	1 Have drums machined by an automotive machine shop
2 Excessive brake disc runout or disc surfaces out-of-parallel	2 Have discs machined by an automotive machine shop
3 Loose or worn wheel bearings	3 Adjust or replace wheel bearings
4 Loose lug nuts	4 Tighten lug nuts

Brakes slow to release

1 Malfunctioning power booster	1 Replace booster
2 Pedal linkage binding	2 Inspect pedal pivot bushing and pushrod, repair/lubricate
3 Malfunctioning proportioning valve	3 Replace proportioning valve
4 Sticking caliper or wheel cylinder	4 Repair or replace calipers or wheel cylinders
5 Kinked or internally split brake hose	5 Locate and replace faulty brake hose

Troubleshooting (continued)

PROBABLE CAUSE	CORRECTIVE ACTION

Brakes grab (one or more wheels)

PROBABLE CAUSE	CORRECTIVE ACTION
1 Grease or brake fluid on brake lining	1 Locate and repair cause of contamination, replace lining
2 Brake lining glazed	2 Replace lining, deglaze disc or drum

Vehicle pulls to one side during braking

PROBABLE CAUSE	CORRECTIVE ACTION
1 Grease or brake fluid on brake lining	1 Locate and repair cause of contamination, replace lining
2 Brake lining glazed	2 Deglaze or replace lining, deglaze disc or drum
3 Restricted brake line or hose	3 Repair line or replace hose
4 Tire pressures incorrect	4 Adjust tire pressures
5 Caliper or wheel cylinder sticking	5 Repair or replace calipers or wheel cylinders
6 Wheels out of alignment	6 Have wheels aligned
7 Weak suspension spring	7 Replace springs
8 Weak or broken shock absorber	8 Replace shock absorbers

Brakes drag (indicated by sluggish engine performance or wheels being very hot after driving)

PROBABLE CAUSE	CORRECTIVE ACTION
1 Brake pedal pushrod incorrectly adjusted	1 Adjust pushrod
2 Master cylinder pushrod (between booster and master cylinder)	2 Adjust pushrod incorrectly adjusted
3 Obstructed compensating port in master cylinder	3 Replace master cylinder
4 Master cylinder piston seized in bore	4 Replace master cylinder
5 Contaminated fluid causing swollen seals throughout system	5 Flush system, replace all hydraulic components
6 Clogged brake lines or internally split brake hose(s)	6 Flush hydraulic system, replace defective hose(s)
7 Sticking caliper(s) or wheel cylinder(s)	7 Replace calipers or wheel cylinders
8 Parking brake not releasing	8 Inspect parking brake linkage and parking brake mechanism, repair as required
9 Improper shoe-to-drum clearance	9 Adjust brake shoes
10 Faulty proportioning valve	10 Replace proportioning valve

Brakes fade (due to excessive heat)

PROBABLE CAUSE	CORRECTIVE ACTION
1 Brake linings excessively worn or glazed	1 Deglaze or replace brake pads and/or shoes
2 Excessive use of brakes	2 Downshift into a lower gear, maintain a constant slower speed (going down hills)
3 Vehicle overloaded	3 Reduce load
4 Brake drums or discs worn too thin	4 Measure drum diameter and disc thickness, replace drums or discs as required
5 Contaminated brake fluid	5 Flush system, replace fluid
6 Brakes drag	6 Repair cause of dragging brakes
7 Driver resting left foot on brake pedal	7 Don't ride the brakes

Brakes noisy (high-pitched squeal)

PROBABLE CAUSE	CORRECTIVE ACTION
1 Glazed lining	1 Deglaze or replace lining
2 Contaminated lining (brake fluid, grease, etc.)	2 Repair source of contamination, replace linings
3 Weak or broken brake shoe hold-down or return spring	3 Replace springs
4 Rivets securing lining to shoe or backing plate loose	4 Replace shoes or pads

PROBABLE CAUSE	CORRECTIVE ACTION

Brakes noisy (high-pitched squeal) (continued)

5 Excessive dust buildup on brake linings	5 Wash brakes off with brake system cleaner
6 Brake drums worn too thin	6 Measure diameter of drums, replace if necessary
7 Wear indicator on disc brake pads contacting disc	7 Replace brake pads
8 Anti-squeal shims missing or installed improperly	8 Install shims correctly

➡ Note: Other remedies for quieting squealing brakes include the application of an anti-squeal compound to the backing plates of the brake pads, and lightly chamfering the edges of the brake pads with a file. The latter method should only be performed with the brake pads thoroughly wetted with brake system cleaner, so as not to allow any brake dust to become airborne.

Brakes noisy (scraping sound)

1 Brake pads or shoes worn out; rivets, backing plate or brake shoe metal contacting disc or drum	1 Replace linings, have discs and/or drums machined (or replace)

Brakes chatter

1 Worn brake lining	1 Inspect brakes, replace shoes or pads as necessary
2 Glazed or scored discs or drums	2 Deglaze discs or drums with sandpaper (if glazing is severe, machining will be required)
3 Drums or discs heat checked	3 Check discs and/or drums for hard spots, heat checking, etc. Have discs/drums machined or replace them
4 Disc runout or drum out-of-round excessive	4 Measure disc runout and/or drum out-of-round, have discs or drums machined or replace them
5 Loose or worn wheel bearings	5 Adjust or replace wheel bearings
6 Loose or bent brake backing plate (drum brakes)	6 Tighten or replace backing plate
7 Grooves worn in discs or drums	7 Have discs or drums machined, if within limits (if not, replace them)
8 Brake linings contaminated (brake fluid, grease, etc.)	8 Locate and repair source of contamination, replace pads or shoes
9 Excessive dust buildup on linings	9 Wash brakes with brake system cleaner
10 Surface finish on discs or drums too rough after machining (especially on vehicles with sliding calipers)	10 Have discs or drums properly machined
11 Brake pads or shoes glazed	11 Deglaze or replace brake pads or shoes

Brake pads or shoes click

1 Shoe support pads on brake backing plate grooved or excessively worn	1 Replace brake backing plate
2 Brake pads loose in caliper	2 Loose pad retainers or anti-rattle clips
3 Also see items listed under Brakes chatter	

Brakes make groaning noise at end of stop

1 Brake pads and/or shoes worn out	1 Replace pads and/or shoes
2 Brake linings contaminated (brake fluid, grease, etc.)	2 Locate and repair cause of contamination, replace brake pads or shoes
3 Brake linings glazed	3 Deglaze or replace brake pads or shoes
4 Excessive dust buildup on linings	4 Wash brakes with brake system cleaner
5 Scored or heat-checked discs or drums	5 Inspect discs/drums, have machined if within limits (if not, replace discs or drums)
6 Broken or missing brake shoe attaching hardware	6 Inspect drum brakes, replace missing hardware

Troubleshooting (continued)

PROBABLE CAUSE	CORRECTIVE ACTION

Rear brakes lock up under light brake application

1 Tire pressures too high	1 Adjust tire pressures
2 Tires excessively worn	2 Replace tires
3 Defective proportioning valve	3 Replace proportioning valve

Brake warning light on instrument panel comes on (or stays on)

1 Low fluid level in master cylinder reservoir (reservoirs with fluid level sensor)	1 Add fluid, inspect system for leak, check the thickness of the brake pads and shoes
2 Failure in one half of the hydraulic system	2 Inspect hydraulic system for a leak
3 Piston in pressure differential warning valve not centered	3 Center piston by bleeding one circuit or the other (close bleeder valve as soon as the light goes out)
4 Defective pressure differential valve or warning switch	4 Replace valve or switch
5 Air in the hydraulic system	5 Bleed the system, check for leaks
6 Brake pads worn out (vehicles with electric wear sensors - small probes that fit into the brake pads and ground out on the disc when the pads get thin)	6 Replace brake pads (and sensors)

Brakes do not self adjust

Disc brakes

1 Defective caliper piston seals	1 Replace calipers. Also, possible contaminated fluid causing soft or swollen seals (flush system and fill with new fluid if in doubt)
2 Corroded caliper piston(s)	2 Same as above

Drum brakes

1 Adjuster screw frozen	1 Remove adjuster, disassemble, clean and lubricate with high-temperature grease
2 Adjuster lever does not contact star wheel or is binding	2 Inspect drum brakes, assemble correctly or clean or replace parts as required
3 Adjusters mixed up (installed on wrong wheels after brake job)	3 Reassemble correctly
4 Adjuster cable broken or installed incorrectly (cable-type adjusters)	4 Install new cable or assemble correctly

Rapid brake lining wear

1 Driver resting left foot on brake pedal	1 Don't ride the brakes
2 Surface finish on discs or drums too rough	2 Have discs or drums properly machined
3 Also see Brakes drag	

3   Anti-lock Brake System (ABS) - general information

GENERAL INFORMATION

▶ **Refer to illustration 3.2**

1   The anti-lock brake system is designed to maintain vehicle steerability, directional stability and optimum deceleration under severe braking conditions on most road surfaces. It does so by monitoring the rotational speed of each wheel and controlling the brake line pressure to each wheel during braking. This prevents the wheels from locking up.

2   The ABS system has three main components - the wheel speed sensors, the electronic control unit (ECU) and the hydraulic unit (see illustration). Four wheel-speed sensors - one at each wheel - send a variable voltage signal to the control unit, which monitors these signals, compares them to its program and determines whether a wheel is about to lock up. When a wheel is about to lock up, the control unit signals the hydraulic unit to reduce hydraulic pressure (or not increase it further) at that wheel's brake caliper. Pressure modulation is handled by electrically-operated solenoid valves.

3   If a problem develops within the system, an "ABS" warning light will glow on the dashboard. Sometimes, a visual inspection of the ABS system can help you locate the problem. Carefully inspect the ABS wiring harness. Pay particularly close attention to the harness and con-

nections near each wheel. Look for signs of chafing and other damage caused by incorrectly routed wires. If a wheel sensor harness is damaged, the sensor must be replaced.

> ## ⁂ WARNING:
>
> **Do NOT try to repair an ABS wiring harness. The ABS system is sensitive to even the smallest changes in resistance. Repairing the harness could alter resistance values and cause the system to malfunction. If the ABS wiring harness is damaged in any way, it must be replaced.**

> ## ⁂ CAUTION:
>
> **Make sure the ignition is turned off before unplugging or reattaching any electrical connections.**

4   Some vehicles come equipped with traction control, which helps prevent wheel spin under acceleration. The traction control system (TCS) utilizes some of the same components as the ABS system. The wheel sensors monitor wheel rotation and transmit data through the same wiring to the ABS control module. The control module compares rotation speeds, then controls the amount of power supplied to the wheels by adjusting fuel settings to the engine.

DIAGNOSIS AND REPAIR

5   If a dashboard warning light comes on and stays on while the vehicle is in operation, the ABS system requires attention. Although special electronic ABS diagnostic testing tools are necessary to properly diagnose the system, you can perform a few preliminary checks before taking the vehicle to a dealer service department.

   a) *Check the brake fluid level in the reservoir.*
   b) *Verify that the computer electrical connectors are securely connected.*
   c) *Check the electrical connectors at the hydraulic control unit.*
   d) *Check the fuses.*
   e) *Follow the wiring harness to each wheel and verify that all connections are secure and that the wiring is undamaged.*

6   If the above preliminary checks do not rectify the problem, the vehicle should be diagnosed by a dealer service department or other quali-

3.2 The ABS hydraulic unit and ECU are located under the master cylinder

fied repair shop. Due to the complex nature of this system, all actual repair work must be done by a qualified automotive technician.

WHEEL SPEED SENSOR - REMOVAL AND INSTALLATION

7   Loosen the wheel lug nuts, raise the vehicle and support it securely on jackstands. Remove the wheel.
8   Make sure the ignition key is turned to the Off position.
9   Trace the wiring back from the sensor, detaching all brackets and clips while noting its correct routing, then disconnect the electrical connector.
10 Remove the mounting bolt and carefully pull the sensor out from the knuckle or, if you're removing the rear wheel speed sensor on a 2010 and earlier front-wheel drive model, from the back of the rear wheel bearing.
11 Installation is the reverse of the removal procedure. Tighten the mounting bolt securely.
12 Install the wheel and lug nuts, tightening them securely. Lower the vehicle and tighten the lug nuts to the torque listed in the Chapter 1 Specifications.

4   Disc brake pads - replacement

▶ **Refer to illustrations 4.5, 4.6a through 4.6i and 4.7a through 4.7i**

> ## ⁂ WARNING:
>
> **Disc brake pads must be replaced on both front or both rear wheels at the same time - never replace the pads on only one wheel. Also, the dust created by the brake system is harmful to your health. Never blow it out with compressed air and don't inhale any of it. An approved filtering mask should be worn when working on the brakes. Do not, under any circumstances, use petroleum-based solvents to clean brake parts. Use brake system cleaner only!**

1   Remove the cap from the brake fluid reservoir. To prevent brake fluid from possibly overflowing the reservoir when the calipers are fully retracted, use a syringe or suction gun to remove brake fluid until the reservoir is approximately half full.
2   Loosen the wheel lug nuts, raise the vehicle and support it securely on jackstands. Block the wheels at the opposite end.
3   Remove the wheels. Work on one brake assembly at a time, using the assembled brake for reference if necessary.
4   Inspect the brake disc carefully as outlined in Section 6. If machining is necessary, follow the information in that Section to remove the disc, at which time the pads can be removed as well.
5   Before disassembling the brake, wash it thoroughly with brake

4.5 Always wash the brakes with brake cleaner before disassembling anything

4.6a Depress the piston into the bottom of its bore in the caliper with a large C-clamp to make room for the new pads (if using a small clamp like this one, alternate from one side to the other to depress the pistons evenly) - make sure the fluid in the master cylinder reservoir doesn't overflow

4.6b Remove the lower caliper mounting bolt . . .

4.6c . . . then rotate the caliper up for access to the pads

4.6d Remove the inner brake pad and shim

4.6e Remove the outer brake pad and shim

system cleaner and allow it to dry (see illustration). Position a drain pan under the brake to catch the residue - DO NOT use compressed air to blow off the brake dust.

FRONT BRAKE PADS (ALL MODELS), REAR BRAKE PADS (2010 AND EARLIER MODELS)

6   For the brake pad replacement sequence, follow the accompanying photos (illustrations 4.6a through 4.6i) for the actual pad replacement procedure. Be sure to stay in order and read the caption under each illustration, then proceed to Step 8.

REAR BRAKE PADS (2011 AND LATER MODELS)

7   For the brake pad replacement sequence, follow Steps 1 through 5, then see illustrations 4.7a through 4.7i. Note the following points:

a)   When removing and installing the brake noise dampener, use only hand tools or the dampener will be damaged.

b)   The parking brake cable is attached to the caliper. The cable does not have to be separated from the caliper in order to change the pads, but be careful not to twist or damage the cable ends when positioning and supporting the caliper to the side.

c)   The manufacturer states that the brake pads are one-time use only. Anytime the brake pads are separated from the caliper, they must be replaced with new pads even if they are not worn out. Brake shudder and noise will occur if pads are reused.

d)   The caliper guide pins are pressed into the mounting bracket (anchor plate). Do not try to remove them or they will be damaged and the mounting bracket will have to be replaced.

e)   The inboard brake pad has a pin on the back. Turn the caliper piston so the notch will line-up with the pin on the backside of the pad.

4.6f Remove and inspect the pad support plates, then reinstall (or replace if necessary) and lubricate them with a light film of high-temperature brake grease

4.6g Clean the caliper mounting bolts (slide the upper bolt from the mounting bracket along with the caliper), then apply a coat of high-temperature brake grease to the sliding surface

4.6h Snap the shims to the back of each pad, then apply anti-squeal compound to the outboard side of the shims

4.6i Install the pads in the bracket, swing the caliper down and install the caliper mounting bolt, tightening it to the torque listed in this Chapter's Specifications

FRONT OR REAR PADS

8   When reinstalling the caliper, be sure to tighten the mounting bolts to the torque listed in this Chapter's Specifications. After the job

has been completed, firmly depress the brake pedal a few times to bring the pads into contact with the disc. Check the level of the brake fluid, adding some if necessary. Check the operation of the brakes carefully before placing the vehicle into normal service.

4.7a Hold the caliper guide pins with one wrench while loosening the caliper mounting bolts (the lower bolt is a noise dampener)

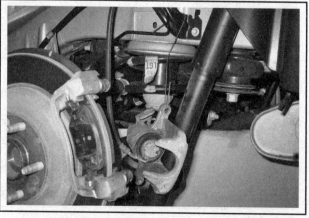

4.7b Remove the caliper and hang it with a length of wire - don't let it hang by the hose

4.7c Use needle-nose pliers or a caliper piston rotating tool to rotate the piston clockwise while pushing it back in the caliper - make sure the fluid in the master cylinder reservoir doesn't overflow

4.7d One of the notches must be at the bottom position to align with the pin on the inner pad

4.7e Remove the outer brake pad

4.7f Remove the inner brake pad

4.7g Remove and inspect the pad support plates, then reinstall (or replace if necessary) and lubricate them with a light film of high-temperature brake grease

4.7h Pull out the caliper guide pins and clean them, then apply a coat of high-temperature grease to the pins and reinstall them in the caliper bracket

4.7i Install the pads and caliper, tightening the caliper mounting bolts to the torque listed in this Chapter's Specifications

5 Disc brake caliper - removal and installation

✳✳ WARNING:

Dust created by the brake system is harmful to your health. Never blow it out with compressed air and don't inhale any of it. An approved filtering mask should be worn when working on the brakes. Do not, under any circumstances, use petroleum-based solvents to clean brake parts. Use brake system cleaner only.

➥ Note: If replacement is indicated (usually because of fluid leakage or damage to a piston boot), it is recommended that the calipers be replaced, not overhauled. New and factory rebuilt units are available on an exchange basis, which makes this job quite easy. Always replace the calipers in pairs - never replace just one of them.

REMOVAL

▶ **Refer to illustrations 5.2 and 5.4**

1   Loosen the wheel lug nuts, raise the vehicle (front or rear) and place it securely on jackstands. Remove the wheels.

2   Remove the banjo fitting bolt and disconnect the brake hose from the caliper (see illustration). Discard the sealing washers from each side of the hose fitting. Plug the brake hose to keep contaminants out of the brake system and to prevent losing any more brake fluid than is necessary.

➥ Note: If the caliper is being removed for access to another component, don't disconnect the hose.

On 2011 and later models, loosen the parking brake cable tension by adjusting the nut on the parking brake equalizer (see Section 11), then disconnect the parking brake cable from the caliper.

3   Start at illustration 4.6a (front) or illustration 4.7a (rear) for the caliper removal procedure. If the caliper is being removed just to access another component, use a piece of wire to securely hang it out of the way (see illustration 4.7b).

✳✳ CAUTION:

Do not let the caliper hang by the brake hose.

4   If you are replacing a rear caliper on a 2011 or later model, disconnect the parking brake cable from the caliper (see illustration).

INSTALLATION

5   Install the caliper by reversing the removal procedure, tightening the mounting bolts to the torque listed in this Chapter's Specifications. Be sure to use new sealing washers and tighten the banjo fitting bolt to the torque listed in this Chapter's Specifications.

6   If you are working on a front caliper, note that the mounting bolts are different sizes. The larger bolt goes in the upper position.

7   Bleed the brake circuit according to the procedure in Section 9. Make sure there are no leaks from the hose connections. Test the brakes carefully before returning the vehicle to normal service.

5.2 Remove the brake line banjo bolt (A), then remove the caliper mounting bolts (B)

5.4 Depress the retaining tangs on the parking brake cable casing and pull the cable through the bracket, then unhook the cable end from the lever (2011 and later models)

6 Brake disc - inspection, removal and installation

INSPECTION

▶ **Refer to illustrations 6.3, 6.4a, 6.4b, 6.5a and 6.5b**

1   Loosen the wheel lug nuts, raise the vehicle and support it securely on jackstands.

2   Remove the brake caliper as outlined in Section 5. It isn't necessary to disconnect the brake hose. After removing the caliper bolts, suspend the caliper out of the way with a piece of wire (see illustration 4.7b).

3   Visually inspect the disc surface for score marks and other damage. Light scratches and shallow grooves are normal after use and may

6.3 The brake pads on this vehicle were obviously neglected, as they wore down completely and cut deep grooves into the disc - wear this severe means the disc must be replaced

6.4a To check disc runout, mount a dial indicator as shown and rotate the disc

6.4b Using a swirling motion, remove the glaze from the disc surface with sandpaper or emery cloth

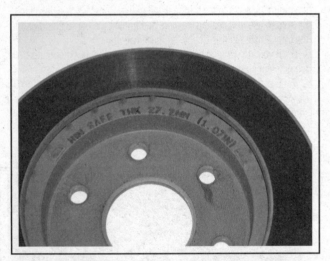

6.5a The minimum thickness dimension is cast into the front or back side of the disc

6.5b Use a micrometer to measure disc thickness

not always be detrimental to brake operation, but deep scoring requires disc removal and refinishing by an automotive machine shop. Be sure to check both sides of the disc (see illustration). If pulsating has been noticed during application of the brakes, suspect disc runout.

4 To check disc runout, reinstall the lug nuts (inverted) and place a dial indicator at a point about 1/2-inch from the outer edge of the disc (see illustration). Set the indicator to zero and turn the disc. The indicator reading should not exceed the specified allowable runout limit. If it does, the disc should be refinished by an automotive machine shop.

➡ Note: The discs should be resurfaced regardless of the dial indicator reading, as this will impart a smooth finish and ensure a perfectly flat surface, eliminating any brake pedal pulsation or other undesirable symptoms related to questionable discs. At the very least, if you elect not to have the discs resurfaced, remove the glaze from the surface with emery cloth or sandpaper, using a swirling motion (see illustration).

5 It's absolutely critical that the disc not be machined to a thickness under the specified minimum thickness. The minimum (or discard) thickness is cast or stamped into the inside of the disc (see illustration).

The disc thickness can be checked with a micrometer (see illustration).

REMOVAL

➤ **Refer to illustrations 6.6a and 6.6b**

6 Remove the caliper mounting bracket (see illustration). Also remove the lug nuts if they were reinstalled for the runout, then remove the disc (see illustration).

➡ Note: If equipped, remove the brake disc screw. If necessary, insert an M10 bolt into the threaded hole, then tighten the bolt to separate the disc from the hub.

INSTALLATION

7 While the disc is off, wire-brush the backside of the center portion that contacts the wheel hub. Also clean off any rust or dirt on the hub face.

6.6a Caliper mounting bracket-to-knuckle bolts

6.6b On models so equipped, remove the screw that secures the disc to the hub

8 Apply small dots of high-temperature anti-seize around the circumference of the hub, and around the raised center portion.
9 Place the disc in position over the threaded studs. On 2011 and later models, install the disc retaining screw and tighten securely.
10 Install the caliper mounting bracket and caliper, tightening the bolts to the torque values listed in this Chapter's Specifications.
11 Install the wheel, then lower the vehicle to the ground. Tighten the lug nuts to the torque listed in the Chapter 1 Specifications. Depress the brake pedal a few times to bring the brake pads into contact with the

disc. Bleeding won't be necessary unless the brake hose was disconnected from the caliper. Check the operation of the brakes carefully before driving the vehicle.
12 If new or resurfaced rear discs are being installed, check the operation of the parking brake and adjust it if necessary (see Section 11).
13 Check the operation of the brakes carefully before driving the vehicle.

7 Master cylinder - removal and installation

REMOVAL

▶ **Refer to illustrations 7.5 and 7.10**

1 The master cylinder is located in the engine compartment, mounted to the power brake booster.
2 Remove the battery and the battery tray (see Chapter 5).
3 Remove the air filter housing and intake duct (see Chaptver 4).
4 Remove as much fluid as you can from the reservoir with a syringe, such as an old turkey baster.

⁂ WARNING:

If a baster is used, never again use it for the preparation of food.

5 Disconnect the brake booster check valve from the brake booster to remove any vacuum from the booster (see illustration).
6 Disconnect the electrical connector at the brake fluid level switch on the master cylinder reservoir.
7 Place rags under the fluid fittings and prepare caps or plastic bags to cover the ends of the lines once they are disconnected.

⁂ CAUTION:

Brake fluid will damage paint. Cover all body parts and be careful not to spill fluid during this procedure.

7.5 Master cylinder mounting details

1 Fluid level warning switch connector
2 Brake line fittings
3 Mounting nut (other nut not visible in photo)
4 Brake booster check valve

8 Loosen the fittings at the ends of the brake lines where they enter the master cylinder (see illustration 7.5). To prevent rounding off the corners on these nuts, the use of a flare-nut wrench, which wraps around the nut, is preferred. Pull the brake lines slightly away from the

7.10 After the reservoir has been removed, replace the O-rings with new ones

7.12 The best way to bleed air from the master cylinder before installing it on the vehicle is with a pair of bleeder tubes that direct brake fluid into the reservoir during bleeding

7.17 Install a new O-ring onto the master cylinder sleeve

master cylinder and plug the ends to prevent contamination.

9   Remove the nuts attaching the master cylinder to the power booster. Pull the master cylinder off the studs and out of the engine compartment. Again, be careful not to spill the fluid as this is done.

10 If a new master cylinder is being installed, remove the reservoir from the old master cylinder and transfer it to the new master cylinder.

➡ Note: **Be sure to install new seals when transferring the reservoir (see illustration).**

INSTALLATION

◗ **Refer to illustrations 7.12 and 7.17**

11 Bench bleed the new master cylinder before installing it. Mount the master cylinder in a vise, with the jaws of the vise clamping on the mounting flange.

12 Attach a pair of master cylinder bleeder tubes to the outlet ports of the master cylinder (see illustration).

13 Fill the reservoir with brake fluid of the recommended type (see Chapter 1).

14 Slowly push the pistons into the master cylinder (a large Phillips screwdriver can be used for this) - air will be expelled from the pressure chambers and into the reservoir. Because the tubes are submerged in

fluid, air can't be drawn back into the master cylinder when you release the pistons.

15 Repeat the procedure until no more air bubbles are present.

16 Remove the bleed tubes, one at a time, and install plugs in the open ports to prevent fluid leakage and air from entering. Install the reservoir cap.

17 Install the master cylinder over the studs on the power brake booster and tighten the attaching nuts only finger tight at this time.

➡ Note: **Be sure to install a new O-ring into the sleeve of the master cylinder (see illustration).**

18 Thread the brake line fittings into the master cylinder. Since the master cylinder is still a bit loose, it can be moved slightly in order for the fittings to thread in easily. Do not strip the threads as the fittings are tightened.

19 Tighten the mounting nuts to the torque listed in this Chapter's Specifications, then tighten the brake line fittings securely.

20 Fill the master cylinder reservoir with fluid, then bleed the master cylinder and the brake system as described in Section 9. To bleed the cylinder on the vehicle, have an assistant depress the brake pedal and hold the pedal to the floor. Loosen the fitting to allow air and fluid to escape. Repeat this procedure on both fittings until the fluid is clear of air bubbles.

✳✳ CAUTION:

Have plenty of rags on hand to catch the fluid - brake fluid will ruin painted surfaces. After the bleeding procedure is completed, rinse the area under the master cylinder with clean water.

21 Test the operation of the brake system carefully before placing the vehicle into normal service.

✳✳ WARNING:

Do not operate the vehicle if you are in doubt about the effectiveness of the brake system. It is possible for air to become trapped in the anti-lock brake system hydraulic control unit, so, if the pedal continues to feel spongy after repeated bleedings or the BRAKE or ANTI-LOCK light stays on, have the vehicle towed to a dealer service department or other qualified shop to be bled with the aid of a scan tool.

8   Brake hoses and lines - inspection and replacement

1   About every six months, with the vehicle raised and placed securely on jackstands, the flexible hoses which connect the steel brake lines with the front and rear brake assemblies should be inspected for cracks, chafing of the outer cover, leaks, blisters and other damage. These are important and vulnerable parts of the brake system and inspection should be complete. A light and mirror will be needed for a thorough check. If a hose exhibits any of the above defects, replace it with a new one.

FLEXIBLE HOSES

▶ **Refer to illustrations 8.3a and 8.3b**

2   Clean all dirt away from the ends of the hose.
3   To remove a brake hose, unscrew the tube nut with a flare-nut wrench, if available, to prevent rounding-off the corners of the nut, then remove the bolt(s) or clip(s) securing the hose to the body (and any suspension components) (see illustrations).
4   Disconnect the hose from the caliper, discarding the sealing washers on either side of the fitting.
5   Using new sealing washers, attach the new brake hose to the caliper. Tighten the banjo fitting bolt to the torque listed in this Chapter's Specifications.

6   Reverse the removal procedure to install the hose, making sure it isn't twisted.
7   Carefully check to make sure the suspension or steering components don't make contact with the hose. Have an assistant push down on the vehicle and also turn the steering wheel lock-to-lock during inspection.
8   Bleed the brake system (see Section 9).

METAL BRAKE LINES

9   When replacing brake lines, be sure to use the correct parts. Don't use copper tubing for any brake system components. Purchase steel brake lines from a dealer parts department or auto parts store.
10   Prefabricated brake line, with the tube ends already flared and fittings installed, is available at auto parts stores and dealer parts departments. These lines can be bent to the proper shapes using a tubing bender.
11   When installing the new line make sure it's well supported in the brackets and has plenty of clearance between moving or hot components.
12   After installation, check the master cylinder fluid level and add fluid as necessary. Bleed the brake system as outlined in Section 9 and test the brakes carefully before placing the vehicle into normal operation.

8.3a To remove a front brake hose, unscrew the brake line fitting (A) while holding the bracket with a pair of pliers, remove the retaining clip (B), remove the mounting bolt from the strut (C), then unscrew the banjo bolt (see illustration 5.2) and detach the hose from the caliper

8.3b To remove a rear brake hose, unscrew the brake line fitting (A) while holding the bracket with a pair of pliers, remove the clip (B), then unscrew the banjo bolt and detach the hose from the caliper

9   Brake hydraulic system - bleeding

▶ **Refer to illustration 9.8**

❊❊ WARNING:

If air has found its way into the hydraulic control unit, the system must be bled with the use of a scan tool. If the brake pedal feels spongy even after bleeding the brakes, or the ABS light on the instrument panel does not go off, or if you have any doubts whatsoever about the effectiveness of the brake system, have

the vehicle towed to a dealer service department or other repair shop equipped with the necessary tools for bleeding the system.

❊❊ WARNING:

Wear eye protection when bleeding the brake system. If the fluid comes in contact with your eyes, immediately rinse them with water and seek medical attention.

9.8 When bleeding the brakes, a hose is connected to the bleed screw at the caliper and submerged in brake fluid - air will be seen as bubbles in the tube and container (all air must be expelled before moving to the next wheel)

➡ Note: Bleeding the brake system is necessary to remove any air that's trapped in the system when it's opened during removal and installation of a hose, line, caliper, wheel cylinder or master cylinder.

1 It will probably be necessary to bleed the system at all four brakes if air has entered the system due to low fluid level, or if the brake lines have been disconnected at the master cylinder.

2 If a brake line was disconnected only at a wheel, then only that caliper or wheel cylinder must be bled.

3 If a brake line is disconnected at a fitting located between the master cylinder and any of the brakes, that part of the system served by the disconnected line must be bled.

4 Remove any residual vacuum (or hydraulic pressure) from the brake power booster by applying the brake several times with the engine off.

5 Remove the master cylinder reservoir cap and fill the reservoir with brake fluid. Reinstall the cap.

➡ Note: Check the fluid level often during the bleeding operation and add fluid as necessary to prevent the fluid level from falling low enough to allow air bubbles into the master cylinder.

6 Have an assistant on hand, as well as a supply of new brake fluid, an empty clear plastic container, a length of plastic, rubber or vinyl tubing to fit over the bleeder valve and a wrench to open and close the bleeder valve.

7 Beginning at the right rear wheel, loosen the bleeder screw slightly, then tighten it to a point where it's snug but can still be loosened quickly and easily.

8 Place one end of the tubing over the bleeder screw fitting and submerge the other end in brake fluid in the container (see illustration).

9 Have the assistant slowly depress the brake pedal and hold it in the depressed position.

10 While the pedal is held depressed, open the bleeder screw just enough to allow a flow of fluid to leave the valve. Watch for air bubbles to exit the submerged end of the tube. When the fluid flow slows after a couple of seconds, tighten the screw and have your assistant release the pedal.

11 Repeat Steps 9 and 10 until no more air is seen leaving the tube, then tighten the bleeder screw and proceed to the left rear wheel, the right front wheel and the left front wheel, in that order, and perform the same procedure. Be sure to check the fluid in the master cylinder reservoir frequently.

12 Never use old brake fluid. It contains moisture which can boil, rendering the brake system inoperative.

13 Refill the master cylinder with fluid at the end of the operation.

14 Check the operation of the brakes. The pedal should feel solid when depressed, with no sponginess. If necessary, repeat the entire process.

✱✱ WARNING:

Do not operate the vehicle if you are in doubt about the effectiveness of the brake system. It is possible for air to become trapped in the anti-lock brake system hydraulic control unit, so, if the pedal continues to feel spongy after repeated bleedings or the BRAKE or ANTI-LOCK light stays on, have the vehicle towed to a dealer service department or other qualified shop to be bled with the aid of a scan tool.

10 Power brake booster - check, removal and installation

OPERATING CHECK

1 Depress the brake pedal several times with the engine off and make sure that there is no change in the pedal reserve distance.

2 Depress the pedal and start the engine. If the pedal goes down slightly, operation is normal.

AIR TIGHTNESS CHECK

3 Start the engine and turn it off after one or two minutes. Depress the brake pedal several times slowly. If the pedal goes down farther the first time but gradually rises after the second or third depression, the booster is airtight.

4 Depress the brake pedal while the engine is running, then stop the engine with the pedal depressed. If there is no change in the pedal reserve travel after holding the pedal for 30 seconds, the booster is airtight.

REMOVAL AND INSTALLATION

▸ **Refer to illustration 10.11**

5 Disassembly of the power unit requires special tools and is not ordinarily performed by the home mechanic. If a problem develops, it's recommended that a new or factory rebuilt unit be installed.

6 Before disconnecting the brake pedal, brake booster or booster pushrod, the brake light switch must be removed. With the brake pedal in the at-rest position, pull very lightly rearward on the brake pedal, rotate the switch clockwise 45-degrees and remove the switch.

7 Remove the master cylinder (see Section 7).

8 Remove the retaining clip holding the hose and wiring harness and position them to the side.

9 Under the dash, remove the lower instrument panel cover.

10 Remove the retaining pin and clip, then disconnect the pushrod from the top of the brake pedal.

➡ **Note: 2011 and later models utilize a one-piece clevis locking pin to connect the push-rod to the brake pedal. Use a 12-point, 11 mm wrench or socket to release the tabs on the pin. The pin is a one-time-use part and must be discarded and replaced if removed.**

11 Remove the booster mounting nuts from inside (see illustration), then carefully lift the booster unit away from the firewall and out of the engine compartment.

12 To install the booster, reverse the removal steps and test the operation of the brakes before placing the vehicle in normal service.

13 When installing the brake light switch, insert the switch into the bracket and rotate the switch 45-degrees counterclockwise. Be careful not to move the brake pedal when installing the switch or damage to the switch can occur.

10.11 To detach the power brake booster from the firewall, remove the four nuts (two nuts not visible here)

11 Parking brake - adjustment

➤ **Refer to illustrations 11.2 and 11.3**

1 The parking brake is adjusted at two locations, one at the parking brake pedal in the driver's compartment and the other at the parking brake equalizer under the vehicle.

➡ **Note: The following dimensions are preliminary adjustments. As the cables age and stretch, it is most likely that these dimensions will have to be exceeded to obtain satisfactory parking brake operation. It's important not to over-adjust the cables, though, as this could cause the brakes to drag.**

2 To adjust the parking brake, first release the parking brake pedal. Use a wrench to tighten the adjusting nut so that the exposed threads equal 5/64-inch (2 mm) (see illustration). When the parking brake cables are old, they may have stretched and require more threads show-ing on the adjuster.

3 Next adjust the cable at the equalizer from under the vehicle. The equalizer is located where the parking brake cable comes through the underside of the vehicle beneath the driver's seat. Use a wrench to tighten the adjusting nut on the equalizer so that the exposed threads equal 51/64-inch (20 mm) (see illustration).

4 Verify the parking brake is actually holding the vehicle when applied. Raise and support the rear of the vehicle and block the front wheels. You can rotate the rear tires by hand to check for proper cable adjustment.

5 Depress the pedal slightly, this should apply noticeable drag on the rear brakes. With the pedal 2/3 to the floor, the rear brakes should be locked. With the parking brake pedal released all the way, there should be no drag on the wheels.

11.2 At the parking brake pedal, turn the adjusting nut until the exposed threads measure 5/64-inch (2 mm)

11.3 Under the vehicle, turn the adjusting nut until the exposed threads measure 51/64-inch (20 mm)

12 Parking brake shoes (2010 and earlier models) - replacement

1   Loosen the wheel lug nuts, raise the rear of the vehicle and support it securely on jackstands. Remove the wheel.
2   Remove the brake disc (see Section 6).
3   Remove the return spring from the parking brake shoe.
4   Remove the parking brake shoe from around the hub and bearing assembly.

5   Installation is the reverse of removal. Check the operation of the parking brake and adjust as necessary (see Section 11).
6   Tighten the wheel lug nuts to the torque listed in the Chapter 1 Specifications.

13 Brake light switch - replacement

▶ **Refer to illustration 13.1**

1   Disconnect the electrical connector at the switch (see illustration).
2   With the brake pedal in the at-rest position, pull very lightly rearward on the brake pedal, rotate the switch clockwise 45-degrees and remove the switch.
3   Insert the switch into the bracket and rotate the switch 45-degrees counterclockwise. Be careful not to move the brake pedal when installing the switch or damage to the switch can occur. The brake light switch is self-adjusting.

➡ **Note: Do not press on the brake pedal during installation of the switch.**

4   Connect the switch electrical connector.

13.1 Disconnect the electrical connector (A) then rotate the switch (B) 45-degrees clockwise to remove it

14 Brake booster vacuum pump - removal and installation

▶ **Refer to illustrations 14.2 and 14.3**

1   Remove the air intake duct (see Chapter 4).
2   Detach the vacuum hose from the fitting on the pump (see illustration).
3   Remove the mounting bolts and detach the pump from the cylin-der head (see illustration).

4   Check the condition of the pump O-ring; if it's in good condition, it can be re-used.
5   Installation is the reverse of the removal procedure. Be sure to align the pump with the slot on the camshaft, and tighten the bolts to the torque listed in this Chapter's Specifications.

14.2 Squeeze the sides of the connector and detach the vacuum hose from the brake booster pump

14.3 Brake booster vacuum pump bolts

Specifications

General

Brake fluid type	See Chapter 1

Disc brakes

Minimum pad lining thickness	See Chapter 1
Disc lateral runout limit	0.002 inch (0.050 mm)
Disc minimum thickness	Cast into disc

Torque specifications	Ft-lbs (unless otherwise indicated)	Nm

➡ **Note: One foot-pound (ft-lb) of torque is equivalent to 12 inch-pounds (in-lbs) of torque. Torque values below approximately 15 foot-pounds are expressed in inch-pounds, because most foot-pound torque wrenches are not accurate at these smaller values.**

Brake line banjo bolt	18	25
Caliper mounting bracket bolts		
Front	98	133
Rear	66	90
Caliper guide pin bolts		
Front	65	88
Rear	19	26
Brake noise dampener	124 in-lbs	14
Master cylinder fluid reservoir pin bolt	53 in-lbs	6
Master cylinder mounting nuts	18	25
Brake line nuts (to master cylinder)	21	28
Power brake booster mounting nuts		
2010 models	18	25
All others	17	23
Brake booster vacuum pump mounting bolts	89 in-lbs	10
Wheel lug nuts	See Chapter 1	

NOTES

10

SUSPENSION AND STEERING SYSTEMS

Section

1   General information

▶ **Refer to illustrations 1.1 and 1.2**

The front suspension is made up of a strut assembly, lower control arm, steering knuckle/hub assembly and a stabilizer bar (see illustration). The strut assembly is made up of a shock absorber and a coil spring. The strut combines several functions into one by supporting the weight of the vehicle, functioning as the spring dampener and providing the pivot point for the steering knuckle.

The rear suspension employs upper and lower control arms, a trailing arm, a toe link, and a coil spring and shock absorber on each side (see illustration).

The rack-and-pinion steering gear is located on the front suspension subframe and actuates the tie-rods, which are attached to the steering knuckles. The inner ends of the tie-rods are protected by rubber boots which should be inspected periodically for secure attachment, tears and leaking lubricant (which would indicate a failed rack seal).

The power assist system consists of a belt-driven pump and associated lines and hoses. The fluid level in the power steering pump reservoir should be checked periodically (see Chapter 1).

The steering wheel operates the steering shaft, which actuates the steering gear through universal joints. Looseness in the steering can be caused by wear in the steering shaft universal joints, the steering gear, the tie-rod ends and loose retaining bolts.

PRECAUTIONS

Frequently, when working on the suspension or steering system components, you may come across fasteners which seem impossible to loosen. These fasteners on the underside of the vehicle are continually

1.1 Front suspension and steering components

1	Strut/coil spring assembly	4	Tie-rod end	6	Control arm bushing
2	Steering knuckle	5	Control arm	7	Steering gear
3	Balljoint				

subjected to water, road grime, mud, etc., and can become rusted or frozen, making them extremely difficult to remove. In order to unscrew these stubborn fasteners without damaging them (or other components), be sure to use lots of penetrating oil and allow it to soak in for a while. Using a wire brush to clean exposed threads will also ease removal of the nut or bolt and prevent damage to the threads. Sometimes a sharp blow with a hammer and punch will break the bond between a nut and bolt threads, but care must be taken to prevent the punch from slipping off the fastener and ruining the threads. Heating the stuck fastener and surrounding area with a torch sometimes helps too, but isn't recommended because of the obvious dangers associated with fire. Long breaker bars and extension, or cheater, pipes will increase leverage, but never use an extension pipe on a ratchet - the ratcheting mechanism could be damaged. Sometimes tightening the nut or bolt first will help to break it loose. Fasteners that require drastic measures to remove should always be replaced with new ones.

Since most of the procedures dealt with in this Chapter involve jack-ing up the vehicle and working underneath it, a good pair of jackstands will be needed. A hydraulic floor jack is the preferred type of jack to lift the vehicle, and it can also be used to support certain components during various operations.

✳✳ WARNING:

Never, under any circumstances, rely on a jack to support the vehicle while working on it. Whenever any of the suspension or steering fasteners are loosened or removed they must be inspected and, if necessary, replaced with new ones of the same part number or of original equipment quality and design. Torque specifications must be followed for proper reassembly and component retention. Never attempt to heat or straighten any suspension or steering components. Instead, replace any bent or damaged part with a new one.

1.2 Rear suspension components

1	Trailing arm	4	Upper suspension arm	7	Lower suspension arm
2	Rear knuckle	5	Stabilizer bar	8	Shock absorber
3	Stabilizer bar link	6	Coil spring		

2 Strut/coil spring assembly (front) - removal, inspection and installation

❋❋ WARNING:

The manufacturer recommends replacing all fasteners with new ones during installation.

REMOVAL

▶ **Refer to illustrations 2.1 and 2.5**

1 In the engine compartment, mark the relationship of one of the mounting studs to the body, then remove the four upper mounting nuts (see illustration).

2 Loosen the wheel lug nuts, raise the vehicle and support it securely on jackstands. Remove the wheel.

3 Unbolt the brake hose bracket from the shock absorber. Remove the wheel speed sensor and detach the wiring harness by removing the clamp bracket bolt.

4 Support the steering knuckle with a floor jack.

5 Unscrew the nuts securing the strut to the steering knuckle, then tap the bolts out with a hammer (see illustration).

❋❋ CAUTION:

Only turn the nuts; the bolts have serrated shoulders, and to turn them could damage the steering knuckle.

6 Use the floor jack to lower the knuckle to allow room to remove

the shock absorber/coil spring assembly, but be careful not to overextend the inner CV joint.

INSPECTION

7 Check the shock body for leaking fluid, dents, cracks and other obvious damage which would warrant replacement.

8 Check the coil spring for chips or cracks in the spring coating (this will cause premature spring failure due to corrosion). Inspect the spring seat for cuts, hardness and general deterioration.

9 If any undesirable conditions exist, proceed to the shock absorber/coil spring disassembly procedure (see Section 3).

INSTALLATION

10 Guide the assembly up into the fenderwell, align the previously made matchmarks and insert the upper mounting studs through the holes in the body. Once the studs protrude, install the *new* nuts so the shock won't fall back through but don't tighten them yet. This is most easily accomplished with the help of an assistant, as the strut is quite heavy and awkward.

11 Use the jack to position the steering knuckle and install the two lower mounting bolts and nuts, then tighten the nuts to the torque listed in this Chapter's Specifications.

12 Install the wheel and lug nuts, then lower the vehicle and tighten the lug nuts to the torque listed in the Chapter 1 Specifications.

13 Tighten the upper mounting nuts to the torque listed in this Chapter's Specifications.

14 Have the front end alignment checked, and if necessary, adjusted.

2.1 Mark the relationship of one of the mounting studs to the body, then remove the upper mounting nuts

2.5 Unscrew the nuts, then drive the bolts out with a hammer (don't turn the bolts - they have serrated shoulders)

3 Strut/coil spring assembly (front) - replacement

▶ **Refer to illustrations 3.3, 3.5a, 3.5b, 3.5c, 3.5d and 3.10**

❋❋ WARNING:

Before attempting to disassemble the shock absorber/coil spring assembly, a tool to hold the coil spring in compression must be obtained. Do not attempt to use makeshift methods. Uncon-

trolled release of the spring could cause damage and personal injury or even death. Use a high-quality spring compressor, and carefully follow the tool manufacturer's instructions provided with it. After removing the coil spring with the compressor still installed, place it in a safe, isolated area. The strut is pressurized; do not apply heat or flame to the assembly or it could explode.

3.3 Make sure the spring compressor tool is on securely

3.5a Remove the upper mount and spring seat . . .

3.5b . . . then remove the spring . . .

3.5c . . . followed by the boot . . .

✳ WARNING:

The manufacturer recommends replacing all fasteners with new ones during installation.

1   If the front suspension shock absorber/coil springs exhibit signs of wear (leaking fluid, loss of damping capability, sagging or cracked coil springs) then they should be disassembled and overhauled as necessary. The shock absorbers themselves cannot be serviced, and should be replaced if faulty; the springs and related components can be replaced individually. To maintain balanced characteristics on both sides of the vehicle, the components on both sides should be replaced at the same time.

2   With the assembly removed from the vehicle (see Section 2), clean away all external dirt but be careful not to damage or remove the protective coating from the spring as this helps prevent corrosion damage.

3   Install the coil spring compressor tools (ensuring that they are fully engaged), and compress the spring until all tension is relieved from the upper mount (see illustration).

4   Hold the shock absorber piston rod with a wrench and unscrew the nut. Do not use an impact wrench as this could damage the shock absorber.

5   Remove the upper mount and spring, followed by the boot, bump

3.5d . . . and the bump stop

stop and lower spring seat (see illustrations).

6   If a new spring is to be installed, the original spring must now be carefully released from the compressor. If it is to be re-used, the spring can be left in compression.

7   With the strut assembly now completely disassembled, examine all the components for wear and damage. Replace components as necessary.

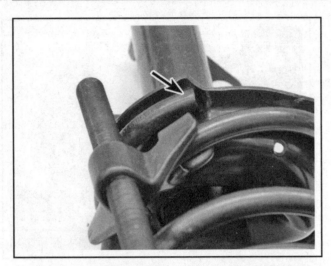

3.10 When installing the spring, make sure the ends fit into the recessed portion of the seats, and keep the gap at 0.39-inch or less

8   Examine the shock for signs of fluid leakage. Check the piston rod for signs of pitting along its entire length, and check the shock body for signs of damage. Test the operation of the shock, while holding it in an upright position, by moving the piston through a full stroke, then through short strokes of 2 to 4 inches. In both cases, the resistance felt should be smooth and continuous. If the resistance is jerky or uneven, or if there is any visible sign of wear or damage, replacement is necessary.

9   To reassemble, install the lower spring seat first, then the bump stop and dust boot onto the shock absorber. Next install the spring and upper mount/upper seat. The arrow (2010 and earlier models) or notch (2011 and later models) on the upper mount must be aligned with the lower mount (pointing out).

10 With the spring compressed, install the rod nut. Position the ends of the spring to within 0.39-inch (10 mm) of the step on both the top and bottom mounts (see illustration). Tighten the nut to the specified torque while maintaining the position at both ends.

11 Release the tension on the spring and re-install the spring assembly in the vehicle.

4   Stabilizer bar and bushings (front) - removal and installation

�֍ WARNING:

The manufacturer recommends replacing all fasteners with new ones during installation.

REMOVAL

▸ **Refer to illustration 4.6, 4.7, 4.9, 4.12, 4.13 and 4.14**

➡ **Note: While the steering column shaft is disconnected, the steering wheel MUST be kept from rotating or damage to the airbag clockspring may occur. If you believe the steering column has rotated, you will need to remove the clockspring and re-center it. See Section 14 for additional information.**

1   Use a steering wheel holding tool to secure the steering wheel in the straight ahead position. An alternative would be to pass the seat belt through the steering wheel, then clip it into place.

2   Loosen the front wheel lug nuts. Raise the front of the vehicle and support it securely on jackstands. Apply the parking brake and block the rear wheels to keep the vehicle from rolling off the stands. Remove the front wheels.

3   Mark the relationship of the steering shaft to the steering gear, then remove the clamp bolt and disconnect the steering shaft from the steering gear.

4   Remove the screws and pin-type fasteners from the front splash guard and right-side fender splash guard and remove the guards.

5   Remove the nuts and separate the lower bumper cover from the subframe.

6   Remove the bolt from the power steering hose bracket (see illustration).

7   Remove the front portion of the exhaust system (see illustration).

4.6 Detach the power steering line bracket from the subframe

4.7 Front exhaust pipe details

1	Flange nuts	3	Hanger
2	Clamp		

4.9 Disconnect the upper and lower stabilizer bar links

4.12 Engine roll restrictor-to-subframe bolt

4.13 Remove the bracket bolts first (A), then remove the subframe nuts (B) and lower the subframe

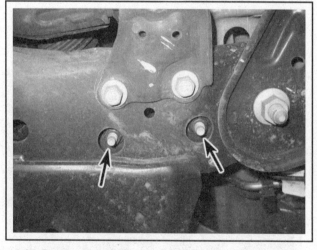

4.14 Remove the stabilizer bar bushing clamp nuts and bolts (left side shown)

8   If you're working on an all-wheel drive model, index-mark the driveshaft, then detach the driveshaft from the transfer case and reposition it out of the way.

9   Detach the stabilizer bar links from the bar (see illustration). If the ballstud turns with the nut, use an Allen wrench to hold the stud.

10 Detach the tie-rod ends from the steering knuckles (see Section 16).

11 Detach the balljoints from the steering knuckles (see Section 5).

12 Remove the engine roll restrictor heat shield, if equipped (the lower nut need only be loosened), then remove the bolt securing the engine roll restrictor to the subframe (see illustration).

13 Mark the location of the front subframe to the underbody at the mounting locations. Support the front subframe with a pair of floor jacks, remove the bolts and nuts from the subframe support brackets, then remove the four subframe nuts. Lower the subframe with the jacks approximately 3 inches (76 mm) (see illustration).

14 Unbolt the stabilizer bar bushing clamps (see illustration). Guide the stabilizer bar out from between the subframe and the body.

15 While the stabilizer bar is off the vehicle, slide off the retainer bushings and inspect them. If they're cracked, worn or deteriorated,

replace them.

16 Clean the bushing area of the stabilizer bar with a stiff wire brush to remove any rust or dirt. Lubricate the inside and outside of the new bushing with vegetable oil (used in cooking) to facilitate reassembly.

※ **CAUTION:**

Don't use petroleum or mineral-based lubricants or brake fluid - they will lead to deterioration of the bushings.

INSTALLATION

17 Installation is the reverse of removal. Tighten the fasteners to the torque values listed in this Chapter's Specifications.

18 When installing the subframe, loosely attach the subframe brackets with the bolts. Use your marks to align the subframe to the body. Tighten the subframe nuts to the torque listed in this Chapter's Specifications, then tighten the remaining support bracket fasteners.

5   Control arm (front) - removal, inspection and installation

REMOVAL

▶ **Refer to illustrations 5.3 and 5.4**

1   Loosen the wheel lug nuts on the side to be disassembled, raise the front of the vehicle, support it securely on jackstands and remove the wheel.

2   Disconnect the stabilizer bar link from the control arm (see Section 4).

3   Remove the nut and bolt to disconnect the lower balljoint from the steering knuckle (see illustration).

4   Remove the control front pivot bolt and spacer (see illustration).

5   Remove the two rear bushing bracket-to-frame bolts and remove the lower arm.

INSPECTION

6   Check the control arm for distortion and the bushings for wear, replacing parts as necessary. Do not attempt to straighten a bent control arm.

INSTALLATION

7   Installation is the reverse of removal. When installing the control arm, leave the three arm-to-frame bolts (two rearward and one forward) finger tight until completing the installation of all other components. Tighten the three control arm fasteners to the specified torque after the vehicle has been lowered with its full weight resting on the ground. As an alternative, raise the outer end of the control arm to simulate normal ride height, then tighten the fasteners.

8   It's a good idea to have the front wheel alignment checked and, if necessary, adjusted after this job has been performed.

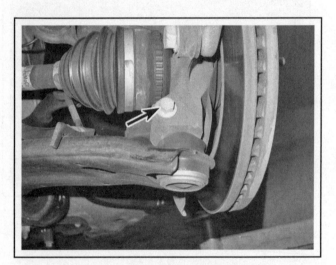

5.3 Remove the nut and the balljoint pinch bolt, and separate the balljoint from the steering knuckle

5.4 Control arm details

1   *Front pivot bolt*   2   *Rear bushing bracket bolts*

6   Steering knuckle and hub - removal and installation

REMOVAL

1   Loosen the wheel lug nuts. Raise the vehicle and support it securely on jackstands, then remove the wheel.

2   With the brake applied to prevent the driveaxle from rotating, remove the driveaxle/hub nut, washer and hub seal. Discard the old seal but do not discard the nut and washer yet.

3   Remove the ABS wheel speed sensor and the wiring harness bracket bolt (see Chapter 9)

4   Disconnect the brake hose bracket from the strut, then remove the brake caliper (don't disconnect the hose), the caliper mounting bracket and the brake disc (see Chapter 9). Hang the caliper from the coil

spring with a piece of wire - don't let it hang by the brake hose.

5   Separate the control arm from the steering knuckle (see Section 5).

6   Separate the tie-rod end from the steering knuckle arm (see Section 16).

7   Separate the driveaxle from the hub using a drive hub remover or an equivalent puller (see Chapter 8).

8   Detach the lower end of the strut from the steering knuckle (see Section 2), then remove the knuckle.

INSTALLATION

9   Guide the knuckle and hub assembly into position, inserting the driveaxle into the hub.

10 Install and tighten the lower strut bolts and nuts.

11 Connect the balljoint to the knuckle and tighten the pinch bolt nut to the torque listed in this Chapter's Specifications.

12 Attach the tie-rod end to the steering knuckle arm (see Section 16). Tighten the nut to the torque listed in this Chapter's Specifications.

13 Install the wheel speed sensor and harness bracket.

14 Install the brake disc and caliper/mounting bracket assembly (see Chapter 9).

15 With the brake applied to prevent the driveaxle from rotating, seat the driveaxle by using the old driveaxle/hub nut and washer and tighten the nut to the torque listed in the Chapter 8 Specifications. Remove and discard the old nut and washer, replace them with new parts and retighten to the specified torque.

➡ **Note: The driveaxle/hub nut must be tightened before lowering the vehicle or damage to the wheel bearings may occur.**

➡ **Note: The driveaxle/hub nut is coated with a one-use locking chemical and cannot be re-used for final assembly. The locking chemical is activated by heat created during tightening. The nut must be tightened to the specified torque within five minutes of starting it on the threads or the locking chemical will not activate properly.**

16 Install the wheel and lug nuts. Lower the vehicle and tighten the lug nuts to the torque listed in the Chapter 1 Specifications.

17 Have the front-end alignment checked and, if necessary, adjusted.

7   Hub and bearing assembly (front) - removal and installation

Due to the special tools and expertise required to press the hub and bearing from the steering knuckle, this job should be left to a professional mechanic. However, the steering knuckle and hub may be removed and the assembly taken to an automotive machine shop or other qualified repair facility equipped with the necessary tools. See Section 6 for the steering knuckle and hub removal procedure.

8   Shock absorber (rear) - removal and installation

▶ **Refer to illustration 8.4**

✳✳ WARNING:

The manufacturer recommends replacing all fasteners with new ones during installation.

1   From inside the rear cargo area, remove the interior quarter trim panel (see Chapter 11).

2   Remove the upper shock absorber mounting nuts.

3   Loosen the wheel lug nuts, raise the vehicle and support it securely on jackstands. Block the front wheels to prevent the vehicle from rolling and remove the rear wheel.

4   Support the rear lower control arm with a floor jack, then remove the lower shock absorber nut and bolt (see illustration).

5   Maneuver the shock out of the vehicle.

6   Installation is the reverse of the removal procedure.

✳✳ CAUTION:

New shock absorbers are gas-filled and come compressed and retained with a fiberglass strap. Do NOT remove the strap until the shock is installed.

8.4 Remove the lower shock absorber nut and bolt

7   When installing the shock absorber, install the upper and lower shock mounting fasteners but leave them loose until after the vehicle has been lowered. Tighten the lower bolt and nut to the specified torque with the full weight of the vehicle on the ground, then tighten the upper mounting nuts to the specified torque.

9 Suspension arms (rear) - removal and installation

✳ WARNING:

The manufacturer recommends replacing all fasteners with new ones during installation.

→ Note: To prevent possible damage to the bushings, always tighten bushing fasteners while the full weight of the vehicle is resting on the wheels.

1   Loosen the wheel lug nuts, raise the vehicle and support it securely on jackstands. Block the front wheels to prevent the vehicle from rolling. Remove the wheel.

UPPER SUSPENSION ARM

▶ Refer to illustrations 9.4 and 9.6

2   On all-wheel drive models, detach the wheel speed sensor, unclip the harness from the retainers on the control arm and reposition it to the side (see Chapter 9).

3   Detach the brake hose bracket.

4   The rear subframe must be lowered in order to remove the inboard bolt. Position a floor jack under the rear subframe. Remove the fasteners holding the subframe bushing bracket and the rearward subframe nut (see illustration). Loosen, but do not remove, the same bolts on the other side of the subframe.

5   Carefully lower the jack to relieve the spring pressure.

6   If you're working on a 2010 or earlier model, remove the outboard nut and bolt from the upper arm. If you're working on a 2011 or later model, remove the upper arm-to-rear knuckle bolts (see illustration). Don't allow the knuckle to fall outward.

7   Remove the inboard bolt and remove the upper arm.

8   Installation is the reverse of removal. Install new inboard and outboard control arm bolts but leave them loose until the vehicle is lowered. Tighten them to the torque listed in this Chapter's Specifications after the full weight is on the wheels and tires. As an alternative, raise the outer end of the lower suspension arm with a floor jack to simulate

normal ride height.

LOWER SUSPENSION ARM

▶ Refer to illustration 9.10

9   Remove the rear coil spring (see Section 10).

10 Mark the position of the cam adjuster bolt to the subframe, then remove the cam adjuster nut and bolt (see illustration). Remove the arm from the vehicle.

11 Installation is the reverse of removal. When installing the cam adjuster bolt, align the matchmarks and install a new nut. Tighten the fasteners to the torque listed in this Chapter's Specifications after the full weight is on the wheels and tires. As an alternative, raise the outer end of the lower suspension arm with a floor jack to simulate normal ride height.

TRAILING ARM

2010 and earlier models

Removal

12 Remove the brake caliper (see Chapter 9) but leave the brake line attached. Use wire to support the caliper and position it to the side.

13 Remove the brake disc.

14 Remove the parking brake shoes, then disconnect the cable.

15 Remove the cable bracket from the back of the stone guard and disconnect the stabilizer bar link.

16 Remove the wheel speed sensor and brake hose bracket and reposition them to the side.

17 If you're working on an all-wheel drive model, remove the inner and outer wheel hub nuts (do not discard the nuts yet) then separate the driveaxle from the hub and bearing using a drive hub remover (see Chapter 8).

9.4 Rear subframe details (left side shown)

1   Bushing bracket bolts
2   Subframe bolts

9.6 Upper arm-to-knuckle bolts

9.10 Mark the position of the cam to the subframe, then remove the lower arm inner pivot bolt

9.35 Trailing arm-to-rear knuckle fasteners

9.36 Remove the pivot bracket bolts

18 Place a floor jack under the lower arm.

✳✳ WARNING:

The lower arm is under considerable pressure from the rear spring. Use caution not to remove or dislodge the jack, and at any time you are working around a loaded spring.

19 Remove the nut and bolt from the lower end of the shock absorber.

20 Remove the fasteners from the outboard upper arm, outboard toe link and outboard lower arm.

21 If you're working on an all-wheel drive model, pull the driveaxle out the back of the knuckle, up through the opening and secure the shaft to the side.

22 Remove the bolts from the trailing arm pivot bracket, noting their positions. Remove the pivot and trailing arm assembly.

23 Remove the nut and bolt from the trailing arm pivot to disconnect the trailing arm from the pivot bracket.

Installation

24 Install the trailing arm pivot bolt and tighten the nut to the specified torque.

25 Install the trailing arm bracket to the frame and tighten the bolts to the specified torque.

26 On all-wheel drive models, place the driveaxle back through the knuckle and into the hub.

27 Loosely install new bolts and nuts into the outboard lower arm, outboard toe link and the lower shock mount.

28 Raise the suspension with the floor jack (if needed) to align and install the upper arm bolt into its mount on the trailing arm; leave the nut loose.

29 Tighten the outboard lower arm bolt to the torque listed in this Chapter's Specifications. Note that the specification is different if installing a new trailing arm.

30 Tighten the bolts to their specified torque in the following order: outboard toe link bolt, shock absorber lower nut then the outboard upper arm nut.

➡ Note: The wheel hub nut must be tightened before lowering the vehicle or damage to the wheel bearings may occur.

31 All-wheel drive models: With the brake applied to prevent the half

shaft from rotating, place the half shaft in the hub. Seat the driveaxle by using the old wheel hub nut and tightening it to 203 Ft-lbs (275 Nm). Remove and discard the old nut, install new inner and outer nuts and retighten to the specified torque.

➡ Note: The wheel hub nut must be tightened before lowering the vehicle or damage to the wheel bearings may occur.

➡ Note: The wheel hub nuts are coated with a one-use locking chemical and cannot be re-used for final assembly. The locking chemical is activated by heat created during tightening. The nuts must be tightened to the specified torque within five minutes of starting it on the threads or the locking chemical will not activate properly.

32 The remainder of the installation is the reverse of removal.

2011 and later models

Removal

▶ Refer to illustrations 9.35 and 9.36

33 Support the lower control arm with a floor jack.

✳✳ WARNING:

The lower arm is under considerable pressure from the rear spring. Use caution not to remove or dislodge the jack, and at any time you are working around a loaded spring.

34 Detach the stabilizer bar link from the trailing arm (see Section 13). Detach the parking brake cable bracket.

35 Remove the trailing arm-to-rear knuckle bolts (see illustration).

36 Remove the bolts from the trailing arm pivot bracket, noting their positions. Remove the pivot and trailing arm assembly (see illustration).

37 Note the angle of the trailing arm in relation to the pivot bracket (measure with a protractor if available), then remove the nut and bolt from the trailing arm pivot to disconnect the trailing arm from the pivot bracket.

Installation

38 If separated, install the trailing arm to the pivot bracket (at the same angle measured in Step 37). Install the trailing arm pivot bolt and tighten the nut to the torque listed in this Chapter's Specifications.

9.42 Toe link fasteners

39 Install the trailing arm bracket to the frame and tighten the bolts to the torque listed in this Chapter's Specifications.

40 Install the trailing arm-to-rear knuckle bolts and tighten the nuts to the torque listed in this Chapter's Specifications.

TOE LINK

▶ **Refer to illustration 9.42**

41 Support the lower control arm with a floor jack and raise it slightly.

42 Mark the position of the adjuster cam to the subframe, then remove the fasteners from the inboard and outboard ends of the toe link (see illustration).

43 Installation is the reverse of removal. Install new inboard and outboard bolts and nuts. Align the marks you made on the cam adjuster and the subframe. Tighten the fasteners to the specified torque after the full weight is on the wheels. As an alternative, raise the outer end of the lower suspension arm with a floor jack to simulate normal ride height.

44 Have the rear wheel alignment checked and, if necessary, adjusted.

---

10 Coil spring (rear) - removal and installation

※※ **WARNING:**

Always replace the springs as a set - never replace just one of them.

※※ **WARNING:**

The manufacturer recommends replacing all fasteners with new ones during installation.

1   Loosen the wheel lug nuts, raise the vehicle and support it securely on jackstands. Block the front wheels to prevent the vehicle from rolling. Remove the wheel.

2010 AND EARLIER MODELS

Removal

2   Remove the brake caliper and the brake disc (see Chapter 9).

3   Remove the brake cable bracket from the rear knuckle and disconnect the stabilizer bar link.

4   Remove the wheel speed sensor and brake hose bracket and reposition them to the side.

5   On all-wheel drive models, remove the inner and outer driveaxle/hub nuts (do not discard the nuts yet), then separate the driveaxle from the hub and bearing using a drive hub remover (see Chapter 8).

6   Place a floor jack under the lower arm.

7   Remove the nut and bolt from the lower end of the shock absorber.

8   Remove the fasteners from the outboard upper arm, outboard toe link and outboard lower arm.

9   On all-wheel drive models. Pull the driveaxle out the back of the knuckle, up through the opening and secure the shaft to the side.

※※ **WARNING:**

The spring is under considerable pressure. Use caution when installing or removing a loaded spring.

10 Slowly lower the jack while pulling out on the knuckle and remove the coil spring.

11 Check the spring for cracks and chips, replacing the springs as a set if any defects are found. Also check the upper and lower seats for damage and deterioration, replacing if necessary.

Installation

12 If a new lower seat is installed, position it in the lower arm by aligning the recess in the seat with the ridge in the lower arm.

13 Install the spring by pulling out on the knuckle and positioning the lower end of the spring no more than 0.39-inch (10 mm) away from the step in the lower spring seat.

14 On all-wheel drive models, place the driveaxle back through the knuckle and into the hub.

15 Raise the jack and loosely install new bolts and nuts into the outboard lower arm, outboard toe link, outboard upper arm and the lower shock mount, then lower the jack.

16 All-wheel drive models: With the brake applied to prevent the driveaxle from rotating, place the driveaxle in the hub. Seat the driveaxle by using the old driveaxle/hub nut and tightening it to 203 Ft-lbs (275 Nm). Remove and discard the old nut, install new inner and outer nuts and retighten to the torque listed in the Chapter 8 Specifications.

➡ **Note: The wheel hub nut must be tightened before lowering the vehicle or damage to the wheel bearings may occur.**

➡ **Note: The wheel hub nuts are coated with a one-use locking chemical and cannot be re-used for final assembly. The locking chemical is activated by heat created during tightening. The nuts must be tightened to the specified torque within five minutes of starting it on the threads or the locking chemical will not activate properly.**

17 The remainder of the installation is the reverse of removal. Tighten the fasteners to the specified torque in the following order after the vehicle has been lowered: outboard toe link bolt, shock absorber lower nut then the outboard upper arm nut.

2011 AND LATER MODELS

Removal

18 Support the lower control arm with a floor jack.

19 Remove the rear knuckle (see Section 12).

20 Slowly lower the jack and allow the coil spring to extend fully. Remove the spring.

21 Check the spring for cracks and chips, replacing the springs as a set if any defects are found. Also check the upper and lower seats for damage and deterioration, replacing if necessary.

Installation

22 If a new lower seat is installed, position it in the lower arm by aligning the recess in the seat with the ridge in the lower arm.

23 Install the spring on the lower arm and position the lower end of the spring no more than 0.39-inch (10 mm) away from the step in the lower spring seat.

24 Raise the jack, then install the rear knuckle (see Section 12).

25 The remainder of installation is the reverse of removal.

ALL MODELS

26 Have the rear wheel alignment checked and, if necessary, adjusted.

11 Hub and bearing assembly (rear) - removal and installation

▶ **Refer to illustration 11.13**

✻✻ WARNING:

The manufacturer recommends replacing all fasteners with new ones during installation.

REMOVAL

➡ **Note: Before beginning the disassembly on 2010 and earlier all-wheel drive models, take a measurement from the center of the rear hub to the lower edge of the bodywork at the top of the wheel opening with the full weight of the vehicle on the ground. This measurement is the normal ride height of the vehicle and will be used when re-assembling the rear suspension components (see illustration 12.1).**

1 Loosen the rear wheel lug nuts. Raise the rear of the vehicle and support it securely on jackstands, then remove the wheel.

2 Remove the brake caliper (see Chapter 9) but leave the brake line attached. Use wire to support the caliper and position it to the side.

3 Remove the brake disc and the brake hose bracket.

4 If you're working on an all-wheel drive model, remove the drive-axle/hub nut(s).

5 Remove the wheel speed sensor (see Chapter 9).

2010 and earlier models

6 Remove the nut and bolt to separate the outboard end of the upper arm from the wheel knuckle.

7 Place a floor jack under the lower arm.

8 Remove the nut and bolt from the lower end of the shock absorber.

9 Remove the fasteners from the upper stabilizer bar link and the outboard toe link.

10 Pull the driveaxle out the back of the knuckle, up through the opening and secure the shaft to the side.

11 On front wheel drive models, remove the wheel speed sensor and brake hose bracket and reposition them to the side.

12 Remove the bolts and detach the wheel bearing and hub assembly from the wheel knuckle (see illustration).

2011 and later models

13 Remove the bolts and detach the wheel bearing and hub assembly from the wheel knuckle (see illustration). If you're working on an all-wheel drive model, simultaneously push the driveaxle from the hub with a suitable puller.

INSTALLATION

2010 and earlier models

14 Install the wheel hub/bearing assembly onto the wheel knuckle and tighten the bolts to the torque listed in this Chapter's Specifications.

15 On all-wheel drive models, place the driveaxle back through the knuckle and into the hub.

16 Loosely install new bolts and nuts into the outboard lower arm, outboard toe link and the lower shock mount.

11.13 Remove the four wheel hub bolts and remove the hub

17 Raise the suspension with the floor jack if needed to align and install the upper arm bolt; leave the nut loose

18 Adjust the height of the jack to attain the ride height measurement taken at the beginning of the procedure and tighten the upper arm nut to the specified torque.

19 Tighten the outboard lower arm bolt to the specified torque. Note that the specification is different if installing a new trailing arm.

20 Tighten the outboard toe link bolt and the shock absorber lower nut to their specified torque.

21 Re-attach the stabilizer bar link and tighten the nut to the specified torque.

22 Install the brake hose bracket and wheel speed sensor followed by the brake disc and brake caliper assembly. Tighten all brake fasteners to the torque values listed in the Chapter 9 Specifications.

23 All-wheel drive models: With the brake applied to prevent the half shaft from rotating, place the half shaft in the hub. Seat the driveaxle by using the old wheel hub nut and tightening it to 203 Ft-lbs (275 Nm). Remove and discard the old nut, install new inner and outer nuts and retighten to the specified torque.

➡ **Note: The wheel hub nut must be tightened before lowering the vehicle or damage to the wheel bearings may occur.**

➡ **Note: The wheel hub nuts are coated with a one-use locking chemical and cannot be re-used for final assembly. The locking chemical is activated by heat created during tightening. The nuts must be tightened to the specified torque within five minutes of starting it on the threads or the locking chemical will not activate properly.**

2011 and later models

24 Install the wheel hub/bearing assembly onto the rear knuckle. If you're working on an all-wheel drive model, guide the end of the driveaxle into the splines as the hub is being installed. Tighten the hub assembly-to-rear knuckle bolts to the torque listed in this Chapter's Specifications

25 The remainder of installation is the reverse of removal. Tighten the brake fasteners to the torque values listed in the Chapter 9 Specifications. If you're working on an all-wheel drive model, tighten the driveaxle/hub nut(s) to the torque listed in the Chapter 8 Specifications.

26 Install the wheel and lug nuts, then lower the vehicle. Tighten the lug nuts to the torque listed in the Chapter 1 Specifications.

12 Rear knuckle (2011 and later models) - removal and installation

▶ **Refer to illustration 12.1**

✳ WARNING:

The manufacturer recommends replacing all fasteners with new ones during installation.

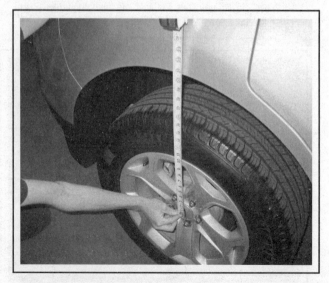

12.1 Measure and record the ride height

1 Before beginning the disassembly, with the full weight of the vehicle on the ground, take a measurement from the center of the rear hub to the lower edge of the bodywork at the top of the wheel opening. This measurement is the normal ride height of the vehicle and will be used when re-assembling the rear suspension components (see illustration).

2 Loosen the rear wheel lug nuts. Raise the rear of the vehicle and support it securely on jackstands, then remove the wheel.

3 Support the lower control arm with a floor jack.

4 Remove the brake caliper (see Chapter 9) but leave the brake line attached. Use wire to support the caliper and position it to the side.

5 Remove the hub and bearing assembly (see Section 11).

6 Disconnect the lower end of the shock absorber from the knuckle (see Section 8).

7 Detach the outer end of the upper control arm from the knuckle (see Section 9).

8 Detach the toe link from the knuckle (see Section 9).

9 Detach the trailing arm from the knuckle (see Section 9).

10 Remove the lower arm-to-knuckle bolt, then use a balljoint separator or other puller to detach the knuckle from the lower arm.

11 Installation is the reverse of the removal procedure, tightening all suspension fasteners to the torque values listed in this Chapter's Specifications with the suspension at normal ride height (this can be simulated by raising the suspension with the floor jack). Tighten the brake fasteners to the torque values listed in the Chapter 9 Specifications. If you're working on an all-wheel drive model, tighten the driveaxle/hub nut(s) to the torque listed in the Chapter 8 Specifications,

12 Install the wheel and lug nuts, then lower the vehicle. Tighten the lug nuts to the torque listed in the Chapter 1 Specifications.

13 Stabilizer bar and bushings (rear) - removal and installation

The manufacturer recommends replacing all fasteners with new ones during installation.

REMOVAL

▶ **Refer to illustrations 13.2 and 13.3**

1   Lift the vehicle on a hoist (if available). Otherwise, back onto a set of ramps and safely block and secure the vehicle, or raise the rear of the vehicle and support it securely on jackstands. Block the front wheels to keep the vehicle from rolling off the stands.

2   Remove the left and right side stabilizer bar links by removing the nuts from the upper and lower ends of the links (see illustration).

3   Remove the nuts holding the stabilizer bar bushing brackets and remove the brackets and the stabilizer bar (see illustration).

4   While the stabilizer bar is off the vehicle, inspect the bushings and replace if cracked, worn or deteriorated.

5   Clean the bushing area of the stabilizer bar with a stiff wire brush to remove any rust or dirt. Lubricate the inside and outside of the new bushing with vegetable oil (used in cooking) to simplify reassembly.

Don't use petroleum or mineral-based lubricants or brake fluid - they will lead to deterioration of the bushings.

6   Installation is the reverse of removal. Tighten the fasteners to the torque values listed in this Chapter's Specifications.

13.2 Rear stabilizer bar link nuts

13.3 Remove the stabilizer bar bushing bracket nuts

14 Steering wheel - removal and installation

These models are equipped with a Supplemental Restraint System (SRS), more commonly known as airbags. Always disable the airbag system before working in the vicinity of any airbag system component to avoid the possibility of accidental deployment of the airbag(s), which could cause personal injury (see Chapter 12).

Do not use a memory saving device to preserve the PCM or radio memory when working on or near airbag system components.

REMOVAL

▶ **Refer to illustrations 14.3, 14.4, 14.6 and 14.8**

1   Turn the ignition key to Off, then disconnect the cable from the negative terminal of the battery. Wait at least two minutes before proceeding.

2   Turn the steering wheel so the wheels are pointing straight ahead and remove the key.

3   Use a small screwdriver or a 3 mm Allen wrench through the holes in the backside of the steering wheel to release the airbag module clips (see illustration). Gently pull the airbag module away from the wheel on the side you have released, then repeat this Step on the other side of the wheel.

14.3 Depress the clips through the holes on each side of the steering wheel to release the airbag

14.4 Pry up the locking tabs, then disconnect the airbag connectors

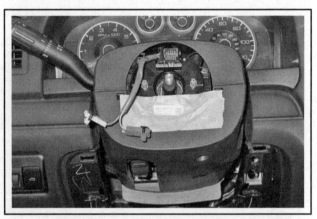

14.8 Apply a piece of tape to the clockspring to prevent it from rotating

4   Pry UP the connector locks and disconnect the airbag module electrical connectors (see illustration).

5   Remove the airbag and set the module in a safe, isolated area.

✳✳ WARNING:

Carry the airbag module with the trim side facing away from you, and set the steering wheel/airbag module down with the trim side facing up. Don't place anything on top of the steering wheel/airbag module.

6   Make match marks on the wheel and the steering shaft, then remove the steering wheel mounting nut and disconnect the electrical connector (see illustration).

7   Try rocking the wheel lightly to remove it from the shaft. If this does not work, use a suitable puller to remove the steering wheel. **Do not** hit the steering shaft with a hammer or you will damage the shaft.

8   Tape the clockspring so that it cannot rotate (see illustration).

✳✳ CAUTION:

Do not rotate the steering shaft at any time while the wheel and airbag are removed or the clockspring could be damaged.

9   If it is necessary to remove the airbag clockspring, remove the steering column covers (see Chapter 11), disconnect the electrical con-

14.6 Mark the position of the steering wheel to the shaft, then use a socket to remove the steering wheel nut

nectors, then remove the screws and take the clockspring off the steering column.

INSTALLATION

10   If the clockspring was removed, install it onto the steering column, making sure the pins on the back of the clockspring engage with the holes in the steering wheel rotation sensor. Install the screws, tightening them securely.

11   New clocksprings come equipped with an anti-rotation pin that holds them in the pre-centered position. If you are installing a new clockspring, don't remove the pin until you are ready to install the steering wheel after the steering column covers have been installed. If you are installing the old clockspring, or are not sure whether or not the clockspring has become uncentered, center the clockspring:

   a) *Turn the inner hub of the clockspring counterclockwise until you feel resistance.*

✳✳ CAUTION:

Don't apply too much force to the hub or you could damage the clockspring ribbon.

   b) *Turn the hub to the 12 o'clock position, then rotate it clockwise three turns, returning it to the 12 o'clock position.*

12   Install the steering column covers, if removed. If you installed a new clockspring, remove the anti-rotation pin.

13   Install the steering wheel by reversing the removal procedure. When placing the steering wheel onto the shaft, be sure to align the match marks you made in Step 6.

14   Tighten the steering wheel nut to the torque listed in this Chapter's Specifications.

✳✳ CAUTION:

Make sure the connectors fit correctly on the airbag module (with the safety tabs still UP). When connecting the airbag connectors, match the key on the connector to the corresponding keyway on the module. Do not push the connectors on if the clips are down. After the clips are secured, push the airbag module down toward the wheel until the retaining clips lock. When seated properly, the gap between the airbag module trim cover and the steering wheel should be even and consistent.

15 Steering column - removal and installation

※ WARNING:

These models are equipped with a Supplemental Restraint System (SRS), more commonly known as airbags. Always disable the airbag system before working in the vicinity of any airbag system component to avoid the possibility of accidental deployment of the airbag(s), which could cause personal injury (see Chapter 12).

※ WARNING:

Do not use a memory saving device to preserve the PCM or radio memory when working on or near airbag system components.

REMOVAL

▶ **Refer to illustrations 15.7 and 15.9**

1   Park the vehicle with the wheels pointing straight ahead. Disconnect the cable from the negative terminal of the battery (see Chapter 5).

2   Remove the steering wheel (see Section 14) and tape the airbag clockspring to prevent it from turning.

※ CAUTION:

If this is not done, the airbag clockspring could be damaged.

3   Remove the steering column covers (see Chapter 11).

4   Remove the knee bolster and reinforcement (see Chapter 11). If the vehicle is equipped with an in-vehicle temperature sensor, disconnect the electrical connector and hose from the sensor.

5   Disconnect the electrical connectors from both sides of the column, then detach the retainer holding the wiring harness and position the harness out of the way.

6   Remove the cover from the lower steering shaft joint.

7   Make a match-mark on the steering column shaft as it relates to the steering gear extension shaft (see illustration).

8   Remove and discard the pinch bolt from the clamp below the U-joint and disconnect the steering column shaft from the steering gear extension shaft.

9   Remove the four steering column mounting fasteners (see illustration). Lower the column and pull it to the rear, making sure nothing is still connected, then remove the column.

INSTALLATION

10 Guide the steering column into position, engaging the U-joint with the bottom of the steering shaft, then install the steering column mounting fasteners and tighten them to the torque listed in this Chapter's Specifications.

➡ **Note: An assistant will be very helpful in this procedure.**

11 Connect the U-joint to the steering gear extension shaft. Install a new pinch bolt, tightening it to the torque listed in this Chapter's Specifications.

12 The remainder of installation is the reverse of removal.

15.7 Mark the U-joint to the steering gear extension shaft, then remove the pinch bolt

15.9 Remove the steering column mounting bolts (one bolt not visible)

16 Tie-rod ends - removal and installation

REMOVAL

▶ **Refer to illustrations 16.2a, 16.2b and 16.4**

1   Loosen the front wheel lug nuts. Apply the parking brake, raise the front of the vehicle and support it securely on jackstands. Remove the front wheel.

2   Hold the tie-rod with a pair of locking pliers or wrench and loosen the jam nut enough to mark the position of the tie-rod end in relation to the threads (see illustrations).

3   Remove the cotter pin and loosen (but don't remove) the nut on the tie-rod end stud.

4   Disconnect the tie-rod end from the steering knuckle arm with a tie-rod end remover (see illustration). Remove the nut and detach the tie-rod end.

5   Unscrew the tie-rod end from the tie-rod.

INSTALLATION

6   Thread the tie-rod end on to the marked position and insert the stud into the steering knuckle arm. Tighten the jam nut securely.

7   Install the nut on the stud and tighten it to the torque listed in this Chapter's Specifications. Install a new cotter pin.

8   Install the wheel and lug nuts. Lower the vehicle and tighten the lug nuts to the torque listed in the Chapter 1 Specifications.

9   Have the alignment checked and, if necessary, adjusted.

16.2a Loosen the jam nut . . .

16.2b . . . then mark the position of the tie-rod end

16.4 Disconnect the tie-rod end from the steering knuckle with a puller

17 Steering gear boots - replacement

▶ **Refer to illustration 17.3**

1   Loosen the lug nuts, raise the vehicle and support it securely on jackstands. Remove the wheel.

2   Remove the tie-rod end and jam nut (see Section 16).

3   Remove the outer steering gear boot clamp with a pair of pliers (see illustration). Cut off the inner boot clamp with a pair of diagonal cutters. Slide off the boot.

4   Before installing the new boot, wrap the threads and serrations on the end of the steering rod with a layer of tape so the small end of the new boot isn't damaged.

5   Slide the new boot into position on the steering gear until it seats in the groove in the steering rod and install new clamps.

6   Remove the tape and install the tie-rod end (see Section 16).

7   Install the wheel and lug nuts. Lower the vehicle and tighten the lug nuts to the torque listed in the Chapter 1 Specifications.

17.3 The outer ends of the steering gear boots are secured by band-type clamps (A); they're easily removed with a pair of pliers. The inner ends are retained by boot clamps (B) which must be cut off and discarded

18 Steering gear - removal and installation

✳✳ WARNING:

These models are equipped with airbags. Always disable the airbag system before working in the vicinity of airbag system components (see Chapter 12). Make sure the steering column shaft is not turned while the steering gear is removed or you could damage the airbag system clockspring. To prevent the shaft from turning, turn the ignition key to the lock position with the steering wheel in the straight ahead position before beginning work.

REMOVAL

♦ **Refer to illustration 18.5**

1 Disconnect the cable from the negative terminal of the battery (see Chapter 5).
2 Loosen the front wheel lug nuts. Raise the vehicle and place it securely on jackstands. Remove both front wheels.
3 Detach the tie-rod ends from the steering knuckles (see Section 16)
4 Remove the front stabilizer bar (see Section 4).
5 Place a drain pan under the steering gear and detach the power steering pressure and return lines (see illustration). Cap the ends to prevent excessive fluid loss and contamination.
6 Index mark the steering shaft to the steering gear input shaft, then disconnect the steering shaft from the steering gear input shaft.
7 Remove the heat shield and the pressure line retainers from the steering gear.
8 Remove the mounting bolts and detach the steering gear from the subframe.

INSTALLATION

9 Installation is the reverse of removal, noting the following points:

18.5 Disconnect the fluid lines from the steering gear

1   *Pressure line*   2   *Return line*

a) *New fasteners should be used in the re-assembly.*
b) *If you're installing a new steering gear, be sure to install a new steering gear turn tube heat wrap.*
c) *Tighten the steering gear mounting bolts to the specified torque in sequence: left rear, right rear, left front, right front.*
d) *When connecting the steering column shaft to the steering gear input shaft, be sure to align the matchmarks, and install a new pinch bolt.*
e) *The banjo bolt and sealing washers on the high-pressure line should be replaced.*
f) *Tighten the banjo bolt to the torque listed in this Chapter's Specifications.*
g) *Fill the power steering reservoir with the recommended fluid (see Chapter 1). Bleed the power steering hydraulic system as described in Section 20.*
h) *Have the front end alignment checked and, if necessary, adjusted.*

19 Power steering pump - removal and installation

V6 MODELS

Removal

1 Disconnect the cable from the negative battery terminal (see Chapter 5).
2 Raise the vehicle and support it securely on jackstands.
3 Using a large syringe or suction gun, suck as much fluid out of the power steering fluid reservoir as possible. Place a drain pan under the vehicle to catch any fluid that spills out when the hoses are disconnected.
4 Remove the drivebelt (see Chapter 1).
5 On all-wheel drive models, first remove the four bolts from the driveshaft coupler and position the driveshaft to the side.
6 Use a floor jack to support the rear of the front subframe. Remove the nuts and bolts from the subframe brackets and remove the brackets.
7 Remove the two middle subframe nuts and slowly lower the jack

to lower the rear of the subframe (see illustration 4.13).
8 Remove the clamp from the power steering pump supply hose and disconnect the hose.
9 Disconnect the electrical connector at the power steering pump.
10 Remove the banjo bolt and disconnect the pressure line.
11 Unscrew and remove the mounting bolts, and withdraw the power steering pump from the engine.

Installation

12 Installation is the reverse of removal, noting the following points:

a) *The banjo bolt and sealing washers on the high-pressure line should be replaced.*
b) *Tighten the mounting bolts and banjo bolt to the torque listed in this Chapter's Specifications.*
c) *Fill the power steering reservoir with the recommended fluid (see Chapter 1). Bleed the power steering hydraulic system as described in Section 20.*

FOUR-CYLINDER MODELS

Removal

▶ **Refer to installation 19.10**

13 Disconnect the cable from the negative battery terminal (see Chapter 5).

14 Using a large syringe or suction gun, suck as much fluid out of the power steering fluid reservoir as possible. Place a drain pan under the vehicle to catch any fluid that spills out when the hoses are disconnected.

15 Remove the drivebelt (see Chapter 1).

16 Detach the pressure and supply hoses from the pump (see illustration).

17 Remove the pump mounting bolts and detach it from the pump from the engine.

Installation

18 Installation is the reverse of removal, noting the following points:

  a) *The banjo bolt and sealing washers on the high-pressure line should be replaced.*

  b) *Tighten the mounting bolts and pressure line fitting bolt to the torque listed in this Chapter's Specifications.*

  c) *Fill the power steering reservoir with the recommended fluid (see Chapter 1). Bleed the power steering hydraulic system as described in Section 20.*

19.10 Power steering pump details (four-cylinder models)

1	*Supply hose clamp*	3 *Upper mounting bolts*
2	*Pressure line fitting bolt*	*(lower bolts not visible)*

20 Power steering system - bleeding

1 The power steering system must be bled whenever a line is disconnected. Bubbles can be seen in power steering fluid that has air in it and the fluid will often have a tan or milky appearance. Low fluid level can cause air to mix with the fluid, resulting in a noisy pump as well as foaming of the fluid.

2 Open the hood and check the fluid level in the reservoir, adding the specified fluid necessary to bring it up to the proper level (see Chapter 1).

3 Start the engine and slowly turn the steering wheel several times from left-to-right and back again. Do not turn the wheel completely from lock-to-lock. Check the fluid level, topping it up as necessary until it remains steady and no more bubbles are visible.

21 Wheels and tires - general information

▶ **Refer to illustration 21.1**

1 All vehicles covered by this manual are equipped with metric-sized fiberglass or steel belted radial tires (see illustration). Use of other size or type of tires may affect the ride and handling of the vehicle. Don't mix different types of tires, such as radials and bias belted, on the same vehicle as handling may be seriously affected. It's recommended that tires be replaced in pairs on the same axle, but if only one tire is being replaced, be sure it's the same size, structure and tread design as the other.

2 Because tire pressure has a substantial effect on handling and wear, the pressure on all tires should be checked at least once a month or before any extended trips (see Chapter 1).

3 Wheels must be replaced if they are bent, dented, leak air, have elongated bolt holes, are heavily rusted, out of vertical symmetry or if the lug nuts won't stay tight. Wheel repairs that use welding or peening are not recommended.

4 Tire and wheel balance is important in the overall handling, braking and performance of the vehicle. Unbalanced wheels can adversely affect handling and ride characteristics as well as tire life. Whenever a tire is installed on a wheel, the tire and wheel should be balanced by a shop with the proper equipment.

21.1 Metric tire size code

22 Wheel alignment - general information

▸ **Refer to illustration 22.1**

A wheel alignment refers to the adjustments made to the wheels so they are in proper angular relationship to the suspension and the ground. Wheels that are out of proper alignment not only affect vehicle control, but also increase tire wear. The front end angles normally measured are camber, caster and toe-in (see illustration). Toe-in and camber are adjustable; if the caster is not correct, check for bent components. Rear toe-in is also adjustable.

Getting the proper wheel alignment is a very exacting process, one in which complicated and expensive machines are necessary to perform the job properly. Because of this, you should have a technician with the proper equipment perform these tasks. We will, however, use this space to give you a basic idea of what is involved with a wheel alignment so you can better understand the process and deal intelligently with the shop that does the work.

Toe-in is the turning in of the wheels. The purpose of a toe specification is to ensure parallel rolling of the wheels. In a vehicle with zero toe-in, the distance between the front edges of the wheels will be the same as the distance between the rear edges of the wheels. The actual amount of toe-in is normally only a fraction of an inch. On the front end, toe-in is controlled by the tie-rod end position on the tie-rod. On the rear end, it's controlled by a cam bolt on the inner end of the toe-link. Incorrect toe-in will cause the tires to wear improperly by making them scrub against the road surface.

Camber is the tilting of the wheels from vertical when viewed from one end of the vehicle. When the wheels tilt out at the top, the camber is said to be positive (+). When the wheels tilt in at the top the camber is negative (-). The amount of tilt is measured in degrees from vertical and this measurement is called the camber angle. This angle affects the amount of tire tread which contacts the road and compensates for changes in the suspension geometry when the vehicle is cornering or traveling over an undulating surface. On the front end it is not adjustable. On the rear end it's adjusted by cam bolts on the inner ends of the lower control arms.

Caster is the tilting of the front steering axis from the vertical. A tilt toward the rear is positive caster and a tilt toward the front is negative caster. Caster isn't adjustable on these vehicles.

CAMBER ANGLE (FRONT VIEW)

CASTER ANGLE (SIDE VIEW)

TOE-IN (TOP VIEW)

22.1 Camber, caster and toe-in angles

A minus B = C (degrees camber)
D = degrees caster
E minus F = toe-in (measured in inches)
G = toe-in (expressed in degrees)

Torque specifications	Ft-lbs (unless otherwise indicated)	Nm

➡ Note: One foot-pound (ft-lb) of torque is equivalent to 12 inch-pounds (in-lbs) of torque. Torque values below approximately 15 foot-pounds are expressed in inch-pounds, because most foot-pound torque wrenches are not accurate at these smaller values.

Front suspension

Lower control arms		
Balljoint-to-knuckle nut	41	55
Lower arm-to-subframe bolts		
Front	111	150
Rear	59	80
Stabilizer bar		
Bracket bolts	46	63
Upper and lower link nuts	66	90
Front wheel speed sensor	See Chapter 9	
Front brake caliper bolts	See Chapter 9	
Driveaxle/hub nut	See Chapter 8	
Strut/coil spring assembly		
Upper mounting nuts	26	35
Lower mounting bolts/nuts	166	225
Piston rod nut	85	115
Front subframe		
Subframe bracket nuts	98	133
Subframe bracket bolts	66	90
Subframe nuts	98	133
Engine roll restrictor-to-subframe fasteners	76	103

Rear suspension

Shock absorber		
Lower bolt/nut		
2010 and earlier models	59	80
2011 and later models	166	225
Upper nuts	18	25
Rear subframe		
Nuts	66	90
Bushing bolts	18	25
Wheel speed sensor bolt	See Chapter 9	
Rear brake caliper bolts	See Chapter 9	
Driveaxle/hub nuts (AWD models)	See Chapter 8	
Upper control arm		
Inner bolt	129	175
Outer bolts	129	175

Torque specifications (continued)	Ft-lbs (unless otherwise indicated)	Nm

➡ **Note:** One foot-pound (ft-lb) of torque is equivalent to 12 inch-pounds (in-lbs) of torque. Torque values below approximately 15 foot-pounds are expressed in inch-pounds, because most foot-pound torque wrenches are not accurate at these smaller values.

Rear suspension (continued)

	Ft-lbs	Nm
Lower control arm		
Inner nut (cam bolt)	111	150
Outer bolt		
If installing onto new rear knuckle		
Step 1	111	150
Step 2	Loosen 180-degrees	
Step 3	59	80
Step 4	Tighten an additional 90-degrees	
If installing onto old rear knuckle		
Step 1	59	80
Step 2	Tighten an additional 90-degrees	
Trailing arm		
Pivot bolt/nut	111	150
Pivot bracket bolts	35	47
Trailing arm-to-rear knuckle bolts/nuts	76	103
Toe link		
Inner bolt	148	200
Outer bolt	129	175
Stabilizer bar		
Bracket nuts	41	55
Upper and lower link nuts	30	40
Rear hub and bearing assembly bolts		
2010 and earlier models	98	133
2011 and later models	85	115

Steering

	Ft-lbs	Nm
Power steering pump mounting bolts	19	26
Power steering pressure line-to-pump fitting bolt (four-cylinder models)	18	25
Power steering pressure line banjo bolts (V6 models)	35	48
Steering shaft U-joint pinch bolt		
2010 and earlier models	177 in-lbs	20
2011 and later models	18	25
Steering column mounting bolts	21	28
Steering wheel nut	26	35
Steering gear heat shield bolts	53 in-lbs	6
Steering gear mounting bolts	76	103
Tie-rod end-to-steering knuckle nut	35	48

Notes

11

BODY

Section

1 General information

Certain body components are particularly vulnerable to accident damage and can be unbolted and repaired or replaced. Among these parts are the hood, doors, tailgate, liftgate, bumpers and front fenders.

Only general body maintenance practices and body panel repair procedures within the scope of the do-it-yourselfer are included in this Chapter.

2 Repair of minor paint scratches

No matter how hard you try to keep your vehicle looking like new, it will inevitably be scratched, chipped or dented at some point. If the metal is actually dented, seek the advice of a professional. But you can fix minor scratches and chips yourself. Buy a touch-up paint kit from a dealer service department or an auto parts store. To ensure that you get the right color, you'll need to have the specific make, model and year of your vehicle and, ideally, the paint code, which is located on a special metal plate under the hood or in the door jamb.

Make sure the damaged area is perfectly clean and rust free. If the touch-up kit has a wire brush, use it to clean the scratch or chip. Or use fine steel wool wrapped around the end of a pencil. Clean the scratched or chipped surface only, not the good paint surrounding it. Rinse the area with water and allow it to dry thoroughly

Thoroughly mix the paint, then apply a small amount with the touch-up kit brush or a very fine artist's brush. Brush in one direction as you fill the scratch area. Do not build up the paint higher than the surrounding paint

If the vehicle has a two-coat finish, apply the clear coat after the color coat has dried

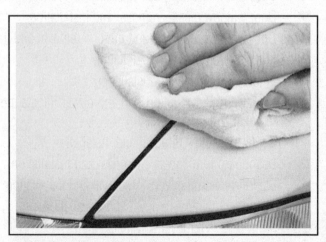

Wait a few days for the paint to dry thoroughly, then rub out the repainted area with a polishing compound to blend the new paint with the surrounding area. When you're happy with your work, wash and polish the area

PLASTIC BODY PANELS

The following repair procedures are for minor scratches and gouges. Repair of more serious damage should be left to a dealer service department or qualified auto body shop. Below is a list of the equipment and materials necessary to perform the following repair procedures on plastic body panels.

Wax, grease and silicone removing solvent
Cloth-backed body tape
Sanding discs
Drill motor with three-inch disc holder
Hand sanding block
Rubber squeegees
Sandpaper
Non-porous mixing palette
Wood paddle or putty knife
Curved-tooth body file
Flexible parts repair material

Flexible panels (bumper trim)

1 Remove the damaged panel, if necessary or desirable. In most cases, repairs can be carried out with the panel installed.

2 Clean the area(s) to be repaired with a wax, grease and silicone removing solvent applied with a water-dampened cloth.

3 If the damage is structural, that is, if it extends through the panel, clean the backside of the panel area to be repaired as well. Wipe dry.

4 Sand the rear surface about 1-1/2 inches beyond the break.

5 Cut two pieces of fiberglass cloth large enough to overlap the break by about 1-1/2 inches. Cut only to the required length.

6 Mix the adhesive from the repair kit according to the instructions included with the kit, and apply a layer of the mixture approximately 1/8-inch thick on the backside of the panel. Overlap the break by at least 1-1/2 inches.

7 Apply one piece of fiberglass cloth to the adhesive and cover the cloth with additional adhesive. Apply a second piece of fiberglass cloth to the adhesive and immediately cover the cloth with additional adhesive in sufficient quantity to fill the weave.

8 Allow the repair to cure for 20 to 30 minutes at 60-degrees to 80-degrees F.

9 If necessary, trim the excess repair material at the edge.

10 Remove all of the paint film over and around the area(s) to be repaired. The repair material should not overlap the painted surface.

11 With a drill motor and a sanding disc (or a rotary file), cut a "V" along the break line approximately 1/2-inch wide. Remove all dust and loose particles from the repair area.

12 Mix and apply the repair material. Apply a light coat first over the damaged area; then continue applying material until it reaches a level slightly higher than the surrounding finish.

13 Cure the mixture for 20 to 30 minutes at 60-degrees to 80-degrees F.

14 Roughly establish the contour of the area being repaired with a body file. If low areas or pits remain, mix and apply additional adhesive.

15 Block sand the damaged area with sandpaper to establish the actual contour of the surrounding surface.

16 If desired, the repaired area can be temporarily protected with several light coats of primer. Because of the special paints and techniques required for flexible body panels, it is recommended that the vehicle be taken to a paint shop for completion of the body repair.

STEEL BODY PANELS

▶ **See photo sequence**

Repair of dents

17 When repairing dents, the first job is to pull the dent out until the affected area is as close as possible to its original shape. There is no point in trying to restore the original shape completely as the metal in the damaged area will have stretched on impact and cannot be restored to its original contours. It is better to bring the level of the dent up to a point that is about 1/8-inch below the level of the surrounding metal. In cases where the dent is very shallow, it is not worth trying to pull it out at all.

18 If the backside of the dent is accessible, it can be hammered out gently from behind using a soft-face hammer. While doing this, hold a block of wood firmly against the opposite side of the metal to absorb the hammer blows and prevent the metal from being stretched.

19 If the dent is in a section of the body which has double layers, or some other factor makes it inaccessible from behind, a different technique is required. Drill several small holes through the metal inside the damaged area, particularly in the deeper sections. Screw long, self-tapping screws into the holes just enough for them to get a good grip in the metal. Now pulling on the protruding heads of the screws with locking pliers can pull out the dent.

20 The next stage of repair is the removal of paint from the damaged area and from an inch or so of the surrounding metal. This is easily done with a wire brush or sanding disk in a drill motor, although it can be done just as effectively by hand with sandpaper. To complete the preparation for filling, score the surface of the bare metal with a screwdriver or the tang of a file or drill small holes in the affected area. This will provide a good grip for the filler material. To complete the repair, see the Section on filling and painting.

Repair of rust holes or gashes

21 Remove all paint from the affected area and from an inch or so of the surrounding metal using a sanding disk or wire brush mounted in a drill motor. If these are not available, a few sheets of sandpaper will do the job just as effectively.

22 With the paint removed, you will be able to determine the severity of the corrosion and decide whether to replace the whole panel, if possible, or repair the affected area. New body panels are not as expensive as most people think and it is often quicker to install a new panel than to repair large areas of rust.

23 Remove all trim pieces from the affected area except those which will act as a guide to the original shape of the damaged body, such as headlight shells, etc. Using metal snips or a hacksaw blade, remove all loose metal and any other metal that is badly affected by rust. Hammer the edges of the hole in to create a slight depression for the filler material.

24 Wire-brush the affected area to remove the powdery rust from the surface of the metal. If the back of the rusted area is accessible, treat it with rust inhibiting paint.

25 Before filling is done, block the hole in some way. This can be done with sheet metal riveted or screwed into place, or by stuffing the hole with wire mesh.

26 Once the hole is blocked off, the affected area can be filled and painted. See the following subsection on filling and painting.

These photos illustrate a method of repairing simple dents. They are intended to supplement Body repair - minor damage in this Chapter and should not be used as the sole instructions for body repair on these vehicles.

1 If you can't access the backside of the body panel to hammer out the dent, pull it out with a slide-hammer-type dent puller. In the deepest portion of the dent or along the crease line, drill or punch hole(s) at least one inch apart . . .

2 . . . then screw the slide-hammer into the hole and operate it. Tap with a hammer near the edge of the dent to help 'pop' the metal back to its original shape. When you're finished, the dent area should be close to its original contour and about 1/8-inch below the surface of the surrounding metal

3 Using coarse-grit sandpaper, remove the paint down to the bare metal. Hand sanding works fine, but the disc sander shown here makes the job faster. Use finer (about 320-grit) sandpaper to feather-edge the paint at least one inch around the dent area

4 When the paint is removed, touch will probably be more helpful than sight for telling if the metal is straight. Hammer down the high spots or raise the low spots as necessary. Clean the repair area with wax/silicone remover

5 Following label instructions, mix up a batch of plastic filler and hardener. The ratio of filler to hardener is critical, and, if you mix it incorrectly, it will either not cure properly or cure too quickly (you won't have time to file and sand it into shape)

6 Working quickly so the filler doesn't harden, use a plastic applicator to press the body filler firmly into the metal, assuring it bonds completely. Work the filler until it matches the original contour and is slightly above the surrounding metal

7 Let the filler harden until you can just dent it with your fingernail. Use a body file or Surform tool (shown here) to rough-shape the filler

8 Use coarse-grit sandpaper and a sanding board or block to work the filler down until it's smooth and even. Work down to finer grits of sandpaper - always using a board or block - ending up with 360 or 400 grit

9 You shouldn't be able to feel any ridge at the transition from the filler to the bare metal or from the bare metal to the old paint. As soon as the repair is flat and uniform, remove the dust and mask off the adjacent panels or trim pieces

10 Apply several layers of primer to the area. Don't spray the primer on too heavy, so it sags or runs, and make sure each coat is dry before you spray on the next one. A professional-type spray gun is being used here, but aerosol spray primer is available inexpensively from auto parts stores

11 The primer will help reveal imperfections or scratches. Fill these with glazing compound. Follow the label instructions and sand it with 360 or 400-grit sandpaper until it's smooth. Repeat the glazing, sanding and respraying until the primer reveals a perfectly smooth surface

12 Finish sand the primer with very fine sandpaper (400 or 600-grit) to remove the primer overspray. Clean the area with water and allow it to dry. Use a tack rag to remove any dust, then apply the finish coat. Don't attempt to rub out or wax the repair area until the paint has dried completely (at least two weeks)

Filling and painting

27 Many types of body fillers are available, but generally speaking, body repair kits which contain filler paste and a tube of resin hardener are best for this type of repair work. A wide, flexible plastic or nylon applicator will be necessary for imparting a smooth and contoured finish to the surface of the filler material. Mix up a small amount of filler on a clean piece of wood or cardboard (use the hardener sparingly). Follow the manufacturer's instructions on the package, otherwise the filler will set incorrectly.

28 Using the applicator, apply the filler paste to the prepared area. Draw the applicator across the surface of the filler to achieve the desired contour and to level the filler surface. As soon as a contour that approximates the original one is achieved, stop working the paste. If you continue, the paste will begin to stick to the applicator. Continue to add thin layers of paste at 20-minute intervals until the level of the filler is just above the surrounding metal.

29 Once the filler has hardened, the excess can be removed with a body file. From then on, progressively finer grades of sandpaper should be used, starting with a 180-grit paper and finishing with 600-grit wet-or-dry paper. Always wrap the sandpaper around a flat rubber or wooden block, otherwise the surface of the filler will not be completely flat. During the sanding of the filler surface, the wet-or-dry paper should be periodically rinsed in water. This will ensure that a very smooth finish is produced in the final stage.

30 At this point, the repair area should be surrounded by a ring of bare metal, which in turn should be encircled by the finely feathered edge of good paint. Rinse the repair area with clean water until all of the dust produced by the sanding operation is gone.

31 Spray the entire area with a light coat of primer. This will reveal any imperfections in the surface of the filler. Repair the imperfections with fresh filler paste or glaze filler and once more smooth the surface

with sandpaper. Repeat this spray-and-repair procedure until you are satisfied that the surface of the filler and the feathered edge of the paint are perfect. Rinse the area with clean water and allow it to dry completely.

32 The repair area is now ready for painting. Spray painting must be carried out in a warm, dry, windless and dust free atmosphere. These conditions can be created if you have access to a large indoor work area, but if you are forced to work in the open, you will have to pick the day very carefully. If you are working indoors, dousing the floor in the work area with water will help settle the dust that would otherwise be in the air. If the repair area is confined to one body panel, mask off the surrounding panels. This will help minimize the effects of a slight mismatch in paint color. Trim pieces such as chrome strips, door handles, etc., will also need to be masked off or removed. Use masking tape and several thickness of newspaper for the masking operations.

33 Before spraying, shake the paint can thoroughly, then spray a test area until the spray painting technique is mastered. Cover the repair area with a thick coat of primer. The thickness should be built up using several thin layers of primer rather than one thick one. Using 600-grit wet-or-dry sandpaper, rub down the surface of the primer until it is very smooth. While doing this, the work area should be thoroughly rinsed with water and the wet-or-dry sandpaper periodically rinsed as well. Allow the primer to dry before spraying additional coats.

34 Spray on the top coat, again building up the thickness by using several thin layers of paint. Begin spraying in the center of the repair area and then, using a circular motion, work out until the whole repair area and about two inches of the surrounding original paint is covered. Remove all masking material 10 to 15 minutes after spraying on the final coat of paint. Allow the new paint at least two weeks to harden, then use a very fine rubbing compound to blend the edges of the new paint into the existing paint. Finally, apply a coat of wax

4 Body repair - major damage

1 Major damage must be repaired by an auto body shop specifically equipped to perform body and frame repairs. These shops have the specialized equipment required to do the job properly.

2 If the damage is extensive, the frame must be checked for proper alignment or the vehicle's handling characteristics may be adversely affected and other components may wear at an accelerated rate.

3 Due to the fact that all of the major body components (hood, fenders, etc.) are separate and replaceable units, any seriously damaged components should be replaced rather than repaired. Sometimes the components can be found in a wrecking yard that specializes in used vehicle components, often at considerable savings over the cost of new parts.

5 Upholstery, carpets and vinyl trim - maintenance

UPHOLSTERY AND CARPETS

1 Every three months remove the floormats and clean the interior of the vehicle (more frequently if necessary). Use a stiff whiskbroom to brush the carpeting and loosen dirt and dust, then vacuum the upholstery and carpets thoroughly, especially along seams and crevices.

2 Dirt and stains can be removed from carpeting with basic household or automotive carpet shampoos available in spray cans. Follow the directions and vacuum again, then use a stiff brush to bring back the "nap" of the carpet.

3 Most interiors have cloth or vinyl upholstery, either of which can be cleaned and maintained with a number of material-specific cleaners or shampoos available in auto supply stores. Follow the directions on

the product for usage, and always spot-test any upholstery cleaner on an inconspicuous area (bottom edge of a backseat cushion) to ensure that it doesn't cause a color shift in the material.

4 After cleaning, vinyl upholstery should be treated with a protectant.

➡ **Note: Make sure the protectant container indicates the product can be used on seats - some products may make a seat too slippery.**

※ **CAUTION:**

Do not use protectant on vinyl-covered steering wheels.

5   Leather upholstery requires special care. It should be cleaned regularly with saddlesoap or leather cleaner. Never use alcohol, gasoline, nail polish remover or thinner to clean leather upholstery.

6   After cleaning, regularly treat leather upholstery with a leather conditioner, rubbed in with a soft cotton cloth. Never use car wax on leather upholstery.

7   In areas where the interior of the vehicle is subject to bright sunlight, cover leather seating areas of the seats with a sheet if the vehicle is to be left out for any length of time.

VINYL TRIM

8   Don't clean vinyl trim with detergents, caustic soap or petroleum-based cleaners. Plain soap and water works just fine, with a soft brush to clean dirt that may be ingrained. Wash the vinyl as frequently as the rest of the vehicle.

9   After cleaning, application of a high-quality rubber and vinyl protectant will help prevent oxidation and cracks. The protectant can also be applied to weather-stripping, vacuum lines and rubber hoses, which often fail as a result of chemical degradation, and to the tires.

6   Fastener and trim removal

▶ **Refer to illustration 6.4**

1   There is a variety of plastic fasteners used to hold trim panels, splash shields and other parts in place in addition to typical screws, nuts and bolts. Once you are familiar with them, they can usually be removed without too much difficulty.

2   The proper tools and approach can prevent added time and expense to a project by minimizing the number of broken fasteners and/or parts.

3   The accompanying illustration shows various types of fasteners that are typically used on most vehicles and how to remove and install them (see illustration). Replacement fasteners are commonly found at most auto parts stores, if necessary.

Fasteners

This tool is designed to remove special fasteners. A small pry tool used for removing nails will also work well in place of this tool

A Phillips head screwdriver can be used to release the center portion, but light pressure must be used because the plastic is easily damaged. Once the center is up, the fastener can easily be pried from its hole

Here is a view with the center portion fully released. Install the fastener as shown, then press the center in to set it

This fastener is used for exterior panels and shields. The center portion must be pried up to release the fastener. Install the fastener with the center up, then press the center in to set it

This type of fastener is used commonly for interior panels. Use a small blunt tool to press the small pin at the center in to release it . . .

. . . the pin will stay with the fastener in the released position

Reset the fastener for installation by moving the pin out. Install the fastener, then press the pin flush with the fastener to set it

This fastener is used for exterior and interior panels. It has no moving parts. Simply pry the fastener from its hole like the claw of a hammer removes a nail. Without a tool that can get under the top of the fastener, it can be very difficult to remove

6.4 These small plastic pry tools are ideal for prying off trim panels

4   Trim panels are typically made of plastic and their flexibility can help during removal. The key to their removal is to use a tool to pry the panel near its retainers to release it without damaging surrounding areas or breaking-off any retainers. The retainers will usually snap out of their designated slot or hole after force is applied to them. Stiff plastic tools designed for prying on trim panels are available at most auto parts stores (see illustration). Tools that are tapered and wrapped in protective tape, such as a screwdriver or small pry tool, are also very effective when used with care.

7   Hood - removal, installation and adjustment

➡ **Note: The hood is awkward to remove and install; at least two people should perform this procedure.**

REMOVAL AND INSTALLATION

▶ **Refer to illustrations 7.2 and 7.3**

1   Open the hood, then place blankets or pads over the fenders and cowl area of the body. This will protect the body and paint as the hood is lifted off.

2   Make marks around the hood hinge to ensure proper alignment during installation (see illustration).

3   Have an assistant support one side of the hood. Grasp the lower corner of the hood and use your shoulder to brace the hood (see illustration). Take turns removing the hinge-to-hood bolts and lift off the hood.

4   Installation is the reverse of removal. Align the hinge bolts with the marks made in Step 2.

ADJUSTMENT

▶ **Refer to illustration 7.8**

5   Fore-and-aft and side-to-side adjustment of the hood is done by moving the hinges after loosening the hinge-to-body bolts.

6   Loosen the bolts and move the hood into correct alignment. Move it only a little at a time. Tighten the hinge bolts and carefully lower the hood to check the position.

7   The hood can also be adjusted vertically so that it's flush with the fenders.

8   Turn each cushion clockwise to lower the hood or counterclockwise to raise the hood (see illustration).

9   The hood latch assembly, as well as the hinges, should be periodically lubricated with white, lithium-base grease to prevent binding and wear.

7.2 Draw alignment marks around the hood hinges to ensure proper alignment of the hood when it's reinstalled

7.3 Support the hood with your shoulder while removing the hood bolts

7.8 There are two vertical height adjustment cushions on the underside of the hood

8   Hood latch and release cable - removal and installation

HOOD LATCH

▶ Refer to illustrations 8.1 and 8.2

1   Open the hood and scribe a line around the latch to aid alignment when installing, then remove the retaining bolts securing the hood latch to the radiator support (see illustration). Remove the latch.
2   Squeeze the cable retainer to release the cable from the latch assembly, then disengage the cable end plug from the latch (see illustration).
3   Installation is the reverse of removal.

RELEASE CABLE

▶ Refer to illustration 8.9

4   Working in the engine compartment, remove the hood latch and disconnect the hood release cable from the latch (see Steps 1 and 2).
5   Detach the two release cable clips from the radiator support.
6   Loosen the left front wheel lug nuts. Raise the vehicle and place it securely on jackstands. Remove the wheel. Remove the inner fender splash shield (see Section 10).
7   Open the two release cable clips in the upper part of the feander opening and detach the release cable from the clips.

8   Disengage the release cable clip from the wiring harness.
➡ **Note: It may be necessary to remove the Smart Junction Box on some models.**

9   Remove the two hood release handle mounting bolts (see illustration). Pull out the handle, then disengage the release cable from the release handle and pull the release cable through the firewall.
10   Installation is the reverse of removal.

8.1 Hood latch bolts

8.2 Hood release cable connection at latch assembly:

1   *Retainer fingers*   2   *Cable end plug*

8.9 Hood release cable and release handle details:

1   *Release handle mounting bolts*   2   *Release cable retainer*   3   *Release cable end plug*

9 Bumper covers - removal and installation

→ Note: Refer to Section 6 for fastener and trim removal.

FRONT BUMPER COVER

▶ Refer to illustrations 9.2, 9.3, 9.6 and 9.7

1 Loosen the front wheel lug nuts, raise the vehicle and support it securely on jackstands.

2 Remove the front wheels. Remove the lower plastic fasteners from under the bumper cover (see illustration).

3 Remove the fasteners that secure the inner fender splash shields to the bumper cover (see illustration).

4 On Edge models, disconnect the electrical connectors to the auxiliary parking lamps, if equipped.

5 Disconnect the electrical connectors from the fog lamps, if equipped (see Chapter 12).

6 Disengage the clips that secure the upper rear edges of the bumper cover to the fender (see illustration).

7 Remove the upper radiator grille bolts and plastic rivets (see illustration).

8 Using a flashlight, do a final inspection and verify that the bumper cover is completely detached, all electrical connectors are disconnected and all wiring harnesses are safely out of the way.

9 With an assistant's help, remove the front bumper cover.

10 Installation is the reverse of removal.

REAR BUMPER COVER

▶ Refer to illustrations 9.12, 9.14 and 9.15

11 Loosen the rear wheel lug nuts, raise the vehicle and support it securely on jackstands. Remove the rear wheels.

9.2 Bumper cover lower fastener locations

9.3 Inner fender splash shield-to-bumper cover fasteners

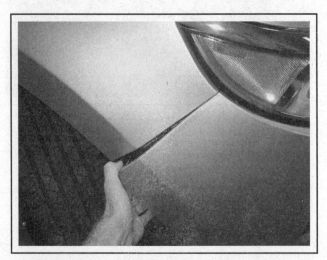

9.6 Pull on the bumper cover to disengage the bumper cover-to-fender clips

9.7 Upper radiator grille bolts and plastic rivet locations

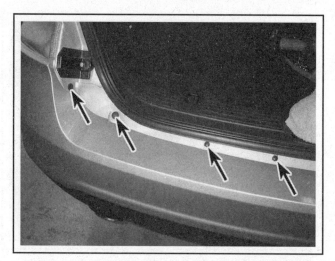

9.12 Remove the plastic push-pin type fasteners along the top of the rear bumper cover

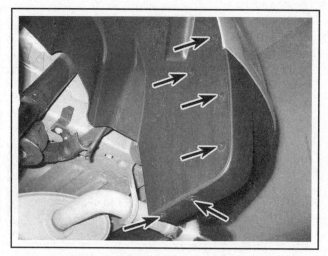

9.14 Remove the wheel well splash shield fasteners

12 Open the rear liftgate and remove the plastic push-pin type fasteners along the top of the rear cover (see illustration).

13 Remove the rear cover mounting bolts from the top of the cover located at the corners of the liftgate opening.

14 Remove the screws from the rear part of the wheel well splash shield (see illustration) and push the shields aside.

15 From under the vehicle, remove the rear cover brace-to-body screws (see illustration).

16 Disconnect the trailer tow connector and parking aid harness connectors, if equipped.

17 Disengage the corners of the bumper cover from the body panel.

18 Using a flashlight, do a final inspection and verify that the bumper cover is completely detached, all electrical connectors are disconnected and all wiring harnesses are safely out of the way.

19 With an assistant's help, remove the rear bumper cover.

20 Installation is the reverse of removal. Again, get help when putting the bumper cover back into position.

9.15 Rear bumper brace mounting bolt

10 Front fender - removal and installation

▶ Refer to illustrations 10.2, 10.3, 10.5, 10.6 and 10.9

➡ **Note: Refer to Section 6 for fastener and trim removal details.**

1 Loosen the front wheel lug nuts. Raise the vehicle, support it securely on jackstands and remove the front wheel.

2 Remove the rocker panel molding end cap mounting screws, and remove the end cap (see illustration).

10.2 Remove the rocker panel molding end cap

10.3 Inner fender splash shield fastener locations

10.5 Front fender mounting bolt locations

10.6 Carefully cut the foam seam along the body and foam covering the inner fender nut – 2011 and later models only

10.9 Upper fender mounting bolts

3 Remove the fasteners that secure the inner fender splash shield (see illustration) and remove the splash shield.

4 Remove the lower fender bolt.

5 Remove the front bumper cover (see Section 9) then remove the front fender mounting bolts (see illustration).

6 On 2011 and later models, carefully cut the foam seam along the body and foam covering the inner fender nut (see illustration). On 2010 and earlier models, remove the inner fender nut.

7 Carefully pry out the rear fender bolt cover, using a plastic trim tool to disengage the cover clips, then remove the upper, rear fender bolt.

8 Remove the cowl panel grille (see Section 12).

9 Remove the upper fender bolts (see illustration), then lift off the fender. It's a good idea to have an assistant support the fender while it's being moved away from the vehicle to prevent damage to the surrounding body panels.

10 Using Flexible Foam repair or equivalent (available from your local dealer or automotive paint store), reseal the area along the seam at the body and around the front fender inner nut.

11 Installation is the reverse of removal. Check the alignment of the fender to the hood and front edge of the door before tightening the bolts.

11 Radiator grille and shutter - removal and installation

1 Remove the front bumper cover (see Section 9).

RADIATOR GRILLE

Edge

2 To remove the manufacturer nameplate, remove the two nuts that secure it to the radiator grille, then pull it off.

3 To remove just the upper and/or lower radiator grille, remove the grille mounting nuts and screws. The lower radiator grille is also secured with plastic push-pin type rivets.

4 To remove the radiator grille reinforcement, disengage the mounting tabs from the bumper cover.

5 Installation is the reverse of removal.

MKX

6 Remove the two upper radiator grille nuts and two center radiator grille nuts.

7 Remove the two badge nuts, then remove the badge.
8 Remove the upper radiator grille from the grille reinforcement.
9 Remove the center radiator grille from the grille reinforcement.
10 Remove the radiator grille reinforcement.
11 Remove the seven lower radiator grille molding clips, then remove the lower radiator grille.
12 Remove the lower radiator grille molding.
13 Remove the front bumper cover valance screws and plastic push-pin type rivets, then remove valance cover.
14 Installation is the reverse of removal.

GRILLE SHUTTER ASSEMBLY (2012 AND LATER MODELS)

15 Remove the grille shutter assembly mounting bolts from each corner of the shutter assembly.
16 Lower the assembly until the grille shutter actuator connector is exposed, then disconnect the electrical connector and remove the shutter assembly.
17 Installation is the reverse of removal.

12 Cowl panels - removal and installation

➡ **Note: Refer to Section 6 for fastener and trim removal techniques.**

UPPER COWL PANEL

▶ **Refer to illustration 12.3**

1 Remove the wiper arms (see Chapter 12).
2 Two small trim pieces fill the gap between the windshield and the front fenders. Both of them must be removed before you can remove the upper cowl panel. Remove them by carefully prying them up.
3 Remove the screws, pin-type retainers and any retainer clips from the upper cowl panel (see illustration).
4 Remove the upper cowl panel.
5 Installation is the reverse of removal.

LOWER COWL PANEL

▶ **Refer to illustration 12.14**

6 Remove the upper cowl panel (see Steps 1 through 4).

7 Remove the windshield wiper motor and linkage assembly (see Chapter 12).
8 Remove the six bolts from the lower cowl panel extensions and remove the left side extension, then the right side extension.
9 Disconnect the wiring harness retaining clips and move the harnesses out of the way.
10 Remove the four lower cowl panel bolts and three nuts, and remove the lower cowl panel.
11 Disconnect the electrical connectors and remove the PCM (see Chapter 6).
12 On 2010 and earlier models, remove the EVAP purge valve and bracket from the center of the lower cowl panel and place it out of the way.
13 On 2011 and later models, remove the radio noise cancellation sensor bracket bolts and move the sensor and bracket out of the way (if equipped).
14 Remove the lower cowl mounting fasteners from inside the cowl panel (see illustration).
15 On 2011 and later models, remove the cowl panel-to-firewall bolt, then move the foam cover off the cowl panel studs.
16 Remove the nuts and remove the cowl panel.
17 Installation is the reverse of removal.

12.3 Upper cowl panel fasteners

12.14 Lower cowl panel mounting bolts

13 Door trim panel - removal and installation

✸ CAUTION:

Wear gloves when working inside the door openings to protect against sharp metal edges.

➡ Note: Refer to Section 6 for fastener and trim removal.

REMOVAL

1 Disconnect the cable from the negative battery terminal (see Chapter 5).

Door trim panels

➡ Note: This procedure applies to both front and rear door trim panels. The only difference is that rear door trim panels do not have a screw at the center of the lower edge of the panel.

2010 and earlier models

▶ Refer to illustrations 13.2a and 13.2b

2 Remove the trim cover from the inside door handle bezel (see illustration) and remove the screw from the bezel. Pull out the bezel and

13.2a Remove the trim cover from the inside door handle and remove the screw

disconnect the electrical connector (see illustration).

3 On MKX models, pry out the door window switch cover.

4 On Edge models, lift up and remove the power window switch mat.

5 Remove the power window switch mounting screw and remove the switch from the panel.

6 Remove the six mounting screws around the trim panel.

7 To detach the door trim panel from its mounting clips, work your way around the outside edge of the trim panel, carefully prying loose the clips with a suitable door trim removal tool.

8 Pull the bottom of the panel outwards and lift the panel up and off of the lock rod, disconnecting any electrical connectors.

2011 and later models

▶ Refer to illustrations 13.9, 13.10, 13.11, 13.13a, 13.13b and 13.14

9 On 2011 and later front doors, carefully pry out the door switch panel and disconnect the electrical connectors (see illustration), then remove the panel mounting bolt.

10 Pry the power window switch panel out of the armrest, starting from the rear end of the switch (see illustration), and lift the switch out of the arm rest.

11 Remove the door panel retaining bolt from the armrest (see illustration).

12 On rear doors, remove the cup holder cover, then remove the panel mounting screw.

13 Remove the trim panel screws from the bottom edge and front edge of the door panel (see illustrations).

➡ Note: On MKX models, remove the applique fasteners and remove the applique from the center of the door.

14 To detach the door trim panel from its mounting clips, work your way around the outside edge of the trim panel, carefully prying loose the clips with a suitable door trim removal tool (see illustration).

15 Pull the bottom of the panel outwards and lift the panel up and off of the lock rod, disconnecting any electrical connectors.

Liftgate trim panel

▶ Refer to illustrations 13.17 and 13.18

16 Support the liftgate in the open position, then remove the power

13.2b Pull out the inside door handle bezel and disconnect the electrical connector

13.9 Pry out the door switch panel and disconnect the electrical connectors

13.10 Pry out the window switch panel from the armrest and disconnect the electrical connectors

liftgate rod nut cover and nut, if equipped.

17 Remove the four mounting screws at the bottom of the liftgate panel (see illustration).

18 Disengage the liftgate trim panel clips using a door panel removal tool (see illustration) and remove the lower section of the panel.

19 Disengage the upper liftgate trim panel clips using a door panel removal tool, and remove the panel.

20 Disconnect the wire connector from the courtesy lamps and remove the trim panel.

INSTALLATION

21 Prior to installation of the door/liftgate trim panel(s), be sure to reinstall any clips which may have come out when you removed the panel.

22 Position the wire harness connectors for the power door lock switch and the power window switch (if equipped) on the back of the panel, then place the panel in position in the door. Press the door panel into place until the clips are seated.

23 The remainder of installation is the reverse of removal.

13.11 Remove the door panel retaining bolt from the armrest

13.13a Remove the trim panel screws from the bottom edge. . .

13.13b . . . and front edge of the door panel (front doors only)

13.14 Carefully pry the door trim panel loose from its mounting clips

13.17 Liftgate trim panel mounting screw locations

13.18 Start from the bottom of the trim panel and work around the perimeter until all the fasteners have been released from the liftgate

14 Door - removal, installation and adjustment

✳✳ WARNING:

The models covered by this manual are equipped with Supplemental Restraint Systems (SRS), more commonly known as airbags. Always disable the airbag system before working in the vicinity of any airbag system component to avoid the possibility of accidental deployment of the airbag, which could cause personal injury (see Chapter 12).

REMOVAL AND INSTALLATION

▶ **Refer to illustrations 14.5 and 14.7**

➡ **Note: The door is heavy and somewhat awkward to remove - at least two people should perform this procedure.**

➡ **Note: This procedure applies to front and rear doors.**

1   Raise the window completely in the door.

2   Disconnect the cable from the negative battery terminal (see Chapter 5).

3   Open the door all the way and support it with a jack or blocks covered with rags to prevent damaging the outer surface.

4   Pull off the rubber conduit that protects the door's wiring harness, then disconnect the connector.

5   Remove the door stop strut mounting bolt (see illustration).

6   Mark around the door hinges with a pen or a scribe to facilitate realignment during reassembly.

7   With an assistant holding the door to steady it, remove the hinge-to-door fasteners (see illustration), and lift off the door.

8   Installation is the reverse of removal.

ADJUSTMENT

▶ **Refer to illustration 14.12**

9   Correct door-to-body alignment is a critical part of a well-functioning door assembly. First check the door hinge pins for excessive play. Fully open the door and lift up and down on the door without lifting the body. If a door has 1/16-inch or more excessive play, replace the hinges.

10   If you need to adjust or replace the hinges for a front door, remove the front fender (see Section 10).

11   Make door-to-body alignment adjustments by loosening the hinge-to-body bolts or hinge-to-door bolts and moving the door. When body alignment is correct, the top of each door is parallel with the roof section, the front door is flush with the fender, the rear door is flush with the rear quarter panel and the bottom of each door is aligned with the lower rocker panel. If you're unable to adjust the door correctly, you might be able to obtain body alignment shims that are inserted behind the hinges to correctly align the door.

12   To adjust the door-closed position, scribe a line or mark around the striker plate (see illustration) to provide a reference point, then verify that the door latch is contacting the center of the striker. If not, adjust the up and down position first. To move the striker, tap it gently with a small hammer.

13   Once the door latch is contacting the center of the striker, adjust the latch striker sideways position, so that the door panel is flush with the center pillar or rear quarter panel and provides positive engagement with the latch mechanism.

14.5 Door stop strut bolt

14.7 Door hinge fasteners

14.12 Adjust the door latch striker by loosening the mounting screws and gently tapping the striker in the desired direction

15 Door latch, lock cylinder and handles - removal and installation

OUTSIDE DOOR HANDLE LEVER

▶ **Refer to illustrations 15.1, 15.2 and 15.3**

➡ **Note: This procedure only applies to the outside door handle lever. If you need to replace the outside door handle reinforcement (the actual mechanism for the outside door handle), see Steps 10 through 15.**

1   Remove the trim cap for the outside handle retaining screw (see illustrativon). Loosen, but don't remove, the screw.
2   Remove the cover from the outside handle (see illustration).
3   Pull the outside door handle out of the door and to the rear to disengage it from the handle reinforcement inside the door (see illustration).
4   Remove and inspect the outside door handle seals. If the seals are cracked, torn or otherwise deteriorated, replace them.
5   Installation is the reverse of removal.

INSIDE DOOR HANDLE

▶ **Refer to illustration 15.7**

6   Remove the door trim panel (see Section 13).
7   Disengage the handle from the regulator module (see illustration).
8   Disconnect the actuator by prying out the bushing. Line up the cable with the slot in the handle lever and pull out the cable end plug.
9   Installation is the reverse of removal.

OUTSIDE DOOR HANDLE REINFORCEMENT

10 Remove the outside door handle lever (see Steps 1 through 3), then remove the door trim panel (see Section 13) and the power window regulator (see Section 17).
11 Disengage the upper lock cylinder actuating rod from the handle reinforcement, if equipped.
12 Disengage the lower exterior door handle reinforcement actuating rod.
13 Disconnect the keyless entry pad harness retaining clip and move

the harness out of the way.
14 Disengage the handle reinforcement-to-window regulator module locking clips and remove the handle reinforcement.
15 Installation is the reverse of removal.

DOOR LOCK CYLINDER

➡ **Note: Before removing the door lock cylinder on these models, be aware that you cannot simply install a new door lock cylinder. Instead, you must discard the old cylinder and build a new unit with the appropriate lock repair package, which you can obtain from your dealer. The lock repair package includes instructions for how to build the new lock cylinder to the key code of the vehicle.**

16 Remove the outside door handle (see Steps 1 through 4).
17 Disengage the release tab and remove the lock cylinder.
18 When installing the rebuilt lock cylinder, align the D-slot in the lock cylinder with the D-slot in the lock cylinder lever.
19 Installation is otherwise the reverse of removal.

15.1 Outside door handle retaining screw

15.2 Remove the outside door handle cover

15.3 To disengage the outside door handle lever from the handle reinforcement inside the door, pull it out of the door and to the rear

15.7 Inside door handle retaining bolts

15.22 Liftgate latch bolt locations

LIFTGATE LATCH

▶ **Refer to illustration 15.22**

20 Remove the trim panel (see Section 13).
21 Disconnect the electrical connector from the liftgate latch.
22 Remove the liftgate latch bolts and remove the latch from the vehicle (see illustration).
23 Installation is the reverse of removal. Perform the de-initialization/initialization procedures (see Section 16).

LIFTGATE RELEASE SWITCH

Power release switch models

24 Remove the liftgate trim panel (see Section 13).
25 Disconnect the electrical connector to the release switch.
26 Remove the two switch molding screws.
27 Depress the tabs on the switch and remove the switch from the molding.
28 Installation is the reverse of removal. Perform the de-initialization/initialization procedures (see Section 16).

Manual release switch models

29 Remove the trim panel (see Section 13).
30 Disconnect the electrical connector to the release switch molding from inside of the liftgate.
31 Remove the six switch molding nuts from the inside of the liftgate and pull the molding off of the outside of the liftgate.
32 Depress the tabs on the switch and remove the switch from the molding.
33 Disconnect the electrical connector to the release switch.
34 Installation is the reverse of removal. Perform the de-initialization/initialization procedures (see Section 16).

KEYLESS ENTRY PAD

35 Remove the upper trim cap for the outside end of the door.
36 Working through the hole, use a screwdriver to release the clip holding the key pad to the reinforcement handle.
37 Pull the key pad out and disconnect the electrical connector.
38 Installation is the reverse of removal.

16 Door window glass - removal and installation

▶ **Refer to illustration 16.4**

1 Remove the door trim panel (see Section 13).
2 Remove the front door speaker (see Chapter 12).
3 Remove the access hole cover plugs from the door module.
4 Lower the window glass until the glass clamp bolts are accessible through the access holes (see illustration). Loosen (but don't remove) both glass clamp bolts, then secure the window in place with tape so that it won't go down.

➡ **Note: If the door window regulator motor is broken or disconnected, you'll have to remove it (see Section 17) and move the window glass manually.**

5 Lower the window regulator, then guide the window up and tilt it outward to remove it through the window opening.
6 Installation is the reverse of removal. Perform the de-initialization/initialization procedures in the following order.

16.4 Front window glass clamp bolts

DE-INITIALIZATION PROCEDURE

7   Turn the ignition key to ON.

8   Activate the power window control switch in the one-touch up-mode and simultaneously remove power from the window motor while the window is moving, by one of the following methods:

a) *Disconnect the battery negative cable while the window is moving.*

b) *Disconnect the power window motor electrical connector while the window is moving.*

c) *Remove the left or right front power window motor fuse while the window is moving.*

9   The power window motor is now de-initialized and the motor is reset to its original factory settings.

10 Reconnect the battery negative cable, power window motor elec-

trical connector or power window motor fuse before proceeding to the initialization procedure.

INITIALIZATION PROCEDURE

11 Turn the ignition key to ON.

12 Press and hold the window control switch until the window glass stalls for two seconds into the glass top run, then release the switch.

13 Pull and hold the power window control switch until the window glass stalls for two seconds at the bottom of its travel, then release the switch.

14 Test the operation of the power window by activating the power window switch in the one-touch up-mode. If the window doesn't operate correctly, repeat this procedure.

17 Door window regulator and motor - removal and installation

REGULATOR MOTOR

▶ **Refer to illustration 17.2**

1   Remove the door trim panel (see Section 13).

2   Disconnect the electrical connector from the regulator motor (see illustration).

3   Secure the window in place with tape.

4   Remove the three regulator motor mounting screws, then remove the motor.

5   Installation is the reverse of removal. Perform the de-initialization/initialization procedures (see Section 16).

REGULATOR MODULE ASSEMBLY

6   Remove the door trim panel (see Section 13).

7   Remove the front door speaker (see Chapter 12).

8   Remove the access hole cover plugs from the door module.

9   Lower the window glass until the glass clamp bolts are accessible through the access holes (see illustration 16.4). Loosen (but don't remove) both glass clamp bolts, then secure the window in place with tape so that it won't go down.

10 Lower the window regulator mechanism until it reaches stops at the bottom of the regulator tracks.

11 Disconnect all electrical wiring harness connectors and harness clips, the power mirror electrical connector (see Section 18), and the harness connection to the A-pillar. Remove the harness grommet retaining bolts.

12 Working through the speaker hole, disengage the retaining clip attaching the harness to the door from the inside. Disengage the clips on the

17.2 Window regulator motor electrical connector

weather strip and feed the harness between the weather strip and the door.

13 Remove the door latch, outside door handle, lock cylinder and keyless entry pad (see Section 15), if equipped.

14 Loosen the exterior door handle reinforcement screw.

15 Remove the regulator module assembly mounting bolts and remove the module from the door.

➡ **Note: If the door window regulator motor is broken or disconnected, you'll have to remove it (see Steps 2 through 4) and move the window glass manually.**

16 Installation is the reverse of removal. Perform the de-initialization/initialization procedures (see Section 16).

18 Mirrors - removal and installation

▶ **Refer to illustrations 18.1 and 18.2**

1 Disengage the sail panel clips and remove the panel (see illustration).

2 Disconnect the electrical connector from the mirror (see illustration).

3 Remove the mirror mounting nuts (see illustration 18.2) and remove the mirror.

4 Installation is the reverse of removal.

18.1 Pry out the sail panel

18.2 Mirror details:

1   Mirror electrical connector   2   Mirror mounting nuts

19 Liftgate - removal and installation

▶ **Refer to illustrations 19.3, 19.7 and 19.8**

➡ **Note: Any time the battery is disconnected, or the liftgate hinges, striker, LTM motor or pinch strip switch are removed or replaced, the liftgate power system must go through the initialization procedure (see Section 20).**

1 Have an assistant support the liftgate in its fully open position.

2 Pull the weatherstrip down away from the liftgate.

3 Pry off the D-pillar trim panels (see illustration).

4 Remove the plastic push-pin type retainers and pull the rear edge of the headliner down enough to disconnect the electrical connectors.

➡ **Note: Do not pull the headliner too far down or it can become creased.**

5 Disconnect the rear washer hose connection.

6 On power liftgate models, disconnect the lift mechanism actuator rod nut and remove the rod from the liftgate (see Section 20).

7 While an assistant supports the liftgate, detach the support struts (see illustration).

8 Mark or scribe around the hinges, then remove the hinge bolts and detach the liftgate from the vehicle (see illustration).

9 Installation is the reverse of removal. Make sure to perform the power liftgate initialization procedure (see Section 20).

10 Close the liftgate and make sure it is in proper alignment with the surrounding body panels. Adjustments are made by changing the position of the hinge bolts in the slots. Loosen the hinge bolts and reposition the hinges (either side-to-side or front and back) the desired amount and retighten the bolts.

11 The engagement of the liftgate can be adjusted by loosening the lock striker bolts, repositioning the striker and retightening the bolts.

19.3 Remove the D-pillar fasteners and pry the trim panel off

19.7 Detach the support strut retaining clips

19.8 Liftgate hinge bolt locations

20 Liftgate/Trunk Module (LTM) and power liftgate motor - removal and installation

➡ **Note: Any time the battery is disconnected, or the liftgate hinges, striker, LTM, motor or pinch strip switch are removed or replaced, the liftgate power system must go through the initialization procedure in this Section.**

LIFTGATE/TRUNK MODULE (LTM)

2010 and earlier models

1 Remove the power liftgate motor (see Steps 9 through 12).
2 Disconnect the module electrical connectors.
3 Remove the three mounting bolts and remove the LTM.
4 Installation is the reverse of removal. Make sure to perform the power liftgate initialization procedure (see Steps 26 through 30).

2011 and later models

5 Remove the driver's side rear quarter panel trim (see Section 26).
6 Disconnect the module electrical connectors.
7 Remove the two mounting bolts and remove the LTM.
8 Installation is the reverse of removal. Make sure to perform the power liftgate initialization procedure (see Steps 26 through 30).

POWER LIFTGATE MOTOR AND ROD

9 Support the liftgate in the open position before disconnecting the power liftgate motor.

2010 and earlier models

Power liftgate rod

10 Remove the driver's side rear quarter panel trim access cover.
11 Squeeze the ends of the liftgate rod-to-motor clip together, then lift the rod assembly up and out of the motor assembly.
12 Remove the cover from the top of the power liftgate rod, then remove the mounting nut and rod.

➡ **Note: On installation, make sure to apply Lock-tight to the threads of the studs and nuts.**

13 Installation is the reverse of removal. Make sure to perform the power liftgate initialization procedure (see Steps 26 through 30).

Power liftgate motor

14 Remove the power liftgate rod (see Steps 9 through 12).

15 Disconnect the liftgate motor electrical connectors.
16 Remove the power liftgate motor mounting bolts and remove the motor.

➡ **Note: Pull the rear section of the quarter panel trim out enough to remove the top bolt on the motor.**

17 Installation is the reverse of removal. Make sure to perform the power liftgate initialization procedure (see Steps 26 through 30).

2011 and later models

18 Remove the driver's side rear quarter panel trim access cover.
19 Disconnect the power liftgate motor from the mount.
20 Disconnect the liftgate motor electrical connector and remove the motor assembly.
21 Installation is the reverse of removal. Make sure to perform the power liftgate initialization procedure (see Steps 26 through 30).

PINCH STRIP SWITCH

22 Remove the liftgate trim panel (see Section 13).
23 Disconnect the switch electrical connector.
24 Remove the plastic pin-type fasteners from the liftgate, then pull the grommet out along with the harness and switch assembly.
25 Installation is the reverse of removal. Make sure to perform the power liftgate initialization procedure (see Steps 26 through 30).

POWER LIFTGATE INITIALIZATION

➡ **Note: Make sure the power liftgate system is turned to the On position in the message center before starting.**

26 Disconnect the battery (see Chapter 5) or remove the LTM fuse for 20-seconds (see the wiring diagrams at the end of Chapter 12).
27 With the battery disconnected or LTM fuse removed, wait 20 seconds, then manually close the liftgate (if it's not already closed).
28 Open the liftgate using the control switch or key fob.
29 Allow the liftgate to fully open, then close the liftgate with the control switch or the key fob.
30 The system should be initialized; if the liftgate does not open or close properly, readjust the liftgate. If a trouble code sets during this time, take the vehicle to your local dealer service department or other qualified repair shop for diagnosis.

21 Center console - removal and installation

2010 AND EARLIER MODELS

1 Raise the seats as high as they can go then slide the front seats all the way forward. Remove the two rear console bolts, then slide the seats all the way rearward.
2 Working around the perimeter of the side panels, use a trim removal tool to carefully pry out the left and right side trim panels from the console.
3 Remove the two front console bolts from each side of the console.

4 On Edge models, carefully pry loose the console finish panel/cup holder and disengage it from the mounting clips
5 On MKX models, remove the storage bin plastic push-type rivets, remove the bin, and disconnect the power socket electrical connector.
6 Remove the console-to-instrument panel bolts.
7 Lift up the console and disconnect all electrical connectors from the console.
8 Remove the center console.
9 Installation is the reverse of removal.

21.12 Pry off the console edge trim from each side – 2011 and later Edge models shown

21.13a Remove the shift lever trim panel screws from the top of the panel . . .

21.13b . . . then disengage the boot tabs

21.14 Pry out the side trim panels – 2011 and later Edge models shown

21.15 Front finish panel fastener locations – 2011 and later Edge models shown

2011 AND LATER MODELS

▶ **Refer to illustrations 21.12, 21.13a, 21.13b, 21.14, 21.15 and 21.22**

10 Apply the parking brake and place the shift lever in the neutral position.

11 Slide the front seats all the way rearward, then place them in the fully reclined position.

12 Using a trim tool, carefully pry off the console edge trim for both sides of the console (see illustration).

Edge models

13 Remove the four mounting screws from the top of the shift lever trim panel, disengage the shift lever boot tabs, and remove the shift lever trim panel (see illustrations).

14 Working around the perimeter of the panels, use a trim removal tool to carefully pry out and remove the left and right side trim panels from the console (see illustration).

➡ **Note: To prevent damage to the console, place a piece of**

cardboard or rag between the panel and the console as they are removed.

15 Remove the three screws from each side of the front finish panel (see illustration).

16 Unclip the ambient light harness from the front finish panel. Rotate the ambient light counterclockwise to remove it. Remove the finish panel.

On MKX models

17 Using a trim tool, carefully pry off the H-shaped console trim between the cup holder and the arm rest.

18 Using a trim removal tool around the perimeter of the panels, carefully pry out and remove the left and right side upper and lower trim panels.

➡ **Note: To prevent damaging the console, place a piece of cardboard or rag between the panels and the console as they are removed.**

19 Remove the four mounting screws from each side of the shift lever trim panel, then pry the shift panel up from the cup holder end until the panel can be removed.

All models

20 Remove the shift cable from the shift lever and bracket (see Chapter 7A).
21 Disconnect the electrical connectors from the console.
22 Remove the console mounting bolts from the base of the console (see illustration).
23 Lift up the console from the rear and remove the center console.
24 Installation is the reverse of removal.

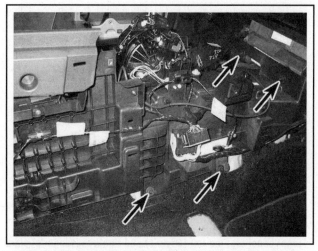

21.22 Remove the console mounting bolts from the base of the console (right side shown, left side similar)

22 Dashboard trim panels - removal and installation

✳✳ WARNING:

Models covered by this manual are equipped with a Supplemental Restraint System (SRS), more commonly known as airbags. Always disable the airbag system before working in the vicinity of any airbag system component to avoid the possibility of accidental deployment of the airbag, which could cause personal injury (see Chapter 12).

➡ Note: Refer to Section 6 for fastener and trim removal.

1 Removing various dashboard trim panels provides access to electrical/electronic components such as the instrument cluster, the audio unit, the heater and air conditioning control unit and various instrument panel-mounted switches. If you're going to remove the entire instrument panel, you'll need to remove all of the trim panels to access the instrument panel mounting bolts.

LEFT OR RIGHT DASHBOARD END TRIM PANELS

▶ Refer to illustration 22.2

2 Carefully pry off the end trim panel (see illustration).
3 Installation is the reverse of removal.

INSTRUMENT CLUSTER TRIM PANEL

2010 and earlier models

4 Disconnect the cable from the negative battery terminal (see Chapter 5).
5 Remove the knee bolster trim panel (see Steps 48 and 49).
6 Remove the steering column covers (see Section 23), then place the steering column in the lowest position.
7 On Edge models, use a trim tool around the perimeter of the panel to disengage the center trim panel spring retaining clips, then remove the panel.

8 The cluster trim panel is a thin, narrow trim piece that runs along the lower edge of the instrument cluster. Disengage the locating tabs from the panel gap trim piece and the instrument cluster trim panel.
9 Remove the screws from the instrument cluster trim panel, then carefully pry off the trim panel.
10 Installation is the reverse of removal.

2011 and later models

Edge models

▶ Refer to illustration 22.15

11 Pry out the left side trim panel below the console.
12 Remove the color console, left side trim panel from the console (see Section 21).
13 Remove the knee bolster trim panel (see Steps 48 and 49).
14 Using a trim tool, disengage the four retaining clips by prying out the corners of the two right appliqués below the console.

22.2 Pry off the end trim panel

15 Remove the screws from the instrument cluster trim panel, then carefully pry off the trim panel (see illustration).

16 Installation is the reverse of removal.

MKX models

17 Remove the left side instrument panel top (see Steps 20 through 32).

18 Remove the screws from the instrument cluster trim panel, then carefully pry off the trim panel.

19 Installation is the reverse of removal.

INSTRUMENT PANEL TOP (2011 AND LATER MKX MODELS ONLY)

➡ **Note: These models are equipped with a two piece instrument panel top; the left (driver's) and right (passenger's) sides are removable separately.**

Left side instrument panel top

20 Pry out the left side instrument panel trim panel, below the instrument cluster.

21 Pry out the left side trim panel just below the vent register. Remove the register mounting screws and pull the register out of the instrument panel.

22 Remove the knee bolster trim cover and disconnect the in-vehicle temperature sensor from the panel.

22.15 Instrument cluster trim panel retaining screw locations – 2011 and later Edge models

22.48 Knee bolster trim panel retaining screw locations

23 Remove the A-pillar trim panel (see illustration 24.2).

24 Remove both floor console upper finish panels (see Section 21).

25 Remove the Front Controls Interface Module (FCIM) (see Chapter 3).

26 Remove the instrument panel speaker (see Chapter 12).

27 Place the steering column in the lowest position.

28 Remove the screws from the lower corners of the top panel.

29 Remove the narrow trim piece that runs along the lower edge of the instrument cluster.

30 Pry out the defroster vent at the top of the instrument panel.

31 Pull the top panel straight back to disengage the clips, and remove the panel.

32 Disconnect the start/stop switch electrical connector, if equipped.

33 Installation is the reverse of removal.

Right side instrument panel top

34 Disconnect the cable from the negative battery terminal (see Chapter 5).

35 Pry out the defroster vent at the top of the instrument panel.

36 Remove the passenger airbag (see Chapter 12).

➡ **Note: To remove the passenger side airbag, the complete instrument panel must be removed (see Section 24). The airbag module may then be removed from underneath the back side of the right side panel top.**

37 Remove the instrument panel top upper screws from the back side of the instrument panel, then remove the A-pillar trim panel (see Section 24).

38 Remove the right appliqué (see Step 44).

39 Pry out the center appliqué next to the vent register. Remove the register mounting screws and pull the register out of the instrument panel.

40 Remove the Front Controls Interface Module (FCIM) (see Chapter 3).

41 Remove the screws from the lower corners of the top panel.

42 Pull the top panel straight back to disengage the clips, and remove the panel.

43 Installation is the reverse of removal.

LEFT, RIGHT AND CENTER APPLIQUÉS

44 Carefully pry off the left, center or right appliqué.

45 Installation is the reverse of removal.

CENTER TRIM PANELS (2010 AND EARLIER MODELS)

46 Carefully pry off the center trim panel, disengaging the retaining clips from the corners of the panel.

➡ **Note: On MKX models, the upper center trim panel must be pried off first.**

47 Installation is the reverse of removal.

KNEE BOLSTER TRIM PANEL AND KNEE BOLSTER

▶ **Refer to illustration 22.48**

48 Remove the two knee bolster trim panel screws, then carefully pry off the trim panel (see illustration).

49 Remove the fasteners securing the knee bolster, and remove the bolster.

50 Installation is the reverse of removal.

22.54 Remove the hinge pins from the bottom of the glove box

22.55 Disengage the damper clip from the left end of the glove box

22.56 Push the corners of the glove box inwards until the stops clear, then pull out the glove box

GLOVE BOX

2010 and earlier models

51 Disengage the damper clip from the right end of the glove box.
52 Lower the glove box, pull it from the hinge clips at the bottom and remove the glove box.
53 Installation is the reverse of removal.

2011 and later models

▶ Refer to illustrations 22.54, 22.55 and 22.56

54 Remove the hinge pins from the bottom of the glove box (see illustration).
55 Disengage the damper clip from the left end of the glove box (see illustration).
56 Firmly grasp the corners of the glove box and push them inwards until the stops clear the sides, and remove the glove box (see illustration).
57 Installation is the reverse of removal.

23 Steering column covers - removal and installation

▶ Refer to illustration 23.2

> ❋❋ **WARNING:**
>
> Models covered by this manual are equipped with a Supplemental Restraint System (SRS), more commonly known as airbags. Always disable the airbag system before working in the vicinity of any airbag system component to avoid the possibility of accidental deployment of the airbag, which could cause personal injury (see Chapter 12).

1 Disconnect the cable from the negative terminal of the battery (see Chapter 5).
2 Remove the bolts from the lower steering column cover (see illustration). Press in on the sides of the upper cover and separate the two covers.
3 To remove the upper column cover, use a trim removal tool to separate it from the instrument cluster trim panel.
4 Installation is the reverse of removal.

23.2 Lower steering column cover retaining bolts

24 Instrument panel - removal and installation

♦ Refer to illustrations 24.2, 24.5, 24.17, 24.18, 24.19, 24.20 and 24.21

❊❊ WARNING:

Models covered by this manual are equipped with a Supplemental Restraint System (SRS), more commonly known as airbags. Always disable the airbag system before working in the vicinity of any airbag system component to avoid the possibility of accidental deployment of the airbag, which could cause personal injury (see Chapter 12).

➡ Note: This is a difficult procedure for the home mechanic. There are many hidden fasteners, difficult angles to work in and many electrical connectors to tag and disconnect/connect. We recommend that this procedure be done only by an experienced do-it-yourselfer.

➡ Note: During removal of the instrument panel, make careful notes of how each piece comes off, where it fits in relation to other pieces and what holds it in place. If you note how each part is installed before removing it, getting the instrument panel back together again will be much easier.

1 Remove the following parts:
   Steering wheel (see Chapter 10)
   All the dashboard trim panels and the glove box (see Section 22)
   Air conditioning and heater control assembly (see Chapter 3)
   Instrument cluster and radio (see Chapter 12)
   Right lower instrument panel insulator
   Front seats (though not absolutely necessary, removing both front seats allows more room to work and eliminates the possibility of damage to the seats during this procedure)
   Center console (see Section 21)

2 Carefully remove the left and right A-pillar (windshield pillar) trim panel and disconnect the tethers from each of the panels (see illustration).

3 Grasp each front door opening sill panel/kick panel and pull them off.

4 Disconnect the two electrical connectors in the left kick panel area as well as the bulkhead electrical connector, antenna cable and satellite antenna, if equipped.

5 Remove the cowl panels (see Section 12), then remove the bolt from the engine compartment side (see illustration).

6 In the glove box area, disconnect all air conditioning system electrical connectors.

7 Disconnect all electrical connectors and wiring harness clips located on the floor between the two front seats.

8 Disconnect any remaining wiring connectors between the vehicle and the instrument panel.

9 Mark the relationship of the upper steering column shaft to the lower shaft, remove the steering column pinch-bolt and separate the upper column shaft from the lower shaft. Discard the old pinch bolt and install a new one when you reassemble the steering column.

10 Remove the two hood release handle screws and set the handle aside (see Section 8).

11 If equipped with an in-vehicle temperature sensor aspirator hose, separate the aspirator hose retaining clips from the heater core/evaporator core housing, then pull the hose away from the housing.

12 Disconnect the shift lever cable from the ball stud and remove the cable from the retaining clips (see Chapter 7A).

13 Remove the center console (see Section 21).

14 Disconnect the electrical connectors from the center console, then remove the center console support.

15 Disconnect the Restraints Control Module (RCM) electrical connector.

16 Remove the plastic pushpin-type retainers and pull the carpet back.

17 Remove the two instrument panel-to-floor bolts and the two instrument panel brace nuts and brace from the left side (see illustration).

18 Remove the instrument panel-to-floor bolt from the right side (see illustration).

19 Completely loosen the left side instrument panel Torx head bolt from inside the driver's door opening (see illustration).

➡ Note: The Torx head bolt can't be completely removed, pull the bolt out far enough to allow the instrument panel to clear it.

24.2 Carefully remove the A-pillar trim panels by prying them off and disconnecting the tethers

24.5 Remove the firewall-to-instrument panel bolt from the engine compartment side

24.17 Left side instrument panel-to-floor bolt (A) and instrument panel brace nut (B) locations

20 Remove the left side instrument panel bolts from inside the driver's door opening (see illustration).

21 Remove the right side instrument panel-to-body bolts (see illustration).

❄ CAUTION:

To avoid damage to the instrument panel, have an assistant support the instrument panel when removing these bolts.

22 With an assistant helping you, remove the instrument panel from the vehicle.

23 Installation is the reverse of removal, except for the following item:

a) When installing the A-pillar trim panels, attach the tethers .

➡ **Note: The trim panels cannot be installed on the A-pillars without putting the clips back where they belong.**

24.18 Right side instrument panel-to-floor bolt locations

24.19 Completely loosen the left side instrument panel Torx head bolt

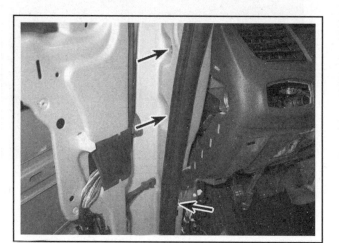

24.20 Left side instrument panel bolt locations (from the driver's door opening)

24.21 Remove the right side instrument panel bolts

25 Front seats - removal and installation

♦ **Refer to illustrations 25.1, 25.2a and 25.2b**

❄ WARNING:

All models covered by this manual are equipped with a Supplemental Restraint System (SRS), more commonly known as airbags. Always disable the airbag system before working in the vicinity of any airbag system component to avoid the possibility of accidental deployment of the airbag, which could cause personal injury (see Chapter 12).

❄ WARNING:

During the removal and installation procedures, if a seat is dropped, or sat in while removed, or if pressure/load is applied to the seat tracks, the Occupant Safety System (OCS) may become damaged and the system may fail in a crash.

✳ CAUTION:

The seats are heavy, so have an assistant handy to help you lift the seat from the vehicle.

➡ **Note:** This procedure applies to the driver and passenger seats.

1   If you're removing the passenger seat, remove the cover from the seatbelt anchor, remove the anchor bolt, and disconnect the seatbelt from the seat (see illustration).
2   Remove the covers from the seat mounting bolts and remove the bolts (see illustrations).
3   Tilt the seat forward and disconnect all electrical connectors underneath the seat.
4   Using a helper, carefully lift the seat out of the vehicle.

✳ WARNING:

The seat is heavy, so trying to remove it by yourself could cause injury.

5   Installation is the reverse of removal.

25.1 Remove the cover from the seatbelt anchor, remove the anchor bolt and disconnect the seatbelt from the front passenger seat

25.2a Remove the bolts from the front . . .

25.2b . . . and the rear of the seat

26 Quarter trim panel - removal and installation

1   On models equipped with a power liftgate, pry the liftgate switch cover off at the bottom of the liftgate rod and disconnect the electrical connector.
2   Remove the power liftgate rod-to-liftgate nut cover and nut (see Section 20).
3   Remove the rear mat and storage tray from the floor, then remove the foam blocks in the spare tire well.
4   Remove the lower seat belt anchor bolt cover, then remove the bolt.

✳ WARNING:

Pay close attention to how the seatbelts are routed. They must be installed exactly the same way. In the event of an acci-

dent, failure to do so could result in serious injury to someone secured by an incorrectly routed seatbelt.

5   Unscrew the cargo net hooks, if equipped.
6   Using a plastic trim tool, disengage the mounting clips and pry out the liftgate scuff plate.
7   Remove the plastic push-pin type retainers.
8   Remove the quarter trim panel and disconnect any electrical connectors.
9   Installation is the reverse of removal.

Section

12

CHASSIS ELECTRICAL SYSTEM

1   General information

The electrical system is a 12-volt, negative ground type. Power for the lights and all electrical accessories is supplied by a lead/acid-type battery that is charged by the alternator.

This Chapter covers repair and service procedures for the various electrical components not associated with the engine. Information on the battery, alternator, ignition system and starter motor can be found in Chapter 5.

It should be noted that when portions of the electrical system are serviced, the negative cable should be disconnected from the battery to prevent electrical shorts and/or fires.

2   Electrical troubleshooting - general information

▶ **Refer to illustrations 2.5a, 2.5b, 2.6 and 2.9**

A typical electrical circuit consists of an electrical component, any switches, relays, motors, fuses, fusible links or circuit breakers related to that component and the wiring and connectors that link the component to both the battery and the chassis. To help you pinpoint an electrical circuit problem, wiring diagrams are included at the end of this Chapter.

Before tackling any troublesome electrical circuit, first study the appropriate wiring diagrams to get a complete understanding of what makes up that individual circuit. Trouble spots, for instance, can often be narrowed down by noting if other components related to the circuit are operating properly. If several components or circuits fail at one time, chances are the problem is in a fuse or ground connection, because several circuits are often routed through the same fuse and ground connections.

Electrical problems usually stem from simple causes, such as loose or corroded connections, a blown fuse, a melted fusible link or a failed relay. Visually inspect the condition of all fuses, wires and connections in a problem circuit before troubleshooting the circuit.

If test equipment and instruments are going to be utilized, use the diagrams to plan ahead of time where you will make the necessary connections in order to accurately pinpoint the trouble spot.

The basic tools needed for electrical troubleshooting include a circuit tester or voltmeter (a 12-volt bulb with a set of test leads can also be used), a continuity tester, which includes a bulb, battery and set of test leads, and a jumper wire, preferably with a circuit breaker incorporated, which can be used to bypass electrical components (see illustrations). Before attempting to locate a problem with test instruments, use the wiring diagram(s) to decide where to make the connections.

VOLTAGE CHECKS

Voltage checks should be performed if a circuit is not functioning properly. Connect one lead of a circuit tester to either the negative battery terminal or a known good ground. Connect the other lead to a connector in the circuit being tested, preferably nearest to the battery or fuse (see illustration). If the bulb of the tester lights, voltage is present, which means that the part of the circuit between the connector and the battery is problem free. Continue checking the rest of the circuit in the same fashion. When you reach a point at which no voltage is present, the problem lies between that point and the last test point with voltage. Most of the time the problem can be traced to a loose connection.

➡ **Note: Keep in mind that some circuits receive voltage only when the ignition key is in the Accessory or Run position.**

FINDING A SHORT

One method of finding shorts in a circuit is to remove the fuse and connect a test light or voltmeter in place of the fuse terminals. There should be no voltage present in the circuit. Move the wiring harness from side-to-side while watching the test light. If the bulb goes on, there is a short to ground somewhere in that area, probably where the insulation has rubbed through. The same test can be performed on each component in the circuit, even a switch.

2.5a   The most useful tool for electrical troubleshooting is a digital multimeter that can check volts, amps, and test continuity

2.5b   A test light is a very handy tool for checking voltage

2.6 In use, a basic test light's lead is clipped to a known good ground, then the pointed probe can test connectors, wires or electrical sockets - if the bulb lights, the part being tested has battery voltage

GROUND CHECK

Perform a ground test to check whether a component is properly grounded. Disconnect the battery and connect one lead of a continuity tester or multimeter (set to the ohms scale), to a known good ground. Connect the other lead to the wire or ground connection being tested. If the resistance is low (less than 5 ohms), the ground is good. If the bulb on a self-powered test light does not go on, the ground is not good.

CONTINUITY CHECK

A continuity check is done to determine if there are any breaks in a circuit - if it is passing electricity properly. With the circuit off (no power in the circuit), a self-powered continuity tester or multimeter can be used to check the circuit. Connect the test leads to both ends of the circuit (or to the power end and a good ground), and if the test light comes on the circuit is passing current properly (see illustration). If the resistance is low (less than 5 ohms), there is continuity; if the reading is 10,000 ohms or higher, there is a break somewhere in the circuit.

2.9 With a multimeter set to the ohms scale, resistance can be checked across two terminals - when checking for continuity, a low reading indicates continuity, a high reading indicates lack of continuity

The same procedure can be used to test a switch, by connecting the continuity tester to the switch terminals. With the switch turned On, the test light should come on (or low resistance should be indicated on a meter).

FINDING AN OPEN CIRCUIT

When diagnosing for possible open circuits, it is often difficult to locate them by sight because the connectors hide oxidation or terminal misalignment. Merely wiggling a connector on a sensor or in the wiring harness may correct the open circuit condition. Remember this when an open circuit is indicated when troubleshooting a circuit. Intermittent problems may also be caused by oxidized or loose connections.

Electrical troubleshooting is simple if you keep in mind that all electrical circuits are basically electricity running from the battery, through the wires, switches, relays, fuses and fusible links to each electrical component (light bulb, motor, etc.) and to ground, from which it is passed back to the battery. Any electrical problem is an interruption in the flow of electricity to and from the battery.

3   Fuses and fusible links - general information

FUSES

▶ **Refer to illustrations 3.1a, 3.1b and 3.3**

The electrical circuits of the vehicle are protected by a combination of fuses, circuit breakers and fusible links. The main fuse/relay panel is in the engine compartment (see illustration), while the interior fuse/relay panel is located inside the passenger compartment (see illustration). Each of the fuses is designed to protect a specific circuit, and the various circuits are identified on the fuse panel itself.

Several sizes of fuses are employed in the fuse blocks. There are small, medium and large sizes of the same design, all with the same blade terminal design. The medium and large fuses can be removed with your fingers, but the small fuses require the use of pliers or the small plastic fuse-puller tool found in most fuse boxes.

If an electrical component fails, always check the fuse first. The

3.1a The engine compartment fuse and relay panel is located at the left side of the engine compartment

3.1b The passenger compartment fuse box is located under the left end of the instrument panel

3.3 When a fuse blows, the element between the terminals melts

best way to check the fuses is with a test light. Check for power at the exposed terminal tips of each fuse. If power is present at one side of the fuse but not the other, the fuse is blown. A blown fuse can also be identified by visually inspecting it (see illustration).

Be sure to replace blown fuses with the correct type. Fuses (of the same physical size) of different ratings may be physically interchangeable, but only fuses of the proper rating should be used. Replacing a fuse with one of a higher or lower value than specified is not recommended. Each electrical circuit needs a specific amount of protection. The amperage value of each fuse is molded into the top of the fuse body.

If the replacement fuse immediately fails, donít replace it again until the cause of the problem is isolated and corrected. In most cases, this will be a short circuit in the wiring caused by a broken or deteriorated wire.

FUSIBLE LINKS

Some circuits are protected by fusible links. The links are used in circuits which are not ordinarily fused, or which carry high current, such as the circuit between the alternator and the battery. Fusible links, which are usually several wire gauges smaller in size than the circuit that they protect, are designed to melt if the circuit is subjected to more current than it was designed to carry. If you have to replace a blown fusible link, make sure that you replace it with one of the same specification. If the replacement fusible link blows in the same circuit, make sure that you troubleshoot the circuit in which the fusible link melted BEFORE installing another fusible link.

4 Circuit breakers - general information

Circuit breakers protect certain circuits, such as the power windows or heated seats. Depending on the vehicle's accessories, there may be one or two circuit breakers, located in the fuse/relay box in the engine compartment.

Because the circuit breakers reset automatically, an electrical overload in a circuit breaker-protected system will cause the circuit to fail momentarily, then come back on. If the circuit does not come back on, check it immediately.

For a basic check, pull the circuit breaker up out of its socket on the fuse panel, but just far enough to probe with a voltmeter. The breaker should still contact the sockets. With the voltmeter negative lead on a good chassis ground, touch each end prong of the circuit breaker with the positive meter probe. There should be battery voltage at each end. If there is battery voltage only at one end, the circuit breaker must be replaced.

Some circuit breakers must be reset manually.

5 Relays - general information

Several electrical accessories in the vehicle, such as the fuel injection system, horns, starter, and fog lamps use relays to transmit the electrical signal to the component. Relays use a low-current circuit (the control circuit) to open and close a high-current circuit (the power cir-

cuit). If the relay is defective, that component will not operate properly. Most relays are mounted in the engine compartment and interior fuse/relay boxes (see illustrations 3.1a and 3.1b).

6   Electrical connectors - general information

Most electrical connections on these vehicles are made with multiwire plastic connectors. The mating halves of many connectors are secured with locking clips molded into the plastic connector shells. The mating halves of some large connectors, such as some of those under the instrument panel, are held together by a bolt through the center of the connector.

To separate a connector with locking clips, use a small screwdriver to pry the clips apart carefully, then separate the connector halves. Pull only on the shell, never pull on the wiring harness, as you may damage the individual wires and terminals inside the connectors. Look at the connector closely before trying to separate the halves. Often the locking clips are engaged in a way that is not immediately clear. Additionally, many connectors have more than one set of clips.

Each pair of connector terminals has a male half and a female half.

When you look at the end view of a connector in a diagram, be sure to understand whether the view shows the harness side or the component side of the connector. Connector halves are mirror images of each other, and a terminal shown on the right side end-view of one half will be on the left side end-view of the other half.

It is often necessary to take circuit voltage measurements with a connector connected. Whenever possible, carefully insert a small straight pin (not your meter probe) into the rear of the connector shell to contact the terminal inside, then clip your meter lead to the pin. This kind of connection is called "backprobing." When inserting a test probe into a terminal, be careful not to distort the terminal opening. Doing so can lead to a poor connection and corrosion at that terminal later. Using the small straight pin instead of a meter probe results in less chance of deforming the terminal connector.

Electrical connectors

Most electrical connectors have a single release tab that you depress to release the connector

Some electrical connectors have a retaining tab which must be pried up to free the connector

Some connectors have two release tabs that you must squeeze to release the connector

Some connectors use wire retainers that you squeeze to release the connector

Critical connectors often employ a sliding lock (1) that you must pull out before you can depress the release tab (2)

Here's another sliding-lock style connector, with the lock (1) and the release tab (2) on the side of the connector

On some connectors the lock (1) must be pulled out to the side and removed before you can lift the release tab (2)

Some critical connectors, like the multi-pin connectors at the Powertrain Control Module employ pivoting locks that must be flipped open

7 Multi-function switch - replacement

♦ Refer to illustration 7.2

✳✳ WARNING:

The models covered by this manual are equipped with Supplemental Restraint Systems (SRS), more commonly known as airbags. Always disable the airbag system before working in the vicinity of any airbag system components to avoid the possibility of accidental deployment of the airbags, which could cause personal injury (see Section 26).

1   Remove the knee bolster trim panel, the knee bolster and the steering column covers (see Chapter 11).
2   Remove the multi-function switch retaining screws and remove the switch (see illustration).
3   Installation is the reverse of removal.

7.2 Remove the switch retaining screws

8 Ignition switch and key lock cylinder - replacement

✳✳ WARNING:

The models covered by this manual are equipped with Supplemental Restraint Systems (SRS), more commonly known as airbags. Always disable the airbag system before working in the vicinity of any airbag system components to avoid the possibility of accidental deployment of the airbags, which could cause personal injury (see Section 26).

8.5 Insert a suitable tool through this hole and push the release button to release the key lock cylinder (key lock cylinder removed for clarity)

1   Disconnect the cable from the negative terminal of the battery (see Chapter 5).
2   Remove the instrument cluster upper and lower trim panels (see Chapter 11).

KEY LOCK CYLINDER

♦ Refer to illustration 8.5

3   Using a small screwdriver, detach the tabs securing the Passive Anti-Theft System (PATS) transceiver to the lock cylinder housing, then pull the transceiver off the housing and disconnect the electrical connector.
4   Insert the ignition key into the lock cylinder and turn the key to the ACC position.
5   Insert an awl or suitable tool into the hole in the underside of the key lock cylinder, then depress the key lock cylinder retaining tab and remove the key lock cylinder (see illustration).
6   To install the key lock cylinder, insert it into the lock cylinder housing and push it in until it clicks into place.
7   Verify that the ignition switch operates correctly in the OFF, ACC, RUN and START positions.
8   Installation is otherwise the reverse of removal.

8.9 Key lock cylinder housing mounting fasteners

8.10 Disconnect the electrical connector for the PATS

IGNITION SWITCH

▶ Refer to illustrations 8.9 and 8.10

✳✳ CAUTION:

Do not remove the ignition switch and the key lock cylinder at the same time. According to the manufacturer, doing so could damage the steering column.

9   Remove the fasteners securing the key lock cylinder housing (see illustration).

10 Disconnect the electrical connector for the Passive Anti-Theft System (PATS) transceiver (see illustration).

11 Disconnect the electrical connector from the ignition switch.

12 Depress the release tabs to detach the ignition switch from the key lock cylinder.

13 When installing the switch, make sure that it snaps into place. Installation is otherwise the reverse of removal.

9   Instrument panel switches - replacement

▶ Refer to illustration 9.3

✳✳ WARNING:

The models covered by this manual are equipped with Supplemental Restraint Systems (SRS), more commonly known as airbags. Always disable the airbag system before working in the vicinity of any airbag system components to avoid the possibility of accidental deployment of the airbags, which could cause personal injury (see Section 26).

1   Disconnect the cable from the negative terminal of the battery (see Chapter 5).

2   Remove the left end trim panel from the instrument panel (see Chapter 11).

3   Reach through the opening in the end of the instrument panel and push on the back of the switch while simultaneously prying the switch out of the dash with a trim removal tool (see illustration). Disconnect the electrical connectors and remove the switch assembly.

4   No further disassembly is possible. If you're replacing the headlight switch, you must replace this assembly.

5   Pop a new instrument panel dimmer switch into the bezel and make sure that it snaps into place. Installation is otherwise the reverse of removal.

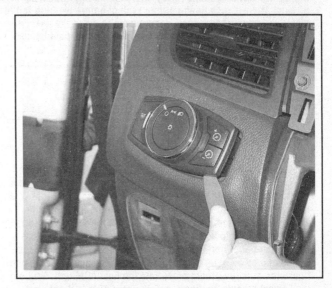

9.3 Use a trim removal tool to pry the headlight switch/instrument panel dimmer switch assembly out of the instrument panel

10 Instrument cluster - removal and installation

▶ **Refer to illustration 10.4**

✳✳ WARNING:

The models covered by this manual are equipped with Supplemental Restraint Systems (SRS), more commonly known as airbags. Always disable the airbag system before working in the vicinity of any airbag system components to avoid the possibility of accidental deployment of the airbags, which could cause personal injury (see Section 26).

1   Disconnect the cable from the negative battery terminal (see Chapter 5).
2   Release the tilt wheel lever and lower the steering wheel to its lowest position.
3   Remove the instrument cluster upper and lower trim panels (see Chapter 11).
4   Remove the instrument cluster mounting screws (see illustration).
5   Carefully pull out the instrument cluster from the instrument panel and disconnect the electrical connectors.
6   Installation is the reverse of removal.

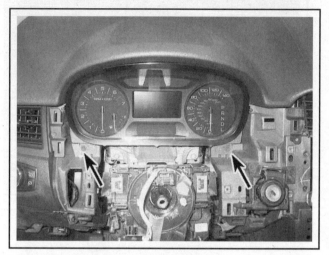

10.4 Instrument cluster mounting screws

11 Radio and speakers - removal and installation

✳✳ WARNING:

The models covered by this manual are equipped with Supplemental Restraint Systems (SRS), more commonly known as airbags. Always disable the airbag system before working in the vicinity of any airbag system components to avoid the possibility of accidental deployment of the airbags, which could cause personal injury (see Section 26).

RADIO

▶ **Refer to illustration 11.3 and 11.4**

➡ **Note: The radio consists of the Front Controls Interface Module (FCIM) and the Audio Control Module (ACM). The FCIM (the controls) is what you see in the center trim panel; the ACM (the radio) is a separate component in the dash behind the FCIM. You can replace the FCIM at home, but not the ACM. You can remove the ACM to access something else, or to remove the instrument panel, but if the ACM must be replaced, it will have to be done by a dealer service department because module configuration must be programmed into the new ACM unit. Without the correct module configuration, the new ACM will not work.**

1   Disconnect the cable from the negative battery terminal (see Chapter 5).
2   Remove the center console side trim moldings (see Chapter 11).
3   Remove the fasteners securing the Front Controls Interface Module (FCIM), remove the FCIM (see illustration), then disconnect the electrical connector

4   If you're removing the ACM, remove the ACM mounting screws (see illustration), then pull out the ACM and disconnect the antenna cable and all electrical connectors.
5   If you're removing the FCIM, remove the FCIM mounting screws (see illustration 11.4), pull out the FCIM and disconnect the electrical connectors.
6   Installation is the reverse of removal.

11.3 FCIM fastener locations

11.4 ACM mounting screws (A) and the FCIM mounting screws (B)

11.8 Door speaker mounting screws

SPEAKERS

Door speakers

♦ **Refer to illustration 11.8**

➡ **Note: This procedure applies to front and rear door speakers.**

7   Remove the door trim panel (see Chapter 11).
8   Remove the speaker mounting screws (see illustration).
9   Pull the speaker out of its enclosure and disconnect the speaker electrical connectors.
10 Installation is the reverse of removal.

12 Antenna - removal and installation

1   The vehicles covered in this manual are equipped with a mast-type antenna attached to the roof.
2   If the antenna is damaged, it can be removed by turning it counterclockwise.
3   The antenna cable runs from the radio up through the passenger-side windshield pillar under the headliner.
4   It's a difficult job for the home mechanic to remove all the panels and the headliner for access to the cables or replacement of the antenna mast base. The procedure is best left to a qualified shop.

13 Headlight bulb - replacement

HALOGEN HEADLIGHTS

♦ **Refer to illustrations 13.2 and 13.3**

⁂ WARNING:

Halogen bulbs are gas-filled and under pressure and might shatter if the surface is scratched or the bulb is dropped. Wear eye protection and handle the bulbs carefully, grasping only the base whenever possible. Don't touch the surface of the bulb with your fingers because the oil from your skin could cause it to overheat and fail prematurely. If you do touch the bulb surface, clean it with rubbing alcohol.

1   Disconnect the cable from the negative battery terminal (see Chapter 5).
2   Remove the bulb access cover (see illustration).

13.2 Rotate the bulb access cover and remove it (headlight housing removed for clarity)

13.3 Rotate the bulb counterclockwise and pull it out of the housing

3   Disconnect the electrical connector, then rotate the bulb counterclockwise and pull it out of the housing (see illustration).
4   Installation is the reverse of removal.

HIGH INTENSITY DISCHARGE (HID) HEADLIGHTS

✳ WARNING:

Some models use High Intensity Discharge (HID) bulbs instead of conventional halogen bulbs. According to the manufacturer, the high voltages produced by this system can be fatal in the event of a shock. Also, the voltage can remain in the circuit even after the headlight switch has been turned to OFF and the ignition key has been removed. Therefore, for your safety, we don't recommend that you replace these bulbs yourself. Instead, have this service performed by a dealer service department or other qualified repair shop.

14 Headlight housing - removal and installation

▶ **Refer to illustration 14.2**

1   Remove the front bumper cover (see Chapter 11).
2   Remove the headlight housing mounting fasteners (see illustration).
3   Pull out the headlight housing and disconnect the electrical connectors.
4   Installation is the reverse of removal.

14.2 Headlight housing mounting fasteners

15 Headlights - adjustment

▶ **Refer to illustrations 15.1 and 15.2**

✳ WARNING:

The headlights must be aimed correctly. If adjusted incorrectly, they could temporarily blind the driver of an oncoming vehicle and cause an accident or seriously reduce your ability to see the road. The headlights should be checked for proper aim every 12 months and any time a new headlight is installed or front-end bodywork is performed. The following procedure is only an interim step to provide temporary adjustment until the headlights can be adjusted by a properly equipped shop.

1   The headlight adjustment screws (see illustration) control up-and-down movement. Left-and-right movement is not adjustable.
2   There are several methods of adjusting the headlights. The sim-plest method requires a blank wall 25 feet in front of the vehicle and a level floor (see illustration).
3   Position masking tape on the wall in reference to the vehicle centerline and the centerlines of both headlights.
4   Measure the height of the headlight reference marks (in the centers of the headlight lenses) from the ground. Position a horizontal tape line on the wall at the same height as the headlight reference marks.

➡ **Note: It may be easier to position the tape on the wall with the vehicle parked only a few inches away.**

5   Adjustment should be made with the vehicle sitting level, the gas tank half-full and no unusually heavy load in the vehicle.
6   Turn on the low beams. Turn the adjusting screw to position the high intensity zone so it is two inches below the horizontal line.
7   Have the headlights adjusted by a dealer service department at the earliest opportunity.

15.1 Vertical adjustment screw location

15.2 Headlight adjustment details

16 Taillight housing - removal and installation

▶ **Refer to illustrations 16.2a and 16.2b**

1 Open the liftgate.
2 Remove the taillight housing mounting fasteners and remove the

taillight housing (see illustrations).
3 Disconnect the electrical connector from the taillight housing.
4 Installation is the reverse of removal.

16.2a Remove the mounting fasteners . . .

16.2b . . . then pull the housing towards you to disengage it from the vehicle

17 Bulb replacement

EXTERIOR LIGHT BULBS

Front turn signal/parking light bulbs

▶ **Refer to illustration 17.1**

1 Turn the bulb holder counterclockwise (see illustration) and remove it from the headlight housing. It's not necessary to disconnect the electrical connector to replace the bulb.

2 To remove the bulb, pull it straight out of the holder.

3 Installation is the reverse of removal.

Taillight bulbs

4 Remove the taillight housing (see Section 16).

5 To remove a taillight bulb socket, rotate it counterclockwise and pull it out of the taillight housing. To remove the bulb from the socket, pull it straight out.

6 Installation is the reverse of removal.

17.1 To remove a front turn signal/parking light bulb, rotate the bulb holder counterclockwise and pull it out (headlight housing removed for clarity)

Bulb removal

To remove many modern exterior bulbs from their holders, simply pull them out

On bulbs with a cylindrical base ("bayonet" bulbs), the socket is spring-loaded; a pair of small posts on the side of the base hold the bulb in place against spring pressure. To remove this type of bulb, push it into the holder, rotate it 1/4-turn counterclockwise, then pull it out

If a bayonet bulb has dual filaments, the posts are staggered, so the bulb can only be installed one way

To remove most overhead interior light bulbs, simply unclip them

Puddle light bulbs

➡ **Note: The puddle lights, which illuminate the ground below the front doors, are located in the outside mirrors.**

7   Release the puddle light housing tab and remove the puddle light housing from the bottom of the mirror housing.

8   Remove the puddle light bulb from its socket and install a new bulb in the socket.

9   To install the bulb socket in the puddle light housing, insert the socket into the housing. You will hear an audible click when the socket is fully seated and locked into place.

License plate light bulbs

10   Using a small screwdriver, unclip the tab at the side of the lens that secures the license plate light housing to the door. Remove the housing.

11   Remove the license plate light socket by rotating it counterclockwise and pulling it out of the license plate light housing. To remove the bulb from the socket, pull it straight out.

12   Installation is the reverse of removal.

17.13 To remove an overhead light lens, carefully pry it off with a trim removal tool or screwdriver

Interior front overhead light bulb

▶ **Refer to illustration 17.13**

13   Carefully pry off the overhead lens (see illustration).

14   Pull the bulb straight out of its socket.

15   Installation is the reverse of removal.

18 Wiper motor - replacement

FRONT WIPER MOTOR

▶ **Refer to illustrations 18.1 and 18.3**

1   Remove the wiper arm nuts and mark the relationship of the wiper arms to their shafts (see illustration). Remove both wiper arms.

2   Remove the plastic cowl cover (see Chapter 11).

3   Disconnect the electrical connector from the wiper motor (see illustration).

4   Remove the two wiper motor and link assembly mounting bolts and remove the wiper motor and link assembly.

5   Using a trim removal tool or a screwdriver, carefully separate the linkage from the motor's crank arm.

6   Remove the nut that secures the crank arm to the motor shaft.

7   Mark the relationship of the crank arm to the motor shaft and remove the crank arm from the shaft.

8   Remove the two motor mounting bolts and remove the motor from its mounting bracket.

9   Installation is the reverse of removal.

18.1 Mark the relationship of the wiper arms to their shafts

18.3 Front wiper motor assembly details

1   Electrical connector
2   Wiper motor assembly mounting bolts

18.12 Rear wiper motor assembly details

1   Electrical connector
2   Wiper motor assembly mounting bolts

REAR WIPER MOTOR

▶ **Refer to illustration 18.12**

10 Remove the wiper arm nut and mark the relationship of the wiper arm to the shaft (see illustration 18.1). Remove the wiper arms.

11 Remove the liftgate trim panel (see Chapter 11).

12 Disconnect the electrical connector from the wiper motor (see illustration).

13 Remove the wiper motor mounting bolts and remove the wiper motor.

14 Installation is the reverse of removal.

19 Horn - replacement

▶ **Refer to illustration 19.3**

➡ **Note: The horn is located at the lower right corner of the vehicle, in the void ahead of the right front wheel well.**

1   Raise the vehicle and place it securely on jackstands.

2   To access the horn, remove the right front fender splash shield fasteners and pull down the splash shield (see Chapter 11).

3   Disconnect the horn electrical connector (see illustration).

4   Remove the horn mounting bolt, then remove the horn.

5   Installation is the reverse of removal.

19.3 Horn assembly details

1   Electrical connector   2   Mounting bolt

20 Rear window defogger - check and repair

1   The rear window defogger consists of a number of horivzontal elements baked onto the glass surface.

2   Small breaks in the element can be repaired without removing the rear window.

CHECK

▶ **Refer to illustrations 20.4, 20.5 and 20.7**

3   Turn the ignition switch and defogger system switches to the ON position. Using a voltmeter, place the positive probe against the defogger grid positive terminal and the negative probe against the ground terminal. If battery voltage is not indicated, check the fuse, defogger switch and related wiring. If voltage is indicated, but all or part of the defogger doesn't heat, proceed with the following tests.

4   When measuring voltage during the next two tests, wrap a piece of aluminum foil around the tip of the voltmeter positive probe and press the foil against the heating element with your finger (see illustration). Place the negative probe on the defogger grid ground terminal.

5   Check the voltage at the center of each heating element (see illustration). If the voltage is 5 or 6-volts, the element is okay (there is no break). If the voltage is zero, the element is broken between the center of the element and the positive end. If the voltage is 10 to 12-volts, the element is broken between the center of the element and ground. Check each heating element.

6   Connect the negative lead to a good body ground. The reading should stay the same. If it doesn't, the ground connection is bad.

7   To find the break, place the voltmeter negative probe against the defogger ground terminal. Place the voltmeter positive probe with the foil strip against the heating element at the positive terminal end and slide it toward the negative terminal end. The point at which the voltmeter deflects from several volts to zero is the point at which the heating element is broken (see illustration).

20.4 When measuring the voltage at the rear window defogger grid, wrap a piece of aluminum foil around the positive probe of the voltmeter and press the foil against the wire with your finger

20.5 To determine if a heating element has broken, check the voltage at the center of each element; if the voltage is 5 or 6 volts, the element is unbroken, but if the voltage is 10 or 12 volts, the element is broken between the center and the ground side. If there is no voltage, the element is broken between the center and the positive side

20.7 To find the break, place the voltmeter negative lead against the defogger ground terminal, place the voltmeter positive lead with the foil strip against the heating element at the positive terminal end and slide it toward the negative terminal end. The point at which the voltmeter reading changes abruptly is the point at which the element is broken

REPAIR

▶ **Refer to illustration 20.13**

8   Repair the break in the element using a repair kit specifically recommended for this purpose, available at most auto parts stores. Included in this kit is plastic conductive epoxy.

9   Prior to repairing a break, turn off the system and allow it to cool off for a few minutes.

10 Lightly buff the element area with fine steel wool, then clean it thoroughly with rubbing alcohol.

11 Use masking tape to mask off the area being repaired.

12 Thoroughly mix the epoxy, following the instructions provided with the repair kit.

13 Apply the epoxy material to the slit in the masking tape, overlapping the undamaged area about 3/4-inch on either end (see illustration).

20.13 To use a defogger repair kit, apply masking tape to the inside of the window at the damaged area, then brush on the special conductive coating

14 Allow the repair to cure for 24 hours before removing the tape and using the system.

21 Power mirror control system - description and check

1   Electric rear view mirrors use two motors to move the glass; one for up and down adjustments and one for left-right adjustments.

2   The control switch has a selector portion which sends voltage to the left or right side mirror. With the ignition ON but the engine OFF, roll down the windows and operate the mirror control switch through all functions (left-right and up-down) for both the left and right side mirrors.

3   Listen carefully for the sound of the electric motors running in the mirrors.

4   If the motors can be heard but the mirror glass doesn't move,

there's probably a problem with the drive mechanism inside the mirror.

5   If the mirrors do not operate and no sound comes from the mirrors, check the fuse (see Section 3).

6   If the fuse is OK, remove the mirror control switch from its mounting without disconnecting the wires attached to it. Turn the ignition ON and check for voltage at the switch. There should be voltage at one terminal. If there's no voltage at the switch, check for an open or short in the circuit between the fuse panel and the switch.

7   If the mirror motor fails to operate as described, replace the mirror assembly (see Chapter 11).

22 Cruise control system - description and check

1   All models have an electronically-controlled throttle body - there is no accelerator cable (or cruise control cable). When you select the speed that you want to maintain, the PCM controls vehicle speed by

opening and closing the throttle plate by means of a computer-controlled solenoid (motor) inside the throttle body.

2   The diagnostic procedures for troubleshooting the cruise control

system are beyond the scope of this manual, but if the system can't be set, or the set speed doesn't cancel when the brake pedal is depressed, check the fuses. Start with the fuses in the engine compartment fuse and relay box, then check the fuses in the under-dash fuse and relay box. If the set speed doesn't cancel when the CANCEL button is depressed, check the fuse for that circuit.

3   Other than checking the fuses, the diagnostic procedures for troubleshooting the cruise control system on these models are beyond the scope of this manual. A dealer service department should handle any further testing.

23 Power window system - description and check

➡ **Note: These models are equipped with a Smart Junction Box (SJB) (manufacturer terminology), otherwise known as a Body Control Module (BCM). Several systems are linked to this centralized control module, which allows simple and accurate troubleshooting, but only with a professional-grade scan tool. The SJB or BCM governs the door locks, the power windows, the ignition lock and security system, the interior lights, the Daytime Running Lights system, the horn, the windshield wipers, the heating/air conditioning system and the power mirrors. In the event of malfunction with this system, have the vehicle diagnosed by a dealership service department or other qualified automotive repair facility.**

1   The power window system operates electric motors, mounted in the doors, which lower and raise the windows. The system consists of the control switches, the motors, regulators, glass mechanisms, the Smart Junction Box (SJB) and associated wiring.

2   The power windows can be lowered and raised from the master control switch by the driver or by remote switches located at the individual windows. Each window has a separate motor that is reversible. The position of the control switch determines the polarity and therefore the direction of operation.

3   The circuit is protected by a fuse and a circuit breaker. Each motor is also equipped with an internal circuit breaker; this prevents one stuck window from disabling the whole system.

4   The power window system will only operate when the ignition switch is ON, and for a period of time after the ignition key has been turned Off (unless one of the doors is opened). In addition, many models have a window lockout switch at the master control switch which, when activated, disables the switches at the rear windows and, sometimes, the switch at the passenger's window also. Always check these items before troubleshooting a window problem.

5   These procedures are general in nature, so if you can't find the problem using them, take the vehicle to a dealer service department or other properly equipped repair facility.

6   If the power windows won't operate, always check the fuse and circuit breaker first.

7   If only the rear windows are inoperative, or if the windows only operate from the master control switch, check the rear window lockout switch for continuity in the unlocked position. Replace it if it doesn't have continuity.

8   Check the wiring between the switches and fuse panel for continuity. Repair the wiring, if necessary.

9   If only one window is inoperative from the master control switch, try the other control switch at the window.

➡ **Note: This doesn't apply to the driver's door window.**

10 If the same window works from one switch, but not the other, check the switch for continuity.

11 If the switch tests OK, check for a short or open in the circuit between the affected switch and the window motor.

12 If one window is inoperative from both switches, remove the switch panel from the affected door. Check for voltage at the switch and at the motor (refer to Chapter 11 for door panel removal) while the switch is operated.

13 If voltage is reaching the motor, disconnect the glass from the regulator (see Chapter 11). Move the window up and down by hand while checking for binding and damage. Also check for binding and damage to the regulator. If the regulator is not damaged and the window moves up and down smoothly, replace the motor. If there's binding or damage, lubricate, repair or replace parts, as necessary.

14 If voltage isn't reaching the motor, check the wiring in the circuit for continuity between the switches and the body control module, and between the body control module and the motors. You'll need to consult the wiring diagram at the end of this Chapter. If the circuit is equipped with a relay, check that the relay is grounded properly and receiving voltage.

15 Test the windows after you are done to confirm proper repairs.

24 Power door lock and keyless entry system - description, check and battery replacement

➡ **Note: These models are equipped with a Smart Junction Box (SJB) (manufacturer terminology), otherwise known as a Body Control Module (BCM). Several systems are linked to this centralized control module, which allows simple and accurate troubleshooting, but only with a professional-grade scan tool. The SJB or BCM governs the door locks, the power windows, the ignition lock and security system, the interior lights, the Daytime Running Lights system, the horn, the windshield wipers, the heating/air conditioning system and the power mirrors. In the event of malfunction with this system, have the vehicle diagnosed by a dealership service department or other qualified automotive repair facility.**

DESCRIPTION AND CHECK

1   The power door lock system operates the door lock actuators mounted in each door. The system consists of the switches, actuators, Smart Junction Box (SJB) and associated wiring. Diagnosis can usually be limited to simple checks of the wiring connections and actuators for minor faults that can be easily repaired.

2   Power door lock systems are operated by bi-directional solenoids located in the doors. The lock switches have two operating positions: Lock and Unlock. These switches send a signal to the SJB, which in turn sends a signal to the door lock solenoids.

3   If you are unable to locate the trouble using the following general

24.14 Using a coin, carefully pry the halves of the transmitter apart

24.15 Carefully pry out the old battery

steps, consult your dealer service department.

4 Always check the circuit protection first. Some vehicles use a combination of circuit breakers and fuses. Refer to the wiring diagrams at the end of this Chapter.

5 Check for voltage at the switches. If no voltage is present, check the wiring between the fuse panel and the switches for shorts and opens.

6 If voltage is present, test the switch for continuity. Replace it if there's not continuity in both switch positions. To remove the switch, use a flat-bladed trim tool to pry out the door/window switch assembly (see Chapter 11).

7 If the switch has continuity, check the wiring between the switch and door lock solenoid.

8 If all but one lock solenoids operate, remove the trim panel from the affected door (see Chapter 11) and check for voltage at the solenoid while the lock switch is operated. One of the wires should have voltage in the Lock position; the other should have voltage in the Unlock position.

9 If the inoperative solenoid is receiving voltage, replace the solenoid.

10 If the inoperative solenoid isn't receiving voltage, check for an open or short in the wire between the lock solenoid and the relavy.

11 On the models covered by this manual, power door lock system communication goes through the Smart Junction Box. If the above tests do not pinpoint a problem, take the vehicle to a dealer or qualified shop with the proper scan tool to retrieve trouble codes from the SJB.

KEYLESS ENTRY SYSTEM

12 The keyless entry system consists of a remote control transmitter that sends a coded infrared signal to a receiver, which then operates the door lock system.

13 Replace the battery when the transmitter doesn't operate the locks at a distance of ten feet. Normal range should be about 30 feet.

KEY REMOTE CONTROL BATTERY REPLACEMENT

▶ **Refer to illustrations 24.14 and 24.15**

14 Use a coin to carefully separate the case halves (see illustration).
15 Replace the battery (see illustration).
16 Snap the case halves together.

TRANSMITTER PROGRAMMING

17 Programming replacement transmitters requires the use of a specialized scan tool. Take the vehicle and the transmitter(s) to a dealer service department or other qualified repair shop equipped with the necessary tool to have the transmitter(s) programmed to the vehicle.

25 Daytime Running Lights (DRL) - general information

The Daytime Running Lights (DRL) system used on some models illuminates the headlights whenever the engine is running. The only exception is with the engine running and the parking brake engaged. Once the parking brake is released, the lights will remain on as long as the ignition switch is on, even if the parking brake is later applied.

The DRL system supplies reduced power to the headlights so they won't be too bright for daytime use, while prolonging headlight life.

26 Airbags - general information

These models are equipped with a Supplemental Restraint System (SRS), more commonly known as airbags. This system is designed to protect the driver and the front seat passenger from serious injury in the event of a head-on or frontal collision. It consists of an airbag module in the center of the steering wheel and another airbag module on the right side of the instrument panel plus, on some and later models, side airbags and curtain shield airbags designed to protect the occupants in a side impact and a sensing/diagnostic module which is mounted in the center of the vehicle below the instrument panel. These models are also equipped with a pair of impact sensors that are located at the front of the vehicle.

Some later models are equipped with seatbelt pre-tensioners, also part of the airbag system. The pre-tensioners are pyrotechnic (explosive) devices designed to retract the seat belts in the event of a collision.

On models equipped with pre-tensioners, do not remove the front seat belt retractor assemblies. Problems with the pre-tensioners will turn on the SRS (airbag) warning light on the dash. If any pre-tensioner problems are suspected, take the vehicle to a dealer service department.

AIRBAG MODULE

Steering wheel-mounted

The airbag inflator module contains a housing incorporating the cushion (airbag) and inflator unit, mounted in the center of the steering wheel. The inflator assembly is mounted on the back of the housing over a hole through which gas is expelled, inflating the bag almost instantaneously when an electrical signal is sent from the system. A spiral cable assembly on the steering column under the module carries this signal to the module. This spiral cable assembly can transmit an electrical signal regardless of steering wheel position.

Instrument panel-mounted

The passenger side airbag is mounted above the glove compartment and designated by the letters SRS (Supplemental Restraint System). It consists of an inflator containing an igniter, a bag assembly, a reaction housing and a trim cover.

The passenger airbag is considerably larger than the steering wheel-mounted unit and is supported by the steel reaction housing. The trim cover has a molded seam which splits when the bag inflates.

Side and curtain airbags

The side airbag and inflator modules are mounted on the sides of the front seats and contain an inflator containing an igniter and bag assembly. The curtain shield airbag assemblies run along the interior of the roof from the front A-pillar to the rear of the passenger compartment. In the event of a side impact, both airbag assemblies are activated by the sensors mounted at the base of the center pillar behind the seats.

SENSING AND DIAGNOSTIC MODULE

The sensing and diagnostic module supplies the current to the airbag system in the event of the collision, even if battery power is cut off. It checks this system every time the vehicle is started, causing the "AIR BAG" light to go on then off, if the system is operating properly. If there is a fault in the system, the light will go on and stay on, flash, or the dash will make a beeping sound. If this happens, the vehicle should be taken to your dealer immediately for service.

SEAT BELT PRE-TENSIONERS

Some models are equipped with pyrotechnic (explosive) units in

the front seat belt retracting mechanisms. During an impact that would trigger the airbag system, the airbag control unit also triggers the seat belt retractors. When the pyrotechnic charges go off, they accelerate the retractors to instantly take up any slack in the seat belt system to more fully prepare the driver and front seat passenger for impact.

The airbag system should be disabled any time work is done to or around the seats.

> ❊❊ WARNING:
>
> **Never strike the pillars or floorpan with a hammer or use an impact-driver tool in these areas unless the system is disabled.**

PRECAUTIONS

Disabling the SRS system

> ❊❊ WARNING:
>
> **Failure to follow these precautions could result in accidental deployment of the airbag and personal injury.**

> ❊❊ WARNING:
>
> **Never install a memory-saver device, used to preserve PCM memory and radio station presets, when working on or around any of the airbag system components.**

Whenever working in the vicinity of the steering wheel, instrument panel or any of the other SRS system components, the system must be disarmed. To disarm the system:

a) *Point the wheels straight ahead and turn the ignition key to the LOCK position.*
b) *Disconnect the cable from the negative terminal of the battery.*
c) *Wait at least two minutes for the back-up power supply capacitor to be depleted.*

Whenever handling an airbag module, always keep the airbag opening (trim side) pointed away from your body. Never place the airbag module on a bench or other surface with the airbag opening facing the surface. Always place the airbag module in a safe location with the airbag opening (trim side) facing up.

Never measure the resistance of any SRS component. An ohmmeter has a built-in battery supply that could accidentally deploy the airbag.

Never use electrical welding equipment on a vehicle equipped with an airbag without first disconnecting the negative battery cable.

Never dispose of a live airbag module. Return it to your dealer for safe deployment, using special equipment, and disposal.

27 Wiring diagrams - general information

Since it isn't possible to include all wiring diagrams for every year covered by this manual, the following diagrams are those that are typical and most commonly needed.

Prior to troubleshooting any circuits, check the fuse and circuit breakers (if equipped) to make sure they're in good condition. Make

sure the battery is properly charged and check the cable connections (see Chapter 1).

When checking a circuit, make sure that all connectors are clean, with no broken or loose terminals. When unplugging a connector, do not pull on the wires. Pull only on the connector housings themselves.

Starting system - 2010 and earlier models

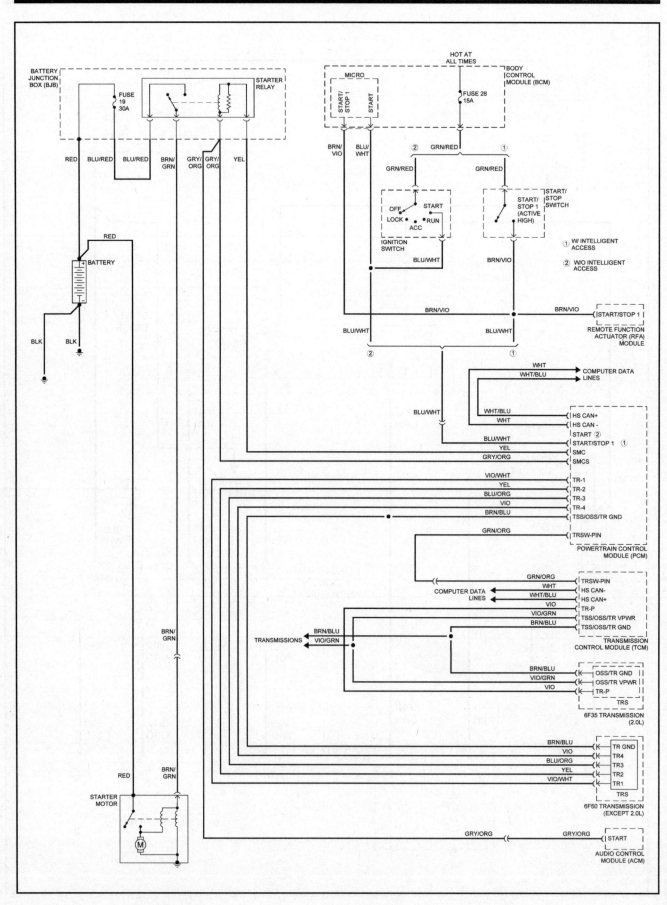

Starting system - 2011 and later models

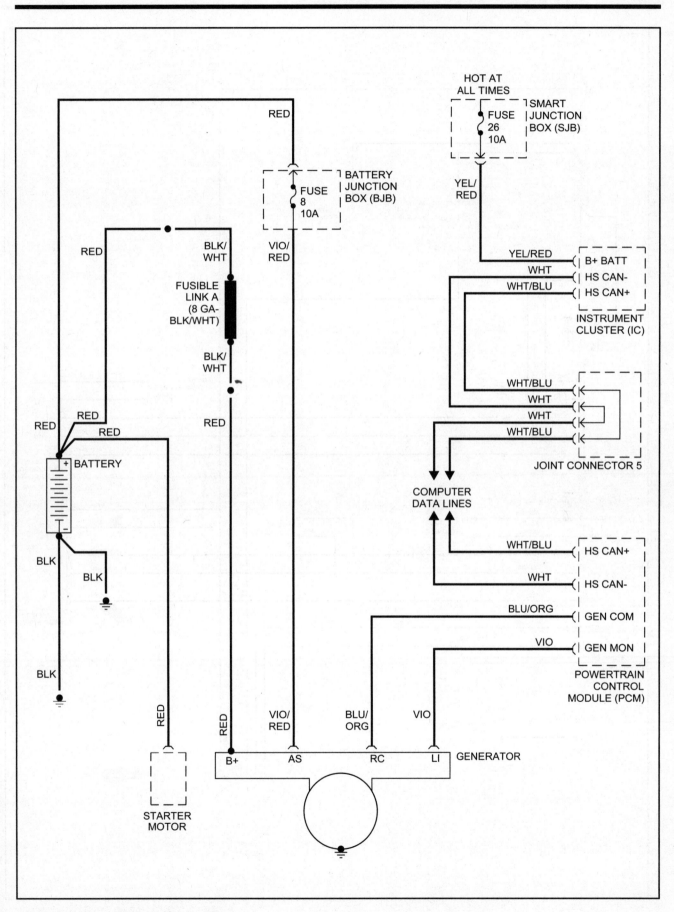

Charging system - 2010 and earlier models

Charging system - 2011 and later models

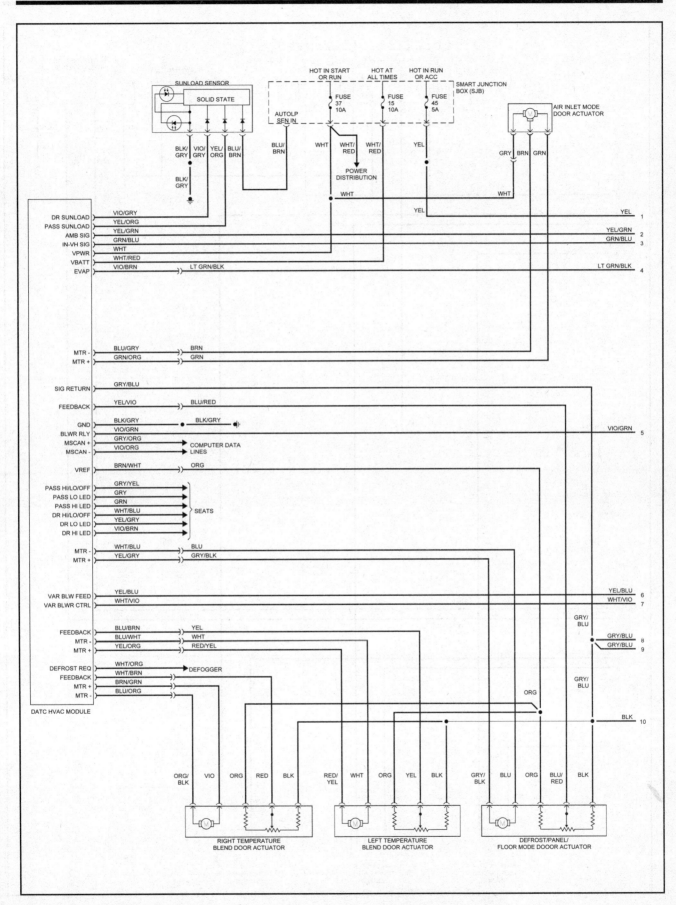

Air conditioning, heating and engine cooling fan system (automatic) - 2010 and earlier models (1 of 3)

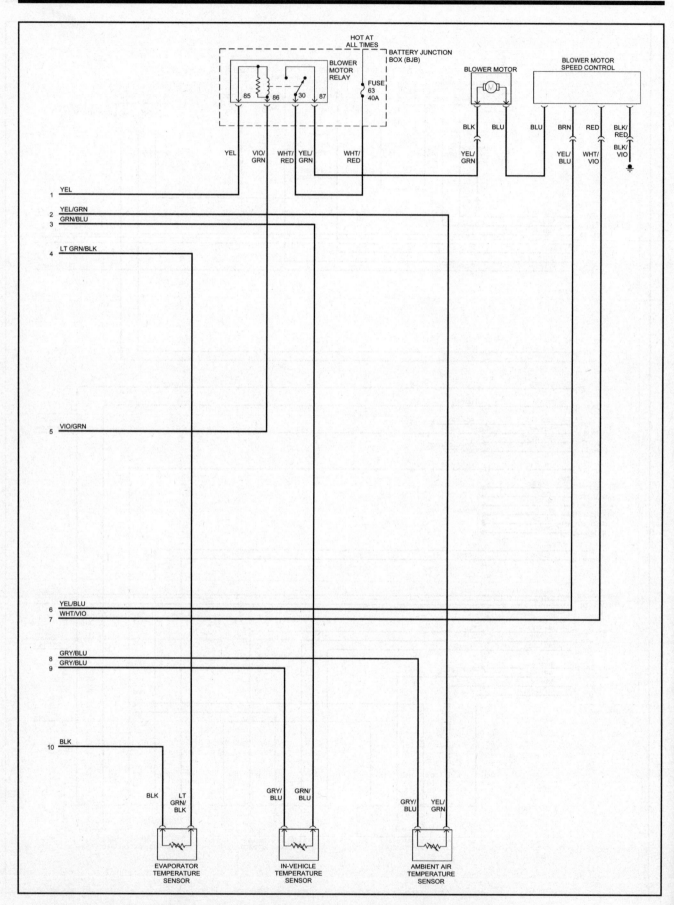

Air conditioning, heating and engine cooling fan system (automatic) - 2010 and earlier models (2 of 3)

Air conditioning, heating and engine cooling fan system (automatic) - 2010 and earlier models (3 of 3)

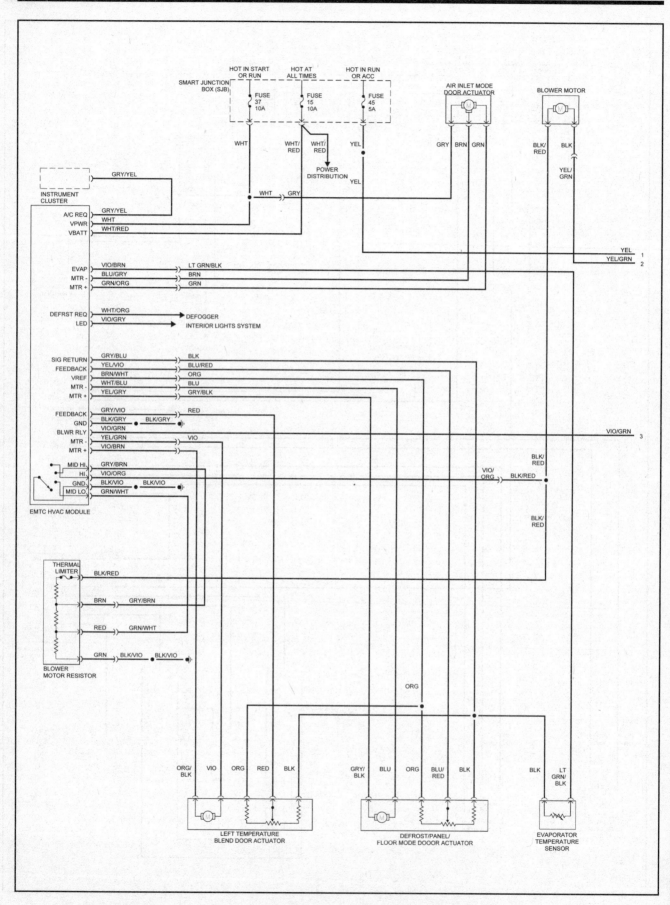

Air conditioning, heating and engine cooling fan system (manual) - 2010 and earlier models (1 of 2)

Air conditioning, heating and engine cooling fan system (manual) - 2010 and earlier models (2 of 2)

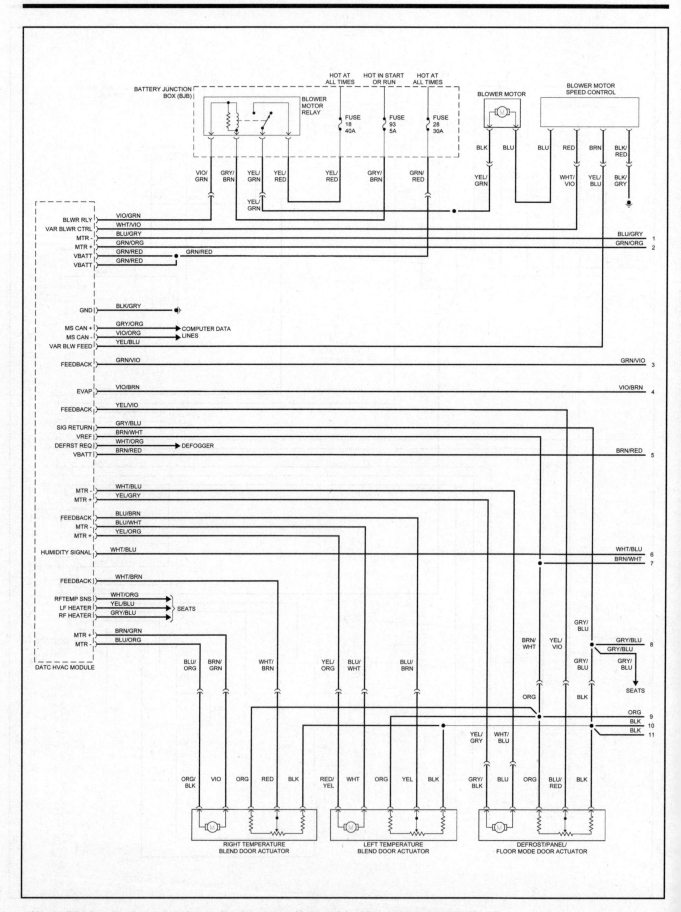

Air conditioning, heating and engine cooling fan system (automatic) - 2011 and later models (1 of 3)

Air conditioning, heating and engine cooling fan system (automatic) - 2011 and later models (2 of 3)

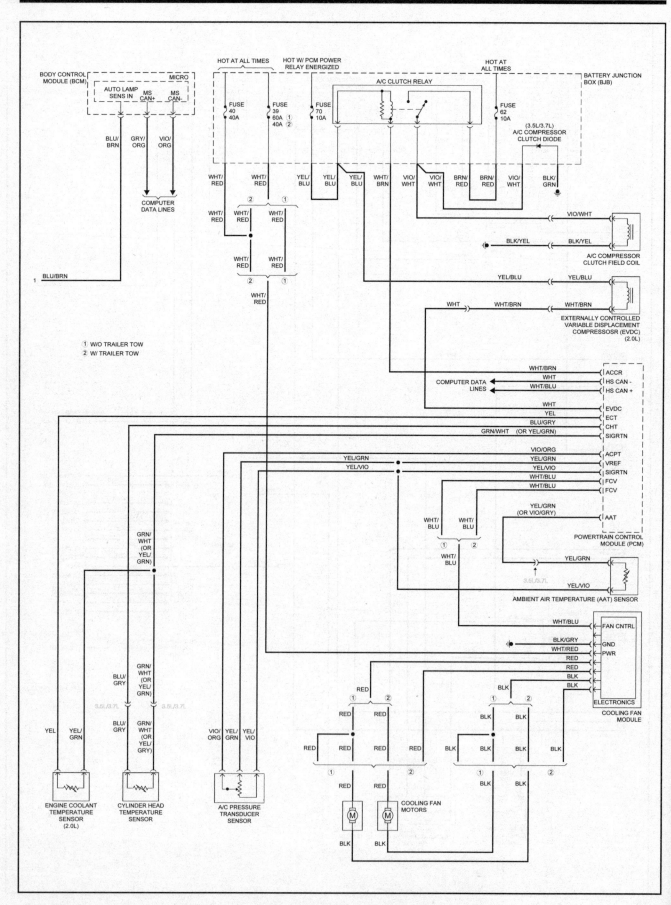

Air conditioning, heating and engine cooling fan system (automatic) - 2011 and later models (3 of 3)

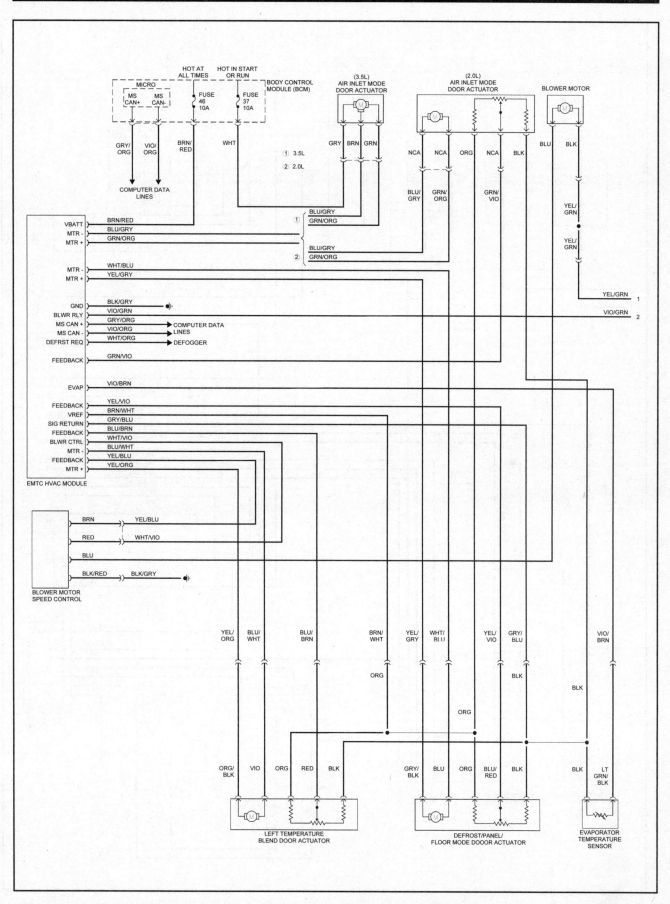

Air conditioning, heating and engine cooling fan system (manual) - 2011 and later models (1 of 2)

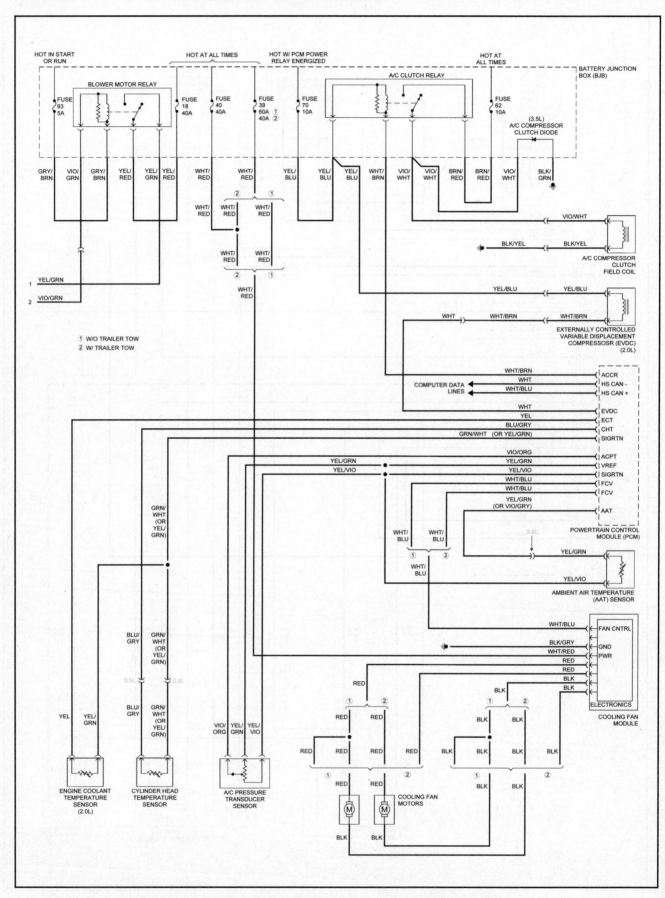

Air conditioning, heating and engine cooling fan system (manual) - 2011 and later models (2 of 2)

Power window system - 2007 models

Power window system - 2008 and later models

Power door lock system - without intelligent access (1 of 2)

Power door lock system - without intelligent access (2 of 2)

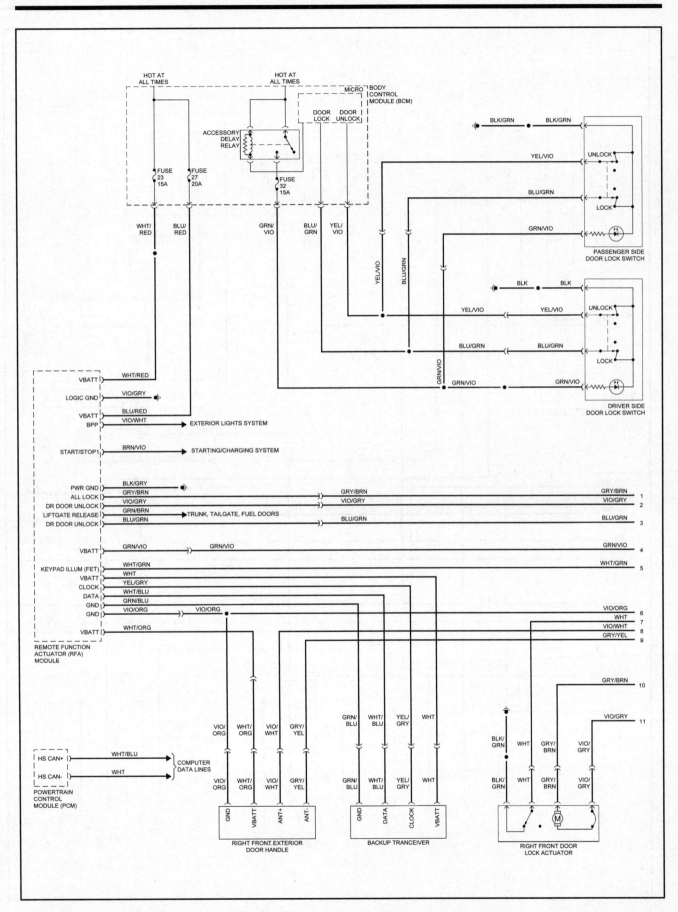

Power door lock system - with intelligent access (1 of 3)

Power door lock system - with intelligent access (2 of 3)

Power door lock system - with intelligent access (3 of 3)

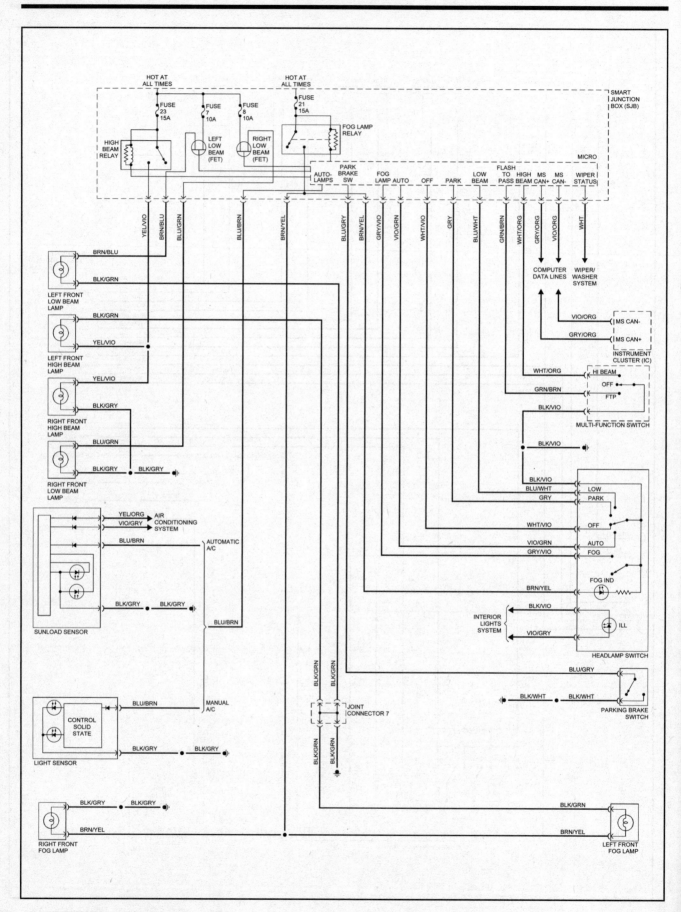

Headlight system - 2010 and earlier models

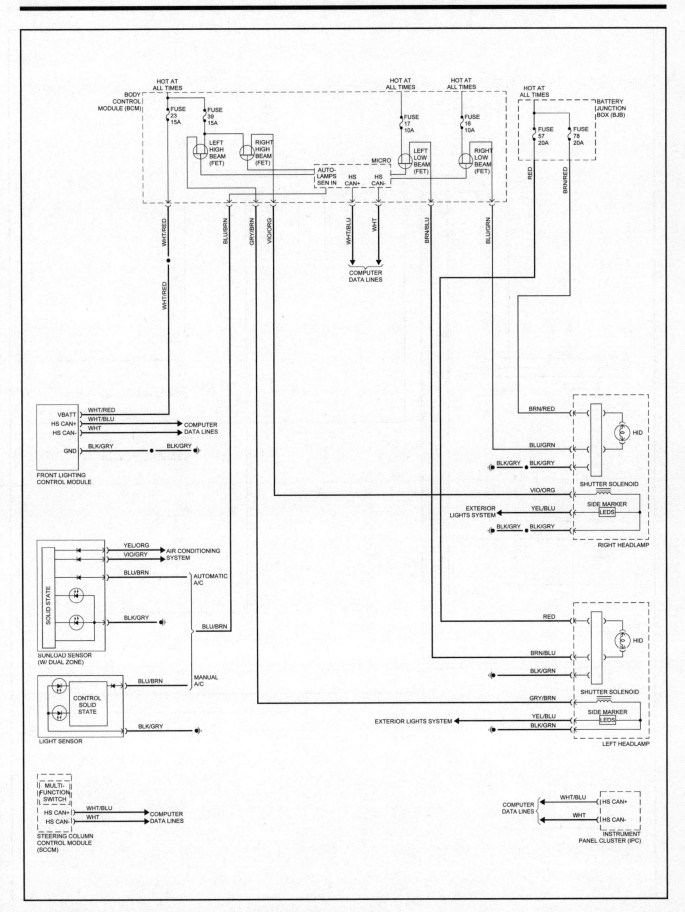

Headlight system - 2011 and later models (with HID headlights)

Headlight system - 2011 and later models (without HID headlights)

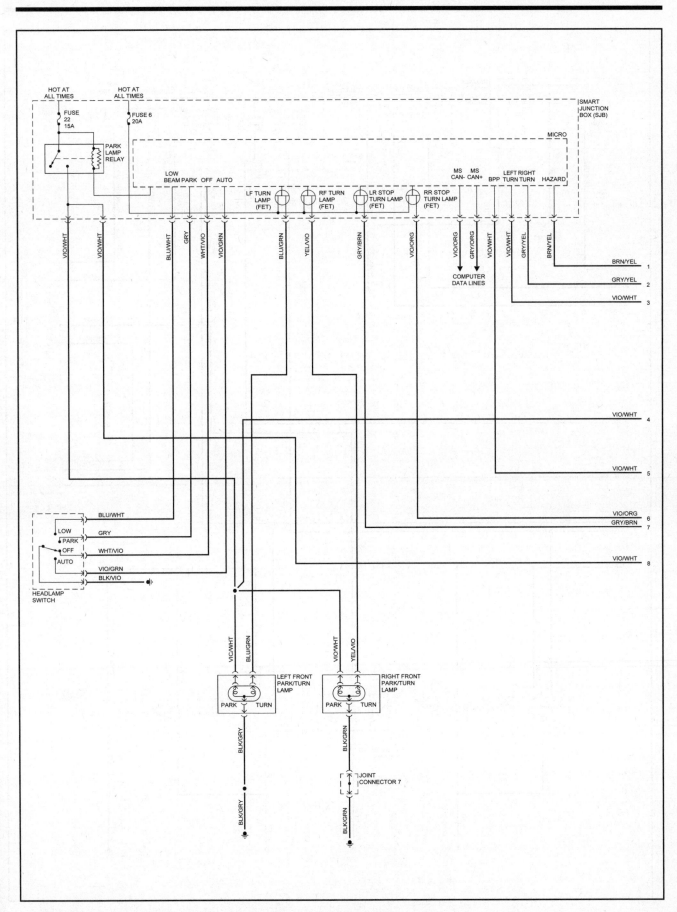

Exterior lighting system (except headlights) - 2010 and earlier models (1 of 2)

Exterior lighting system (except headlights) - 2010 and earlier models (2 of 2)

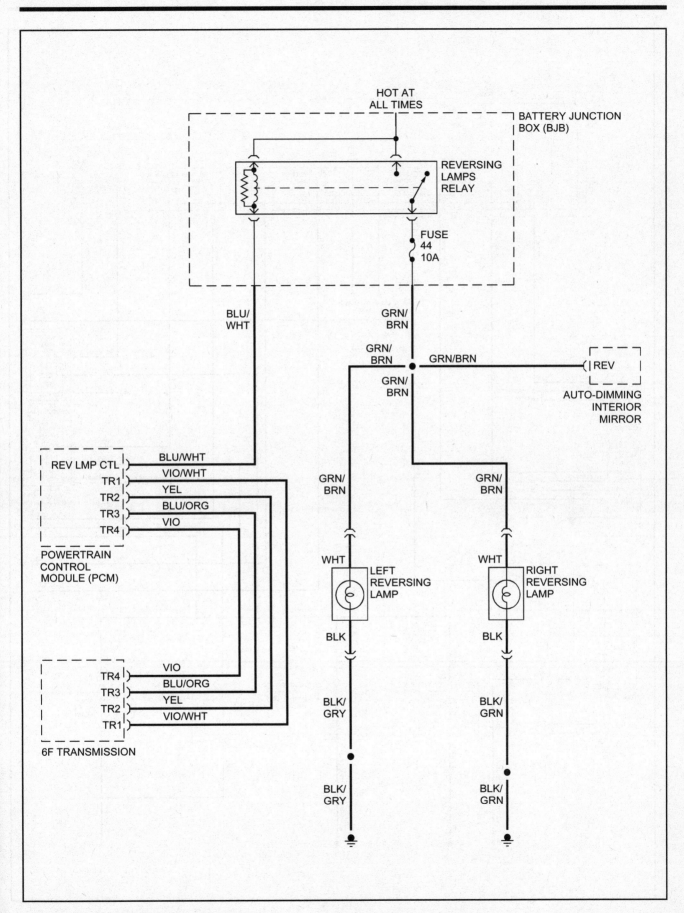

Back-up light system - 2010 and earlier models

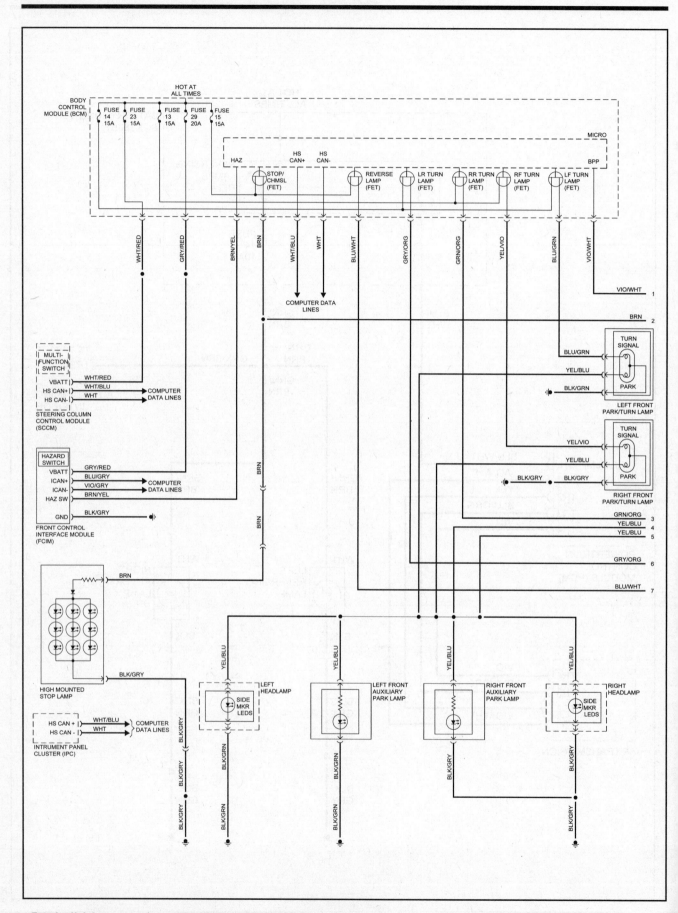

Exterior lighting system (except headlights) - 2011 and later models (1 of 2)

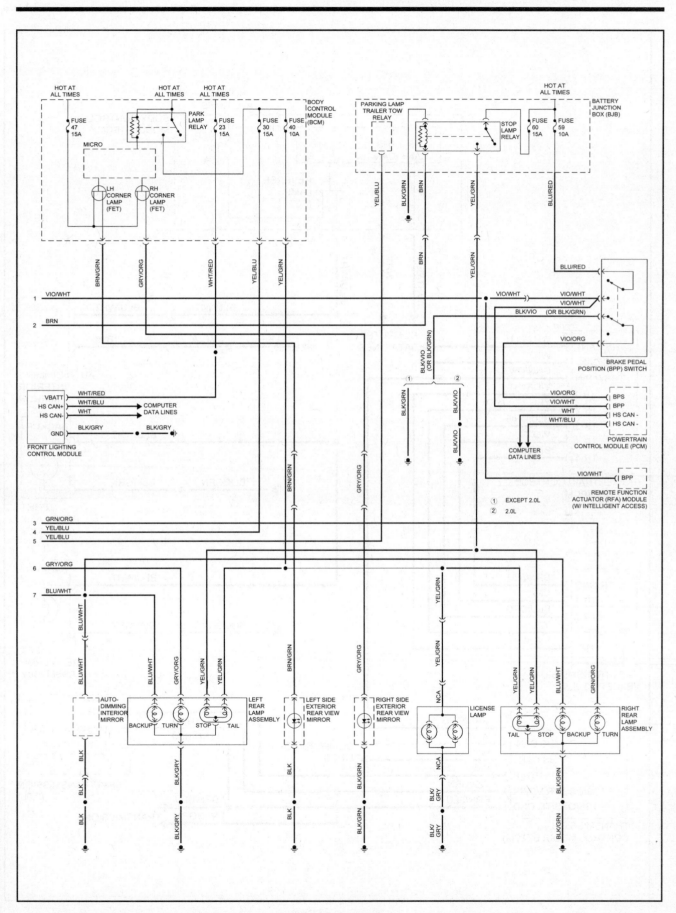

Exterior lighting system (except headlights) - 2011 and later models (2 of 2)

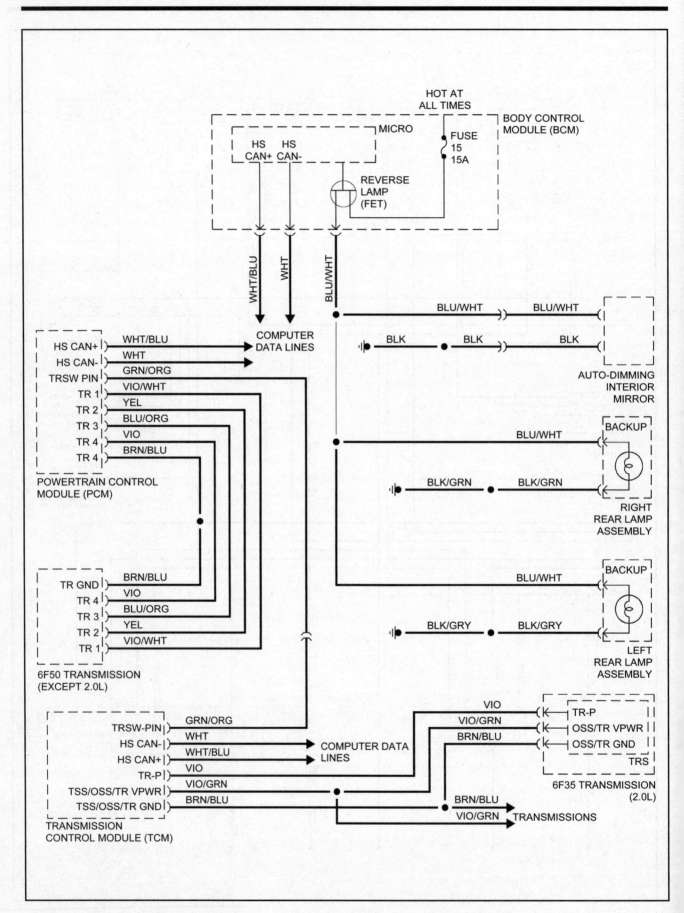

Back-up light system - 2011 and later models

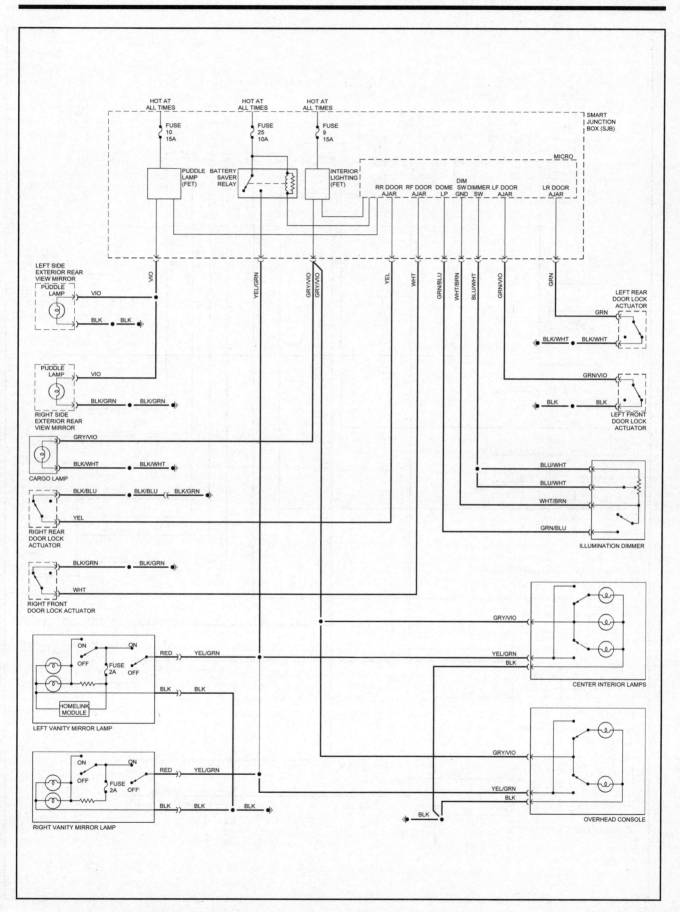

Interior lighting system - 2007 and 2008 models

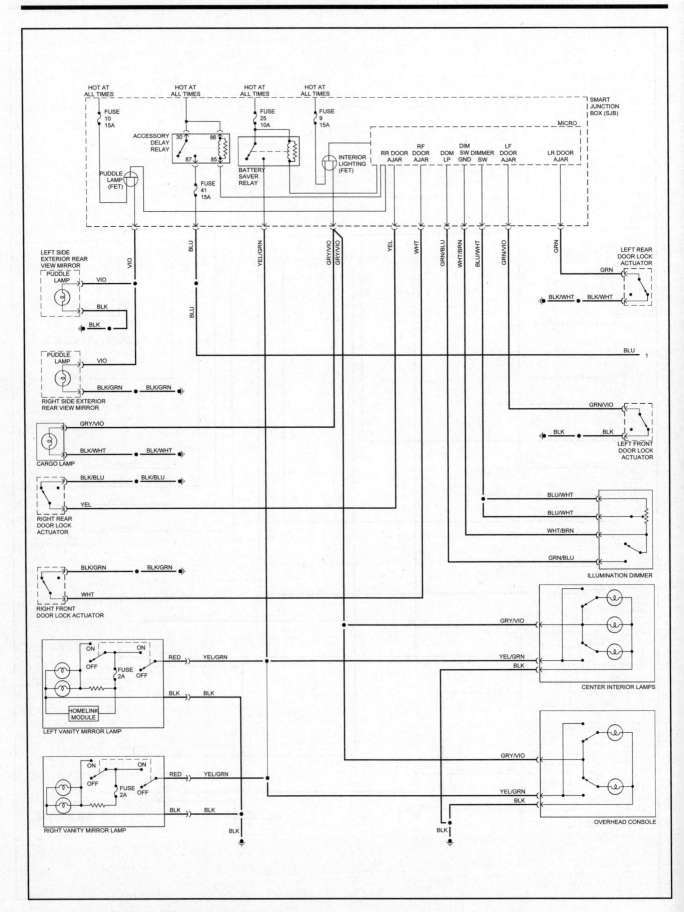

Interior lighting system - 2009 and 2010 models (1 of 2)

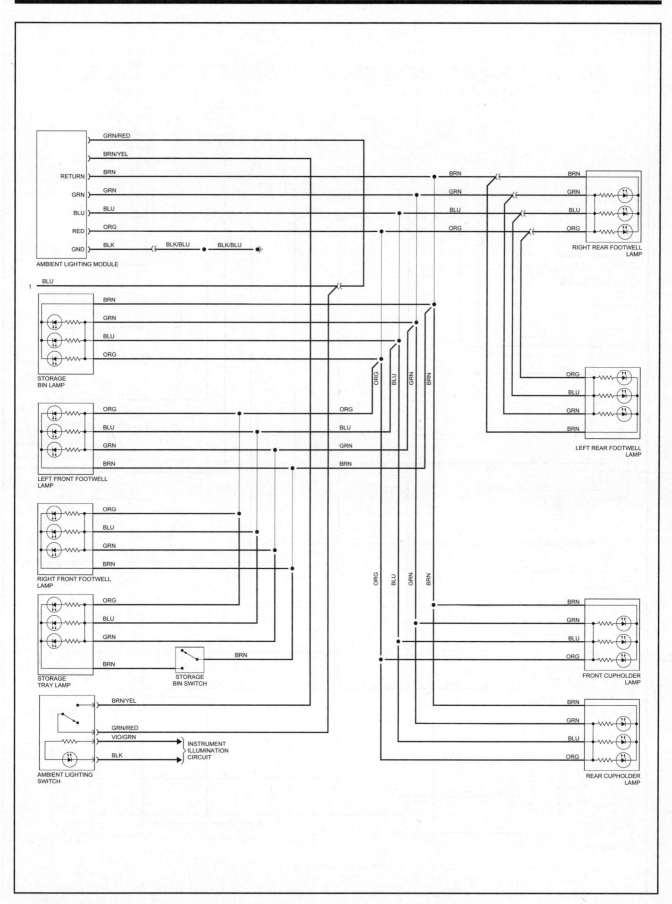

Interior lighting system - 2009 and 2010 models (2 of 2)

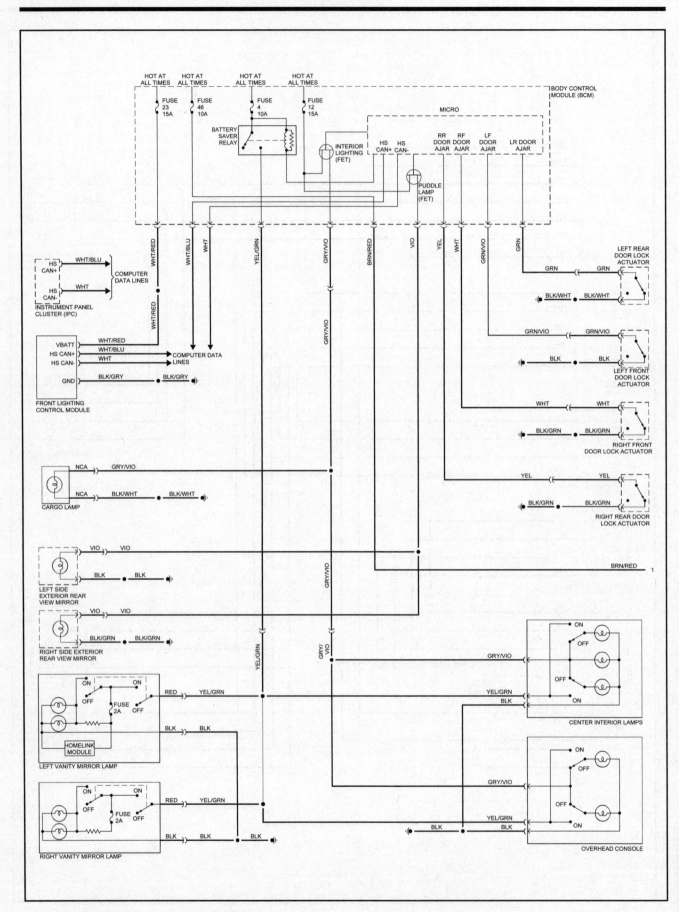

Interior lighting system - 2011 and later models (1 of 3)

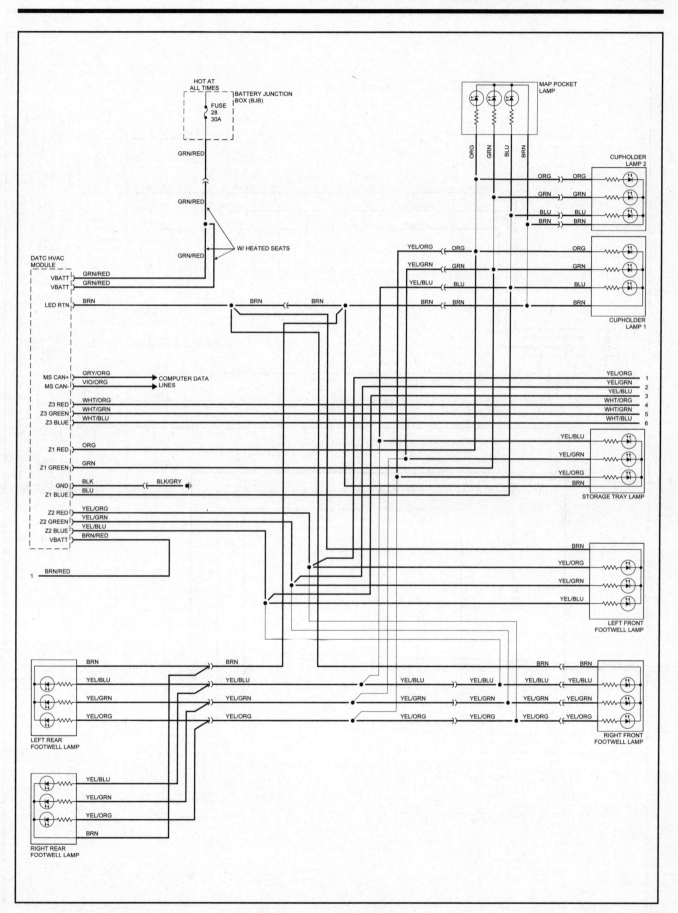

Interior lighting system - 2011 and later models (2 of 3)

Interior lighting system - 2011 and later models (3 of 3)

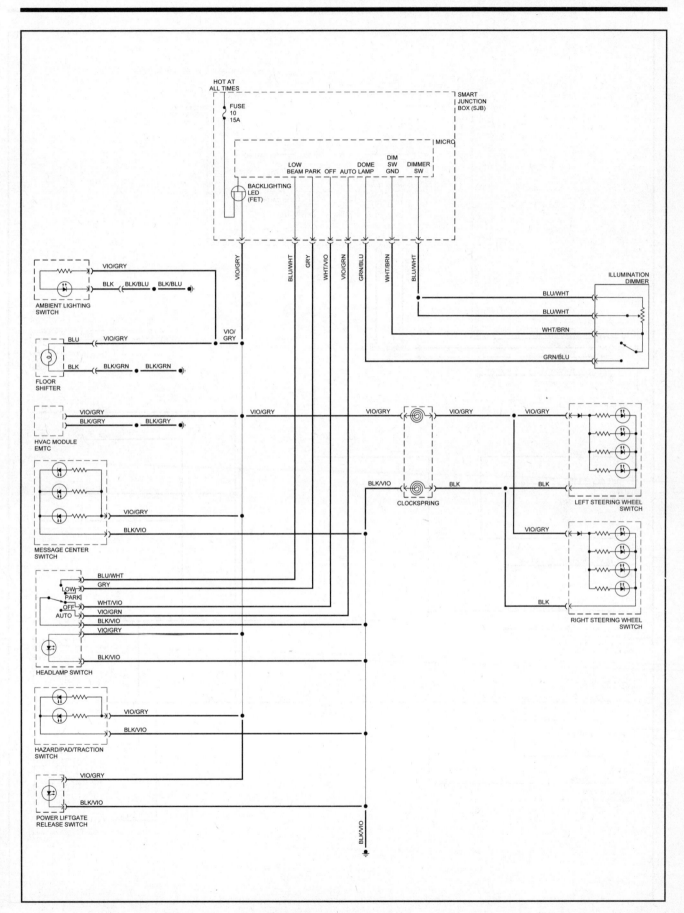

Instrument panel and switch illumination - 2010 and earlier models

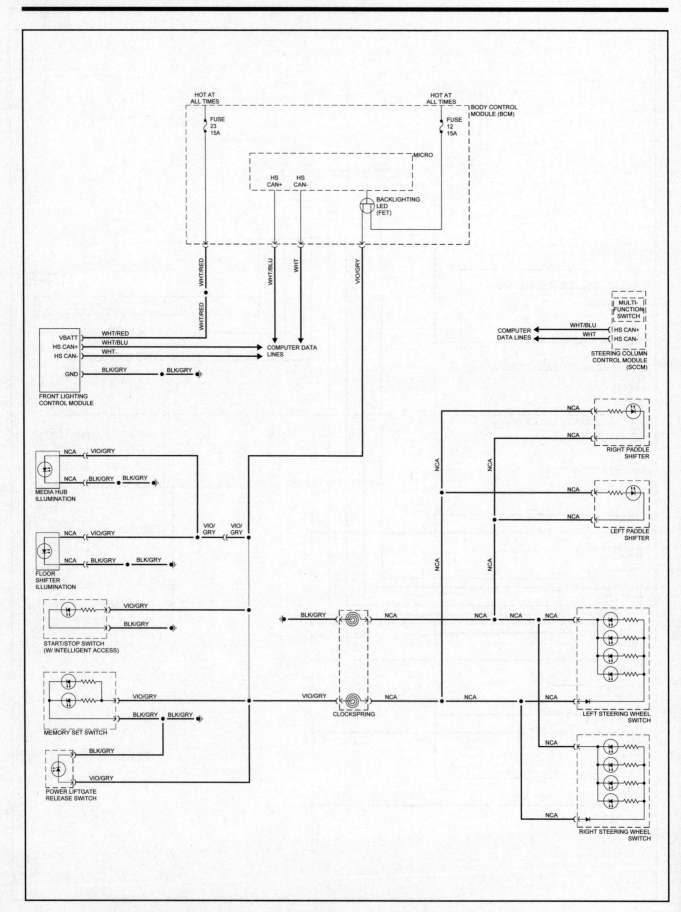

Instrument panel and switch illumination - 2011 and later models

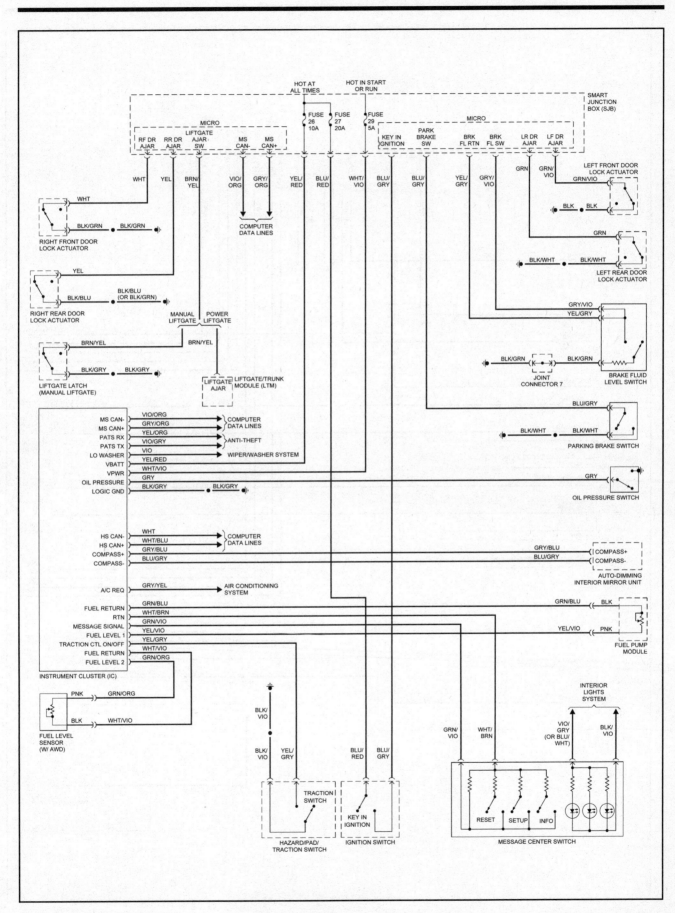

Instrument cluster and related systems - 2010 and earlier models

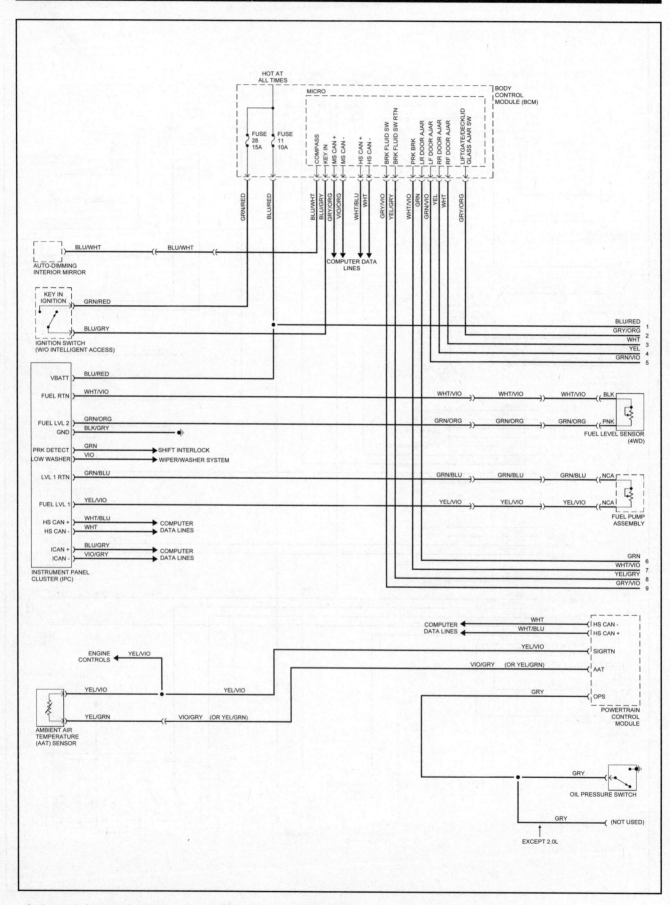

Instrument cluster and related systems - 2011 and later models (1 of 2)

Instrument cluster and related systems - 2011 and later models (2 of 2)

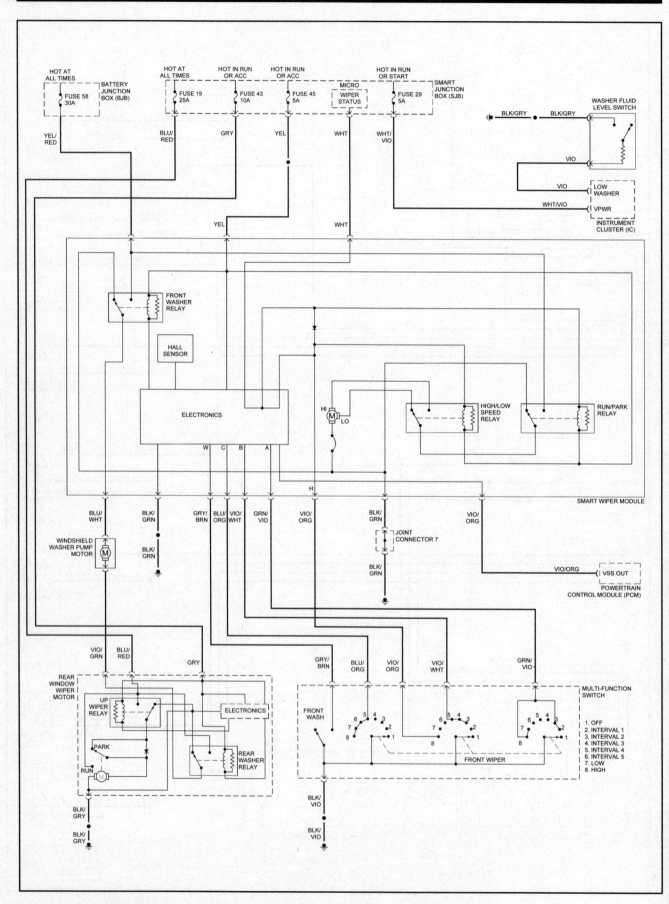

Windshield wiper/washer system - 2010 and earlier models

Rear window wiper/washer system - 2010 and earlier models

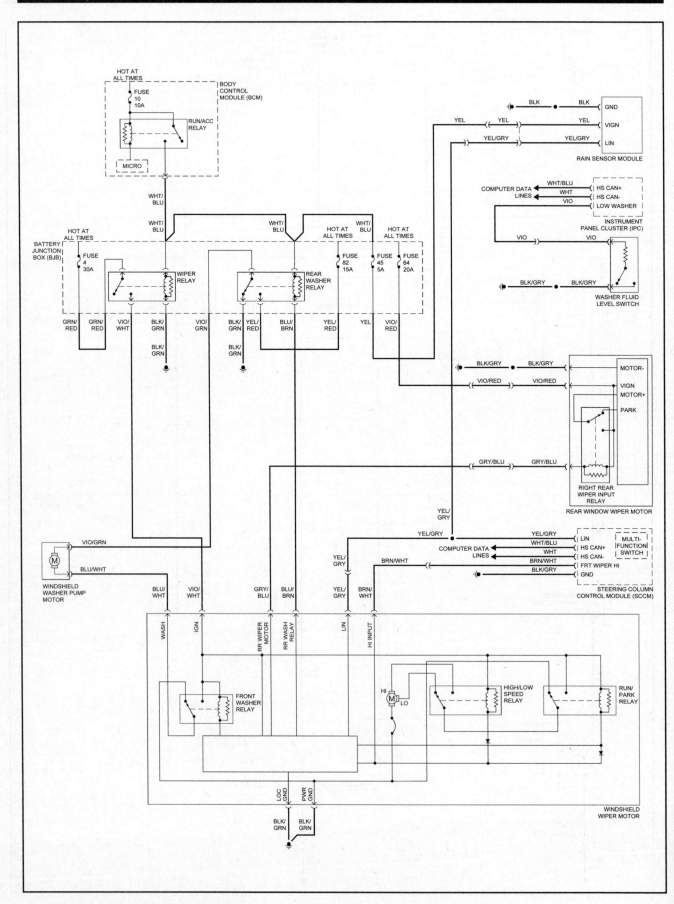

Wiper/washer systems - 2011 and later models

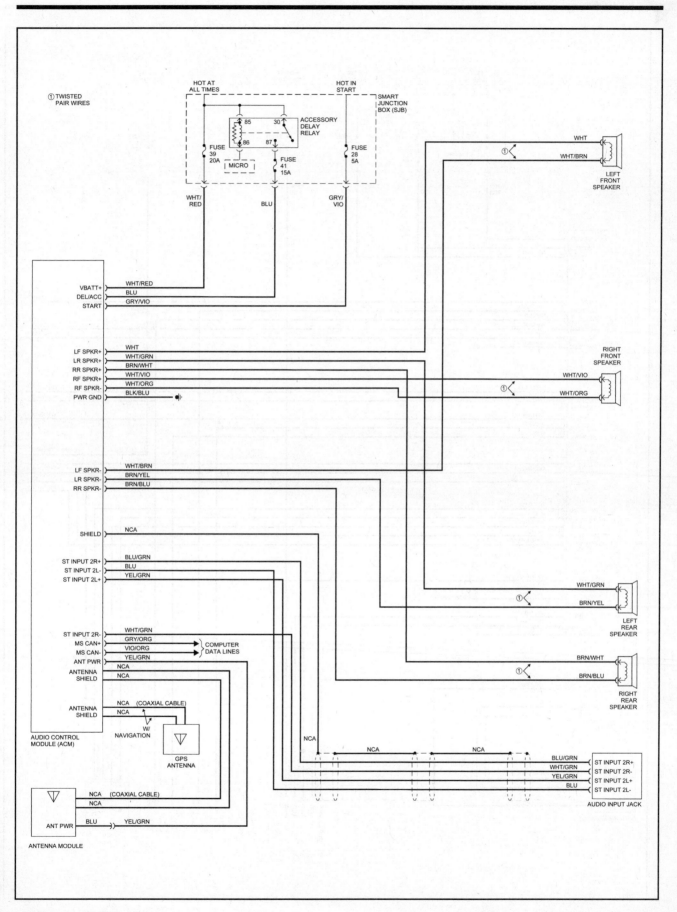

Audio system - 2007 and 2008 models

Audio system - 2009 and 2010 models (1 of 2)

Audio system - 2009 and 2010 models (2 of 2)

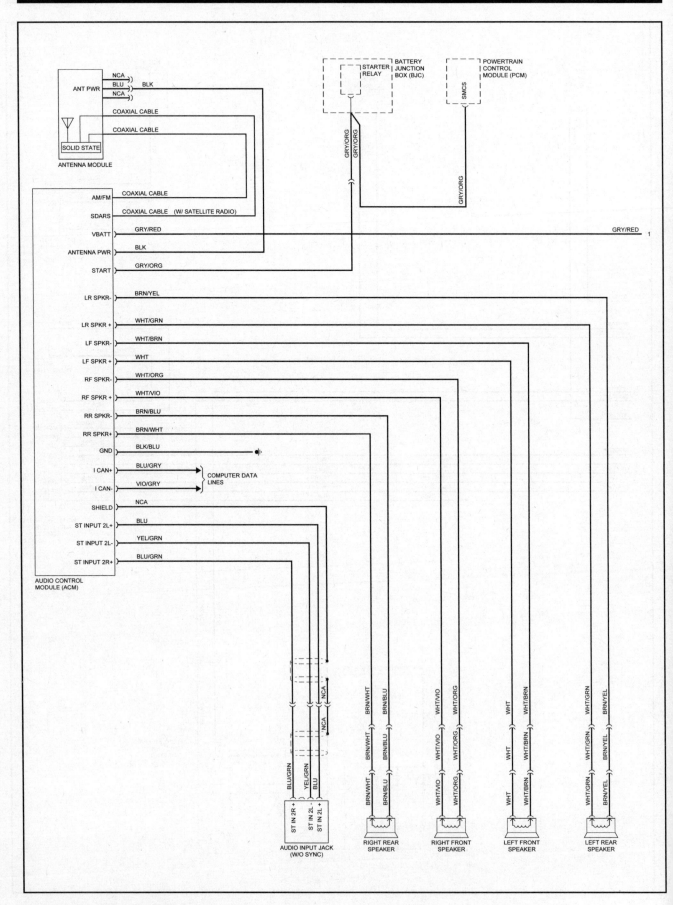

Audio system - 2011 and later models (1 of 2)

Audio system - 2011 and later models (2 of 2)

Notes

GLOSSARY

AIR/FUEL RATIO: The ratio of air-to-gasoline by weight in the fuel mixture drawn into the engine.

AIR INJECTION: One method of reducing harmful exhaust emissions by injecting air into each of the exhaust ports of an engine. The fresh air entering the hot exhaust manifold causes any remaining fuel to be burned before it can exit the tailpipe.

ALTERNATOR: A device used for converting mechanical energy into electrical energy.

AMMETER: An instrument, calibrated in amperes, used to measure the flow of an electrical current in a circuit. Ammeters are always connected in series with the circuit being tested.

AMPERE: The rate of flow of electrical current present when one volt of electrical pressure is applied against one ohm of electrical resistance.

ANALOG COMPUTER: Any microprocessor that uses similar (analogous) electrical signals to make its calculations.

ARMATURE: A laminated, soft iron core wrapped by a wire that converts electrical energy to mechanical energy as in a motor or relay. When rotated in a magnetic field, it changes mechanical energy into electrical energy as in a generator.

ATMOSPHERIC PRESSURE: The pressure on the Earth's surface caused by the weight of the air in the atmosphere. At sea level, this pressure is 14.7 psi at 32°F (101 kPa at 0°C).

ATOMIZATION: The breaking down of a liquid into a fine mist that can be suspended in air.

AXIAL PLAY: Movement parallel to a shaft or bearing bore.

BACKFIRE: The sudden combustion of gases in the intake or exhaust system that results in a loud explosion.

BACKLASH: The clearance or play between two parts, such as meshed gears.

BACKPRESSURE: Restrictions in the exhaust system that slow the exit of exhaust gases from the combustion chamber.

BAKELITE: A heat resistant, plastic insulator material commonly used in printed circuit boards and transistorized components.

BALL BEARING: A bearing made up of hardened inner and outer races between which hardened steel balls roll.

BALLAST RESISTOR: A resistor in the primary ignition circuit that lowers voltage after the engine is started to reduce wear on ignition components.

BEARING: A friction reducing, supportive device usually located between a stationary part and a moving part.

BIMETAL TEMPERATURE SENSOR: Any sensor or switch made of two dissimilar types of metal that bend when heated or cooled due to the different expansion rates of the alloys. These types of sensors usually function as an on/off switch.

BLOWBY: Combustion gases, composed of water vapor and unburned fuel, that leak past the piston rings into the crankcase during normal engine operation. These gases are removed by the PCV system to prevent the buildup of harmful acids in the crankcase.

BRAKE PAD: A brake shoe and lining assembly used with disc brakes.

BRAKE SHOE: The backing for the brake lining. The term is, however, usually applied to the assembly of the brake backing and lining.

BUSHING: A liner, usually removable, for a bearing; an anti-friction liner used in place of a bearing.

CALIPER: A hydraulically activated device in a disc brake system, which is mounted straddling the brake rotor (disc). The caliper contains at least one piston and two brake pads. Hydraulic pressure on the piston(s) forces the pads against the rotor.

CAMSHAFT: A shaft in the engine on which are the lobes (cams) which operate the valves. The camshaft is driven by the crankshaft, via a belt, chain or gears, at one half the crankshaft speed.

CAPACITOR: A device which stores an electrical charge.

CARBON MONOXIDE (CO): A colorless, odorless gas given off as a normal byproduct of combustion. It is poisonous and extremely dangerous in confined areas, building up slowly to toxic levels without warning if adequate ventilation is not available.

CARBURETOR: A device, usually mounted on the intake manifold of an engine, which mixes the air and fuel in the proper proportion to allow even combustion.

CATALYTIC CONVERTER: A device installed in the exhaust system, like a muffler, that converts harmful byproducts of combustion into carbon dioxide and water vapor by means of a heat-producing chemical reaction.

CENTRIFUGAL ADVANCE: A mechanical method of advancing the spark timing by using flyweights in the distributor that react to centrifugal force generated by the distributor shaft rotation.

CHECK VALVE: Any one-way valve installed to permit the flow of air, fuel or vacuum in one direction only.

CHOKE: A device, usually a moveable valve, placed in the intake path of a carburetor to restrict the flow of air.

CIRCUIT: Any unbroken path through which an electrical current can flow. Also used to describe fuel flow in some instances.

CIRCUIT BREAKER: A switch which protects an electrical circuit from overload by opening the circuit when the current flow exceeds a predetermined level. Some circuit breakers must be reset manually, while most reset automatically.

COIL (IGNITION): A transformer in the ignition circuit which steps up the voltage provided to the spark plugs.

COMBINATION MANIFOLD: An assembly which includes both the intake and exhaust manifolds in one casting.

COMBINATION VALVE: A device used in some fuel systems that routes fuel vapors to a charcoal storage canister instead of venting them into the atmosphere. The valve relieves fuel tank pressure and allows fresh air into the tank as the fuel level drops to prevent a vapor lock situation.

COMPRESSION RATIO: The comparison of the total volume of the cylinder and combustion chamber with the piston at BDC and the piston at TDC.

CONDENSER: 1. An electrical device which acts to store an electrical charge, preventing voltage surges. 2. A radiator-like device in the air conditioning system in which refrigerant gas condenses into a liquid, giving off heat.

CONDUCTOR: Any material through which an electrical current can be transmitted easily.

CONTINUITY: Continuous or complete circuit. Can be checked with an ohmmeter.

COUNTERSHAFT: An intermediate shaft which is rotated by a mainshaft and transmits, in turn, that rotation to a working part.

CRANKCASE: The lower part of an engine in which the crankshaft and related parts operate.

CRANKSHAFT: The main driving shaft of an engine which receives reciprocating motion from the pistons and converts it to rotary motion.

CYLINDER: In an engine, the round hole in the engine block in which the piston(s) ride.

CYLINDER BLOCK: The main structural member of an engine in which is found the cylinders, crankshaft and other principal parts.

CYLINDER HEAD: The detachable portion of the engine, usually fastened to the top of the cylinder block and containing all or most of the combustion chambers. On overhead valve engines, it contains the valves and their operating parts. On overhead cam engines, it contains the camshaft as well.

DEAD CENTER: The extreme top or bottom of the piston stroke.

DETONATION: An unwanted explosion of the air/fuel mixture in the combustion chamber caused by excess heat and compression, advanced timing, or an overly lean mixture. Also referred to as "ping".

DIAPHRAGM: A thin, flexible wall separating two cavities, such as in a vacuum advance unit.

DIESELING: A condition in which hot spots in the combustion chamber cause the engine to run on after the key is turned off.

DIFFERENTIAL: A geared assembly which allows the transmission of motion between drive axles, giving one axle the ability to turn faster than the other.

DIODE: An electrical device that will allow current to flow in one direction only.

DISC BRAKE: A hydraulic braking assembly consisting of a brake disc, or rotor, mounted on an axle, and a caliper assembly containing, usually two brake pads which are activated by hydraulic pressure. The pads are forced against the sides of the disc, creating friction which slows the vehicle.

DISTRIBUTOR: A mechanically driven device on an engine which is responsible for electrically firing the spark plug at a predetermined point of the piston stroke.

DOWEL PIN: A pin, inserted in mating holes in two different parts allowing those parts to maintain a fixed relationship.

DRUM BRAKE: A braking system which consists of two brake shoes and one or two wheel cylinders, mounted on a fixed backing plate, and a brake drum, mounted on an axle, which revolves around the assembly.

DWELL: The rate, measured in degrees of shaft rotation, at which an electrical circuit cycles on and off.

ELECTRONIC CONTROL UNIT (ECU): Ignition module, module, amplifier or igniter. See Module for definition.

ELECTRONIC IGNITION: A system in which the timing and firing of the spark plugs is controlled by an electronic control unit, usually called a module. These systems have no points or condenser.

END-PLAY: The measured amount of axial movement in a shaft.

ENGINE: A device that converts heat into mechanical energy.

EXHAUST MANIFOLD: A set of cast passages or pipes which conduct exhaust gases from the engine.

FEELER GAUGE: A blade, usually metal, or precisely predetermined thickness, used to measure the clearance between two parts.

FIRING ORDER: The order in which combustion occurs in the cylinders of an engine. Also the order in which spark is distributed to the plugs by the distributor.

FLOODING: The presence of too much fuel in the intake manifold and combustion chamber which prevents the air/fuel mixture from firing, thereby causing a no-start situation.

FLYWHEEL: A disc shaped part bolted to the rear end of the crankshaft. Around the outer perimeter is affixed the ring gear. The starter drive engages the ring gear, turning the flywheel, which rotates the crankshaft, imparting the initial starting motion to the engine.

FOOT POUND (ft. lbs. or sometimes, ft.lb.): The amount of energy or work needed to raise an item weighing one pound, a distance of one foot.

FUSE: A protective device in a circuit which prevents circuit overload by breaking the circuit when a specific amperage is present. The device is constructed around a strip or wire of a lower amperage rating than the circuit it is designed to protect. When an amperage higher than that stamped on the fuse is present in the circuit, the strip or wire melts, opening the circuit.

GEAR RATIO: The ratio between the number of teeth on meshing gears.

GENERATOR: A device which converts mechanical energy into electrical energy.

HEAT RANGE: The measure of a spark plug's ability to dissipate heat from its firing end. The higher the heat range, the hotter the plug fires.

HUB: The center part of a wheel or gear.

HYDROCARBON (HC): Any chemical compound made up of hydrogen and carbon. A major pollutant formed by the engine as a byproduct of combustion.

HYDROMETER: An instrument used to measure the specific gravity of a solution.

INCH POUND (inch lbs.; sometimes in.lb. or in. lbs.): One twelfth of a foot pound.

INDUCTION: A means of transferring electrical energy in the form of a magnetic field. Principle used in the ignition coil to increase voltage.

INJECTOR: A device which receives metered fuel under relatively low pressure and is activated to inject the fuel into the engine under relatively high pressure at a predetermined time.

INPUT SHAFT: The shaft to which torque is applied, usually carrying the driving gear or gears.

INTAKE MANIFOLD: A casting of passages or pipes used to conduct air or a fuel/air mixture to the cylinders.

JOURNAL: The bearing surface within which a shaft operates.

KEY: A small block usually fitted in a notch between a shaft and a hub to prevent slippage of the two parts.

MANIFOLD: A casting of passages or set of pipes which connect the cylinders to an inlet or outlet source.

MANIFOLD VACUUM: Low pressure in an engine intake manifold formed just below the throttle plates. Manifold vacuum is highest at idle and drops under acceleration.

MASTER CYLINDER: The primary fluid pressurizing device in a hydraulic system. In automotive use, it is found in brake and hydraulic clutch systems and is pedal activated, either directly or, in a power brake system, through the power booster.

MODULE: Electronic control unit, amplifier or igniter of solid state or integrated design which controls the current flow in the ignition primary circuit based on input from the pick-up coil. When the module opens the primary circuit, high secondary voltage is induced in the coil.

NEEDLE BEARING: A bearing which consists of a number (usually a large number) of long, thin rollers.

OHM: (Ω) The unit used to measure the resistance of conductor-to-electrical flow. One ohm is the amount of resistance that limits current flow to one ampere in a circuit with one volt of pressure.

OHMMETER: An instrument used for measuring the resistance, in ohms, in an electrical circuit.

OUTPUT SHAFT: The shaft which transmits torque from a device, such as a transmission.

OVERDRIVE: A gear assembly which produces more shaft revolutions than that transmitted to it.

OVERHEAD CAMSHAFT (OHC): An engine configuration in which the camshaft is mounted on top of the cylinder head and operates the valve either directly or by means of rocker arms.

OVERHEAD VALVE (OHV): An engine configuration in which all of the valves are located in the cylinder head and the camshaft is located in the cylinder block. The camshaft operates the valves via lifters and pushrods.

OXIDES OF NITROGEN (NOx): Chemical compounds of nitrogen produced as a byproduct of combustion. They combine with hydrocarbons to produce smog.

OXYGEN SENSOR: Use with the feedback system to sense the presence of oxygen in the exhaust gas and signal the computer which can reference the voltage signal to an air/fuel ratio.

PINION: The smaller of two meshing gears.

PISTON RING: An open-ended ring with fits into a groove on the outer diameter of the piston. Its chief function is to form a seal between the piston and cylinder wall. Most automotive pistons have three rings: two for compression sealing; one for oil sealing.

PRELOAD: A predetermined load placed on a bearing during assembly or by adjustment.

PRIMARY CIRCUIT: the low voltage side of the ignition system which consists of the ignition switch, ballast resistor or resistance wire, bypass, coil, electronic control unit and pick-up coil as well as the connecting wires and harnesses.

PRESS FIT: The mating of two parts under pressure, due to the inner diameter of one being smaller than the outer diameter of the other, or vice versa; an interference fit.

RACE: The surface on the inner or outer ring of a bearing on which the balls, needles or rollers move.

REGULATOR: A device which maintains the amperage and/or voltage levels of a circuit at predetermined values.

RELAY: A switch which automatically opens and/or closes a circuit.

RESISTANCE: The opposition to the flow of current through a circuit or electrical device, and is measured in ohms. Resistance is equal to the voltage divided by the amperage.

RESISTOR: A device, usually made of wire, which offers a preset amount of resistance in an electrical circuit.

RING GEAR: The name given to a ring-shaped gear attached to a differential case, or affixed to a flywheel or as part of a planetary gear set.

ROLLER BEARING: A bearing made up of hardened inner and outer races between which hardened steel rollers move.

ROTOR: 1. The disc-shaped part of a disc brake assembly, upon which the brake pads bear; also called, brake disc. 2. The device mounted atop the distributor shaft, which passes current to the distributor cap tower contacts.

SECONDARY CIRCUIT: The high voltage side of the ignition system, usually above 20,000 volts. The secondary includes the ignition coil, coil wire, distributor cap and rotor, spark plug wires and spark plugs.

SENDING UNIT: A mechanical, electrical, hydraulic or electromagnetic device which transmits information to a gauge.

SENSOR: Any device designed to measure engine operating conditions or ambient pressures and temperatures. Usually electronic in nature and designed to send a voltage signal to an on-board computer, some sensors may operate as a simple on/off switch or they may provide a variable voltage signal (like a potentiometer) as conditions or measured parameters change.

SHIM: Spacers of precise, predetermined thickness used between parts to establish a proper working relationship.

SLAVE CYLINDER: In automotive use, a device in the hydraulic clutch system which is activated by hydraulic force, disengaging the clutch.

SOLENOID: A coil used to produce a magnetic field, the effect of which is to produce work.

SPARK PLUG: A device screwed into the combustion chamber of a spark ignition engine. The basic construction is a conductive core inside of a ceramic insulator, mounted in an outer conductive base. An electrical charge from the spark plug wire travels along the conductive core and jumps a preset air gap to a grounding point or points at the end of the conductive base. The resultant spark ignites the fuel/air mixture in the combustion chamber.

SPLINES: Ridges machined or cast onto the outer diameter of a shaft or inner diameter of a bore to enable parts to mate without rotation.

TACHOMETER: A device used to measure the rotary speed of an engine, shaft, gear, etc., usually in rotations per minute.

THERMOSTAT: A valve, located in the cooling system of an engine, which is closed when cold and opens gradually in response to engine heating, controlling the temperature of the coolant and rate of coolant flow.

TOP DEAD CENTER (TDC): The point at which the piston reaches the top of its travel on the compression stroke.

TORQUE: The twisting force applied to an object.

TORQUE CONVERTER: A turbine used to transmit power from a driving member to a driven member via hydraulic action, providing changes in drive ratio and torque. In automotive use, it links the driveplate at the rear of the engine to the automatic transmission.

TRANSDUCER: A device used to change a force into an electrical signal.

TRANSISTOR: A semi-conductor component which can be actuated by a small voltage to perform an electrical switching function.

TUNE-UP: A regular maintenance function, usually associated with the replacement and adjustment of parts and components in the electrical and fuel systems of a vehicle for the purpose of attaining optimum performance.

TURBOCHARGER: An exhaust driven pump which compresses intake air and forces it into the combustion chambers at higher than atmospheric pressures. The increased air pressure allows more fuel to be burned and results in increased horsepower being produced.

VACUUM ADVANCE: A device which advances the ignition timing in response to increased engine vacuum.

VACUUM GAUGE: An instrument used to measure the presence of vacuum in a chamber.

VALVE: A device which control the pressure, direction of flow or rate of flow of a liquid or gas.

VALVE CLEARANCE: The measured gap between the end of the valve stem and the rocker arm, cam lobe or follower that activates the valve.

VISCOSITY: The rating of a liquid's internal resistance to flow.

VOLTMETER: An instrument used for measuring electrical force in units called volts. Voltmeters are always connected parallel with the circuit being tested.

WHEEL CYLINDER: Found in the automotive drum brake assembly, it is a device, actuated by hydraulic pressure, which, through internal pistons, pushes the brake shoes outward against the drums.

A

MASTER INDEX

NOTES